P9-BBQ-266

The Great Documents of Western Civilization

The Great Documents of Western Civilization

Milton Viorst

This edition published by Barnes & Noble, Inc.,
by arrangement with Wylie, Aitken & Stone.

1994 Barnes & Noble Books

ISBN 1-56619-559-4

Printed and bound in the United States of America

M 9 8 7

To My Sons

ANTHONY and NICHOLAS

FOR WHOM I WANT CIVILIZATION PRESERVED

Foreword

ONE OF THE most heartening of recent trends in the teaching of history has been the increasing use of source materials to supplement textbooks and instructors' lectures. While textbooks remain essential to give unity to a course, and lectures are even more necessary for interpretation and explanation, neither can give the student the sense of intimacy with events provided by original documents. Who, for example, can have a real comprehension of the import of Magna Charta without reading the Charter itself, or understand the significance of the Edict of Nantes without examining its actual provisions?

The book for which these paragraphs serve as an introduction presents a remarkable collection of materials illustrating the history of Western man from the rise of Christianity to the present day. With a rare sense of discrimination the author has chosen nearly all the significant documents which show the evolution of the contemporary world to what it is. The divisions, conflicts, failures, and triumphs in the struggle for laws and institutions that would bring peace and justice are skillfully exemplified in neat and suggestive array. The book fulfills a vital need.

EDWARD MCNALL BURNS

Dr. Burns is Professor Emeritus of Political Science at Rutgers University and former chairman of the department of history and political science. His book, Western Civilizations: Their History and Their Cultures, *is regarded as a classic study. It is in use in many colleges and universities throughout the country.*

Acknowledgments

I WOULD LIKE to thank the countless scholars who, by preceding me in recording the history of Western civilization, made this work possible; the many librarians and friends who advised and helped me in my search for the appropriate documents; my wife Judy, who read every word of the manuscript and gave me the benefit of her invaluable suggestions.

* * *

For permission to include certain documentary material, I wish to thank the following:

Harvard University Press, Cambridge, Mass. for *The Secret Treaties of Austria-Hungary, 1879–1914* by Alfred Pribram, 1920.

University of Pennsylvania Press, Philadelphia, Pa. for *A Source Book of Medieval History* by Frederick Ogg, 1907, and *European History, Vol. I* by James H. Robinson, 1904, from its "Translations and Reprints" Series.

American Book Company, New York, N.Y. also for *A Source Book of Medieval History* by Frederick Ogg, 1907.

Rutgers University Press, New Brunswick, N.J. for *Documents of German History* by Louis L. Snyder, 1958.

Century Company, New York, N.Y. for *Documents of Russian History* by F. A. Golder, 1927.

Ginn and Company, Boston, Mass. for *Readings in European History, Vol. II* by James Harvey Robinson, 1904–6 and *Readings in Modern European History, Vols. I & II* by James Harvey Robinson and Charles A. Beard, 1908–09.

Random House, Inc., Alfred A. Knopf, Inc. for "Tsar Nicholas II Announces His Policy, 1894" copyright 1917 by Alfred A. Knopf, Inc. Reprinted from *Modern Russian History* by Alexander Kornilov, translated by Alexander S. Kaun, by permission of the publisher.

University of California Press for "The Decembrist Manifesto" from *The First Russian Revolution* by A. G. Mazour.

M. V.

Washington, D.C.
June, 1965

Contents

List of Documents

The Great Documents of Western Civilization

INTRODUCTION

From Hammurabi to Augustus

The sources of Western civilization lie in the Near East, in the fertile valleys of the Nile, the Tigris and the Euphrates, where Egyptian, Sumerian and Babylonian cultures flourished three thousand years before the Christian era. It was here that men first learned to use the plow, yoke oxen, construct wheeled carts and cross the seas by sail. It was here that they first dug canals to irrigate their fields and built cities for the conduct of their trade and the practice of their craft. They invented writing, metal instruments, bureaucracy and methods of accounting. They generated ideas that, for good or bad, have become the legacy of hundreds of generations who have followed them.

No idea was more significant than the concept of a written law to regulate the relations between human beings. As the cultures of the ancient civilizations became more complex, so did the jurisprudence by which they were ruled. Most famous of the early codes was that of the Babylonian King Hammurabi, who fixed a legal system about 1750 B.C. that passed more or less intact from one Mediterranean people to another over the course of centuries. Hammurabi's Code, engraved on a stone column in 3600 lines of cuneiform, was found by an archaeologist in Persia in 1901 and taken to Paris for permanent display at the Louvre.

Some of the provisions of Hammurabi's Code illustrate the primitive, retributive justice of Mesopotamian civilization. Still, in its concern for widows, orphans and other helpless persons, it is remarkably humane. The civilization for which it was prepared possessed a rigid class structure, a highly developed commerce and a well-developed, if harsh, sense of ethics. The first provision expresses the famous "eye for an eye" philosophy of justice, which long remained part of the Western heritage.

> If a noble has destroyed the eye of an aristocrat, his eye shall be destroyed.
>
> If he has destroyed the eye of a commoner or broken the bone of a commoner, he shall pay one mina of silver.

If he has destroyed the eye of a noble's slave or broken the bone of a noble's slave, he shall pay one half his value.

If a son has struck his father, they shall cut off his hand.

If a noble charges another noble with murder but fails to prove it, the accuser shall be put to death.

If a builder constructs a house for a noble and does not make his work strong, with the result that the house collapses and so causes the death of the owner, the builder shall be put to death.

If it has caused the death of a son of the owner, the son of the builder shall be put to death.

If a woman has so hated her husband that she has declared, "You may not have me," her record shall be investigated at her city council, and if she was careful and not at fault, even though her husband has gone out and disparaged her greatly, she may, without incurring any blame at all, take her dowry and go off to her father's house.

Hammurabi's code is a noteworthy event in social development if only because it excludes the arbitrary administration of justice. Each member of society, whether in his personal or professional dealings, has standing in a system of law that is both public and specific. Codes such as Hammurabi's transmitted to Western civilization the notion that all members of society, if not equal before the law, must have at least assured recourse to law.

If fixed law was one side of a coin, the ancient civilizations of the Near East also offered to the West the reverse side. These societies exalted divine rulers and dominating priests. Fearful of the desert nomads who periodically swept into their valleys, they yielded their freedom to their generals and their armies. Their days of vigor were followed by an early middle-age of intense conservatism and dull conformity. They substituted superstition and magic for free inquiry and the totalitarian state for the dignity of the individual. Ultimately the debilitating view prevailed that religion, the arts, learning and the citizen existed to serve the ruling class. These ancient civilizations died rejecting innovation, failing in adaptability, drained of vigor.

To these stifled systems of the Near East, the Greeks issued a vigorous challenge. In response to the handicaps of inhospitable terrain and unfertile soil, Greek-speaking tribes, beginning a millenium before Christ, formed city-states that derived their sustenance from specialized cultivation, quality craftsmanship and commerce that radiated throughout the Mediterranean basin. Full of energy and daring, the Greeks pressed westward to found colonies in North Africa, Italy and Sicily, Provence and Spain, but never did they set out to dominate the world. Theirs was a sea culture, characterized by war and piracy as well as by enterprise but always adventurous and stimulating to the spirit. Theirs was also an urban culture, leisured enough and wealthy enough to permit the luxury of thought. The Greeks exalted the individual and never, before or since, has the human spirit been more free.

Greek thinkers, conscious of a contest with the physical environment, first gave their attention to overcoming the obstacles that astringent nature imposed on them. Divesting themselves of the burdens of superstition and magic inherited from the East, they devised techniques of exact observation and abstract analysis. They founded astronomy and physics and made the first original discoveries in the medical sciences. From practical rationality they moved on to the realm of ethical and philosophical speculation. The Greeks reveled in exercises of the mind, found tonic in the clash of wits. It is no coincidence that the Greeks created masterpieces of thought which to this day remain vibrant and exciting stimulants to the West.

The Greek contribution to the soul of the West is so magnificent that it is often forgotten that Greek fighting men merit the credit for saving the West from an Orientalization that would have changed profoundly the character of Western civilization. Five hundred years before Christ the Persian emperor Darius, who had achieved dominion over all of Western Asia and Egypt, turned to the conquest of Europe. Only the Greek city-states, small and fragile, stood in his way. In 490 B.C. a Greek army composed principally of Athenians defeated a Persian force six times its size on the battlefield of Marathon. A decade later the Persians returned to overwhelm a heroic force of Spartans and Thespians at Thermopolae and to take Athens, but then to lose their fleet to the Athenian navy at Salamis and their army of occupation to a mixed army of Greeks at Plataea. By defeating the Persians, the Greeks thwarted the first major attempt of the East to overrun Europe. They thereby assured Western civilization a development free of Oriental domination.

Victory over the Persians put an end to the temporary unity the Greeks had achieved and polarized the city-states around the two principal powers of the peninsula, Athens and Sparta. It was in Athens, after the Persian wars, that Greek civilization reached its spiritual pinnacle, while Sparta at the same time was becoming more tyrannical and militaristic. For all their intellectual genius, the Greeks never succeeded in transcending the city-state as a political form. Even as Athens was developing a system of democracy, which provided the West with a vital though long dormant tradition, the rivalry among the city-states was becoming more and more threatening. Inept at making allies or retaining their loyalty, Athens found itself virtually alone when the great Peloponnesian War began in 431 B.C. In the long conflict that followed, Athens ultimately succumbed. Not until the legions of Macedon arrived in 338 B.C. did the Greek peninsula again know real peace.

The Athenian leader Pericles, after war had ravaged the Greek lands for a year, explained the wonderful balance that Hellenic culture at its best sought to achieve. His oration over the Athenian dead, transmitted by the historian Thucydides, remains one of the most elegant representations of the Greek civilization.

> We are lovers of beauty without extravagance and lovers of wisdom without unmanliness. Wealth to us is not mere material for vainglory but opportunity for achievement. . . . Instead of looking on discussion

as an obstacle to action, we think of it as an indispensible preliminary to any wise action. Other men are bold in ignorance, while reflection will paralyze them; but the bravest are surely those who have the clearest vision of what lies before them, glory and danger alike, and yet go out to meet it. . . . In short, I say that as a city we are the school of Hellas. Athenians yield to none, man for man, in independence of spirit, versatility of attainment and complete self-reliance of brain and limb. . .

The ideals expressed by Pericles, too exalted for easy reach and violated in such instances as the execution of Socrates, produced the brilliant philosophy of Plato and Aristotle, the deathless drama of Sophocles and Euripides, the penetrating history of Heroditus and Thucydides and the breathtaking beauty of the Parthenon and other works of art. They failed to produce the political union necessary to prevent civil war. The city-states fell but not before they had implanted their culture throughout the West.

While Athens was leading Greece to magnificence, the citizens of a city-state in central Italy were driving out their foreign rulers and establishing a primitive republic. Under an energetic and ambitious Senate, aristocratic and patrician rather than democratic, Rome began its spectacular career by conquering its neighbors, then by setting as its objective the entire known world. Romans first met the superior culture of Greece in the Hellenic settlements they overran along the Mediterranean shores. In the course of the third and fourth centuries B.C., Roman legions had marched far enough east to encounter the full impact of Greek civilization. The Hellenization of Rome is one of the important events in the development of the West. It assured the survival of the humanistic and rational traditions of Athens, as well as the Greek monuments of literature and art. The soul of Greece, transmitted to the West through the medium of the superb Latin tongue, therefore remained alive to enrich the new civilization that was to rise in Europe from Rome's ashes.

Rome's destiny was fixed by its victories in the Punic Wars. By destroying Carthage in a conflict that erupted thrice in a century, Rome acquired hegemony over Spain, the north shore of Africa and all the lands that bordered the Mediterranean Sea. By the middle of the second century B.C., Rome had no serious challengers to its dreams of limitless dominion. To rule its vast empire, the Romans developed a magnificent system of law, a noble testimonial to a civilization and the most lasting heritage to its successors. But Rome was far less successful in dispensing social justice. The Senate governed the provinces not for the benefit of Romans but for the enrichment of the ruling classes. Several times the slaves revolted, only to be repressed with incredible brutality. In 133 B.C., Tiberius Gracchus led a revolt of free farmers to obtain a redistribution of the land that had been concentrated in the hands of a few oligarchs. It was a memorable uprising, important to the revolutionary tradition that has become part of Western man's endless struggle for social justice. In a great revolutionary oration to the disinherited of Rome, recorded by the historian Plutarch, Gracchus declared:

> The beasts of the field and the birds of the air have their holes and their hiding places; but the men who fight and die for Italy enjoy only the light and the air. Our generals urge their soldiers to fight for the graves and the shrines of their ancestors. The appeal is idle and false. You cannot point to a paternal altar. You have no ancestral tomb. You fight and die to give wealth and luxury to others. You are called the masters of the world, but there is not a foot of ground that you can call your own.

The revolt of the Gracchi failed, as did the other uprisings against the senatorial ruling classes. But the days of the senatorial oligarchy were numbered. The empire it had won had become too widespread for it to handle. Constant disorder had undermined its authority. Ambitious military chiefs fought to usurp its power. Brutus, in literature, may have been the symbol of Republican virtue but he was also the defender of senatorial privilege. Caesar, by tradition, may be the symbol of tyranny yet he was also the champion of the masses, from whom he drew his political strength. When Caesar emerged in the middle of the first century B.C. as undisputed ruler, Rome was ready for another stage of its development—the Empire—a stage of autocracy, tyranny and, finally, dissolution.

The anarchy that followed Caesar's assassination in 44 B.C. brought forth, as the strong man of Rome, Octavian, who took the title of Augustus, or Emperor. Augustus, as he is known to history, initiated a period of peace that lasted some two centuries. This celebrated *pax romana* the West would forever seek to emulate. In Augustus' time, the Roman Empire extended from Ireland to the Arabian desert, from the Elbe and the Carpathians to the Sahara. Augustus reorganized the provincial government and the army and instituted the construction of the great highway system that went unequaled until our own day. Under Augustus the Roman Empire became a single nation. So thorough was Rome's domination over the known world that the notion became all but fixed that political unity was the natural condition of the West. Long after Rome's disintegration, the Augustan concept of empire remained alive, as much an ideal for the future as a reminder of the past.

The Empire enjoyed moments of glory after the early emperors but they became more and more rare with the decline of imperial leadership. Roman rule grew to resemble the oriental despotisms which had once seemed a relic of the dark past. The Emperor Constantine, symbolically at least, consummated the process of orientalization by transferring the capital of the Empire to the shores of the Bosporus. There a splendid civilization flourished, but in its tyranny, bureaucracy and orthodoxy it was more like the ancient states of the Near East than the soaring spirit of Greece.

The ancient world had come full circle. It had performed great feats and mean ones. It had produced magnificent ideas and base ones. It justified optimism and pessimism for the future. It transmitted each of its characteristics, with their many contradictions, to the new civilization emerging from the ruins of Rome. From the East once again came the fresh idea and the vitality to inspire Europe. The new element in the old mixture was Christianity, which brought life out of stagnation. Christianity created a new dynamism in the exhausted heritage that Rome had brought forth from its Eastern roots. By the third or fourth century after Christ, Rome was moribund and Western civilization was being born.

I

The Rise of Christianity and the Papacy

I

The Rise of Christianity and the Papacy

Western civilization was born of Christianity. The Christian religion is the thread that winds through the diverse communities of the West. For every trait in common, for every value shared, these communities probably have ten on which they differ. But all spring from the Judeo-Christian tradition of the East, modified and transmitted to them by the Church of Rome. Roman Christianity is the mother of Western civilization, however harshly her children throughout two milleniums have treated one another. Western Christianity has made of this civilization, whatever its internal disparities, a cultural unity, with attitudes and ambitions different from those of any other civilization of history.

Correspondence between Pliny and Trajan, 112

For the first three centuries of its existence, Christianity was officially banned and persecuted by Rome. The state religion was a type of political polytheism, though Rome did not insist on rigid conformity to any specific form of worship. It permitted, without interference, a great variety of pagan cults to thrive. During the period of its apogee, when the Empire extended from Britain to the Persian Gulf, many forms of paganism flourished under the aegis of the Roman state. But if Rome was tolerant of religious diversity, it was keenly alert to political subversion. Rome regarded the security of the state as the objective of religion. It enforced on the pagan cults only one rule: that the Roman emperor be included among the panoply of gods to which homage was paid. The pagans, to whom one god more or less made little difference, adjusted without difficulty to the Roman stipulation. But Christianity, which like Judaism recognized only one God, could accept no such condition. Christians took their one God very seriously, more seriously than they took the state. They refused military service and rejected the obligations of Roman citizenship. Rome thus believed it was necessary to persecute Christians, as it persecuted Jews.

For two and a half centuries, the policy of persecution was pursued fitfully. Christianity was not regarded as a real menace. A few martyrs were made, most notably St. Peter, who by tradition gave his life in the mad Emperor Nero's blood bath after establishing the Church of Rome. Other emperors oppressed Christians, but more out of a sense of administrative efficiency and reform, to keep at bay any challenge to their authority, than out of a spirit of religious intolerance. Most Roman rulers, from indifference, simply let Christians alone. Though the policy of persecution remained officially in effect, public tranquility was usually easier to maintain, in the provinces as well as in Rome, by ignoring the Christian heresy. Christianity, during its early years, was thus favored by an atmosphere throughout the Empire that was by no means hostile to its growth.

A celebrated exchange of letters that took place about 112 A.D. between Pliny the Younger, governor of the province of Bithynia, and the Emperor Trajan reveals something of Rome's attitude toward the Christian heretics. Pliny, after a thorough study of Christian practices, concluded that this constantly growing religion represented a threat to the state. "The contagion of that superstition," he wrote, "has penetrated not the cities only, but the villages and the country." With the conventional view of a Roman administrator, however, he was confident that Christianity could be contained by leniency and forced repentance. He wrote to Trajan, his Emperor, for confirmation of this policy.

Document 1A

It is my custom, lord emperor, to refer to you all questions whereof I am in doubt. Who can better guide me when I am at a stand, or enlighten me if I am in ignorance? In investigations of Christians I have never taken part; hence I do not know what is the crime usually punished or investigated, or what allowances are made. So I have had no little uncertainty whether there is any distinction of age, or whether the very weakest offenders are treated exactly like the stronger; whether pardon is given to those who repent, or whether a man who has once been a Christian gains nothing by having ceased to be such; whether punishment attaches to the mere name apart from secret crimes, or to the secret crimes connected with the name. Meantime this is the course I have taken with those who were accused before me as Christians. I asked them whether they were Christians, and if they confessed, I asked them a second and third time with threats of punishment. If they kept to it, I ordered them for execution; for I held no question that whatever it was that they admitted, in any case obstinacy and unbending perversity deserve to be punished. There were others of the like insanity; but as these were Roman citizens, I noted them down to be sent to Rome.

Before long, as is often the case, the mere fact that the charge was taken notice of made it commoner, and several distinct cases arose. An unsigned paper was presented, which gave the names of many. As for those who said that they neither were nor ever had been Christians, I thought it right to let them go, since they recited a prayer to the gods at my dictation, made supplication with incense and wine to your statue, which I had ordered to be brought into court for the purpose together with the images of the gods, and moreover cursed Christ—things which (so it is said) those who are really Christians cannot be made to do. Others who were named by the informer said that they were Christians and then denied it, explaining that they had been, but had ceased to be such, some three years ago, some a good many years, and a few even twenty. All these too both worshipped your statue and the images of the gods, and cursed Christ.

They maintained, however, that the amount of their fault or error had been this, that it was their habit on a fixed day to assemble before daylight and recite by turns a form of words to Christ as a god; and that they bound themselves with an oath, not for any crime, but not to commit theft or robbery or adultery, not to break their word, and not to deny a deposit when demanded. After this was done, their custom was to depart, and to meet again to take food, but ordinary and harmless food; and even this (they said) they had given up doing after the issue of my edict, by which in accordance with your commands I had forbidden the existence of clubs. On this I considered it the more necessary to find out from two maid-servants who were called deaconesses and that by torments, how far this was true: but I discovered nothing else than a perverse and extravagant superstition. I therefore adjourned the case and hastened to consult you. The matter seemed to me worth deliberation, especially on account of the number of those in danger; for many of all ages and every rank, and also of both sexes are brought into present or future danger. The contagion of that superstition has penetrated not the cities only, but the villages and country; yet it seems possible to stop it and set it right. At any rate it is certain enough that the almost deserted temples begin to be resorted to, that long disused ceremonies of religion are restored, and that fodder for victims finds a market, whereas buyers till now were very few. From this it may easily be supposed, what a multitude of men can be reclaimed, if there be a place of repentance.

Trajan, in his brief reply, affirmed Pliny's judgment. It is interesting to note, in his final sentence, how Trajan, faithful to Roman legal procedures—what we now call "rights"—condemned anonymous accusations. Trajan clearly believed that the result of an active policy of persecution would be domestic unrest. Tranquility was his goal. For this reason, he ruled against oppression.

Document 1B

You have adopted the proper course, my dear Secundus, in your examination of the cases of those who were accused to you as Christians, for indeed nothing can be laid down as a general ruling involving something like a set form of procedure. They are not to be sought out; but if they are accused and convicted, they must be punished—yet on this condition, that whoso denies himself to be a Christian, and makes the fact plain by his action, that is, by worshipping our gods, shall obtain pardon on his repentance, however suspicious his past conduct may be. Papers, however, which are presented unsigned ought not to be admitted in any charge, for they are a very bad example and unworthy of our time.

Emperor Galerius' Edict of Toleration, 311

By the middle of the third century, conditions had changed. Rome, having for a variety of reasons lost its vigor, was suffering through its last great decline. Its population was diminishing. Its trade was stagnating. The administration of the Empire was disintegrating and enemies threatened at its borders. Panic was setting in and the state needed a scapegoat. Christianity was the most likely candidate.

As Rome tired, Christianity showed spectacular energy. A mystic, religious feeling—perhaps the consequence of loss of confidence in the state—seems to have swept across the Empire. Wherever Roman civilization had penetrated, the new faith followed, traveling over the great highways that Roman engineers had built. The movements of conversion took on two patterns. The Hellenic tradition was carried by Greek-speaking Christians from the eastern Mediterranean throughout Asia Minor and Syria, then northeast into Armenia and southern Russia, northwest into Rumania and south into Egypt. Starting a century later, Latin-speaking Christianity swept from Italy west into Spain and Gaul, north into Germany and Britain and south across the top of Africa. Conversions, coming faster and faster, were not limited to the lower classes as they first had been but began to pierce the middle and upper classes and even the governing aristocracy. By the middle of the third century, Christianity was still the religion of only a tenth of the population of the Empire but it was dynamic and its members were dedicated and determined.

The Emperor Decius, having decided on his scapegoat, in 250 A.D. undertook the first concerted program to destroy Christianity. His persecution was the most terrible that Christians had thus far to endure. The oppression he initiated lasted under a series of Roman rulers for two decades, after which there was a respite. But at the beginning of the fourth century, the repression in its full fury was resumed. Still, it failed to serve its purpose. The new religion seemed to thrive on the blood of its martyrs. No matter how cruel the persecution, the Christian religion and the Church that had by now been organized to lead it continued to grow stronger.

The Emperor Galerius (305–311 A.D.), himself one of the severest persecutors, was the first to acknowledge that the battle against the Christians was futile. He apparently believed that Christianity could be manipulated to serve the Empire's purposes, for already Christians and their Church had overcome their aversion to accepting civic responsibilities. Galerius issued the first edict of toleration of Christianity. That it appeared near the end of a long illness, a few days before he died, has led to the speculation that he was actually seeking mercy from the Christians' God. The final paragraph of the edict, in which Christians are called upon to pray for their emperor and the state, seems to substantiate this interpretation. But whatever his motives, Galerius' edict of toleration of 311 A.D., the text of which is given here, remains one of the major steps in Christianity's conquest of the West.

Document 2

Amongst our other measures for the advantage of the Empire, we have hitherto endeavored to bring all things into conformity with the ancient laws and public order of the Romans. We have been especially anxious that even the Christians, who have abandoned the religion of their ancestors, should return to reason. For they have fallen, we know not how, into such perversity and folly that, instead of adhering to those ancient institutions which possibly their own forefathers established, they have arbitrarily made laws of their own and collected together various peoples from various quarters.

After the publication, on our part, of an order commanding Christians to return to the observance of the ancient customs, many of them, it is true, submitted in view of the danger, while many others suffered death. Nevertheless, since many of them have continued to persist in their opinions and we see that in the present situation they neither duly adore and venerate the gods nor yet worship the god of the Christians, we, with our wonted clemency, have judged it is wise to extend a pardon even to these men and permit them once more to become Christians and reëstablish their places of meetings; in such manner, however, that they shall in no way offend against good order. We propose to notify the magistrates in another mandate in regard to the course that they should pursue.

Wherefore it should be the duty of the Christians, in view of our clemency, to pray to their god for our welfare, for that of the Empire, and for their own, so that the Empire may remain intact in all its parts, and that they themselves may live safely in their habitations.

Edicts from the Theodosian Code, beginning 312

In the struggles for the imperial throne that characterized Rome's declining years, Christianity and the Church quite naturally became a factor. One of the principal schemers, even before Galerius' death, was Constantine, a successful general who somehow managed to strike an alliance with Christian power. When Constantine defeated his rivals at the famous Battle of the Milvian Bridge in 312, Christianity was acknowledged a share in the victory. As emperor, Constantine first confirmed the policy of toleration of Christianity. He then embarked on a program that made Christianity the favored religion of the state and led to his own conversion a decade later.

Though the first Christian emperor, Constantine accepted the traditional Roman notion that religion must serve the needs of the state, which was precisely the reverse of the Christian view. Nonetheless, the Church accepted Constantine's authority. For its part, the Church taught the duty of the believer was to submit to the civil power. Constantine, in return, suppressed not only the pagan cults but also the various Christian heresies that threatened the growing dominance of the Roman Church. In this new alliance of Church and state, Christianity flourished and the Empire enjoyed one of its last moments of brilliance.

Constantine's edicts, collected many years later under the Emperor Theodosius II, illustrate Christianity's step-by-step triumph over the rival religions of the Empire. Selected edicts from the Theodosian Code are presented below.

The first relieves the Christian clergy of taxation and other public burdens, making them a privileged class in society. Interestingly, the edict was subsequently amended to exclude wealthy clergymen, presumably because the priesthood had become a device used by the rich to evade the payment of taxes.

Document 3A

Those who exercise the functions of divine worship, that is to say those who are called clerics (*clerici*), shall be exempt from all public burdens, lest otherwise they might be called away from their sacred duties through some one's malicious interference. (A.D. 319)

The right of the Church to receive legacies was established in the following edict, dated 321 A.D. It permitted the Church at Rome, within a few years, to assemble the greatest concentration of wealth in the Empire. This wealth remained within the Church, the corporate character of which was now acknowledged. In their power to dispose of extensive property and vast sums of money, the Catholic bishops acquired enormous influence of a non-spiritual nature.

Document 3B

Every one shall have the right, when he is dying, to leave so much of his goods as he will to the holy and Catholic Church . . . (A.D. 321)

In the following edict, issued in 321 A.D., Constantine extended to all Roman citizens the prerogative of following the Christian practice of refraining from work on Sunday. The action considerably simplified the effort to convert heathens to the new religion.

Document 3C

Just as it appears to Us most unseemly that the Day of the Sun which is celebrated on account of its own veneration should be occupied with legal altercations and with noxious controversies of the litigation of contending parties, so it is pleasant and fitting that those acts which are especially desired shall be accomplished on that day. Therefore all men shall have the right to emancipate and to manumit on this festive day, and the legal formalities thereof are not forbidden. Given on 3 July at Cagliari in the second consulship of Crispus and Constantine Caesars (321 A.D.).

Constantine demonstrated his devotion to the concept of Christian orthodoxy during the bitter Arian controversy, when Eastern and Western Christianity came close to splitting over a doctrinal disagreement on the substance of Jesus. Anxious to preserve the unity of the Empire, Constantine in 325 convoked the Council of Nicea, where he personally presided over all the bishops of Christendom. Under his influence, the Council devised a formula aimed at achieving maximum acceptance among the contending parties. The Nicene formula, a theological compromise, has remained church doctrine to this day. Constantine made the state responsible for enforcing this doctrine. His edict of 326, reflecting his insistence upon religious conformity, indicates the degree of union that had been achieved between church and state in Rome.

Document 3D

The privileges that have been granted in consideration of religion must benefit only the adherents of the Catholic faith. It is Our will moreover, that heretics and schismatics shall not only be alien from these privileges but shall also be bound and subjected to various compulsory public services (326 A.D.).

Decretal of Pope Siricius, 385

Important as were Constantine's efforts in behalf of the Western Church, his greatest contribution to its development was unintentional. In 330, Constantine decided for political and military reasons to move his capital from the banks of the Tiber to the shores of the Bosporus, straddling Europe and Asia. There, in the city soon to be known as Constantinople, he gave the Roman Empire a new start. From Constantinople, he extended his influence over the eastern branch of Christianity, until he came almost to dominate it. But at the same time his relaxation of control in the West left the Roman Church free to develop virtually independent of any civil constraint. When the imperial government moved to Constantinople, the Bishop of Rome became the principal figure in the crumbling Western empire. Constantine, having by his decrees enabled the Church to become wealthy and powerful, provided by default of his own authority the conditions to make it autonomous.

The Church of Rome, since its founding early in the first century, had always been an extraordinary church, far more prominent than the other churches throughout the Empire. Situated in the capital, it basked at first in the glory reflected from the state. It was the largest and richest church in the West, always extending its influence by endowing missionary activities and founding new churches. But perhaps most important, the Church of Rome firmly pressed the claim that, having been founded by St. Peter, Christ's chief apostle, it was heir to the authority of Jesus himself. Successive bishops of Rome, designating their domain the Apostolic See, insisted that the power to guide the Christian church had been assigned to them by the frequently cited passage in Matthew xvi 18–19, in which Christ said: "Thou art Peter, and upon this rock I will build my church; and the gates of hell shall not prevail against it. And I will give unto thee the keys of the kingdom of heaven . . ." On the basis of this passage, they claimed not only the spiritual leadership of Christianity but the right to rule the entire Church organization.

By as early as 90 A.D., records indicate that the Bishop of Rome had already established a precedent of openly intervening in the affairs of lesser churches. In succeeding years, the Roman bishops again and again attempted to impose their will on churches throughout the Empire. In 343, an ecclesiastical council meeting in Sardica (now Sofia, Bulgaria) empowered the Bishop of Rome to rule on decisions appealed from local church councils. The Sardica council thereby established the principle that the Bishop of Rome possessed the power of supreme judge of the Catholic Church. The Empire offered the model for the future development of the office which became known as the Papacy (from *papa*, "father"). It seemed natural for the Bishop of Rome to develop authority over the church parallel to that which the Roman Emperor exercised over the state.

In 385, Pope Siricius issued, in reply to the questions of a Spanish bishop, a papal ordinance or "decretal," in which he discussed sternly the "general orders which I have addressed to you." It is clear that Siricius expected to be obeyed, not only by the bishop to whom the decretal was addressed but by "all our brethren." The following document, the decretal of Siricius, is the earliest papal decree that remains in existence.

Document 4

I believe that I have now given a sufficient answer to the various questions which you have referred to the Roman church as to the head of your body. Now we would stimulate you, our brother, more and more carefully to observe the canons and adhere to the decretals which have been ordained. Moreover, we would have you bring to the attention of all our fellow-bishops those things which we have written in reply to your questions, not only to those bishops who are within your dioceses, but to all the Carthaginians, Bæticans, Lusitanians, and Gallicians, as well as to those in the neighboring provinces. Let all the matters which have been duly settled by us be transmitted to them through letters from you. For although no priest of God is likely to remain in ignorance of the decrees of the Apostolic See and the venerable decisions of the canons, it will be more expedient and more to the glory of the ancient station which you occupy if those general orders which I have addressed to you individually should be brought through you to the attention of all our brethren. In this way those things which have been ordained by us with the utmost circumspection and caution, after due deliberation and by no means hastily, shall be permanently observed, and thus all possibility of those excuses which might otherwise reach us shall be removed.

Edict of Emperor Valentinian, 455

From Constantinople, the imperial government was able to exercise little control over the church at Rome. In contrast, the Empire made of the Eastern Church a virtual instrumentality of the state. In 451, the imperial government convoked an ecclesiastical council at Chalcedon and persuaded the bishops to declare the Church of Constantinople the equal in power of the Church of Rome. But, in fact, Rome augmented its autonomy and became stronger while its eastern rival fell further and further behind.

As the barbarian tribes nibbled away at the Empire's western frontiers, the Roman Church rose to the challenge and made what is perhaps its greatest contribution to Western civilization. Roman missionaries infiltrated the barbarian ranks, converting the tribes to Christianity as they approached the capital. While the Empire crumbled, the Church thereby saved Roman civilization from total destruction. The Church thus extended its own influence into uncharted areas to bridge the way to a new era.

The wane of the Empire left a vacuum of power into which the Papacy quite naturally stepped. Pope Leo I (440–461), one of the strongest of the early popes, vigorously asserted claims of temporal power for the Church. Shortly after he intervened with the Hun chief, Attila, to save the city of Rome from sacking, Emperor Valentinian III, in gratitude, issued an edict which put the force of Roman law behind papal decisions. Valentinian's edict, issued in 455, tightened the bond between Church and state. At the same time, it reveals how thoroughly the Church, once at the mercy of the state, had come to dominate its relationship with the Empire. Valentinian III's edict follows.

Document 5

Since, then, the primacy of the Apostolic See is established by the merit of St. Peter (who is the chief among the bishops), by the majesty of the city of Rome, and finally by the authority of a holy council, no one, without inexcusable presumption, may attempt anything against the authority of that See. Peace will be secured among the churches if every one recognize his ruler.

[After a reference to the independent action of certain prelates of Gaul, the edict continues.] Lest even a slight commotion should arise in the churches, or the religious order be disturbed, we herewith permanently decree that not only the bishops of Gaul, but those of the other provinces, shall attempt nothing counter to ancient custom without the authority of the venerable father of the Eternal City. Whatever shall be sanctioned by the authority of the Apostolic See shall be law to them and to everyone else; so that if one of the bishops be summoned to the judgment of the Roman bishop and shall neglect to appear, he shall be forced by the moderator of his province to present himself. In all respects let the privileges be maintained which our deified predecessors have conferred upon the Roman church.

Pope Gelasius I's Letter to the Emperor, 494

By the end of the fifth century, the Papacy had become sufficiently secure in its dominion to challenge the supremacy of the state.

The Empire had by now given up all pretense to exercising authority in Rome, where a barbarian king sat on the throne. The Roman Church was not strong enough to press with vigor its claims of hegemony over Eastern Christianity. As a consequence, the battle over whether church or state exercised the superior power, so bitterly waged during the Middle Ages, was still somewhat theoretical. Nonetheless, the groundwork was being laid for this conflict.

Nowhere is this more evident than in the letter dispatched by Pope Gelasius I to the Emperor Anastasius in 494. Haughty and censorious, the Pope demanded of the Emperor the "obedience due to the bishop of that See which the Most High ordained to be above all others." The political doctrine enunciated by Gelasius—that even in temporal matters the authority of the Pope was superior to that of civil rulers—plagued Western civilization for the succeeding fourteen hundred years. It occasionally recurs to this day.

Document 6

. . . There are two powers, august Emperor, by which this world is chiefly ruled, namely, the sacred authority of the priests and the royal power. Of these, that of the priests is the more weighty, since they have to render an account for even the kings of men in the divine judgment. You are also aware, dear son, that while you are permitted honorably to rule over human kind, yet in things divine you bow your head humbly before the leaders of the clergy and await from their hands the means of your salvation. In the reception and proper disposition of the heavenly mysteries you recognize that you should be subordinate rather than superior to the religious order, and that in these matters you depend on their judgment rather than wish to force them to follow your will.

If the ministers of religion, recognizing the supremacy granted you from heaven in matters affecting the public order, obey your laws, lest otherwise they might obstruct the course of secular affairs by irrelevant considerations, with what readiness should you not yield them obedience to whom is assigned the dispensing of the sacred mysteries of religion. Accordingly, just as there is no slight danger in the case of the priests if they refrain from speaking when the service of the divinity requires, so there is no little risk for those who disdain—which God forbid—when they should obey. And if it is fitting that the hearts of the faithful should submit to all priests in general who properly administer divine affairs, how much the more is obedience due to the bishop of that See which the Most High ordained to be above all others, and which is consequently dutifully honored by the devotion of the whole Church.

II

Feudalism and the Frankish State

II

Feudalism and the Frankish State

Vigorous Germanic tribes replaced the power of Rome in western Europe. In the third century they began migrating southward in a constantly rising tide, sometimes in search of new lands and food, sometimes fleeing from fiercer races invading from the east. Tribal names such as Burgundian, Thuringian, Bavarian, Angle, Jute, Saxon and Frank entered European history at this juncture and have ever since remained. But these Germans did not overthrow the Roman Empire, even though they occasionally defeated Roman legions on the battlefield. Rome, somehow, destroyed itself. Its population diminished, its trade routes lay still, its land went untilled. Somehow the fiber that had made Rome great had rotted. The magnificent Roman army, once a conqueror of the known world, took barbarian mercenaries into its ranks in such numbers that they soon became its leaders. More often than by war, the Germans took over Roman territories through peaceful migration, often at the invitation of the enervated Romans themselves. Far from hungering to destroy Roman civilization, the barbarian tribes were with few exceptions anxious to accept it as their own. Largely through the medium of Christianity, the Germans who came into contact with Rome were transformed. Their barbarian culture was softened and imbued with new values. By the fifth century Roman power in the West was dead but Rome lived on in the new civilization that the Germanic peoples established on the soil of Europe.

The Coronation of Pepin the Short, 750

More than any other tribe, the Franks emerged as the principal heirs to the traditions of Rome. Their tribal seat was the lower e and, unlike most other Germanic nomads, they retained their con- t with the homeland and its rude culture as they moved southward. The rst great king of the Franks was Clovis, who in 481 began a campaign of expansion which led ultimately to recognition by almost all the Germanic tribes of Frankish suzerainty and of Frankish dominion over territory that encompasses most of present-day France, Germany and the Low Countries. Even more important than Clovis's conquests was his conversion to Roman Christianity. As a Christian, Clovis became the Papacy's chief defender of orthodoxy, not only against paganism but against the greater menace of Eastern Christianity, which missionaries from the east were actively propagating among the tribes. That Clovis performed his duty by bloodshed and treachery did not trouble the Church. "Thus did God each day deliver his enemies into his hands and increase his realm," wrote the pious Bishop Gregory of Tours of the Frankish king, "because he walked with a perfect heart before Him and did what was right in His sight." By the sword of Clovis, Roman Christianity and Roman culture were spread throughout Gaul. For the first time since the retreat of the Roman legions, Clovis restored political unity to western Europe. More important, he made western Europe a religious and cultural entity again.

It was not until 751, however, that the alliance between the Papacy and the Frankish state was formally consecrated. Clovis's heirs, the Merovingian line of succession, had become worthless monarchs. Power had for some generations been exercised by the royal official known as the Mayor of the Palace. When the Papacy found itself threatened by the Lombards, an ambitious Germanic tribe that aspired to rule all of Italy, it turned naturally to the Mayor of the Palace for help. In 739, Charles Martel, one of the great Palace Mayors, rejected a plea for assistance from Pope Gregory III, for Martel relied on the Lombards to help drive the invading Saracens from Europe. But a few years later a new Pope, Zacharias, made a similar appeal to Martel's son, Pepin the Short, who reacted quite differently.

Pepin, thirsty for the honors as well as the substance of power, wanted to be king. Reluctant to usurp the throne openly, he desired Papel sanction for his action. Pepin entered into negotiations with the Pope's emissary, the brilliant Benedictine monk Boniface, a tireless and effective servant of Rome who, in 751 or 752, anointed Pepin King of the Franks. In January, 754, Pope Stephen II, successor to Zacharias, personally reanointed Pepin at the Frankish court near Metz. He also conferred on him the Roman title of Patricius, which implied that the Frankish monarchy had taken over from Constantinople the responsibility for the rule and protection of Italy. By accepting the crown from the Pope's hands, Pepin acknowledged an obligation to the Church and, to a degree at least, some Papal authority over his own throne. After his coronation he marched into Italy and defeated the Lombards. Two years later he made the famous Donation of Pepin, granting to the Pope the rule of a wide territory—which was by no means his to give—surrounding the city of Rome. By guaranteeing protection of this temporal domain of the Church, Pepin effectively thwarted the Lombardian effort to unite Italy. The importance of the Donation cannot be overestimated, for it was more than 1100 years before the Popes could be divested of their lands and Italy fused into a single state.

The following account of Pepin's coronation by Boniface was written by a Benedictine monk from the monastery at Lorsch, near Heidelberg. The "annals" produced in the monasteries are among the best and most reliable records of the Middle Ages. The Benedictines were, in an age of general ignorance and illiteracy, almost the only servants of enlightenment. Though they often made mistakes, such as recording in this document the date of the coronation as 750, the monks were indispensable to the preservation of Western culture. This document vividly describes one of the great events of the Middle Ages.

Document 7

In the year of the Incarnation of our Lord, 750, Pepin sent ambassadors to Pope Zacharias to ask his opinion in the matter of the kings of the Franks, who, though of the royal line, and called kings, enjoyed in truth no power in the realm except that official documents were issued in their name. Otherwise they were destitute of power, and did only what the mayor of the palace told them.

Only upon the day when the people, according to ancient usage, were wont to bring gifts to their sovereign on the March Field, did the king, surrounded by the army, sit in his chair, the mayor of the palace standing before him, and proclaim such laws as had been established by the Franks. The next day he returned home, and stayed there during the remainder of the year.

Pope Zacharias, therefore, in virtue of apostolic authority, told the ambassadors that he judged it better and more advantageous that he should be king and be called king who had the power rather than he who was falsely called king.

The said pontiff accordingly enjoined the king and the people of the Franks that Pepin, who already exercised the regal power, should be called king and raised to the throne.

And this was done by St. Boniface, the archbishop, who anointed him king in the City of Soissons. And so it came about that Pepin was called king, while Childeric, falsely called king, was shaven and sent to the monastery.

Charlemagne Made Roman Emperor, 799–801

Pepin's son Charles—known to history as Charles the Great or Charlemagne—extended the work of Clovis to unite the Germanic peoples under the Frankish throne. He conquered the Lombards, the menace to the integrity of Rome. He incorporated Bavaria into his realm and subdued the fierce Saxons in a series of brutal, bloody wars. Wherever Charlemagne's legions went, the missionaries of the Church followed, sharing in his conquests. His dominion and that of the Church were imposed over all the Germanic peoples except the Anglo-Saxons in Britain and the heathen Scandinavians. His frontiers, by the end of the eighth century, pressed against the Arabs in the south and the Slavs in the east. Charlemagne had become the first undisputed leader of Europe since the days of the Roman emperors.

Rome found in Charlemagne's conquests a grandiose prospect for the Church. But Pope Leo III had a more immediate reason for courting the king. In 799 Leo ran afoul of charges of corruption in the Papal office and looked to Charlemagne for help. Facing physical danger from his enemies, Leo hastened across the Alps to seek Charlemagne's protection, but even at the Frankish court charges of adultery and perjury rang in his ears. The king, promising to reflect on the dispute, sent the pope back to Rome under escort and spent the next year at his normal violent pursuits. In November, 800, Charlemagne arrived in Rome and allowed Pope Leo to clear himself of his alleged crimes by taking an oath in St. Peter's Church. On Christmas Day the Pope, in gratitude, crowned Charlemagne Emperor of the Romans, heir to Caesar, Aurelius and Constantine.

Charlemagne appears to have attached little significance to his coronation as Roman Emperor, but the act looms large in European history. Constantinople had continued to exercise theoretical hegemony over the Western Empire, a sort of mythical rule to which Europe rendered homage long after all real power was gone. The coronation of Charlemagne transferred the crown of the Western Empire to a German king. To Charlemagne's contemporaries it meant the reëstablishment of the Roman Empire in the west. It planted so firmly the notion that the German kings were the heirs to the throne of Rome that a thousand years would pass—during which the Holy Roman Empire was nothing more than a fiction—before the idea would die. It was not until Napoleon that this vestige of a departed civilization disappeared, only to be resurrected by Adolph Hitler as the *Third*

Reich (Empire). Charlemagne's coronation created a political myth that long remained an integral part of Western civilization.

The account of the coronation presented here was written by Einhard, Charlemagne's court biographer. Einhard claims that if the king had known of the Pope's intention, he would not have entered the church on that fateful Christmas day. Most historians regard that view with skepticism. Charlemagne probably took no pleasure in receiving the imperial crown from the Pope, of whose authority he was scornful, but it is not considered likely that he was taken by surprise. Einhard, one of the greatest of the medieval writers, vividly describes the events which led to Charlemagne's becoming Emperor.

Document 8

As Pope Leo [III] was riding from the Lateran in Rome to service in the church of St. Lawrence, called "the Gridiron," he fell into an ambush which the Romans had set for him in the neighborhood of this church. He was dragged from off his horse and, as some would have it, his eyes put out, his tongue cut off, and he was then left lying in the street, naked and half dead. Afterward the instigators of this deed ordered that he should be taken into the monastery of the holy martyr Erasmus to be cared for. His chamberlain Albinus succeeded, however, in letting him down over the wall at night, whereupon Duke Winigis of Spoleto, who had hurried to Rome on hearing of this deed of sacrilege, took him into his charge and carried him to Spoleto.

When the king [Charlemagne] received news of this occurrence, he gave orders that the Roman pope, the successor of St. Peter, should be brought to him, with all due honor. He did not, however, give up on this account the expedition into Saxony which he had undertaken. He held a general assembly at a place called Lippeham, on the Rhine; he then crossed the river and pushed on with his entire army to Paderborn where he set up his camp and awaited the pope. In the meantime he sent his son Charles, with a part of the army, to the Elbe to settle certain matters with the Wilzer and Abodrites and to receive into his charge certain of the North Saxons.

While he was awaiting his son's return, the pope arrived, was honorably received, and remained several days with him. After he had laid before the king all the reasons for his coming, he was accompanied back to Rome by the king's ambassadors and reinstated in his authority there. . . .

* * *

When spring came again, about the middle of March, the king left Aix-la-Chapelle and journeyed toward the coast of Gaul. Off this coast, which was being devastated by the piratical Northmen, he built and manned a fleet. Easter he celebrated in St. Riquier at the shrine of St. Richard. From here he traveled along the coast to the city of Rouen, where he crossed the Seine and betook himself to Tours in order to perform his devotions at the shrine of St. Martin. On account of the illness of his wife, Luitgarda, who died and was buried here, he was forced to remain some days in this place; she died on the 4th of June. From here he returned, by way of Orleans and Paris, to Aix-la-Chapelle; early in August he reached Mayence, where he held a diet and announced his intended journey to Italy.

From Mayence he went with his army to Ravenna, where he stayed only seven days and whence he dispatched his son Pepin, with the army, into the country of Beneventum. He and his son left Ravenna together, but at Ancona they parted company and he betook himself to Rome.

On the very day of his arrival Pope Leo went to meet him at Nomentum. He received the pope with great reverence, and they dined together. Then he remained behind while the pope returned to the city in order that he might be waiting to receive him the next morning on the steps of St. Peter's, together with the bishops and all the clergy.

When he appeared and dismounted from his horse, the pope received him with gratitude and thanksgiving and conducted him into the church, while all the people glorified God in hymns of praise. This was on the 24th day of November. Seven days later, the king publicly proclaimed, in an assembly which he had called together, all the reasons why he had come to Rome, and thenceforth he labored daily to carry out all that he had come to do.

He began with the most serious and difficult matter, namely, the investigation into the offenses of which the pope had been accused. But since no one could be found who was willing to substantiate the charges, the pope, carrying the Gospels in his hand, mounted the pulpit in St. Peter's and before all the people, and in the name of the Holy Trinity, took an oath to clear himself from the crimes imputed to him. . . .

On the most holy day of the birth of our Lord, the king went to mass at St. Peter's, and as he knelt in prayer before the alter Pope Leo set a crown upon his head, while all the Roman populace cried aloud, "Long life and victory to the mighty Charles, the great and pacific Emperor of the Romans, crowned of God!" After he had been thus acclaimed, the pope did homage to him, as had been the custom with the early rulers, and henceforth he dropped the title of Patrician and was called Emperor and Augustus. . . .

The Oaths of Strasbourg and the Treaty of Verdun, 842–3

A. The Oaths of Strasbourg

Charlemagne's empire, called Carolingian after its first emperor, was unable to survive intact its leader's death in 814. The Germanic peoples, lacking a strong chief to bind them together, proved too disparate and too undisciplined to remain united as a nation. Equally divisive was the inability of the Carolingians, including Charlemagne himself, to make a distinction between their personal possessions and their realm. It was the custom of the German tribes for the father to divide his wealth among his heirs. Thus the Carolingians divided their empire.

Charlemagne's single surviving son, Louis the Pious, inherited his father's throne in its entirety. But hardly had Louis become Emperor than he began to make provision for distributing his domain among his three sons: Lothair, Ludwig the German and Pepin. Lothair, the eldest, was to inherit the title of Emperor and rule over all but Aquitaine and Bavaria, which his two brothers were to receive. But while Ludwig and Pepin grumbled at the inequity of the division, a fourth claimant appeared, King Louis's son by a second marriage, known as Charles the Bald. His father's favorite, Charles the Bald benefited by a succession of changes in the King's testament, each giving him, at the expense of his brothers, a larger share than before.

In 838 Pepin died, reducing the contending brothers to three, and in 840 King Louis died, eliminating the last restraint to civil war. Ludwig the German and Charles the Bald allied themselves against Lothair, claimant to the imperial title, and on the battlefield of Fontenay, near Auxerre, bested him in 841. To cement their alliance until Lothair could be crushed, Ludwig and Charles met at Strasbourg in 842 to swear, in the presence of their armies, oaths of mutual fidelity. Ludwig's men were almost pure German. Charles's army was composed principally of Gallo-Romans and Franks from the south and west of France. So that Charles's men would understand him, Ludwig spoke the oath in a language called *lingua romana*, precursor of contemporary French, Spanish and Italian. Charles spoke, for Ludwig's army, in the *lingua teudisca*, forebear of contemporary German, Dutch and English. Ludwig and Charles also gave oaths to each other in their own tongues. The Strasbourg Oaths, foreshadowing the great political divisions of Europe, demonstrate how the German and Latin cultures had already become both distinctive and self-conscious.

The Strasbourg Oaths were preserved by the historian Nithardus, who fought for Charles the Bald at Fontenay and later played an important part in the negotiations between the two allied brothers. The document below contains a portion of Nithardus's account of the meeting at Strasbourg, followed by the text of the oaths taken before the armies, first in the original languages, then in English translation.

Document 9A

On the fifteenth of February Ludwig and Charles came together in the city formerly called Argentoratum, now known as Strasbourg, and there they took the mutual oaths which are given herewith, Ludwig in the *lingua romana* and Charles in the *lingua teudisca*. Before the exchange of oaths they addressed the assembled people, each in his own language, and Ludwig, being the elder, thus began:

"How often, since the death of our father, Lothair has pursued my brother and myself and tried to destroy us, is known to you all. So, then, when neither brotherly love, nor Christian feeling, nor any reason whatever could bring about a peace between us upon fair conditions, we were at last compelled to bring the matter before God, determined to abide by whatever issue He might decree. And we, as you know, came off victorious; our brother was beaten, and with his followers got away, each as best he could. Then we, moved by brotherly love and having compassion on our Christian people, were not willing to pursue and destroy them; but, still, as before, we begged that justice might be done to each. He, however, after all this, not content with the judgment of God, has not ceased to pursue me and my brother with hostile purpose, and to harass our peoples with fire, plunder, and murder. Wherefore we have been compelled to hold this meeting, and, since we feared that you might doubt whether our faith was fixed and our alliance secure, we have determined to make our oaths thereto in your presence. And we do this, not from any unfair greed, but in order that, if God, with your help, shall grant us peace, we may the better provide for the common welfare.

But if, which God forbid, I shall dare to violate the oath which I shall swear to my brother, then I absolve each one of you from your allegiance and from the oath which you have sworn to me."

After Charles had made the same speech in the *lingua romana*, Ludwig, as the elder of the two, swore first to be faithful to his alliance:

THE OATH OF LUDWIG

Pro Deo amur et pro christian poblo et nostro commun salvament, dist di in avant, in quant Deus savir et podir me dunat, si salvaraeio cist meon fradre Karlo et in adiudha et in cadhuna cosa, si cum om per dreit son fradra salvar dist in o quid il mi altresi fazet; et ab Ludher nul plaid numquam prindrai, qui meon vol cist meon fradre Karle in damno sit.

When Ludwig had taken this oath, Charles swore the same thing in the *lingua teudisca.*

THE OATH OF CHARLES

In Godes minna ind in thes christianes folches ind unser bedhero gealtnissi, fon thesemo dage frammordes, so fram so mir Got gewizci indi madh furgibit, so haldih tesan minan bruodher, soso man mit rehtu sinan bruodher scal, in thiu, thaz er mig sosoma duo; indi mit Ludheren in nohheiniu thing ne gegango, the minan willon imo ce scadhen werhen.

THE OATH TAKEN BY THE SUBJECTS OF THE TWO KINGS

The oath which the subjects of the two kings then took, each (people) in its own language, reads thus in the *lingua romana:*

Si Lodhwigs sagrament qua son fradre Karlo jurat, conservat, et Karlus meos sendra, de suo part, non lo stanit, si io returnar non lint pois, ne io ne neuls cui eo returnar int pois, in nulla aiudha contra Lodhuwig nun li iver.

And in the *lingua teudisca:*

Oba Karl then eid then, er sineno bruodher Ludhuwige gesuor, geleistit, indi Ludhuwig min herro then er imo gesuor, forbrihchit, obih ina es irwenden ne mag, noh ih no thero nohhein then ih es irwended mag, widhar Karle imo ce follusti ne wirdhic.

The translation of the first oath is as follows: "For the love of God, and for the sake as well of our peoples as of ourselves, I promise that from this day fourth, as God shall grant me wisdom and strength, I will treat this my brother as one's brother ought to be treated, provided that he shall do the same by me. And with Lothair I will not willingly enter into any dealings which may injure this my brother."

The second oath, taken by the followers of the two kings, may be thus translated: "If Ludwig (or Charles) shall observe the oath which he has sworn to his brother Charles (or Ludwig), and Charles (or Ludwig), our lord, on his side, should be untrue to his oath, and we should be unable to hold him to it, neither we nor any whom we can deter, shall give him any support." The oath taken by the two armies was the same, with only the names of the kings interchanged.

B. The Treaty of Verdun

After the meeting at Strasbourg, Ludwig the German and Charles the Bald advanced on Lothair and overtook him near the town of Chalons-sur-Saone. Aware that he was hopelessly outnumbered, Lothair proposed to his brothers that they negotiate a peace. His only conditions were that he take the imperial title and, to maintain its dignity, slightly more territory than the others would receive. Ludwig and Charles accepted the terms and, in 843, met at Verdun to arrange the peaceful partition of the Empire.

The Treaty of Verdun divided Charlemagne's realm into three parts. Lothair, recognized by his brothers as Emperor, emerged from the bargaining with a wide center strip without geographic or ethnic unity that ran from Rome across the Alps, down the west bank of the Rhine to the North Sea. Ludwig took the part of the Empire to the east, Charles the Bald the part to the west. Ludwig's East Frankish kingdom was the beginning of modern Germany and Charles's West Frankish domain the beginning of modern France. The middle kingdom was the beginning of trouble. The imperial crown, which soon became a German institution, proved a curse to the German people throughout most of a thousand years, while the territories, especially those along the Rhine, remained a French-German battlefield throughout the ages. The Treaty of Verdun truly opened the era of modern modern European political history.

Unfortunately, the text of the Treaty of Verdun has not survived. Its most important provisions, however, were recorded by the chroniclers of the period. The following two short passages, the first written by Saint Bertin and the second by Rudolph of Fulda, provide the essence of the document.

Document 9B

(a)

Charles set out to find his brothers, and they met at Verdun. By the division there made Ludwig received for his share all the country beyond the Rhine, and on this side Speyer, Worms, Mainz, and the territories belonging to these cities. Lothair received that which is between the Scheldt and the Rhine toward the sea, and that lying beyond Cambrésis, Hainault, and the counties adjoining on this side of the Meuse, down to the confluence of the Saône and Rhone, and thence along the Rhone to the sea, together with the adjacent counties. Charles received all the remainder, extending to Spain. And when the oath was exchanged they went their several ways.

(b)

The realm had from early times been divided in three portions, and in the month of August the three kings, coming together at Verdun in Gaul, redivided it among themselves. Ludwig received the eastern part, Charles the western. Lothair, who was older than his brothers, received the middle portion. After peace was firmly established and oaths exchanged, each brother returned to his dominion to control and protect it. Charles, presuming to regard Aquitaine as belonging properly to his share, was given much trouble by his nephew Pepin, who annoyed him by frequent incursions and caused great loss.

Formulae of Commendation, Immunity and Fiefdom

The all-pervasive social, economic and political system known as feudalism—one of the crucial developments of Western history—spread over Europe as the central government of the Carolingian empire disintegrated. The feudal system was not the product of a single leader or a conscious political idea. It had its institutional roots in the Roman Empire and Germanic tribal life and had already appeared in primitive form when Charlemagne's rule interrupted its growth. In the ninth and tenth centuries, feudalism attained full development in France, Italy, Christian Spain, and Germany. Later it passed into England, eastern Europe and Scandinavia. Feudalism was medieval Europe's substitute for government and its response to the threat of economic and social anarchy. It left influences on European society that are perceptible today.

Though its characteristics varied from region to region, feudalism from the North Sea to the Mediterranean had a common foundation: it grew out of the need to preserve order, as central authority disappeared. The kings, unable to control the nobles, assigned them the powers of government in return for military service and personal loyalty. Theoretically bound to him, the nobles dispensed justice, collected taxes and in general ruled their territories or "fiefs" under "immunity" from royal jurisdiction. Feudalism established an intricate system of personal bondage; the king, in theory, at the top of the hierarchy, the serfs at bottom, and any number of lords and vassals in between, all tied to one another by mutual obligations, the principle of which was protection. Law enforcement under feudalism was thus based on a contract between individuals, not on a relationship between individuals and the state. It was basic to the nature of feudalism that these relationships possessed a formal, legal quality, confirmed by ceremony and ritual. The feudal oath, with its semi-mystical connotations, set the duties and obligations of the two individuals entering into a feudal compact.

Commendation

"Commendation" was the act establishing a union between lord and vassal. This was the fundamental feudal relationship. In the eighth century, when the Merovingian regime was crumbling, large numbers of freemen sought protection by entering the service of a stronger lord. In the debris of the Carolingian regime a century later, more freemen sought refuge in vassalage from rampaging Northmen, Hungarians and Saracens, as well as from rapacious lords and bands of outlaws. By the tenth century, scarcely a freeman was left in western Europe.

The formula of commendation given here dates from the Merovingian period. Note in the last paragraph the vassal's insistence on retaining his "free condition," a stipulation that was not then regarded as inherently contradictory. The terms of the contract are limited to the life of the vassal. But within a few centuries, vassalage had become generally hereditary and the "free condition" existed no more.

Document 10A

To that magnificent lord ________, I, ________. Since it is well known to all how little I have wherewith to feed and clothe myself, I have therefore petitioned your piety, and your good-will has decreed to me, that I should hand myself over, or commend myself, to your guardianship, which I have thereupon done; that is to say, in this way, that you should aid and succor me, as well with food as with clothing, according as I shall be able to serve you and deserve it.

And so long as I shall live I ought to provide service and honor to you, compatible with my free condition; and I shall not, during the time of my life, have the right to withdraw from your control or guardianship; but must remain during the days of my life under your power or defense. Wherefore it is proper that if either of us shall wish to withdraw himself from these agreements, he shall pay ______ shillings to the other party, and this agreement shall remain unbroken.

Immunity

"Immunity" was the renunciation by the crown of its legal jurisdiction over a territory given to a vassal as his fief. Beginning with Clovis, the kings had made such grants to land-holding bishops as expressions of piety. The practice was later extended to laymen, the grant usually being made in return for or in promise of some important military service. The king's chief object in granting each immunity was to win the favor of an ecclesiastic or a noble. In return for the fiefs, the king could count on the support of armed contingents, supplied by both his clerical and his lay vassals. But every grant weakened the king's authority over his domain, until the kings during the high periods of feudalism often had less power than their vassals and sometimes had no power at all.

The following formula provides for a grant of an immunity from the king to a bishop. The "you" referred to is meant as a warning to any rival claimants of the land which the fief occupies.

Document 10B

We believe that we give our royal authority its full splendor if, with benevolent intentions, we bestow upon churches—or upon any persons—the favors which they merit, and if, with the aid of God, we give a written assurance of the continuance of these favors. We wish, then, to make known that at the request of a prelate, lord of ______ [the estate named] and bishop of ________ [the church named], we have accorded to him, for the sake of our eternal salvation, the following benefits: that in the domains of the bishop's church, both those which it possesses to-day and those which by God's grace it may later acquire, no public official shall be permitted to enter, either to hold courts or to exact fines, on any account; but let these prerogatives be vested in full in the bishop and his successors. We ordain therefore that neither you nor your subordinates, nor those who come after you, nor any person endowed with a public office, shall ever enter the domains of that church, in whatever part of our kingdom they may be situated, either to hold trials or to collect fines. All the taxes and other revenues which the royal treasury has a right to demand from the people on the lands of the said church, whether they be freemen or slaves, Romans or barbarians, we now bestow on the said church for our future salvation, to be used by the officials of the church forever for the best interests of the church.

Fiefdom

The system of granting fiefs was fundamental to property holding under feudalism. It made perfect sense during the medieval era for title over property to be vested in one person and the rights of usage in another. A fief could be almost anything. One man, for example, might grant to another the right to collect tolls on a bridge or at a mill on his estate. But characteristically a fief meant land.

In the following document, Thiebault grants as a fief to Jocelyn d'Avalon the feudal estate of Gillencourt, which was part of the land surrounding the castle of La Ferté-sur-Aube. Thiebault promises Jocelyn to take away none of the men from the estate. Jocelyn, for his part, became Thiebault's liege man or vassal, with all its implied obligations of service. But note that these obligations were hedged by Jocelyn's earlier commitments. Jocelyn's service as a vassal to three other lords demonstrates the complexity that feudal relationships often assumed.

Document 10C

I, Thiebault, count palatine of Troyes, make known to those present and to come that I have given in fee to Jocelyn d'Avalon and his heirs the manor which is called Gillencourt, which is of the castellaneire of La Ferté-sur-Aube; and whatever the same Jocelyn shall be able to acquire in the same manor I have granted to him and his heirs in enlargement of that fief. I have granted, moreover, to him that in no free manor of mine will I retain men who are of this gift. The same Jocelyn, moreover, on account of this has become my liege man, saving, however, his allegiance to Gerad d'Arcy, and to the lord duke of Burgundy, and to Peter, count of Auxerre. Done at Chouaude, by my own witness, in the year of the Incarnation of our Lord 1200, in the month of January. Given by the hand of Walter, my chancellor.

Truce of God, 1083

Despite feudalism's elaborate administrative machinery, disorder remained a characteristic of medieval life. Feudal nobles, far from maintaining the peace within their jurisdictions, engaged constantly in private warfare which endangered not only their own lives but those of peasants, merchants and churchmen.

Late in the tenth century, the Church began to take the leadership in an effort to end the chronic strife. Church councils, under the influence of the Cluniac movement for ecclesiastical reform, issued decrees known as the Peace of God, designed to reduce violence, particularly against the defenseless members of society. Even with the force of the Church behind it, however, the Peace of God was not very successful.

The Church then decided on a shift in emphasis in order to prohibit violence during certain portions of the week and certain times of the year. At first only Sunday was designated. Then the ban was extended from Wednesday evening to Monday morning. Holidays were gradually added, with an eye to protecting the peasant during the season he spent in the field and the merchant when he was on the road. It is difficult to determine whether the Truce of God had any impact. At best, its influence was not great.

Feudalism, from its beginning to its end, remained a way of life dangerous to its members. Public safety was not restored until, over the succeeding centuries, strong central governments pre-empted the anarchy of the nobles.

The Truce of God presented here was issued by a church council held at Cologne in 1083. The passages quoted provide eloquent evidence of conditions of medieval life.

Document 11

Inasmuch as in our own times the Church, through its members, has been extraordinarily afflicted by tribulations and difficulties, so that tranquillity and peace were wholly despaired of, we have endeavored with God's help to come to its aid, in the midst of its sufferings and perils. And by the advice of our faithful subjects we have at length provided this remedy, so that we might to some extent reëstablish, on certain days at least, the peace which, because of our sins, we could not make enduring. Accordingly we have enacted and set forth the following:

Having called together those under us to a legally summoned council, which was held at Cologne, the chief city of our province, in the church of St. Peter, in the 1083d year of our Lord's Incarnation, in the sixth indiction, on the twelfth day before the Kalends of May, after arranging other business, we have caused to be read in public what we proposed to do in this matter. After this had been fully discussed by all, both clergy and people with God's aid reached an agreement, and we set forth in what manner and during what parts of the year the peace should be observed, namely:

That from the first day of the Advent of our Lord through Epiphany, and from the beginning of Septuagesima to the eighth day after Pentecost and through that whole day, and throughout the year on every Sunday, Friday, and Saturday, and on the fast days of the four seasons, and on the eve and the day of all the apostles, and on all days canonically set apart—or which shall in future be set apart—for fasts or feasts, this decree of peace shall be observed; so that both those who travel and those who remain at home may enjoy security and the most entire peace, so that no one may commit murder, arson, robbery, or assault, no one may injure another with a sword, club, or any kind of weapon. Let no one, however irritated by wrong, presume to carry arms, shield, sword, or lance, or any kind of armor, from the Advent of our Lord to the eighth day after Epiphany, and from Septuagesima to the eighth day after Pentecost. On the remaining days, indeed, namely, on Sundays, Fridays, apostles' days, and the vigils of the apostles, and on every day set aside, or to be set aside for fasts or feasts, arms may be carried, but on this condition that no injury shall be done in any way to any one.

If it shall be necessary for any one, during the period of the peace,—i.e. from the Advent of our Lord to the eighth day after Epiphany, and from Septuagesima to the eighth day after Pentecost,—to go from one bishopric into another in which the peace is not observed, he may bear arms, but on the condition that he shall not injure any one, except in self-defense if he is attacked; and when he returns into our diocese he shall immediately lay aside his arms. If it shall happen that any castle is besieged during the days which are included within the peace, the besiegers shall cease from attack unless they are set upon by the besieged and compelled to beat the latter back.

And in order that this statute of peace should not be violated by any one rashly or with impunity, a penalty was fixed by the common consent of all, namely. If a free man or noble violates it, i.e. commits homicide, or wounds any one, or is at fault in any manner whatever, he shall be expelled from his lands, without any indulgence on account of the payment of money or the intercession of friends, and his heirs shall take all his property. If he holds a fief, the lord to whom it belongs shall receive it again. Moreover, if it appear that his heirs after his expulsion have furnished him any support or aid, and if they are convicted of it, the estate shall be taken from them and revert to the king. But if they wish to clear themselves of the charge against them, they shall take oath, with twelve who are equally free or equally noble . . .

The statute of this noble peace is especially enacted for the safety of those engaged in feuds; but after the end of the peace they are not to dare to rob and plunder in the villages and houses, since the laws and penalties enacted before the institution of the peace are still legally valid to restrain them from crime, and, moreover, because robbers and highwaymen are excluded from this divine peace, and indeed from any peace.

If any one attempt to oppose this pious institution and is unwilling to promise peace to God with the others, or to observe it, no priest in our diocese shall presume to say a mass for him, or shall take any care for his salvation; if he is sick, no Christian shall dare to visit him; on his deathbed he shall not receive the eucharist, unless he repents. The supreme authority of the peace pledged to God and generally extolled by all will be so great that it will be observed not only in our times, but forever among our posterity, because if any one shall presume to infringe or violate it, either now or ages hence, until the end of the world, he is irrevocably excommunicated by us.

The responsibility for carrying out the above-mentioned penalties against the violators of the peace rests no more with the counts, local judges, or officials than with the whole people in general. They are to be especially careful not to show friendship or hatred, nor to do anything contrary to justice in punishing, nor to conceal crimes, which may be hidden, but to bring them to light. No one is to receive money for the release of those taken in fault, or to attempt to aid the guilty by any favor of any kind, because whoever does this incurs the intolerable damnation of his soul; and all the faithful ought to remember that this peace has not been promised to men, but to God, and therefore must be observed so much the more rigidly and firmly. Wherefore we exhort all in Christ to guard inviolably this necessary contract of peace, and if any one hereafter presumes to violate it, let him be damned by the ban of irrevocable excommunication and by the anathema of eternal perdition. . . .

Pope Urban II Initiates the First Crusade, 1095

The medieval world, inferring from its hardy, brawling social life, was clearly bursting with energy. Whoever could manage to channel that energy would have at his disposal a mighty force. Throughout Europe, the monarchies were too enfeebled, the nobility too divided to mobilize any substantial strength. It took the Papacy to direct Europe's brimming vigor into Crusades to the Holy Land, one of the strangest and most exciting phenomena in all Western history.

Shortly after the death of Mohammed in 632, Palestine was overrun by Arabs and Jerusalem passed into Moslem hands. The Arabs, however, shared the Christian's veneration for Biblical holy places. Not only did the Arabs protect these places but they tolerated frequent Christian pilgrimages to them. The Arabs evoked little crusading zeal in Europe.

But in the eleventh century, Jerusalem, after a brief liberation from Mohammedan rule by a Byzantine emperor, was once again taken by infidels, this time the Seljuk Turks, who had become the fiercest champions of the Moslem faith. Pilgrims returning from the Holy Land told terrifying tales of treatment suffered at the hands of the new conqueror. In 1095, the Byzantine emperor dispatched a plea to Pope Urban II to save the Eastern Empire and the Eastern Church from the rampaging Turkish infidels. Urban, who was probably indifferent to the fate of the Eastern Empire, was fascinated by the prospect of rescuing the Eastern Church and incorporating it into the Roman Catholic system. Without doubt, he recognized that his own leadership of a great crusade would solidify his power in Europe. Pope Urban responded affirmatively to the Byzantine appeal.

Urban's success in persuading the European nobility, particularly the French, to join him is somewhat difficult to understand. Still, there are explanations. Trips to the Holy Land, despite its distance, were reasonably common throughout the Middle Ages, and had, in fact, been growing in popularity. One hundred seventeen pilgrimages were noted in the eleventh century alone. Religious zeal, in a measure difficult for the modern mind to comprehend, undoubtedly motivated many of the Crusaders. It would not have been unusual for them to conceive of their voyage simply as an armed pilgrimage. Some Crusaders undoubtedly had less noble motives. Some went for profit, to take advantage of the newly reopened trade routes to the east. Some went for adventure. Some went for escape, either from social convention or from punishment for crime. But it would be unjust to overemphasize the secular objectives. The Crusades were probably a facet of the same missionary drive within Christianity that took the faith from the Middle East to the Atlantic and now was taking it back again.

Urban personally launched the First Crusade in a speech before the Council of Clermont in 1095. It has been described as the most effective speech ever delivered and, judging by its result, may very well have been. A Frenchman facing an audience of Frenchmen, Urban abandoned the ecclesiastical Latin to speak in his native tongue. He appealed to every emotion of his listeners: racial pride, religious ardor, military fervor, social dissatisfaction and base avarice. The Council was deeply moved. By April, 1096, a vast horde of warriors was on its way east, directed by the organizing genius of the Church.

Urban's brilliant speech is reproduced in translation here in the version transmitted by Robert the Monk of Rheims. One of several variations extant, it is generally regarded as the best.

Document 12

In the year of our Lord's Incarnation one thousand and ninety-five, a great council was convened within the bounds of Gaul, in Auvergne, in the city which is called Clermont. Over this Pope Urban II presided, with the Roman bishops and cardinals. This council was a famous one on account of the concourse of both French and German bishops, and of princes as well. Having arranged the matters relating to the Church, the lord Pope went forth into a certain spacious plain, for no building was large enough to hold all the people. The Pope then, with sweet and persuasive eloquence, addressed those present in words something like the following, saying:

"Oh, race of Franks, race beyond the mountains [the Alps], race beloved and chosen by God (as is clear from many of your works), set apart from all other nations by the situation of your country, as well as by your Catholic faith and the honor you render to the holy Church: to you our discourse is addressed, and for you our exhortations are intended. We wish you to know what a serious matter has led us to your country, for it is the imminent peril threatening you and all the faithful that has brought us hither.

"From the confines of Jerusalem and from the city of Constantinople a grievous report has gone forth and has been brought repeatedly to our ears; namely, that a race from the kingdom of the Persians, an accursed race, a race wholly alienated from God, 'a generation that set not their heart aright, and whose spirit was not steadfast with God,' has violently invaded the lands of those Christians and has depopulated them by pillage and fire. They have led away a part of the captives into their own country, and a part they have killed by cruel tortures. They have either destroyed the churches of God or appropriated them for the rites of their own religion. They destroy the altars, after having defiled them with their uncleanness. . . . The kingdom of the Greeks [the Eastern Empire] is now dismembered by them and has been deprived of territory so vast in extent that it could not be traversed in two months' time.

"On whom, therefore, rests the labor of avenging these wrongs and of recovering this territory, if not upon you—you, upon whom, above all other nations, God has conferred remarkable glory in arms, great courage, bodily activity, and strength to humble the heads of those who resist you? Let the deeds of your ancestors encourage you and incite your minds to manly achievements—the glory and greatness of King Charlemagne, and of his son Louis [the Pious], and of your other monarchs, who have destroyed the kingdoms of the Turks and have extended the sway of the holy Church over lands previously pagan. Let the holy sepulcher of our Lord and Saviour, which is possessed by the unclean nations, especially arouse you, and the holy places which are now treated with ignominy and irreverently polluted with the filth of the unclean. Oh most valiant soldiers and descendants of invincible ancestors, do not degenerate, but recall the valor of your ancestors.

"But if you are hindered by love of children, parents, or wife, remember what the Lord says in the Gospel, 'He that loveth father or mother more than me is not worthy of me.' 'Every one that hath forsaken houses, or brethren, or sisters, or father, or mother, or wife, or children, or lands, for my name's sake, shall receive an hundred-fold, and shall inherit everlasting life.' Let none of your possessions restrain you, nor anxiety for your family affairs. For this land which you inhabit, shut in on all sides by the seas and surrounded by the mountain peaks, is too narrow for your large population; nor does it abound in wealth; and it furnishes scarcely food enough for its cultivators. Hence it is that you murder and devour one another, that you wage war, and that very many among you perish in civil strife.

"Let hatred, therefore, depart from among you; let your quarrels end; let wars cease; and let all dissensions and controversies slumber. Enter upon the road of the Holy Sepulcher; wrest that land from the wicked race, and subject it to yourselves. That land which, as the Scripture says, 'floweth with milk and honey' was given by God into the power of the children of Israel. Jerusalem is the center of the earth; the land is fruitful above all others, like another paradise of delights. This spot the Redeemer of mankind has made illustrious by His advent, has beautified by His sojourn, has consecrated by His passion, has redeemed by His death, has glorified by His burial.

"This royal city, however, situated at the center of the earth, is now held captive by the enemies of Christ and is subjected, by those who do not know God, to the worship of the heathen. She seeks, therefore, and desires to be liberated, and ceases not to implore you to come to her aid. From you especially she asks succor, because, as we have already said, God has conferred upon you, above all other nations, great glory in arms. Accordingly, undertake this journey eagerly for the remission of your sins, with the assurance of the reward of imperishable glory in the kingdom of heaven."

When Pope Urban had skilfully said these and very many similar things, he so centered in one purpose the desires of all who were present that all cried out, "It is the will of God! It is the will of God!" When the venerable Roman pontiff heard that, with eyes uplifted to heaven, he gave thanks to God and, commanding silence with his hand, said:

"Most beloved brethren, to-day is manifest in you what the Lord says in the Gospel. 'Where two or three are gathered together in my name, there am I in the midst of them.' For unless God had been present in your spirits, all of you would not have uttered the same cry; since, although the cry issued from numerous mouths, yet the origin of the cry was one. Therefore I say to you that God, who implanted this in your breasts, has drawn it forth from you. Let that, then, be your war cry in battle, because it is given to you by God. When an armed attack is made upon the enemy, let this one cry be raised by all the soldiers of God: 'It is the will of God! It is the will of God!'

"And we neither command nor advise that the old or feeble, or those incapable of bearing arms, undertake this journey. Nor ought women to set out at all without their husbands, or brothers, or legal guardians. For such are more of a hindrance than aid, more of a burden than an advantage. Let the rich aid the needy; and according to their wealth let them take with them experienced soldiers. The priests and other clergy, whether secular or regular, are not to go without the consent of their bishop; for this journey would profit them nothing if they went without permission. Also, it is not fitting that laymen should enter upon the pilgrimage without the blessing of their priests.

"Whoever, therefore, shall decide upon this holy pilgrimage, and shall make his vow to God to that effect, and shall offer himself to Him for sacrifice, as a living victim, holy and acceptable to God, shall wear the sign of the cross of the Lord on his forehead or on his breast. When he shall return from his journey, having fulfilled his vow, let him place the cross on his back between his shoulders. Thus shall ye, indeed, by this twofold action, fulfill the precept of the Lord, as He commands in the Gospel, 'He that taketh not his cross, and followeth after me, is not worthy of me'."

III

The Struggle Between Monarchs and Popes

III

The Struggle Between Monarchs and Popes

A. Germany—Nationalism Defeated

While feudalism flourished in France, in Germany the monarchy struggled to maintain a centralized state. From the tenth to the twelfth centuries, the German crown was the strongest and most dynamic in Europe. But it was never secure. Not long after Charlemagne's time, the Germans returned to the old tribal practice of electing kings. As long as the tribal chieftains possessed a taste for independence the system precluded the development of a powerful dynasty. In contrast to the situation in France, the tribes in Germany, though now sedentary, had retained the deep tribal patriotism of their nomadic days. The nobles who ruled them defended their prerogatives fiercely. It was only because a succession of forceful men mounted the throne that the German monarchy was able to make a fight of it against the dispersive pressure of the tribal nobility.

Gregory VII's Dictatus Papae, 1075

In 936, the crown went to the ambitious Otto I of Saxony, who aspired not only to found a Saxon dynasty to rule over Germany but to follow the path of Charlemagne in reestablishing the Empire. But Otto, a king who was powerless to tax his country and who lacked a landed fortune of his own, was in a poor position to suppress his tribal rivals. The strategy he adopted was to strike an alliance with the Church. Otto initiated a policy of buying the support of the German bishops by constantly increasing their properties and their immunities. Since ecclesiastical fiefs were not hereditary, he gambled that he could retain their support through the appointment of his own candidates to vacant bishoprics, a common medieval practice known as "lay investiture." The ecclesiastical feudal system over which Otto presided provided him with prestige and troops. His policy was sound so long as he and his successors could dominate the German Church. Since there was no certainty that the Church would not emerge the dominant partner, King Otto—though he may have had no alternative—had clearly embarked the monarchy on a dangerous course.

In 962 Otto complemented his domestic alliance with the Church by leading an army across the Alps, as Clovis had done before him, to protect the Papacy. In gratitude Pope John XII crowned him Emperor and assured him that henceforth no Pope would be elected without the approval of the imperial throne. Otto, in effect, had appended Italy to the German state. He controlled the bishops at home and the Pope in Rome. But he had mortgaged the monarchy's future by tying it to the destiny of the Papacy and the Church.

By the tenth century the Cluniac movement for ecclesiastical reform, aimed at changing the scandalous state into which the Church had fallen, was beginning to sweep through Europe. The movement, inspired by the Benedictine monastery of Cluny in Burgundy, was dedicated not only to putting an end to clerical corruption but to restoring the independence of the Church. The Cluniac determination to assert the prerogatives of the Papacy and the Church hierarchy meant an inevitable clash with the ambitions of the German monarchy.

King Henry III, who mounted the German throne a century after Otto, made the mistake in his dealings with Rome that was to prove fatal to royal aspirations. Though the Papacy was now a German institution, he allowed it to fall under the influence of the monk Hildebrand, a leader of the Cluniac reformers. Henry, who at home dominated the nobles and succeeded in expanding German frontiers, seems—apparently out of pure religious faith—to have consciously chosen to violate his own self-interest in Rome. He took no action when, in 1059, Hildebrand forced the adoption of new procedures for the election of Popes which virtually eliminated German ascendency. He stood by passively when Hildebrand, to reduce the Papacy's dependence on German arms, concluded a military alliance with the Norman dukes. In 1073 Hildebrand was himself elected Pope, taking the name of Gregory VII. The battle was thereby joined.

As Pope, the monk Hildebrand embarked almost at once on a campaign to make western Europe into a theocratic state under Papal rule. The Cluniac movement, now at its apogee, had come to demand general recognition of Papal supremacy over the temporal powers. The principal obstacle to achieving this goal was, of course, the German monarchy. The Papacy was now ready to turn on its former master to reduce it to subservience.

Gregory's conception of Papal prerogatives was expressed in a document known as *Dictatus Papae*, or the Pope's Dictate, which appears to have been published about 1075. The more important of its twenty-seven propositions are presented here.

Document 13

1. That the Roman Church was founded by God alone.

2. That the Roman bishop alone is properly called universal.

3. That he alone has the power to depose bishops and reinstate them.

4. That his legate, though of inferior rank, takes precedence of all bishops in council, and may give sentence of deposition against them.

5. That the Pope has the power to depose [bishops] in their absence.

6. That we should not even stay in the same house with those who are excommunicated by him. . . .

8. That he alone may use the imperial insignia.

9. That the Pope is the only person whose feet are kissed by all princes. . . .

11. That the name which he bears belongs to him alone.

12. That he has the power to depose emperors.

13. That he may, if necessity require, transfer bishops from one see to another. . . .

16. That no general synod may be called without his consent.

17. That no action of a synod, and no book, may be considered canonical without his authority.

18. That his decree can be annulled by no one, and that he alone may annul the degrees of any one.

19. That he can be judged by no man.

20. That no one shall dare to condemn a person who appeals to the apostolic see. . . .

22. That the Roman Church has never erred, nor ever, by the testimony of Scripture, shall err, to all eternity. . . .

26. That no one can be considered Catholic who does not agree with the Roman Church.

27. That he [the Pope] has the power to absolve the subjects of unjust rulers from their oath of fidelity.

Gregory VII's Letter Denouncing Henry IV, 1075

The dispute between Gregory VII and Henry III's successor, Henry IV, soon came to focus on the issue of lay investiture, the practice that the German kings rightly regarded as essential to the perpetuation of their authority. Although Papal opposition to the practice was not new, Gregory was the first Pope to insist on exercising the power to fill vacant bishoprics. At a synod in Rome in February, 1075, he excommunicated five of Henry IV's advisors for trafficking in ecclesiastical offices and suspended six bishops whom Henry had appointed. The king clearly could not submit to this intrusion. Half of the land and wealth of Germany was in ecclesiastical hands. If he lost control of it, he faced certain defeat in the monarchy's long-standing competition with the nobility.

Having recently quelled a tribal rebellion, Henry was feeling particularly confident. Defying the Pope, he not only continued to associate with his excommunicated advisors but put his own candidates into Italian bishoprics, within the shadow of Rome itself. Gregory, of course, was outraged.

In December, 1075, the Pope addressed a letter across the Alps to Henry IV protesting the royal action. But though the tone of the letter was firm, it was also conciliatory. Gregory VII was determined to have his way but he was not yet ready to provoke a break. Note, in the text presented below, how Gregory VII both scolds and cajoles. Especially interesting is the snide opening, in which he conditions his apostolic benediction on Henry's obedience.

Document 14

Gregory, bishop, servant of the servants of God, to Henry, the King, greeting and apostolic benediction,—that is, if he be obedient to the apostolic see as is becoming in a Christian king:

It is with some hesitation that we have sent you our apostolic benediction, knowing that for all our acts as pope we must render an account to God, the severe judge. It is reported that you have willingly associated with men who have been excommunicated by decree of the Pope and sentence of a synod. If this be true, you are very well aware that you can receive the blessing neither of God nor of the Pope until you have driven them from you and have compelled them to do penance, and have also yourself sought absolution and forgiveness for your transgressions with due repentance and good works. Therefore we advise you that, if you realize your guilt in this matter, you immediately confess to some pious bishop, who shall absolve you with our permission, prescribing for you penance in proportion to the fault, and who shall faithfully report to us by letter, with your permission, the nature of the penance required.

We wonder, moreover, that you should continue to assure us by letter and messengers of your devotion and humility; that you should call yourself our son and the son of the holy mother Church, obedient in the faith, sincere in love, diligent in devotion; and that you should commend yourself to us with all zeal of love and reverence—whereas in fact you are constantly disobeying the canonical and apostolic decrees in important matters of the faith. . . . Since you confess yourself a son of the Church, you should treat with more honor the head of the Church, that is, St. Peter, the prince of the apostles. If you are one of the sheep of the Lord, you have been entrusted to him by divine authority, for Christ said to him: "Peter, feed my sheep" and again: "And I will give unto thee the keys of the kingdom of Heaven; and whatsoever thou shalt bind on earth shall be bound in heaven; and whatsoever thou shalt loose on earth shall be loosed in heaven." And since we, although an unworthy sinner, exercise his authority by divine will, the words which you address to us are in reality addressed directly to him. And although we read or hear only the words, he sees the heart from which the words proceed. Therefore your highness should be very careful that no insincerity be found in your words and messages to us; and that you show due reverence, not to us, indeed, but to omnipotent God, in those things which especially make for the advance of the Christian faith and the well-being of the Church. For our Lord said to the apostles and to their successors: "He that heareth you heareth me, and he that despiseth you despiseth me." For no one will disregard our admonitions if he believes that the decrees of the Pope have the same authority as the words of the apostle himself. . . .

Now in the synod held at the apostolic seat to which the divine will has called us (at which some of your subjects also were present) we, seeing that the Christian religion had been weakened by many attacks and that the chief and proper motive, that of saving souls, had for a long time been neglected and slighted, were alarmed at the evident danger of the destruction of the flock of the Lord, and had recourse to the decrees and the doctrine of the holy fathers. We decreed nothing new, nothing of our invention; but we decided that the error should be abandoned and the single primitive rule of ecclesiastical discipline and the familiar way of the saints should be again sought out and followed. For we know that no other door to salvation and eternal life lies open to the sheep of Christ than that which was pointed out by Him who said: "I am the door: by me if any man enter in he shall be saved, and find pasture"; and this, we learn from the gospels and from the sacred writings, was preached by the apostles and observed by the holy fathers. And we have decided that this decree—which some, placing human above divine honor, have called an unendurable weight and an immense burden, but which we call by its proper name, that is, the truth and light necessary to salvation—is to be received and observed not only by you and your subjects, but also by all princes and peoples of the earth who confess and worship Christ; for it is greatly desired by us, and would be most fitting to you, that as you are greater than others in glory, and in virtue so you should be more distinguished in devotion to Christ.

Nevertheless, that this decree may not seem to you beyond measure grievous and unjust, we have commanded you by your faithful ambassadors to send to us the wisest and most pious men whom you can find in your kingdom, so that if they can show or instruct us in any way how we can temper the sentence promulgated by the holy fathers without offense to the eternal King or danger to our souls, we may consider their advice. But, even if we had not warned you in so friendly a manner, it would have been only right on your part, before you violated the apostolic decrees, to ask justice of us in a reasonable manner in any matter in which we had injured or affected your honor. But from what you have since done and decreed it is evident how little you care for our warnings, or for the observance of justice.

But since we hope that, while the long-suffering patience of God still invites you to repent, you may become wiser and your heart may be turned to obey the commands of God, we warn you with fatherly love that, knowing the rule of Christ to be over you, you should consider how dangerous it is to place your honor above His, and that you should not interfere with the liberty of the Church which He has deigned to join to Himself by heavenly union, but rather with faithful devotion you should offer your assistance to the increasing of this liberty to omnipotent God and St. Peter, through whom also your glory may be enhanced. You ought to recognize what you undoubtedly owe to them for giving you victory over your enemies, that as they have gladdened you with great prosperity, so they should see that you are thereby rendered more devout. And in order that the fear of God, in whose hands is all power and all rule, may affect your heart more than these our warnings, you should recall what happened to Saul, when, after winning the victory which he gained by the will of the prophet, he glorified himself in his triumph and did not obey the warnings of the prophet, and how God reproved him; and, on the other hand, what grace King David acquired by reason of his humility, as well as his other virtues.

Henry IV's Violent Reply, 1076

Far from being intimidated by the Pope's letter, Henry reacted angrily and determined to strike back sharply. He summoned a council of German bishops on January 24, 1076, at Worms. He found that the bishops would back him, for their own status depended on royal control of Germany's ecclesiastical offices. At Henry's urging, the bishops addressed a letter to "Brother Hildebrand," renouncing their obedience to him "since, as thou didst publicly proclaim, none of us has been to thee a bishop, so thou henceforth will be Pope to none of us."

Henry IV then addressed his own letter to Pope Gregory. It is probably one of the most stinging letters on record from one public figure to another. Like that of the bishops, it demanded Gregory's abdication. Henry's letter, the text of which follows, created an irreparable breach between Papacy and throne, which could only lead to a test of strength.

Document 15

Henry, king not by usurpation, but by the holy ordination of God, to Hildebrand, not pope, but false monk.

This is the salutation which you deserve, for you have never held any office in the Church without making it a source of confusion and a curse to Christian men, instead of an honor and a blessing. To mention only the most obvious cases out of many, you have not only dared to lay hands on the Lord's anointed, the archbishops, bishops, and priests, but you have scorned them and abused them, as if they were ignorant servants not fit to know what their master was doing. This you have done to gain favor with the vulgar crowd. You have declared that the bishops know nothing and that you know everything; but if you have such great wisdom you have used it not to build but to destroy. Therefore we believe that St. Gregory, whose name you have presumed to take, had you in mind when he said: "The heart of the prelate is puffed up by the abundance of subjects, and he thinks himself more powerful than all others." All this we have endured because of our respect for the papal office, but you have mistaken our humility for fear, and have dared to make an attack upon the royal and imperial authority which we received from God. You have even threatened to take it away, as if we had received it from you, and as if the Empire and kingdom were in your disposal and not in the disposal of God. Our Lord Jesus Christ has called us to the government of the Empire, but He never called you to the rule of the Church. This is the way you have gained advancement in the Church: through craft you have obtained wealth; through wealth you have obtained favor; through favor, the power of the sword; and through the power of the sword, the papal seat, which is the seat of peace; and then from the seat of peace you have expelled peace. For you have incited subjects to rebel against their prelates by teaching them to despise the bishops, their rightful rulers. You have given to laymen the authority over priests, whereby they condemn and depose those whom the bishops have put over them to teach them. You have attacked me, who, unworthy as I am, have yet been anointed to rule among the anointed of God, and who, according to the teaching of the fathers, can be judged by no one save God alone, and can be deposed for no crime except infidelity. For the holy fathers in the time of the apostate Julian [Roman Emperor 361–363] did not presume to pronounce sentence of deposition against him, but left him to be judged and condemned by God. St. Peter himself said, "Fear God, honor the king." But you, who fear not God, have dishonored me, whom He hath established. St. Paul, who said that even an angel from heaven should be accursed who taught any other than the true doctrine, did not make an exception in your favor, to permit you to teach false doctrines. For he says, "But though we, or an angel from heaven, preach any other gospel unto you than that which we have preached unto you, let him be accursed." Come down, then, from that apostolic seat which you have obtained by violence; for you have been declared accursed by

St. Paul for your false doctrines, and have been condemned by us and our bishops for your evil rule. Let another ascend the throne of St. Peter, one who will not use religion as a cloak of violence, but will teach the life giving doctrine of that prince of the apostles. I, Henry, king by the grace of God, with all my bishops, say unto you: "Come down, come down, and be accursed through all the ages."

Gregory VII Deposes Henry IV, 1076

Gregory VII wasted no time in striking back. Before a synod of churchmen in Rome in February, 1076, he announced the excommunication of the king and the release from any allegiance to him of all Christian subjects. In a decree addressed to St. Peter, he defended his own record and put Henry under curse. The text of the Papal decree discloses the depth of Gregory's feeling toward King Henry.

Document 16

St. Peter, prince of the apostles, incline thine ear unto me I beseech thee, and hear me, thy servant, whom thou hast nourished from mine infancy and hast delivered from mine enemies that hate me for my fidelity to thee. Thou art my witness, as are also my mistress, the mother of God, and St. Paul thy brother, and all the other saints, that the Holy Roman Church called me to its government against my own will, and that I did not gain thy throne by violence; that I would rather have ended my days in exile than have obtained thy place by fraud or for worldly ambition. It is not by my efforts, but by thy grace, that I am set to rule over the Christian world which was especially intrusted to thee by Christ. It is by thy grace, and as thy representative that God has given to me the power to bind and to loose in heaven and in earth. Confident of my integrity and authority, I now declare in the name of the omnipotent God, the Father, Son, and Holy Spirit, that Henry, son of the Emperor Henry, is deprived of his kingdom of Germany and Italy. I do this by thy authority and in defense of the honor of thy

Church, because he has rebelled against it. He who attempts to destroy the honor of the Church should be deprived of such honor as he may have held. He has refused to obey as a Christian should; he has not returned to God from whom he had wandered; he has had dealings with excommunicated persons; he has done many iniquities; he has despised the warnings which, as thou art witness, I sent to him for his salvation; he has cut himself off from thy Church, and has attempted to rend it asunder; therefore, by thy authority; I place him under the curse. It is in thy name that I curse him, that all people may know that thou art Peter, and upon thy rock the Son of the living God has built his Church, and the gates of Hell shall not prevail against it.

Gregory's Account of Henry's Submission at Canossa, 1077

Gregory VII's excommunication of Henry IV proved an effective weapon. Many of the king's ecclesiastical allies, faced with a dilemma of conscience, submitted to the wishes of the Pope. The rebellious nobles were encouraged to intensify their challenge to the throne. Henry seemed powerless to halt the defections and became progressively more isolated.

In October, 1076, the king announced his capitulation to Gregory in a meeting of German princes at Tribur. He retracted his condemnation of the Pope and swore that he would forever be obedient. But the princes, anxious to be rid of him for good, were not satisfied. They decided that if the Pope did not lift Henry's excommunication by February 22, 1077, they would meet again in the city of Augsburg to elect a new king. Furthermore, they invited Pope Gregory to preside over the election meeting.

Henry obviously had to move quickly if he was to forestall his deposition. He headed at once for Italy to intercept the Pope, who had begun his journey to Augsburg as soon as the invitation reached him. In one of the bitterest of winters Henry, accompanied by his wife and young son, secretly crossed the Alps. He found the Pope at the castle of Canossa near Parma in northern Italy. Dressed as a penitent, Henry begged for absolution for three days before the castle gate. Gregory knew that the excommunication represented the chief obstacle to the king's ambitions. But bound by the rules of the Church to recognize repentence, he surrendered to Henry's entreaties. Having restored the king to favor with the Church, the Pope had no choice but to cancel the trip to Germany.

In a letter to the German nobility, both ecclesiastical and lay, Pope Gregory described the events at Canossa. The letter, presented below, contains the oath of fidelity that Henry IV gave to the Pope at the moment of surrender.

DOCUMENT 17

Gregory, bishop, servant of the servants of God, to all the archbishops, bishops, dukes, counts, and other princes of the realm of the Germans who defend the Christian faith, greeting and apostolic benediction.

Inasmuch as for love of justice you assumed common cause and danger with us in the struggle of Christian warfare, we have taken care to in-inform you, beloved, with sincere affection, how the king, humbled to penance, obtained the pardon of absolution and how the whole affair has progressed from his entrance into Italy to the present time.

As had been agreed with the legates who had been sent to us on your part, we came into Lombardy about twenty days before the date on which one of the commanders was to come over the pass to meet us, awaiting his advent that we might cross over to the other side. But when the period fixed upon had already passed, and we were told that at this time on account of many difficulties—as we can readily believe—an escort could not be sent to meet us, we were involved in no little perplexity as to what would be best for us to do, having no other means of coming to you.

Meanwhile, however, we learned that the king was approaching. He also, before entering Italy, sent to us suppliant legates, offering in all things to render satisfaction to God, to St. Peter and to us. And he renewed his promise that, besides amending his way of living, he would observe all obedience if only he might deserve to obtain from us the favor of absolution and the apostolic benediction. When, after long postponing a decision and holding frequent consultations, we, through all the envoys who passed, had severely taken him to task for his excesses, he came at length of his own accord, with a few followers, showing nothing of hostility or boldness, to the town of Canossa where we were tarrying. And there, having laid aside all the belongings of royalty, wretchedly, with bare feet and clad in wool, he continued for three days to stand before the gate of the castle. Nor did he desist from imploring with many tears, the aid and consolation of the apostolic mercy until he had moved all of those who were present there, and whom the report of it reached, to such pity and depth of compassion that, interceding for him with many prayers and tears, all wondered indeed at the unaccustomed hardness of our heart, while some actually cried out that we were exercising, not the dignity of apostolic severity, but the cruelty, as it were, of a tyrannical madness.

Finally, won by the persistency of his suit and by the constant supplications of all who were present, we loosed the chain of the anathema and at length received him into the favor of communion and into the lap of the holy mother Church, those being accepted as sponsors for him whose names are written below.

Having thus accomplished these matters, we desire at the first opportunity to cross over to your country in order that, by God's aid, we may more fully arrange all things for the peace of the Church and the concord of the kingdom, as has long been our wish. For we desire, beloved, that you should know beyond a doubt that the whole question at issue is as yet so little cleared up—as you can learn from the sponsors mentioned—that both our coming and the concurrence of your counsels are extremely necessary. Wherefore strive ye all to continue in the faith in which you have begun and in the love of justice; and know that we are not otherwise committed to the king save that, by word alone, as is our custom, we have said that he might have hopes from us in those matters in which, without danger to his soul or to our own, we might be able to help him to his salvation and honor, either through justice or through mercy.

Oath of King Henry

I, King Henry, on account of the murmuring and enmity which the archbishops and bishops, dukes, counts and other princes of the realm of the Germans, and others who follow them in the same matter of dissension, bring to bear against me, will, within the term which our master Pope Gregory has constituted, either do justice according to his judgment or conclude peace according to his counsels—unless an absolute impediment should stand in his way or in mine. And on the removal of this impediment I shall be ready to continue in the same course. Likewise, if that same lord Pope Gregory shall wish to go beyond the mountains [into Germany], or to any other part of the world, he himself, as well as those who shall be in his escort or following, or who are sent by him, or come to him from any parts of the world whatever, shall be secure while going, remaining, or returning, on my part, and on the part of those whom I can constrain, from every injury to life or limb, or from capture. Nor shall he, by my consent, meet any other hindrance that is contrary to his dignity; and if any such be placed in his way I will aid him according to my ability. So help me God and this holy gospel.

Concordat of Worms, 1122

Henry's humiliation at Canossa, one of the most dramatic episodes of the Middle Ages, remains among the most difficult to evaluate. Ostensibly it was a victory for the Pope. Bismarck, seven hundred years later, expressed such an interpretation when, during his own struggle with the Papacy, he immortalized the words: "I shall not go to Canossa." But to the medieval mind, it was not a great indignity to submit to the Church. Henry's contemporaries made relatively little of the incident. More consequential, it seemed to them, was the king's success in thwarting the effort by the Papacy and the nobility to depose him.

Despite the climactic quality of Canossa, the struggle for power between the king and his enemies continued. In 1080, Pope Gregory VII tried once again to overthrow Henry IV, this time asserting the principle that Germany and Italy had been granted to the king as Papal fiefs. But on this occasion he overreached himself. Henry crossed the Alps again, not in sackcloth but in armor, deposed Gregory and established a Papal rival in Rome. A few years later Gregory VII died in exile, heartbroken. His successors, for a while, ignored Germany and devoted their attention to Crusades. The fight with Gregory, however, had drained the German monarchy of its energy and its esteem. The investiture struggle did not end with a Papal victory. But in strengthening the feudal nobility, the German monarchy became the loser.

The investiture struggle formally ended after Henry's death in what was ostensibly a compromise. In the Concordat of Worms, concluded between Henry V and Pope Calixtus, the Papacy recognized the obligation of each bishop to swear fealty to the king and accept the secular obligations of a feudal vassal. More important, the king lost all but a fraction of his former power over the selection of candidates to fill episcopal vacancies. The Concordat, by depriving the king of the assurance of ecclesiastical loyalty, ended the alliance between the monarchy and the Church in Germany. The bishops tended now to gravitate to the nobles for protection. The monarchy was doomed to impotence.

The principal concessions of the Concordat of Worms are translated below. The Concordat affirmed that the bishops had both spiritual and temporal loyalties. By empowering the king to confer the *regalia*, it acknowledged his sovereignty over temporal matters. But the king's power over episcopal election was now limited to cases of disagreement among electors, when he could give "support to the party which shall seem to you to have the better case."

Document 18

I, Bishop Calixtus, servant of the servants of God, do grant to thee, by the grace of God august Emperor of the Romans, the right to hold the elections of the bishops and abbots of the German realm who belong to the kingdom, in thy presence, without simony, and without any resort to violence; it being agreed that, if any dispute arise among those concerned, thou, by the counsel and judgment of the metropolitan (the archbishop) and the suffragan bishops, shalt extend favor and support to the party which shall seem to you to have the better case. Moreover, the person elected may receive from thee the *regalia* through the scepter without any exaction being levied; and he shall discharge his rightful obligations to thee for them.

He who is consecrated in other parts of the Empire shall receive the *regalia* from thee through the scepter, within six months, and without any exaction, and shall discharge his rightful obligations to thee for them; those rights being excepted, however, which are known to belong to the Roman Church. In whatever cases thou shalt make complaint to me and ask my aid I will support thee according as my office requires. To thee, and to all those who are on thy side, or have been, in this period of strife, I grant a true peace.

* * *

In the name of the holy and indivisible Trinity, I, Henry, by the grace of God august Emperor of the Romans, for the love of God and of the holy Roman Church and of our lord Pope Calixtus, and for the saving of my soul, do give over to God, and to the holy apostles of God, Peter and Paul, and the holy Catholic Church, all investiture through ring and staff; and do concede that in all the churches that are in my kingdom or empire there shall be canonical election and free consecration.

All the property and *regalia* of St. Peter which, from the beginning of this conflict until the present time, whether in the days of my father or in my own, have been confiscated, and which I now hold, I restore to the holy Roman Church. And as for those things which I do not now hold, I will faithfully aid in their restoration. The property also of all other churches and princes and of every one, whether lay or ecclesiastical, which has been lost in the struggle, I will restore as far as I hold it, according to the counsel of the princes, or according to considerations of justice. I will also faithfully aid in the restoration of those things which I do not hold.

And I grant a true peace to our lord Pope Calixtus, and to the holy Roman Church, and to all those who are, or have been, on its side. In matters where the holy Roman Church shall seek assistance, I will faithfully render it, and when it shall make complaint to me I will see that justice is done.

The Golden Bull of Charles IV, 1356

The last major effort to unify Germany was undertaken by the Hohenstaufen emperors of Swabia, a province that encompassed much of contemporary Switzerland, southwest Germany and western Austria. King Frederick I (1152–1190). known—thanks to his red beard—as Barbarossa, was its outstanding representative. His goal was to make of Germany a federation of duchies tied to him by vassalage. By defeating his chief rival, the Welf family, by reestablishing royal dominance over the Church, and by consolidating his own territories, he made a promising start toward regaining the ground lost by the German kings in the previous centuries. But Frederick's attention, like that of his predecessors, was diverted by the imperial dream. Determined to extend his rule into Italy, he challenged the new, vigorous cities of Lombardy and the always dangerous Papacy. He thus forced into alliance against him two natural Italian rivals, whom together he could not overcome. Barbarossa neither achieved his imperial objectives nor made his regime at home secure enough to prevent a bitter civil war after his death.

By the time Frederick II, Barbarossa's grandson, succeeded to the crown in 1211, monarchical power in Germany had already receded significantly. Frederick II, a man remarkable for his vast culture and wide range of interests, was half Latin by blood, fonder of Sicily than Germany and even more imperial in outlook than his forebears. His Italian policies earned him the enmity of the Papacy and the Lombardian cities, while his efforts at home to buy off the churchmen and to divert the energy of the nobles to war against the Slavs failed to win him the independence he sought. By the end of the thirteenth century, the Hohenstaufen effort, both national and imperial, had collapsed.

The Hohenstaufens, however, left their mark on Germany. By encouraging expansion to the east, they set in motion a shift in the balance of power away from the west. Ultimately Germany's eastern provinces would dominate the country. The Hohenstaufen collapse also left the way open in Germany for the triumph of feudalism—and an extreme form of feudalism it became. The feudal duchies, successor to the ancient tribes, broke up into a multitude of petty sovereignties, both lay and ecclesiastical, as well as an increasing number of free cities. Henceforth German history would be the history of its individual principalities. Not until the nineteenth century would another serious effort be made to unite the local sovereignties under a single crown.

The monarchical institution remained, however, and for a while an undefined group of sovereigns elected the German king and the Holy Roman Emperor, but by the beginning of the fourteenth century the number of electors had been fixed at seven. They were the archbishops of Mainz, Trier and Cologne, the king of Bohemia, the margrave of Brandenburg, the duke of Saxony and the count palatine of the Rhine. These seven became the most powerful men in Germany, imposing on the crown whatever conditions they chose, deposing emperors at will, at times buying and selling the throne, always keeping as their objective a monarchy too feeble to challenge their own independence. In 1356, the Emperor Charles IV legitimized the electoral system and made it permanent. The decree known as the Golden Bull of Charles IV was Germany's constitution throughout the Middle Ages. It remained fundamental law until 1806.

The Golden Bull dealt with such diverse matters as the power of the electors within their domains, the rules of private warfare, protocol among German sovereigns and the privileges of the free cities. The following selection discusses the procedure for electing "a king of the Romans and future emperor, to be ruler of the world and of the Christian people." In these empty words, the electors resolved the contradiction between the universality of the Holy Roman Emperor, with his mythical empire, and the provinciality of the German king, without power even over his own kingdom.

Document 19

I. 1. We decree and determine by this imperial edict that, whenever the electoral princes are summoned according to the ancient and praiseworthy custom to meet and elect a king of the Romans and future emperor, each one of them shall be bound to furnish on demand an escort and safe-conduct to his fellow electors or their representatives, within his own lands and as much farther as he can, for the journey to and from the city where the election is to be held. Any electoral prince who refuses to furnish escort and safe-conduct shall be liable to the penalties for perjury and to the loss of his electoral vote for that occasion.

2. We decree and command also that all other princes who hold fiefs from the Empire, by whatever title, and all counts, barons, knights, clients, nobles, commoners, citizens, and all corporations of towns, cities, and territories of the Empire, shall furnish escort and safe-conduct for this occasion to every electoral prince or his representatives, on demand, within their own lands and as much farther as they can. . . .

16. When the news of the death of the king of the Romans has been received at Mainz, within one month from the date of receiving it the archbishop of Mainz shall send notices of the death and the approaching election to all the electoral princes. But if the archbishop neglects or refuses to send such notices the electoral princes are commanded on their fidelity to assemble on their own motion and without summons at the city of Frankfort, within three months from the death of the emperor, for the purpose of electing a king of the Romans and future emperor.

17. Each electoral prince or his representatives may bring with him to Frankfort at the time of the election a retinue of 200 horsemen, of whom not more than 50 shall be armed.

18. If any electoral prince, duly summoned to the elections, fails to come, or to send representatives with credentials containing full authority, or if he (or his representatives) withdraws from the place of the election before the election has been completed, without leaving behind substitutes fully accredited and empowered, he shall lose his vote in that election.

II. 1. (This section specified that Mass be celebrated the day following the arrival of the electors at Frankfort, and that the archbishop of Mainz should administer to his six colleagues the oath which he himself has taken, as specified in section 2.)

2. "I, archbishop of Mainz, archchancellor of the Empire for Germany, electoral prince, swear on the holy gospels here before me and by the faith which I owe to God and to the Holy Roman Empire, that with the aid of God, and according to my best judgment and knowledge, I will cast my vote, in this election of the king of the Romans and future emperor, for a person fitted to rule the Christian people. I will give my voice and vote freely, uninfluenced by any agreement, price, bribe, promise, or anything of the sort, by whatever name it may be called. So help me God and all the saints."

3. After the electors have taken this oath, they shall proceed to the

election, and shall not depart from Frankfort until the majority have elected a king of the Romans and future emperor, to be ruler of the world and of the Christian people. If they have not come to a decision within thirty days from the day on which they took the above oath, after that they shall live upon bread and water and shall not leave the city until the election has been decided.

IV. 1. In the imperial diet, at the council-board, table, and all other places where the emperor or king of the Romans meets with the electoral princes, the seats shall be arranged as follows: On the right of the emperor, first, the archbishop of Mainz, or of Cologne, according to the province in which the meeting is held, as arranged above; second, the king of Bohemia, because he is a crowned and anointed prince; third, the count palatine of the Rhine; on the left of the emperor, first, the archbishop of Cologne, or of Mainz; second, the duke of Saxony; third, the margrave of Brandenburg.

2. When the imperial throne becomes vacant, the archbishop of Mainz shall have the authority, which he has had from of old, to call the other electors together for the election. It shall be his peculiar right also, when the electors have convened for the election, to collect the votes, asking each of the electors separately in the following order: first, the archbishop of Trier, who shall have the right to the first vote, as he has had from of old; then the archbishop of Cologne, who has the office of first placing the crown upon the head of the king of the Romans; then the king of Bohemia, who has the priority among the secular princes because of his royal title; fourth, the count palatine of the Rhine; fifth, the duke of Saxony; sixth, the margrave of Brandenburg. Then the princes shall ask the archbishop of Mainz in turn to declare his choice and vote. At the diet, the margrave of Brandenburg shall offer water to the emperor or king, to wash his hands; the king of Bohemia shall have the right to offer him the cup first, although, by reason of his royal dignity, he shall not be bound to do this unless he desires; the count palatine of the Rhine shall offer him food; and the duke of Saxony shall act as his marshal in the accustomed manner.

B. France—Nationalism Triumphant

The political development of France during the Middle Ages took a direction almost precisely opposite that of Germany.

The Gallo-Roman or western segment of Charlemagne's empire quickly disintegrated into feudal fragments. Throughout most of the period, Carolingian kings continued to sit on the throne but they were frequently incompetent and invariably impotent. When the German monarchy was at its apogee, the king of France was just another feudal lord, usually a minor one and often under the tutelage of the German crown. France had no central government and showed no prospects of acquiring one.

Adalbero's plea to elect Hugh Capet, 987

But in 987 the last Carolingian died and French history took an important turn. The contenders for the throne were Duke Charles of Lower Lorraine, an uncle of the late king, and Hugh Capet, Count of Paris, whose family had helped drive off the rampaging Northmen in the ninth century and had held the crown in the intervals when no Carolingians were immediately available. Because Charles was a German vassal, Hugh was the heavy favorite. Not only did the French clergy and nobility object to having a German on the throne but the German king himself opposed Charles in order to keep French influence out of Lorraine. In this competition for the French throne, we thus detect faint but genuine signs of what can be characterized as national feelings.

Charles of Lorraine did not easily give up his wish to be king. He campaigned vigorously at the meeting of feudal magnates, called at Senlis to select the new monarch. The competition, however, was too keen. The decisive plea appears to have been made by Adalbero, archbishop of Rheims. Note the appeal to nationalism in his speech, recorded here by the monk Richer. Hugh Capet was elected. He founded a dynasty that united France and ruled it for 350 years, then provided successors who sat on the throne until 1848.

Document 20

Meanwhile the nobles of Gaul who had taken the oath came together at the appointed time at Senlis; when they had all taken their places in the assembly, the duke, having made a sign to [Adalbero] the archbishop of Rheims, the latter expressed himself as follows: "King Louis, of divine memory, left no children; we must therefore take counsel as to the choice of a successor, in order that the country shall not come to ruin through neglect and the lack of a pilot. Our deliberations on this subject were recently postponed, by common consent, in order that each one might here voice the sentiments with which God might inspire him, and that from all these individual opinions a general and collective decision might be reached.

"Now that we are once more assembled together, let us endeavor, in all prudence and rectitude, not to sacrifice reason and truth to our personal likes or dislikes. We know that Charles has his partisans, who claim that the throne belongs to him by right of birth. Regarding the question from this point of view, we reply that the throne cannot be acquired by hereditary right. Nor should one be placed upon it who is not distinguished alike by nobility of body and wisdom of mind, and by his good faith and magnanimity. We see in the annals of history rulers of illustrious origin deposed on account of their unworthiness, and replaced by incumbents of equal, or even of inferior, birth.

"And what is there to recommend Charles of Lorraine? He is feeble and without honor, faith, or character; he has not blushed to become the servitor of a foreign king [the emperor], nor to take to wife a girl of only knightly rank. How could the great duke bear that a woman belonging to the lowest rank of his vassals should be queen and rule over him? How could he give precedence to a woman, when his equals and even his superiors in birth bend the knee before him and place their hands beneath his feet? If you consider this matter carefully, you will see that Charles' fall has been brought about through his own fault rather than that of others.

"Make a choice, therefore, that shall insure the welfare of the state instead of being its ruin. If you wish ill to your country, choose Charles; if you wish to see it prosperous, make Hugh, the glorious duke, King. Do not let yourselves be misled by your sympathy for Charles, nor blinded to the common good by hatred of the duke. For if you blame the good, how can you praise the bad? If you praise the bad, how despise the good? Remember the words of the Scripture: 'Woe unto them that call evil good, and good evil; that put darkness for light, and light for darkness.' Choose the duke, therfore; he is the most illustrious among us all by reason of his exploits, his nobility, and his military following. Not only the state, but every individual interest, will find in him a protector. His great-heartedness will render him a father to you all. Who has ever fled to him for aid and been disappointed? Who that has been left in the lurch by his friends has he ever failed to restore to his rights?"

This discourse was received with universal applause, and by unanimous consent the duke was raised to the throne. He was crowned at Noyon on the first of June, by the archbishop and the other bishops, as king of the Gauls, the Bretons, the Danes [Normans], the Aquitanians, the Goths, the Spaniards, and the Gascons. Surrounded by the nobles of the kingdom, he issued decrees and made laws according to royal custom, judging and disposing of all matters with success.

The Charter of Lorris, 1155

The territory over which Hugh Capet ruled directly was known as the Ile de France, the chief city of which was Paris. It was small and weak compared to the neighboring fiefs but, unlike the domains of the German kings, it was compact and had the strategic advantage of a central location. The Capetians enjoyed the additional advantage over the German kings in that their rivals were too busy fighting each other to unite against the throne. Bit by bit, the Capetians consolidated their holdings and, by defeating all attempts by the nobles to emulate the Germans and make the monarchy elective, also succeeded in perpetuating their dynasty and their power.

The formation of the French nation, as it exists today, began in the reign of the Capetian king, Philip Augustus (1180–1223). Shrewd and ambitious, Philip determined to destroy the great empire that the Angevin kings of England had built in France. By playing off rival claimants to the English throne one against another, he acquired first small portions of the Angevin holdings. Later he declared open war against the English and drove them from the northern provinces of Normandy, Brittany, Anjou, Maine and Touraine. When the English tried to regain their territory by making an alliance with the German emperor, Philip joined forces with a dissident German prince and defeated his rivals at Bouvines in one of the decisive battles of the Middle Ages. In just a few years, the Capetian domain was tripled in size and the monarchy at a new pinnacle of prestige.

One of the sources of Philip Augustus' power lay in his appreciation of the changes taking place in feudal society, the most important of which was the rise of the city. As Moslem control of the Mediterranean receded, the pace of European commerce quickened. The cities became the gathering place of the new middle-class, living in a money economy and demanding sufficient freedom to trade. Philip, far more clearly than the German kings, saw in the cities military and financial assets of vast potential. At first the townspeople were subject, like other feudal folk, to the rule of the local lord, but in the twelfth century the practice of granting town charters was initiated. These charters provided guarantees of liberty, property and self-government that were otherwise unknown within feudal society. Philip Augustus granted no less than seventy-eight such charters during his reign, in return for which he received money or other assistance that liberated him from dependence on the feudal lords.

The town of Lorris, several miles east of Orleans, was granted a charter by King Louis VII in 1155. Reproduced in its essentials here, the charter became a model for Philip Augustus and his Capetian successors.

The first provision set the annual tax due the king, in the fashion of the traditional lord-vassal relationship; the second, ninth and fifteenth protect the burgher from other financial burdens, while the third virtually exempts him from military service. The fourth and sixth are meant to promote interurban commerce. The fifth and the seventeenth guarantee the burgher's property. The twelfth, sixteenth and thirty-fifth constitute a kind of primitive bill of rights. The eighteenth established protection for runaway serfs. It suggests a royal invitation to flee the feudal manor, a major step in the disintegration of the feudal system.

Document 21

1. Every one who has a house in the parish of Lorris shall pay as *cens* sixpence only for his house, and for each acre of land that he possesses in the parish.

2. No inhabitant of the parish of Lorris shall be required to pay a toll or any other tax on his provisions; and let him not be made to pay any measurage fee on the grain which he has raised by his own labor.

3. No burgher shall go on an expedition, on foot or on horseback, from which he cannot return the same day to his home if he desires.

4. No burgher shall pay toll on the road to Étampes, to Orleans, to Milly (which is in the Gâtinais), or to Melun.

5. No one who has property in the parish of Lorris shall forfeit it for any offense whatsoever, unless the offense shall have been committed against us or any of our vassels.

6. No person while on his way to the fairs and markets of Lorris, or returning, shall be arrested or disturbed, unless he shall have committed an offense on the same day.

9. No one, neither we nor any other, shall exact from the burghers of Lorris any tallage, tax, or subsidy.

12. If a man shall have had a quarrel with another, but without breaking into a fortified house, and if the parties shall have reached an agreement without bringing a suit before the provost [the king's chief legal officer in the town] no fine shall be due to us or our provost on account of the affair.

15. No inhabitant of Lorris is to render us the obligation of *corvée*, except twice a year, when our wine is to be carried to Orleans, and not elsewhere.

16. No one shall be detained in prison if he can furnish surety that he will present himself for judgment.

17. Any burgher who wishes to sell his property shall have the privilege of doing so; and having received the price of the sale, he shall have the right to go from the town freely and without molestation, if he so desires, unless he has committed some offense in it.

18. Any one who shall dwell a year and a day in the parish of Lorris, without any claim having pursued him there, and without having refused to lay his case before us or our provost, shall abide there freely and without molestation.

35. We ordain that every time there shall be a change of provosts in the town the new provost shall take an oath faithfully to observe these regulations; and the same thing shall be done by new deputies every time that they are installed.

The Unam Sanctam of Pope Boniface VIII, 1302

To develop a strong national state, the French monarchy had not only to control the nobility but to make itself independent of the Papacy. The concept of the sovereign nation clashed directly with the medieval notion of the omnipotent, universal Church, exalted by such forceful Popes as Gregory VII (1073–1085) and Innocent III (1198–1216). In 1200, the Papacy was still strong enough to humble the popular and dynamic King Philip Augustus. It forced him by means of an *interdict* to submit to the Church on a marriage question. A century later, however, the

Papacy could no longer exert such influence in France. National feeling had flowered and society had taken on a more secular quality. When Pope Boniface VIII (1294–1303) invoked Church rights over national rights, a bitter struggle ensued which wounded the Papacy so severely that it never completely recovered.

The dispute began when King Philip IV, known as Philip the Fair, proposed taxing the French church to help finance his continuing war against England. Though Rome taxed the French clergy for its own political objectives—always referred to as "crusades"—it claimed exemption for the local churches from any royal exactions. After French churchmen sided with the king, Pope Boniface issued the bull *Clericis laicos*, in which he asserted that any ruler seeking to tax the Church without Papal permission automatically incurred a sentence of excommunication. Such Papal weapons as excommunication and interdict had laid the German monarchy low two centuries before. They no longer possessed that power. Philip retaliated by forbidding the export from France of all money and precious metals, which threatened the Papacy's solvency. Boniface backed away by suspending enforcement of the bull.

Five years later, Philip provoked a resumption of the contest by arresting Bernard Saisset, Bishop of Pamiers, on a charge of treason. In response to protests from the French clergy, the king agreed to remand the case to Rome but Boniface was not satisfied. He reinstated *Clericis laicos* and issued a second bull, *Ausculta fili*, in which he censured and insulted Philip and reasserted the Papal claim to determine the policies of the state. Philip, by distributing a garbled version of the bull and his own sneering reply, summoned on his behalf the power of public opinion, a relatively new factor in politics. He then called the first meeting of the Estates-General, an assembly of lay and episcopal nobles and representatives of the towns, to send a solemn protest to Rome. But his action only provoked Boniface the more. The Pope proceeded to issue still another bull, *Unam Sanctam*, which announced in terms never surpassed in boldness the Papal claims to temporal supremacy.

Philip decided to counter by deposing Boniface. He sent William of Nogaret, his chief advisor, to Italy to seize the Pope and return him to France as a prisoner, after which Philip planned to choose a new and more pliant Pope. Nogaret captured Boniface in his home town of Agnani but the next day the townspeople rallied and drove the French away. The Pope was conducted triumphantly back to Rome, only to die a few days later from the strain of events. Philip, winner by dint of circumstances, consolidated his victory by selecting a French archbishop to mount the Papal throne.

As Clement V, the new Pope took up residence not in Rome but in the Provençal city of Avignon where, for a time at least, the Papacy followed the king's instructions. The vigorous French monarchy had defeated the Papacy as decisively as the Papacy had itself defeated the German emperors two centuries before.

Presented below is *Unam sanctam*, which is regarded as the classic medieval expression of Papal aspirations. Events, however, had made its doctrine obsolete, so that its promulgation proved to be the pursuit of a cause long since lost.

Document 22

The true faith compels us to believe that there is one holy Catholic Apostolic Church and this we firmly believe and plainly confess. And outside of her there is no salvation or remission of sins, as the Bridegroom says in the Song of Solomon: "My dove, my undefiled, is but one; she is the only one of her mother, she is the choice one of her that bore her" which represents the one mystical body, whose head is Christ, but the head of Christ is God. In this Church there is "one Lord, one faith, one baptism." For in the time of the flood there was only one ark, that of Noah, prefiguring the one Church, and it was "finished above in one cubit" and had but one helmsman and master, namely, Noah. And we read that all things on the earth outside of this ark were destroyed. This Church we venerate as the only one, since the Lord said by the prophet: "Deliver my soul from the sword; my darling from the power of the dog." He prayed for his soul, that is, for himself, the head; and at the same time for the body, and he named his body, that is, the one Church, because there is but one Bridegroom, and because of the unity of the faith, of the sacraments, and of his love for the Church. This is the seamless robe of the Lord which was not rent but parted by lot.

Therefore there is one body of the one and only Church, and one head, not two heads, as if the Church were a monster. And this head is Christ, and his vicar, Peter and his successor; for the Lord himself said to Peter: "Feed my sheep." And he said "my sheep," in general, not these or those sheep in particular; from which it is clear that all were committed to him. If, therefore, Greeks [i.e., the Greek or Eastern Church] or any one else say that they are not subject to Peter and his successors, they thereby necessarily confess that they are not of the sheep of Christ. For the Lord says in the Gospel of John, that there is one fold and only one shepherd. By the words of the gospel we are taught that the two swords, namely, the spiritual authority and the temporal, are in the power of the Church. For when the apostles said "Here are two swords"—that is, in the Church since it was the apostles who were speaking—the Lord did not answer, "It is too much," but "It is enough." Whoever desires that the temporal sword is in the power of Peter does not properly understand the word of the Lord when He said: "Put up thy sword into the sheath." Both swords, therefore, the spiritual and the temporal, are in the power of the Church. The former is to be used by the Church, the latter for the Church; the one by the hand of the priest, the other by the hand of kings and knights, but at the command and permission of the priest. Moreover, it is necessary for one sword to be under the other, and the temporal authority to be subjected to the spiritual; for the apostle says, "For there is no power but of God: and the powers that be are ordained of God"; but they would not be ordained unless one were subjected to the other, and, as it were, the lower made the higher by the other.

For, according to St. Dionysius, it is a law of divinity that the lowest is made the highest through the intermediate. According to the law of the universe all things are not equally and directly reduced to order, but the lowest are fitted into their order through the intermediate, and the lower through the higher. And we must necessarily admit that the spiritual power surpasses any earthly power in dignity and honor, because spiritual things surpass temporal things. We clearly see that this is true from the paying of tithes, from the benediction, from the sanctification, from the receiving of the power, and from the governing of these things. For the truth itself declares that the spiritual power must establish the temporal power and pass judgment on it if it is not good. Thus the prophecy of Jeremiah concerning the Church and the ecclesiastical power is fulfilled: "See, I have this day set thee over the nations and over the kingdoms, to root out, and to pull down, and to destroy, and to throw down, to build, and to plant."

Therefore if the temporal power errs, it will be judged by the spiritual power, and if the lower spiritual power errs, it will be judged by its superior. But if the highest spiritual power errs, it cannot be judged by men, but by God alone. For the apostle says: "But he that is spiritual judgeth all things, yet he himself is judged of no man." Now this authority, although it is given to man and exercised through man, is not human, but divine. For it was given by the word of the Lord to Peter, and the rock was made firm to him and his successors, in Christ himself, whom he had confessed. For the Lord said to Peter: "Whatsoever thou shalt bind on earth shall be bound in heaven; and whatsoever thou shalt loose on earth shall be loosed in heaven."

Therefore, whosoever resisteth this power thus ordained of God resisteth the ordinance of God, unless there are two principles, as Manichæus pretends there are. But this we judge to be false and heretical. For Moses says that, not in the beginnings, but in the beginning, God created the heaven and the earth. We therefore declare, say, and affirm that submission on the part of every man to the bishop of Rome is altogether necessary for his salvation.

Declaration of the Council of Pisa, 1409

Though humbled by the French monarchy, the Papacy soon renewed its claims to temporal supremacy, its control over Church administration and its insistence on doctrinal orthodoxy. Disparaged as the "Babylonian Captivity," the period the Papacy spent in Avignon was actually characterized by distinguished Papal leadership and rigorous maintenance of Papal prerogatives. If, as the pontiffs regained their independence, they chose not to return to Rome, it was more the consequence of disorder in the Holy City and in Italy than of any coercion on the part of the French kings.

Still, it was at Avignon that the Papacy committed itself to the degrading practices that ultimately turned most of Europe against it. Removed from its chief sources of revenue in Italy, the Papacy had to seek new methods for raising funds. Besides increasing the taxation of the local churches, the Popes lent themselves to the practice of selling ecclesiastical offices. If they themselves did not profit from these sharp dealings, they tolerated a degree of luxury and frivolity at the Avignon Court that equalled the extravagance of any in Europe. The Catholic Church came thereby to be increasingly associated with scandal and corruption. Not only the populace but the clergy regarded the condition of the Church as a disgrace, requiring thorough reform.

In 1378, Pope Gregory XI, no longer able to withstand the pressure to reestablish the Holy See in Rome, at last abandoned Avignon. When he died the following year, the majority of the Cardinals, who were French, seriously considered the election of a French Pope and a return of the court to France. But the Roman mobs so violently opposed this proposal that the Cardinals chose instead the Italian Archbishop of Bari, a narrow-minded and tactless zealot who took the name of Urban VI. The Cardinals quickly had reason to repent their choice, since the new Pope wanted to correct at once the ecclesiastical abuses to which they had become happily accustomed. The French Cardinals therefore deposed Urban VI, on the grounds that his election had been forced on them by the threatening mobs. They selected in his place a young French bishop, who took the name of Clement VII and moved himself and his retinue back to Avignon. But, to the Cardinals' astonishment, Pope Urban VI refused to accept his deposition and continued to reign as pontiff in Rome.

The Papal schism was certainly the most humiliating event in Church history and undoubtedly the incident that most debased the Papacy in popular eyes. There were now not only two Popes but rival colleges of cardinals and two Papal courts. There were two sets of Papal legates and competing sets of Papal tax collectors. Each Pope belligerently claimed his own legitimacy while excommunicating the other. Rather than one taking up the cause of virtue and reform, each side seemed to try to exceed the other in abuse and corruption. While the demand for unity was virtually unanimous, the means to achieve it could not be devised.

In 1409, the majority of French and Roman Cardinals withdrew from their respective Popes and met in a general council at Pisa to discuss proposals made by savants at the University of Paris. They voted to depose Gregory XII, then reigning at Rome, and Benedict XIII, then reigning at Avignon, and elected as new Pope the Cardinal of Milan, who took the name of Alexander V. Neither of the deposed Popes, however, recognized the authority of the Council of Pisa. The following year Alexander V died and the Cardinals chose to replace him an Italian known more for his piracy than his piety, a Pope who called himself John XXIII, hardly the man to restore Papal unity. The Church was now in the utterly ludicrous position of having not one, not two, but three Popes. The confusion was incalculable.

The Declaration of the Council of Pisa symbolized the disintegration of the power of the Papacy. The claim of the Council to rule for the Church challenged the thousand year trend toward Papal centralization. The Declaration at Pisa was, in effect, an act of clerical revolution. It sought to remake the Church constitution to deprive the Pope of powers he had asserted since the days of the Roman Empire and to replace them with what is known as the "conciliar theory"—rule by council—of ecclesiastical government. The Council of Pisa was, in some measure, a reflection of contemporaneous European experiments with parliaments, estates-general and diets, which aimed to share the responsibilities of government with the kings. The Papacy, however, rejected the doctrine of sharing any of its power. In succeeding years, the Popes conspired with considerable success to destroy the conciliar theory but they failed to put commensurate effort into reforming the conditions that evoked it. The Declaration of the Council of Pisa follows.

Document 23

This holy and general council, representing the universal Church, decrees and declares that the united college of cardinals was empowered to call the council, and that the power to call such a council belongs of right to the aforesaid holy college of cardinals, especially now when there is a detestable schism. The council further declares that this holy council, representing the universal Church, caused both claimants of the papal throne to be cited in the gates and doors of the churches of Pisa to come and hear the final decision (in the matter of the schism) pronounced, or to give a good and sufficient reason why such sentence should not be rendered.

The Council of Constance, 1415

The Council of Constance, which brought together the representatives of the entire European Church, succeeded in 1415 in achieving what the Council of Pisa had failed to do six years earlier, restore the unity of the Papacy. The Council of Constance tried and convicted Pope John XXIII on fifty-four charges—among them fornication, adultery, incest and sodomy—and forced him from the throne. Shortly afterward Pope Gregory XII of Rome abdicated. Benedict XII of Avignon proved more stubborn and only after much threatening did he finally step down. In November, 1417, the Council elevated to the Papacy the Italian Cardinal Otto Colonna, who took the name Martin V.

The Council of Constance's interest in reform, however, was limited to ending the schism and establishing its own dominance within the Church. Far from pursuing any doctrinal innovation, the Council lured the Czech reformer John Hus to Constance where, after he refused to renounce his heretical ideas, it burned him at the stake. After unity was restored, the Council appeared more indifferent than ever to eradicating corruption from the Church. The Council of Constance declared itself the supreme authority within the Church, empowered to review all Papal decisions. In the succeeding years, much of the energy of the Church was devoted to the struggle for power between Pope and Council. The struggle, the martyrdom of Hus, the growing scandal and the official indifference to reform were steps that led irresistibly in the next century to the greatest challenge to the Church's existence, the Protestant Reformation.

The following statement was issued by the Council of Constance in 1415.

Document 24

This holy synod of Constance, being a general council, and legally assembled in the Holy Spirit for the praise of God and for ending the present schism, and for the union and reformation of the Church of God in its head and in its members, in order more easily, more securely, more completely. and more fully to bring about the union and reformation of the Church of God, ordains, declares, and decrees as follows: First it declares that this synod, legally assembled, is a general council, and represents the Catholic church militant and has its authority directly from Christ; and everybody, of whatever rank or dignity, including also the pope, is bound to obey this council in those things which pertain to the faith, to the ending of this schism, and to a general reformation of the Church in its head and members. Likewise it declares that if any one, of whatever rank, condition, or dignity, including also the pope, shall refuse to obey the commands, statutes, ordinances, or orders of this holy council, or of any other holy council properly assembled, in regard to the ending of the schism and to the reformation of the Church, he shall be subject to the proper punishment, and, unless he repents, he shall be duly punished, and, if necessary, recourse shall be had to other aids of justice.

The Pragmatic Sanction of Bourges, 1438

In the years following the Council of Constance, the Popes were not strong enough to keep further councils from meeting, nor were the councils strong enough to dominate the Popes. The Council of Pavia in 1423, which later adjourned to Siena, and the Council of Basel in 1431 became the scene of fierce battles between Papacy and clergy. When the Council of Basel deposed Pope Eugenius IV and elected in his place Amadeus VIII, a rich widower with several children, it was more than most of Europe would tolerate. It became the opportunity for the French monarchy to free itself of Church interference in matters of state.

In 1438, King Charles VIII of France called together a synod at Bourges which, after careful deliberation, issued a "pragmatic sanction," a directive issued in the name of the sovereign and the church assembly. The Pragmatic Sanction of Bourges established the superiority of national church councils over the Papacy, the diminishing of Papal patronage, restrictions on Papal taxation and the limitation of judicial appeals to Rome. Together the affirmations of the Pragmatic Sanction embody the principle known as "Gallicanism," the applications of which are the "Gallican liberties," which the French Church maintained in its relations with the Papacy. The Pragmatic Sanction meant that the French Church would henceforth be ruled not by the Pope but by the king of France. It became thereby more a monarchical than a Papal institution.

The Pragmatic Sanction of Bourges, though modified from time to time, remained the basis for church-state relations throughout the history of the French monarchy. It was the symbol of the French crown's triumph over the Papacy. The Pragmatic Sanction ended Papal claims of superiority over the temporal sovereigns. Though a few German princes took advantage of it, the Pragmatic Sanction came far too late to repair the damage the Papacy had already done to German nationalism. In France, however, the Papacy's universal state had been routed and nationalism was triumphant.

The text printed below contains an abstract of the thirty-three sections of the Pragmatic Sanction of Bourges. The *réserve* and the *grâce expectative* mentioned in the introduction refer to the Papal practices of raising funds by filling ecclesiastical offices, in the first case, over which Rome had no jurisdiction and, in the second, which were not yet vacant. The canonships cited in point 5 had given Rome undue influence over local church organizations. The annates mentioned in point 7 were the first year's revenues from an office, which the Pope claimed. The very practices that are prohibited reveal the Papacy's techniques for raising money. The descriptions presented testify to the profound corruption that had afflicted the Church.

Document 25

The king declares that, according to the oath taken at their coronation, kings are bound to defend and protect the holy Church, its ministers and its sacred offices, and zealously to guard in their kingdoms the decrees of the holy fathers. The general council assembled at Basel to continue the work begun by the councils of Constance and Siena, and to labor for the reform of the Church, in both its head and members, having had presented to it numerous decrees and regulations, with the request that it accept them and cause them to be observed in the kingdom, the king has convened an assembly composed of prelates and other ecclesiastics representing the clery of France and of the Dauphiné. He has presided in person over its deliberations, surrounded by his son, the princes of the blood, and the principal lords of the realm. He has listened to the ambassadors of the Pope and the council. From the examination of prelates and the most renowned doctors, and from the thoroughgoing discussions of the assembly, it appears that, from the falling into decay of the early discipline, the churches of the kingdom have been made to suffer from all sorts of insatiable greed; that the *réserve* and the *grâce expectative* have given rise to grievous abuses and unbearable burdens; that the most notable and best endowed benefices have fallen into the hands of unknown men, who do not conform at all to the requirement of residence and who do not understand the speech of the people committed to their care, and consequently are neglectful of the needs of their souls, like mercenaries who dream of nothing whatever but temporal gain; that thus the worship of Christ is declining, piety is enfeebled, the laws of the Church are violated, and buildings for religious uses are falling in ruin. The clergy abandon their theological studies, because there is no hope of advancement. Conflicts without number rage over the possession of benefices, plurality of which is coveted by an execrable ambition. Simony is everywhere glaring; the prelates and other collators are pillaged of their rights and their ministry; the rights of patrons are impaired; and the wealth of the kingdom goes into the hands of foreigners, to the detriment of the clergy.

Since, in the judgment of the prelates and other ecclesiastics, the decrees of the holy council of Basel seemed to afford a suitable remedy for all these evils, after mature deliberation, we have decided to accept them —some without change, others with certain modifications—without wishing to cast doubt upon the power and authority of the council, but at the same time taking account of the necessities of the occasion and of the customs of the nation.

1. General councils shall be held every ten years, in places to be designated by the pope.

2. The authority of the general council is superior to that of the pope in all that pertains to the faith, the extirpation of schism, and the reform of the Church in both head and members.

3. Election is reestablished for ecclesiastical offices, but the king, or the princes of his kingdom, without violating the canonical rules, may make recommendations when elections are to occur in the chapters or the monasteries.

4. The popes shall not have the right to reserve the collation of benefices, or to bestow any benefice before it becomes vacant.

5. All grants of benefices made by the pope in virtue of the *droit d'expectative* are hereby declared null. Those who shall have received such benefices shall be punished by the secular power. The popes shall not have the right to interfere by the creation of canonships.

6. Appeals to Rome are prohibited until every other grade of jurisdiction shall have been exhausted.

7. Annates are prohibited.

IV

The Reformation

IV

The Reformation

The Middle Ages, in which the Catholic Church was the dominant institution, was by the year 1500 expiring. Strong states in France, England, Spain and Portugal had replaced the fragmented governments of feudalism. Patriotism had supplanted religion as the most deeply seated popular emotion. The spiritual, anti-intellectual, parochial outlook of medieval times was, in considerable measure, giving way to a worldly, intellectual and sensual spirit, generated largely by the Italian Renaissance. The rational, anti-dogmatic philosophy of humanism and a new emphasis on individualism had already had a significant impact on Europe's leaders. Some thinkers questioned whether the Church, as an institution, was necessary at all. Western civilization was passing through a revolution of the mind.

Perhaps the single most important factor in the transition from the Medieval to the Modern world was the rise of capitalism and a dynamic middle-class. Capitalism expanded as trade quickened, as cities arose, as industries sprouted up and, finally, as the oceans were conquered and new worlds discovered. Fresh commercial techniques, based on the extension of credit and aimed at the acquisition of profit, developed in response to the intensification of economic activity. European monarchs, recognizing the power inherent in wealth and the potential for freeing themselves from their traditional rivals, engaged their countries in a race for gold and silver. By 1500 capitalism had already made significant progress toward overthrowing Europe's feudal economy.

Had the Church had its affairs in order, it might have dealt successfully with this revolution in Western society. It could somehow have made its accommodation to the modern world and, as it had in earlier times of social upheaval, retained its leadership. But the Church, at the beginning of the sixteenth century, was sick. Debilitated by internal and external struggles for power, the Church lacked the resilience to turn events to its advantage. While the Papacy was itself caught in the quest for riches, the national monarchies were both depriving it of its normal sources of revenue and dispossessing the local churches of their wealth. Catholicism, at the same time, continued to stand for an earlier ideal, basically resistant to the pursuit of material gain and particularly opposed to the practice of lending money for interest. The Church thus faced the insoluble dilemma of preaching against the rise of capitalism while itself contributing to it.

Tetzel's Instructions on Selling Indulgences, 1517

The Papacy resorted to every sort of device to get money, frequently utilizing as its agents the most aggressive banking houses and the most unscrupulous financiers. Among the most detested of its fund-raising methods was the sale of Papal indulgences. An indulgence was a promise of remission of punishment after death. Normally, to obtain an indulgence, a sinner would have to do penance, such as the recitation of certain prayers or the performance of "good works." But on the eve of the Reformation, the most conspicuous of "good works" was the payment of money to the Papacy. The sale of indulgences had become a great scandal.

In 1517, Pope Leo X, anxious to raise money to rebuild St. Peter's Church in Rome, struck the bargain with the Archibishop of Mainz that precipitated the revolt against the Papacy. The Archbishop was heavily indebted to the Fugger banking house for the office he had just purchased from the Pope. Leo X agreed to issue a "plenary indulgence," the profits from which he planned to divide equally with the Archbishop in return for his handling the sale. To John Tetzel, a Dominican preacher of great eloquence and persuasiveness but with few scruples, was entrusted the responsibility for promotion of the indulgence. Tetzel promised to potential buyers remission not only of their own sins but also of those of their departed relatives. His theological swindles disgusted Martin Luther, an Augustinian monk, who refused to accept the indulgence as penance. Luther's indignation lit the spark that fired the Reformation.

The following excerpt is from the instructions that Tetzel and his band of peddlers, whom he designated his "penitentiaries and confessors," carried with them. It is based on the bull issued by Pope Leo X to announce the sale of the plenary indulgence. The selections here cover the high-pressure selling techniques that Tetzel recommended to his men.

Document 26

The first grace is the complete remission of all sins; and nothing greater than this can be named, since man, who lives in sin and forfeits the favor of God, obtains complete remission by these means and once more enjoys God's favor; moreover, through this remission of sins the punishment which one is obliged to undergo in purgatory on account of the affront to the Divine Majesty is all remitted, and the pains of purgatory completely blotted out. And although nothing is precious enough to be given in exchange for such a grace,— in order that Christian believers may be the more easily induced to procure the same, we establish the following rules, to wit: . . .

Respecting, now, the contribution to the chest, for the building of the said church of the chief of the apostles (St. Peter's), the penitentiaries and confessors, after they have explained to those making confession the full remission and privileges, shall ask of them for how much money or other temporal goods they would conscientiously pay for the said most complete remission and privileges; and this shall be done in order that hereafter they may be brought the more easily to contribute. And because the conditions and occupations of men are so manifold and diverse that we cannot consider them individually, and impose specific rates accordingly, we have therefore concluded that the rates should be determined according to the recognized classes of persons.

Kings and queens and their offspring, archbishops and bishops, and other great rulers, provided they seek the places where the cross is raised, or otherwise present themselves, shall pay at least five and twenty Rhenish guilders in gold. Abbots and the great prelates of cathedral churches, counts, barons, and others of the higher nobility, together with their consorts, shall pay for each letter of indulgence ten such guilders. Other lesser prelates and nobles, as also the rectors of celebrated places, and all others who, either from permanent incomes or merchandise, or otherwise, enjoy a total yearly revenue of five hundred gold guilders, shall pay six such guilders. Other citizens and tradespeople and artisans, who have individual incomes and families of their own, shall pay one such guilder; those of less means, only a half. . . .

All other persons are confided to the discretion of the confessors and penitentiaries, who should have ever in view the advancement of this building, and should urge their penitents to a free contribution, but should let no one go away without some portion of grace, because the happiness of Christian believers is here concerned not less than the interests of the building. And those that have no money shall supply their contribution with prayer and fasting; for the kingdom of heaven should be open to the poor not less than to the rich. . . .

It is, furthermore, not necessary that the persons who place their contributions in the chest for the dead should be contrite in heart and have orally confessed, since this grace is based simply on the state of grace in which the dead departed, and on the contribution of the living, as is evident in the text of the bull. Moreover preachers shall exert themselves to give this grace the widest publicity, since through the same, help will surely come to departed souls, and the construction of the church of St. Peter will be abundantly promoted at the same time. . . .

Luther's Ninety-Five Theses

Luther, who regarded himself as a loyal if somewhat disaffected Catholic, did not rush at once to the theological barricades. Rather he refrained from expressing himself openly for six months, so that he could reflect not only on Tetzel's disgraceful huckstering but also on the general theory of indulgences. He concluded that the true penitent, with or without an indulgence, would receive God's pardon. The intercession of the Pope was therefore superfluous. Luther came to believe that the indulgence was an ecclesiastical fraud and the Papacy seriously in error. Though he was not immediately willing to acknowledge it, Luther had questioned the very foundation of the Catholic Church. For the moment, however, he preferred to regard himself as a doctrinal reformer, rather than a heretic and a rebel.

Luther decided that his best tactic was to provoke debate on his ideas. Instead of issuing an open challenge to the Church, he chose to phrase his dissent in the form of debating theses. He composed his famous Ninety-Five Theses, which subsequently became Protestantism's declaration of independence. To invite argument on them, he posted them on the door of the church in the Saxon town of Wittenberg on the evening of October 31, 1517, just before the annual church festival. Though they were written in Latin, they were immediately translated into German. With the help of the new invention, the printing press, copies were quickly distributed all over Germany. Within a month, Luther's imputations were known throughout Europe. Tetzel's sales dropped dramatically and he himself had to hide from angry mobs. The great struggle of the Reformation had begun.

The following extracts provide the essence of the Ninety-Five Theses. Though they were meant to evoke argument, so that Luther might reconcile himself with orthodoxy, it is clear that they were too harsh and too basic to what was essential in Catholic doctrine for the Church establishment to tolerate.

DOCUMENT 27

In the desire and with the purpose of elucidating the truth, a disputation will be held on the underwritten propositions at Wittenberg, under the presidency of the Reverend Father Martin Luther, monk of the order of St. Augustine, Master of Arts and of Sacred Theology, and ordinary lecturer in the same at that place. He therefore asks those who cannot be present and discuss the subject with us orally to do so by letter in their absence. In the name of our Lord Jesus Christ. Amen.

1. Our Lord and Master Jesus Christ in saying "Repent ye" (*poenitentiam agite*), intended that the whole life of believers should be penitence (*poenitentia*).

2. This word (*poenitentia*) cannot be understood as sacramental penance, that is, the confession and satisfaction which are performed under the ministry of priests. . . .

5. The pope has neither the will nor the power to remit any penalties except those which he has imposed by his own authority, or by that of the canons. . . .

20. Therefore the pope, when he speaks of the plenary remission of all penalties, does not mean really of all, but only of those imposed by himself.

21. Thus those preachers of indulgences are in error who say that by the indulgences of the pope a man is freed and saved from all punishment. . . .

23. If any entire remission of all penalties can be granted to any one, it is certain that it is granted to none but the most perfect,—that is, to very few. . . .

27. They preach man (rather than God) who say that the soul flies out of purgatory as soon as the money rattles in the chest.

28. It is certain that, when the money rattles in the chest, avarice and gain may be increased, but the effect of the intercession of the Church depends on the will of God alone. . . .

39. It is a very difficult thing, even for the most learned theologians, to exalt at the same time, in the eyes of the people, the ample effect of pardons and the necessity of true contrition.

40. True contrition seeks and loves punishment, while the ampleness of pardons relaxes it and causes men to hate it, or at least gives occasion for them to do so. . . .

43. Christians should be taught that he who gives to a poor man, or lends to a needy man, does better than if he bought pardons.

44. Because by works of charity, charity increases and the man becomes better, while by means of pardons he does not become better, but only freer from punishment. . . .

50. Christians should be taught that, if the pope were acquainted with the exactions of the preachers of pardons he would prefer that the basilica of St. Peter should be burnt to ashes rather than that it should be built up with the skin, flesh, and bones of his sheep.

51. Christians should be taught that as it would be the duty, so it would be the wish of the pope even to sell, if necessary, the basilica of St. Peter, as well as to give of his own money to very many of those from whom the preachers of pardons extract money. . . .

56. The treasures of the Church, whence the pope grants indulgences, are neither sufficiently discussed nor understood among the people of Christ.

57. It is clear that they are at least not temporal treasures, for these are not so readily lavished, but only accumulated, by many of the preachers. . . .

62. The true treasure of the Church is the holy gospel of the glory and grace of God.

63. This treasure, however, is naturally most hateful because it makes the first to be last;

64. While the treasure of indulgences is naturally most acceptable, because it makes the last to be first. . . .

81. This license in the preaching of pardons makes it no easy thing, even for learned men, to protect the reverence due to the pope against the calumnies, or, at all events, the keen questionings of the laity.

82. As, for instance: Why does not the pope empty purgatory for the sake of his most holy charity and of the supreme necessity of souls,—this being the most just of all reasons,—if he redeems an infinite number of souls for the sake of that most fatal thing, money, to be spent on building a basilica,—this being a very slight reason? . . .

86. Again: Why does not the pope, whose riches are at this day more ample than those of Croesus, build the basilica of St. Peter with his own money rather than with that of poor believers?

87. Again: What greater good could the Church receive than if the pope were to bestow these remissions and participations a hundred times a day, instead of once, as he does now, on any one of the faithful? . . .

90. To repress these scruples and arguments of the laity by force alone, and not to solve them by giving reasons, is to expose the Church and the pope to the ridicule of their enemies and to make Christian men unhappy.

91. If then pardons were preached according to the spirit and wish of the pope, all these questions would be solved with ease; nay, would not exist.

Luther's Address to the German Nobility, 1520

Luther's ideas found a receptive audience among the Germans. Patriotism in Germany contained, to a degree greater than elsewhere in Europe, a distinctly anti-Papal flavor. In addition to their long-standing grievances against Rome, Germans resented the particular advantage the Papacy had taken of them because they had no strong state to protect them. Germany presented a curious paradox of hostility and submission to the Papacy. Luther provided the justification for throwing off the burden of submission.

For two years Luther's challenge simmered, without coming to a boil. Reluctant to commit an irrevocable act, Luther maintained communication with Rome, appeared inclined to compromise and, at one point, even agreed to write the Pope a letter of conciliation. The Pope, unwilling himself to provoke a break, made several attempts to persuade Luther to recant. But in a debate with the prominent theologian John Eck at Leipzig in June, 1519, Luther was forced to admit that his views closely resembled those of Wycliffe and the martyred Hus, the great heretics of an earlier day. Luther maintained that the relationship between man and God did not require the intercession of the Church and that the Papacy was not a divine but a human institution. Having done so, it was obvious that no hope remained for his reconciliation with the Church. Luther was now prepared to acknowledge the rupture and to undertake ardently his revolutionary mission.

In 1520, Luther issued a stirring appeal for support to Charles V, the

Holy Roman Emperor, and to the German nobility. If the Ninety-Five Theses was Protestantism's psychological declaration of independence, Luther's *Address to the Nobility of the German Nation* was the formal act of secession from the Catholic Church. When the Pope retaliated by excommunication, the diet of the Holy Roman Empire rejected Luther's plea and declared him an outlaw. Luther, however, burned the bull of excommunication and received asylum from the Elector of Saxony, his native province. He had now become a national hero and the Protestant revolution was a fact.

In his *Address to the Nobility*, excerpts of which are presented below, Luther calls on the temporal sovereigns to take the leadership in reforming Germany's religious, social and economic life. Denouncing the theory of a sacred priesthood, he proposes the creation of a national church, free of Roman exploitation and clerical rule. In hard, incisive German, Luther cites three fallacious "walls of defense" set up by the "Romanists" against reform: the independence of the spiritual from the temporal authority, the exclusive right of the Pope to interpret the Scriptures, the exclusive power of the Pope to summon a Church council. By emphasizing the wealth of the Church, Luther sought to whet the appetite of the Emperor and the nobles. What is quite clear is that the *Address to the Nobility*, though a foundation stone of Protestantism, was a German document, concerned principally with German conditions. But once a German base was established, the Reformation was free to spread.

Document 28

The time for silence is gone, and the time to speak has come, as we read in Ecclesiastes (3:7). I have, in conformity with our resolve, put together some few points concerning the reformation of the Christian estate, with the intent of placing the same before the Christian nobility of the German nation, in case it may please God to help His Church by means of the laity, inasmuch as the clergy, whom this task rather befitted, have become quite careless. . . .

It is not out of mere arrogance and perversity that I, an individual poor man, have taken upon me to address your lordships. The distress and misery that oppress all the Christian estates, more especially in Germany, have led not only myself, but every one else, to cry aloud and to ask for help, and have now forced me, too, to cry out and to ask if God would give His Spirit to any one to reach a hand to His wretched people. Councils have often put forward some remedy, but it has adroitly been frustrated, and the evils have become worse, through the cunning of certain men. Their malice and wickedness I will now, by the help of God, expose, so that, being known, they may henceforth cease to be so obstructive and injurious. . . .

The Romanists have, with great adroitness, drawn three walls round themselves, with which they have hitherto protected themselves, so that no one could reform them, whereby all Christendom has fallen terribly. . . .

Firstly, if pressed by the temporal power, they have affirmed and maintained that the temporal power has no jurisdiction over them, but on the contrary, that the spiritual power is above the temporal.

Secondly, if it were proposed to admonish them with the Scriptures, they objected that no one may interpret the Scriptures but the Pope.

Thirdly, if they are threatened with a council, they pretend that no one may call a council but the Pope. . . .

Now may God help us, and give us one of those trumpets that overthrew the walls of Jericho, so that we may blow down these walls of straw and paper, and that we may set free our Christian rods for the chastisement of sin, and expose the craft and deceit of the devil, so that we may amend ourselves by punishment and again obtain God's favor.

THE FIRST WALL

That the Temporal Power Has No Jurisdiction over the Spirituality. . . .

It has been devised that the Pope, bishops, priests, and monks are called the *spiritual estate*, princes, lords, artificers, and peasants are the *temporal estate.* This is an artful lie and hypocritical device, but let no one be made afraid by it, and that for this reason: that all Christians are truly of the spiritual estate, and there is no difference among them, save of office alone. . . .

It follows . . . that between laymen and priests, princes and bishops, or, as they call it, between spiritual and temporal persons, the only real difference is one of office and function, and not of estate, for they are all of the same spiritual estate, true priests, bishops, and popes, though their functions are not the same—just as among priests and monks every man has not the same functions. . . . Therefore I say: Forasmuch as the temporal power has been ordained by God for the punishment of the bad and the protection of the good, therefore we must let it do its duty throughout the whole Christian body, without respect of persons, whether it strike popes, bishops, priests, monks, nuns, or whoever it may be.

THE SECOND WALL

That No One May Interpret the Scriptures But the Pope

The second wall is even more tottering and weak: that they alone pretend to be considered masters of the Scriptures; although they learn nothing of them all their lives. They assume authority, and juggle before us with impudent words, saying that the Pope cannot err in matters of faith, whether he be evil or good, albeit they cannot prove it by a single letter. . . . We will quote the Scriptures. St. Paul says, "If any thing be revealed to another that sitteth by, let the first hold his peace" (I Cor. 14: 30). What would be the use of this commandment, if we were to believe him alone that teaches or has the highest seat? Christ Himself says, "And they shall be all taught of God" (John 6: 45). Thus it may come to pass that the Pope and his followers are wicked and not true Christians, and not being taught by God, have no true understanding, whereas a common man may have true understanding. Why should we then not follow him? Has not the Pope often erred? . . .

Therefore it is a wickedly devised fable—and they cannot quote a single letter to confirm it—that it is for the Pope alone to interpret the Scriptures or to confirm the interpretation of them. They have assumed the authority of their own selves. And though they say that this authority was given to St. Peter when the keys were given to him, it is plain enough that the keys were not given to St. Peter alone, but to the whole community.

THE THIRD WALL

That No One May Call a Council But the Pope

The third wall falls of itself, as soon as the first two have fallen; for if the Pope acts contrary to the Scriptures, we are bound to stand by the Scriptures, to punish and to constrain him, according to Christ's commandment, "Moreover, if thy brother shall trespass against thee, go and tell him his fault between thee and him alone; if he shall hear thee, thou hast gained thy brother. But if he will not hear *thee*, then take with thee one or two more, that in the mouth of two or three witnesses every word may be established. And if he shall neglect to hear them, tell it unto the Church; but if he neglect to hear the Church, let him be unto thee as an heathen man and a publican" (Matt. 18: 15–17). Here each member is commanded to take care for the other, much more then should we do this, if it is a ruling member of the community that does evil, which by its evil-doing causes great harm and offense to the others. If then I am to accuse him before the Church, I must collect the Church together. . . .

Let us now consider the matters which should be treated in the councils, and with which popes, cardinals, bishops, and all learned men should occupy themselves day and night, if they love Christ and His Church. . . .

1. It is a distressing and terrible thing to see that the head of Christendom, who boasts of being the vicar of Christ and the successor of St. Peter, lives in a worldly pomp that no king or emperor can equal. . . .

2. What is the use in Christendom of the people called "cardinals?" I will tell you. In Italy and Germany there are many rich convents, endowments, fiefs, and benefices, and as the best way of getting these into the hands of Rome, they created cardinals, and gave them the sees, convents, and prelacies, and thus destroyed the service of God. That is why Italy is almost a desert now.

What has brought us Germans to such a pass that we have to suffer this robbery and the destruction of our property by the Pope?

Long ago the emperors and princes of Germany allowed the Pope to claim the *annates* from all German benefices, that is, half of the first year's income from every benefice. The object of this concession was that the Pope should collect a fund with all this money to fight against the Turks and infidels, and to protect Christendom, so that the nobility should not have to bear the burden of the struggle alone, and that the priests should also contribute. The popes have made such use of this good simple piety of the Germans that they have taken this money for more than one hundred years, and have now made of it a regular tax . . . [for] posts and offices at Rome. . . .

Now though I am too lowly to submit articles that could serve for the reformation of these fearful evils, I will yet sing out my fool's song, and will show, as well as my wit will allow, what might and should be done by the temporal authorities or by a general council.

1. Princes, nobles, and cities should promptly forbid their subjects to pay the *annates* to Rome and should even abolish them altogether. . . .

3. It should be decreed by an imperial law that no episcopal cloak and no confirmation of any appointment shall for the future be obtained from Rome. The order of the most holy and renowned Nicene Council must again be restored, namely that a bishop must be confirmed by the two nearest bishops or by the archbishop. . . .

9. The Pope should have no power over the Emperor, except to anoint and crown him at the altar, as a bishop crowns a king. . . .

14. We see also . . . how many a poor priest is encumbered with a woman and children and burdened in his conscience, and no one does anything to help him . . . therefore I say: According to the ordinances of Christ and His Apostles, every town should have a minister or bishop, as St. Paul plainly says (Titus 1), and this minister should not be forced to live without a lawful wife, but should be allowed to have one, as St. Paul writes, saying: "A bishop then must be blameless, the husband of one wife . . . having his children in subjection with all gravity" (I Tim. 3). . . .

25. The universities also require a good, sound reformation. I must say this, let it vex whom it may. The fact is that whatever the papacy has ordered or instituted is only designed for the propagation of sin and error. . . .

Peasants' Manifesto, 1524

The Peasants' Revolt of 1524, like the Reformation itself, grew out of the disintegration of the medieval world. To the German peasantry, the rise of capitalism meant only increased taxes and decreased protection. When Luther urged the princes to seize the possessions of the Church, the peasants naturally saw an opportunity to grab a share of the spoils. Luther had no objection to their depradations, as long as they confined them to Church property. But as soon as the peasants made demands on the temporal sovereigns, Luther showed on whose side he stood and vigorously backed the established classes.

The Peasants' Manifesto of 1524 illustrates vividly the economic dilemma in which the peasants found themselves. In severe economic distress, they were crushed between dynamic capitalism and stagnant feudalism. Unaware that they were the victims of economic transition they asked, on the one hand, for the restoration of certain feudal rights and, on the other, for new capitalist freedoms. Woven through and inseparable from the other provisions of the Manifesto are demands for Luther's theological reforms. The Manifesto, of which extracts follow, demonstrates brilliantly how closely linked were the economic and religious aspects of the Protestant revolution.

Though the peasants' demands were moderate enough, Luther saw in them a grave threat to his own movement. When the peasants rose up to take by force what they could not acquire by negotiation, Luther authorized the nobles to "smite, strangle or stab, secretly or publicly" to put them down. The Peasants' Revolt was crushed in 1525 with the slaughter of an estimated 50,000 persons. It condemned the German peasantry to an existence as grim and depressed as any in Europe. The ruthless suppression turned many peasants away from Luther, especially in the south of Germany, and paradoxically persuaded some conservative princes that Luther's radical appeals ought to be resisted. The Peasants' Revolt helped check the spread of Lutheranism in Germany. Its failure revealed Protestantism as a vehicle for middle-class, not lower-class, revolution.

Document 29

Peace to the Christian reader and the grace of God through Christ:

There are many evil writings put forth of late which take occasion, on account of the assembling of the peasants, to cast scorn upon the gospel, saying, "Is this the fruit of the new teaching, that no one should obey but that all should everywhere rise in revolt, and rush together to reform, or perhaps destroy altogether, the authorities, both ecclesiastic and lay?" The articles below shall answer these godless and criminal fault-finders, and serve, in the first place, to remove the reproach from the word of God and, in the second place, to give a Christian excuse for the disobedience or even the revolt of the entire peasantry.

In the first place, the gospel is not the cause of revolt and disorder, since it is the message of Christ, the promised Messiah; the word of life, teaching only love, peace, patience, and concord. Thus all who believe in Christ should learn to be loving, peaceful, long-suffering, and harmonious. Thus is the foundation of all the articles of the peasants (as will be seen), who accept the gospel and live according to it. How then can the evil reports declare the gospel to be a cause of revolt and disobedience? That the authors of the evil reports and the enemies of the gospel oppose themselves to these demands is due, not to the gospel, but to the devil, the worst enemy of the gospel, who causes this opposition by raising doubts in the minds of his followers, and thus the word of God, which teaches love, peace, and concord, is overcome. . . .

The First Article. First, it is our humble petition and desire as also our will and resolution, that in the future we should have power and authority so that each community should choose and appoint a pastor, and that we should have the right to depose him should he conduct himself improperly. The pastor thus chosen should teach us the gospel pure and simple, without any addition, doctrine, or ordinance of man.

The Second Article. According as the just tithe is established by the Old Testament and fulfilled in the New, we are ready and willing to pay the fair tithe of grain. The word of God plainly provides that in giving rightly to God and distributing to his people the services of a pastor are required. We will that for the future our church provost whomsoever the community may appoint, shall gather and receive this tithe. From this he shall give to the pastor elected by the whole community, a decent and sufficient maintenance for him and his, as shall seem right to the whole community. What remains over shall be given to the poor of the place, as the circumstances and the general opinion demand. Should anything farther remain, let it be kept, lest any one should have to leave the country from poverty. The small tithes, whether ecclesiastical or lay, we will not pay at all, for the Lord God created cattle for the free use of man. We will not, therefore, pay farther any unseemly tithe which is of man's invention.

The Third Article. It has been the custom hitherto for men to hold us as their own property, which is pitiable enough, considering that Christ has delivered and redeemed us all, without exception, by the shedding of his precious blood, the lowly as well as the great. Accordingly it is consistent with Scripture that we should be free and should wish to be so. Not that we would wish to be absolutely free and under no authority. God does not teach us that we should lead a disorderly life in the lusts of the flesh, but that we should love the Lord our God and our neighbors. We would gladly observe all this as God has commanded us in the celebration of the communion. He has not commanded us not to obey the authorities, but rather that we should be humble, not only towards those in authority, but towards everyone. We are thus ready to yield obedience according to God's law to our elected and regular authorities in all proper things becoming to a Christian. We therefore take it for granted that you will release us from serfdom as true Christians, unless it should be shown us from the gospel that we are serfs.

The Fourth Article. In the fourth place, it has been the custom heretofore that no poor man should be allowed to touch venison or wild fowl, or fish in flowing water, which seems to us quite unseemly and unbrotherly as well as selfish and not agreeable to the word of God. In some places the authorities preserve the game to our great annoyance and loss, recklessly permitting the unreasoning animals to destroy to no purpose our crops, which God suffers to grow for the use of man; and yet we must submit quietly. This is neither godly nor neighborly. . . .

The Sixth Article. Our sixth complaint is in regard to the excessive services which are demanded of us and which are increased from day to day. We ask that this matter be properly looked into, so that we shall not continue to be oppressed in this way, but that some gracious consideration be given us, since our forefathers were required only to serve according to the word of God.

The Seventh Article. Seventh, we will not hereafter allow ourselves to be farther oppressed by our lords, but will let them demand only what is just and proper according to the word of the agreement between the lord and the peasant. The lord should no longer try to force more services and other dues from the peasant without payment, but permit the peasant to enjoy his holding in peace and quiet. The peasant should, however, help the lord when it is necessary and at proper times, when it will not be disadvantageous to the peasant, and for a suitable payment.

The Eighth Article. In the eighth place, we are greatly burdened by holdings which cannot support the rent exacted from them. The peasants suffer loss in this way and are ruined; and we ask that the lords may appoint persons of honor to inspect these holdings, and fix a rent in accordance with justice, so that the peasant shall not work for nothing since the laborer is worthy of his hire. . . .

The Tenth Article. In the tenth place, we are aggrieved by the appropriation by individuals of meadows and fields which at one time belonged to a community. These we will take again into our own hands. It may, however, happen that the land was rightfully purchased. When, however, the land has unfortunately been purchased in this way, some brotherly arrangement should be made according to circumstances. . . .

Conclusion. In the twelfth place, it is our conclusion and final resolution that if any one or more of the articles here set forth should not be in agreement with the word of God, as we think they are, such article we will willingly retract if it is proved really to be against the word of God by a clear explanation of the Scripture. Or if articles should now be conceded to us that are hereafter discovered to be unjust, from that hour they shall be dead and null and without force. Likewise, if more complaints should be discovered which are based upon truth and the Scriptures and relate to offenses against God and our neighbor, we have determined to reserve the right to present these also, and to exercise ourselves in all Christian teaching. For this we shall pray to God, since he can grant our demands, and he alone. The peace of Christ abide with us all.

England's Act of Supremacy, 1534

The Reformation spread quickly throughout Europe, finding more hospitality in some regions than in others. Like all disruptions, it invariably generated hatreds and, in some cases, civil war. Wherever it went, it encountered particular political or economic conditions which frequently determined the form it took. Often Reformation doctrine became the weapon of one side or another in an economic or political struggle. In many arenas Protestantism won or lost against Catholicism for reasons far removed from the theological question.

Nowhere was this more true than in England, where King Henry VIII found Luther's challenge a useful precedent in his own battle against Rome. The king, anxious to preserve the Tudor dynasty, fretted because his only surviving heir was a girl and thus regarded as an unsuitable successor. In 1527 he determined to be rid of Catherine of Aragon, his wife for eighteen years, so he could marry the black-eyed Anne Boleyn, a maid-in-waiting at the court. Henry, who looked on himself as a loyal Catholic, petitioned Pope Clement VII for an annulment, claiming that because Catherine was the widow of his older brother the marriage had never been legal. The Pope, battling defections all over Europe, was loathe to refuse Henry's request, but Italy, at that moment, was held by the Holy Roman Emperor, Charles V, a nephew of the unwanted queen. After much procrastination, Pope Clement VII, deciding in Catherine's favor, denied the annulment.

Henry made up his mind at once that if the Pope did not reverse the decision he would break with the Church. Backed by Parliament, he put through a series of statutes that weakened the tie between the English churches and Rome. When the Pope reaffirmed his original position, Henry named Thomas Cranmer, a Lutheran by conviction, as Archbishop of Canterbury, the most important ecclesiastical office in the realm. Cranmer proceeded to declare the royal marriage annulled and the king lawfully wedded to Anne Boleyn. Later that year another girl, the Princess Elizabeth, was born to the newlyweds. The English Church was by now, for all practical purposes, independent.

Henry VIII legalized the secession from Rome in 1534 in a series of parliamentary statutes that established the Anglican Church with the king as its head. His own orthodox tastes kept all but a little Lutheranism from creeping into its ceremonies and doctrine. Except for its substitution of the king for the Pope, the Anglican Church remained theologically Catholic and did not change significantly until the reign of Henry's daughter, Queen Elizabeth (1558–1603). The Reformation in England was little concerned with religious questions for, from start to finish, its aims were political.

The Act of Supremacy of 1534, presented below, ratified what King Henry VIII had actually done on his own some time before. Nonetheless, it established the legal basis for the assumption by the English monarchs of the title and powers of "the Supreme Head of the Church of England."

Document 30

Albeit the king's Majesty justly and rightfully is and ought to be the supreme head of the Church of England, and so is recognized by the clergy of this realm in their convocations, yet nevertheless, for corroboration and confirmation thereof, and for increase of virtue in Christ's religion within this realm of England, and to repress and extirpate all errors, heresies, and other enormities and abuses heretofore used in the same, be it enacted, by authority of this present Parliament, that the king, our sovereign lord, his heirs and successors, kings of this realm, shall be taken, accepted, and reputed the only supreme head in earth of the Church of England, called *Anglicana Ecclesia;* and shall have and enjoy, annexed and united to the imperial crown of this realm, as well the title and style thereof, as all honors, dignities, preëminences, jurisdictions, privileges, authorities, immunities, profits, and commodities to the said dignity of the supreme head of the same Church belonging and appertaining; and that our said sovereign lord, his heirs and successors, kings of this realm, shall have full power and authority from time to time to visit, repress, redress, record, order, correct, restrain, and amend all such errors, heresies, abuses, offenses contempts and enormities, whatsoever they be, which by any manner of spiritual authority or jurisdiction ought or may lawfully be reformed, repressed, ordered, redressed, corrected, restrained, or amended, most to the pleasure of Almighty God, the increase of virtue in Christ's religion, and for the conservation of the peace, unity, and tranquillity of this realm; any usage, foreign land, foreign authority, prescription, or any other thing or things to the contrary hereof notwithstanding.

Religious Peace of Augsburg, 1555

In Germany, Luther at first met general opposition to his challenge to Rome from the countless temporal sovereigns of the realm. The princes, in traditional fashion, rushed to the defense of the Pope. In 1521 they summoned Luther to appear before the Diet of the Empire, meeting at Worms, and there ordered him to recant. He refused and fled into hiding. Over the succeeding years, Lutheranism spread throughout the country and the German people, long divided politically, had thrust upon them a deep religious issue to divide them more.

As a rule, the success or failure of Protestantism in Germany followed the boundaries of the principalities. In many of the sovereignties, Lutheranism actually became the state church, functioning under the leadership of the temporal ruler. In others, the princes remained loyal to Catholicism and, with varying degrees of vigor, tried to stamp out the Lutheran heresy.

Charles V, the Holy Roman Emperor, favored the Catholic cause and formed a loose alliance of Catholic sovereigns to fight the Protestants. In 1531 the Lutheran princes, in retaliation, established their own defensive federation, called the Schmalkaldic League. Over the ensuing years the two coalitions engaged in desultory civil war. Under Charles V, the Catholics were getting the better of the fight until the Protestant sovereigns made a pact with the king of France, Henry II, who was himself warring with the Emperor over control of Italy. The French king, backed by his new German allies, struck hard at the Emperor and defeated him. Charles V had now to acknowledge that he could no longer attain his goal of uniting Germany as the secular arm of the Church. The compromise to which he agreed in 1555 was called the Religious Peace of Augsburg. It confirmed the division of Germany into Protestant and Catholic provinces.

The Religious Peace of Augsburg affirmed the right of the German princes to subscribe to the creed of the Lutheran Church, known as the Confession of Augsburg of 1530. It empowered each prince to determine the religion of his subjects, although it authorized any dissenter from the prince's choice to emigrate to a territory of his choice. The agreement confirmed all seizures of Catholic property by Protestant churches prior to 1552, established Lutheranism as the only permissible form of Protestantism in Germany and required Catholic clerics who converted to Protestantism to surrender their offices and any ecclesiastical wealth they possessed. The Religious Peace of Augsburg, the major provisions of which are given below, was negotiated by King Ferdinand, brother of the Holy Roman Emperor, apparently because Charles V could not accept for himself this humiliation to the Empire and the Church.

Document 31

Constitution of the Peace between their Imperial and Royal Majesties, on the one hand, and the electors and estates of the realm, on the other:

We, Ferdinand, by God's grace king of the Romans and at all times widener of the empire, king of Germany, Hungary, Bohemia, Dalmatia, Croatia, and Slavonia, infanta of Spain, archduke of Austria, etc., etc.,—Whereas, at all the diets held during the last thirty years and more, and at several special sessions besides, there have often been negotiations and consultations to establish between the estates of the Holy Empire a general, continuous, and enduring peace in regard to the contending religions; and several times terms of peace were drawn up, which, however, were never sufficient for the maintenance of peace, but in spite of them the estates of the Empire remained continually in bitterness and distrust toward each other, from which not a little evil has had its origin; . . . to secure again peace and confidence, in the minds of the estates and subjects toward each other, and to save the German nation, our beloved fatherland, from final dissolution and ruin; we, on the one hand, have united and agreed with the electors, the princes and estates present, and with the deputies and embassies of those absent, as they, on the other hand, with us.

1. We therefore establish, will, and command that from henceforth no one, whatsoever his rank or character, for any cause, or upon any pretense whatsoever, shall engage in feuds, or make war upon, rob, seize, invest, or besiege another. Nor shall he, in person or through any agent, descend upon any castle, town, manor, fortification, villages, estates, hamlets, or against the will of that other seize them wickedly with violence, or damage them by fire or in other ways. Nor shall any one give such offenders counsel or help, or render them aid and assistance in any other way. Nor shall one knowingly or willingly show them hospitality, house them, give them to eat or drink, keep or suffer them. But every one shall love the other with true friendship and Christian love.

It is provided also that no estate or member of the Holy Empire shall deprive or cut off any other estate from free access to provisions and food, or interfere with its trade, rents, money, or income; for justice should be administered not irregularly but in suitable and fixed places. In every way shall his Imperial Majesty, and we and all the estates, mutually adhere to all the contents of this present religious and general constitution for securing the peace of the land.

2. And in order that such peace, which is especially necessary in view of the divided religions, as is seen from the causes before mentioned, and is demanded by the sad necessity of the Holy Roman Empire of the German nation, may be the better established and made secure and enduring between his Roman Imperial Majesty and us, on the one hand, and the electors, princes, and estates of the Holy Empire of the German nation on the other, therefore his Imperial Majesty, and we, the electors, princes, and estates of the Holy Empire, will not make war upon any estate of the empire on account of the Augsburg Confession and the doctrine, religion, and faith of the same, nor injure nor do violence to those estates that hold it, nor force them, against their conscience, knowledge, and will, to abandon the religion, faith, church usages, ordinances, and ceremonies of the Augsburg Confession, where these have been established or may hereafter be established, in their principalities, lands, and dominions. Nor shall we, through mandate or in any other way, trouble or disparage them, but shall let them quietly and peacefully enjoy their religion, faith, church usages, ordinances, and ceremonies, as well as their possessions, real and personal property, lands, people, dominions, governments, honors, and rights. . . .

3. On the other hand, the estates that have accepted the Augsburg Confession shall suffer his Imperial Majesty, us, and the electors, princes, and other estates of the Holy Empire, adhering to the old religion, to abide in like manner by their religion, faith, church usages, ordinances, and ceremonies. They shall also leave undisturbed their possessions, real and personal property, lands, people, dominions, government, honors, and rights, rents, interest, and tithes. . . .

5. But all others who are not adherents of either of the above-mentioned religions are not included in this peace, and shall be altogether excluded.

6. And since, in the negotiation of this peace, there has been disagreement about what should be done when one or more of the spiritual estates should abandon the old religion, on account of the archbishoprics,

bishoprics, prelacies, and benefices that were held by them, about which the adherents of both religions could not come to an agreement; therefore, by the authority of the revered Roman Imperial Majesty, fully delegated to us, we have established and do hereby make known, that where an archbishop, bishop, prelate, or other spiritual incumbent shall depart from our old religion, he shall immediately abandon, without any opposition or delay, his archbishopric, bishopric, prelacy, and other benefices, with the fruits and incomes that he may have had from it—nevertheless without prejudice to his honor.

7. But since certain estates or their predecessors have confiscated certain foundations, monasteries, and other spiritual possessions, and have applied the income of these to churches, schools, charitable institutions, and other purposes, such confiscated property, which does not belong to them, shall (if the holders are immediately subject to the empire and are estates of the empire, and if the clergy did not have possession of the said property at the time of the convention of Passau [1552] or since that time) be included in this agreement of peace, shall be considered as confiscated, and shall be regulated by the rules governing each estate in dealing with confiscated properties. . . .

10. No estate shall urge another estate, or the subject of the same, to embrace its religion.

11. But when our subjects and those of the electors, princes, and estates, adhering to the old religion or to the Ausburg Confession, wish, for the sake of their religion, to go with wife and children to another place in the lands, principalities, and cities of the electors, princes, and estates of the Holy Empire, and settle there, such going and coming and the sale of property and goods, in return for reasonable compensation for serfdom and arrears of taxes, . . . shall be everywhere unhindered, permitted, and granted. . . .

13. And in such peace the free knights who are immediately subject to his Imperial Majesty and us, shall also be included; and it is further provided that they shall not be interfered with, persecuted, or troubled by any one on account of either of the aforesaid religions.

14. But since in many free and imperial cities both religions—namely, our old religion and that of the Augsburg Confession—have hitherto come into existence and practice, the same shall remain hereafter and be held in the same cities; and citizens and inhabitants of the said free and imperial cities, whether spiritual or secular in rank shall peacefully and quietly dwell with one another; and no party shall venture to abolish the

religion, church customs, or ceremonies of the other, or persecute them therefor. . . .

19. And also herewith, and by the authority of this our imperial edict we command and order the judges of the imperial courts, and their colleagues, to hold and conduct themselves in conformity with this treaty of peace, as well as to give fitting and necessary relief of the law to the appealing suitors themselves, no matter to which of the aforesaid religions they belong, and against all such to recognize and decree no citation, mandate, or process. . . .

Given in the imperial city of Augsburg belonging to us (namely, Charles V), King Ferdinand, and to the Holy Empire, on the twenty-fifth day of the month of September, since the birth of Christ our dear Lord one thousand five hundred and fifty-five in the twenty-fifth year of our reign as emperor and in the twenty-ninth as ruler of our other realms.

FERDINAND

Decrees of the Council of Trent, 1545

That the Catholic Church succeeded in salvaging much of Europe from the debris of the Reformation and even in winning back some Protestant regions was tribute to the vigor of those inside the Church who would delay reform no longer. The reformers were divided between those who favored compromise with the Protestants and those who wanted a rigorous rededication to medieval Church doctrine. The second group triumphed. The Catholic or Counter Reformation was not an accommodation to the modern world but a reaffirmation of ecclesiastical orthodoxy.

The Catholic Reformation's chief inspiration came from Spain. In contrast to Germany, in Spain the Church was associated not with oppression but with nationalism and unity. The Spanish, under constant seige by the Moors from across the Mediterranean, looked to the Church for leadership in their wars of liberation. The Spanish sovereigns, though sufficiently nationalistic to insist on ecclesiastical submission, nonetheless regarded the Church less as a rival than as an ally. When a movement began to purify the Spanish Church, the kings lent their authority and their support. Spain thus proved to be an excellent base for the radiation of a Catholic reform movement around Europe.

The reformers, overwhelmingly, called for convocation of a council to set new rules for the Church's regeneration. The contending reformist factions, as well as some Protestants, each hoped to dominate the council and give Christianity a push in the direction it favored. Emperor Charles V, another factor in the mixture, looked to a council to restore his influence in the schismatic German provinces. But the Pope, recognizing that the worst abuses existed at his own doorstep and possessing the Papacy's traditional reluctance to abet both conciliar and imperial power, delayed any decision as long as possible. At last, aware that further procrastination might cost him the initiative, he called a Church council to meet in the northern Italian city of Trent on March 15, 1545.

The Council of Trent was spread over a period of eighteen years, with long lapses between meetings. The Jesuits, a new religious order from Spain, quickly established their dominance over the proceedings, frustrating both the liberals and the Protestants. Dedicated, capable and energetic, the Jesuits answered the demand for a rejuvenation of the Church by calling for a rejection of all modern ecclesiastical ideas. Under their influence, the Council surrendered nothing of ancient Catholic dogma. It made only a few small compromises on Church procedures. Its only significant reform legislation was aimed at restoring the Church's purity and religious zeal. The Council of Trent provided for the elimination of the shady practices that had so debased the reputation of the Catholic Church. It set standards for recruiting and training an able, educated, upright clergy. In winning repudiation of all the tenets of the Lutheran revolt, the Jesuits could triumphantly go forth throughout Europe to perform their mission of salvation. They became the principal instrument of the Catholic Reformation. But in following their leadership, the Council of Trent confirmed the break between Catholics and Protestants. From that day to this, every effort at Christian reconciliation—however thoughtful and sincere—has ended in failure.

The decrees of the Council of Trent constitute the most important monument to the Catholic Reformation. Of those presented here, the first condemns various Protestant doctrines, the second establishes ceremonial responsibilities for priests and the third sets standards for clerical conduct.

Document 32

If any one saith that the New Testament does not provide for a distinct, visible priesthood, or that this priesthood has not any power of consecrating and offering up the true body and blood of the Lord, and of forgiving and retaining sins, but is only an office and bare ministry of preaching the gospel; or that those who do not preach are not priests at all; let him be anathema. . . .

If any one saith that by sacred ordination the Holy Ghost is not given, and that vainly therefore do the bishops say, "Receive ye the Holy Ghost"; or that a character is not imprinted by that ordination; or that he who has once been a priest can again become a layman; let him be anathema. . . .

If any one saith that in the Catholic Church there is not a hierarchy instituted by divine ordination, consisting of bishops, priests, and ministers; let him be anathema.

If any one saith that the sacraments of the new law were not all instituted by Jesus Christ, our Lord; or that they are more or less than seven, to wit, baptism, confirmation, the eucharist, penance, extreme unction, orders, and matrimony; or even that any one of these seven is not truly and properly a sacrament; let him be anathema.

* * *

In order that the faithful may approach and receive the sacraments with greater reverence and devotion of mind, this holy Council enjoins on all bishops that, not only when they are themselves about to administer them to the people they shall first explain in a manner suited to the capacity of those who receive them, the efficacy and use of those sacraments, but they shall endeavor that the same be done piously and prudently by every parish priest; and this even in the vernacular tongue, if need be, and if it can be conveniently done.

Such instruction shall be given in accordance with the form which will be prescribed for each of the sacraments by this holy Council in a catechism, which the bishops shall take care to have faithfully translated into the vulgar tongue, and to have expounded to the people by all parish priests. They shall also explain in the said vulgar tongue, during the solemnization of mass, or the celebration of the divine offices, of all festivals or solemnities, the sacred oracles and the maxims of salvation; and, setting aside all unprofitable questions, they shall endeavor to impress them on the hearts of all, and to instruct their hearers in the law of the Lord.

* * *

It is to be desired that those who undertake the office of bishop should understand what their portion is, and comprehend that they are called, not to their own convenience, not to riches or luxury, but to labors and cares, for the glory of God. For it is not to be doubted that the rest of the faithful also will be more easily excited to religion and innocence if they shall see those who are set over them not fixing their thoughts on the things of this world, but on the salvation of souls and on their heavenly country. Wherefore this holy Council, being minded that these things are of the greatest importance towards restoring ecclesiastical discipline, admonishes all bishops that, often meditating thereon, they show themselves conformable to their office by their actual deeds and the actions of their lives; which is a kind of perpetual sermon; but, above all, that they so order their whole conversation that others may thence be able to derive examples of frugality, modesty, continency, and of that holy humility which so much commends us to God.

Wherefore, after the example of our fathers in the Council of Carthage [third century, A.D.], this Council not only orders that bishops be content with modest furniture, and a frugal table and diet, but that they also give heed that in the rest of their manner of living, and in their whole house, there be nothing seen which is alien to this holy institution, and which does not manifest simplicity, zeal toward God, and a contempt of vanities.

It strictly forbids them, moreover, to strive to enrich their own kindred or domestics out of the revenues of the Church, seeing that even the canons of the apostles forbid them to give to their kindred the property of the Church, which belongs to God; but if their kindred be poor, let them distribute to them thereof as poor, but not misapply or waste the Church's goods for their sakes: yea, this holy Council, with the utmost earnestness, admonishes them completely to lay aside all this human and carnal affection towards brothers, nephews, and kindred, which is the seed plot of many evils in the Church. And what has been said of bishops, the same is to be observed by all who hold ecclesiastical benefices, whether secular or regular, each according to the nature of his rank. . . .

Edict of Nantes, 1598

France was deeply rent by the Reformation. By the middle of the sixteenth century, an estimated 300,000 to 400,000 Frenchmen —known as Huguenots—had adopted Calvinism, a particularly rigorous form of Protestantism. Their influence—near the throne, in the nobility, in the bourgeoisie—was out of proportion to their numbers. It never occurred to either Catholics or Protestants in these first days of the modern era that each might live in the same land at peace with the other. Each believed they had to crush the others to survive. The Catholic opposition, led by the House of Guise from Lorraine, was not only fanatical and cunning but was supported by the Catholic monarch of Spain. Catholics and Protestants fought throughout most of the second half of the sixteenth century. The Wars of Religion, cruel and exhausting, left tens of thousands dead, great monuments in ruin, enormous riches destroyed, and France in a state of impotence.

France lacked a substantial leader throughout the period of the Religious Wars. Weak kings sat on the throne, making alliances with this faction and that in order to retain power. When Henri of Navarre, leader of the nation's Protestants, became through the normal processes of dynastic succession the heir-apparent, the Duke of Guise, the Catholic leader, decided to usurp the crown himself. King Henri II, the last of the Valois dynasty, heard of the plan and, in the accepted practice of the time, had Guise assassinated, only to be assassinated himself shortly afterward. Henri of Navarre thereupon succeeded him as Henri IV. He continued to wage war for five more years, then decided that for the good of France he would convert to Catholicism. "Paris was well worth a mass," was the irreverent remark he made famous. The Wars of Religion were over at last.

In 1598, Henri IV pacified the Protestant minority by issuing the Edict of Nantes, the first significant act of religious toleration in Western Europe. The Edict, the major provisions of which are presented below, did not put Protestantism on an equal footing with Catholicism but it gave to Protestants the right to religious worship in fixed places under set conditions and guaranteed a number of other important civic privileges. Certain secret articles, meant to give assurances of safety, empowered the Protestants to keep 150 fortified places in France, which created the dangerous condition of a state within a state. But since Henri IV's objective in issuing the Edict of Nantes was "the pacification of the troubles in his realm," he had good reason to provide the Protestants the safeguards they considered necessary. The Edict, whatever its troubled history, stands as one of the milestones on the road to religious liberty.

Document 33

Henry, by the grace of God king of France and of Navarre, to all to whom these presents come, greeting:

Among the infinite benefits which it has pleased God to heap upon us, the most signal and precious is his granting us the strength and ability to withstand the fearful disorders and troubles which prevailed on our advent in this kingdom. The realm was so torn by innumerable factions and sects that the most legitimate of all the parties was fewest in numbers. God has given us strength to stand out against this storm; we have finally surmounted the waves and made our port of safety,—peace for our state. For which his be the glory all in all, and ours a free recognition of his grace in making use of our instrumentality in the good work. . . . We implore and await from the Divine Goodness the same protection and favor which he has ever granted to this kingdom from the beginning. . . .

We have, by this perpetual and irrevocable edict, established and proclaimed and do establish and proclaim:

I. First, that the recollection of everything done by one party or the other between March, 1585, and our accession to the crown, and during all the preceding period of troubles, remain obliterated and forgotten, as if no such things had ever happened. . . .

III. We ordain that the Catholic Apostolic and Roman religion shall be restored and reëstablished in all places and localities of this our kingdom and countries subject to our sway, where the exercise of the same has been interrupted, in order that it may be peaceably and freely exercised, without any trouble or hindrance; forbidding very expressly all persons, of whatsoever estate, quality, or condition, from troubling, molesting, or disturbing ecclesiastics in the celebration of divine service, in the enjoyment or collection of tithes, fruits, or revenues of their benefices, and all other rights and dues belonging to them; and that all those who during the troubles have taken possession of churches, houses, goods or revenues, belonging to the said ecclesiastics, shall surrender to them entire possession and peaceable enjoyment of such rights, liberties, and sureties as they had before they were deprived of them. . . .

VI. And in order to leave no occasion for troubles or differences between our subjects, we have permitted, and herewith permit, those of the said religion called Reformed [Protestant] to live and abide in all the cities and places of this our kingdom and countries of our sway, without being annoyed, molested, or compelled to do anything in the matter of religion contrary to their consciences, . . . upon condition that they comport themselves in other respects according to that which is contained in this our present edict.

VII. It is permitted to all lords, gentlemen, and other persons making profession of the said religion called Reformed, holding the right of high justice (or a certain feudal tenure), to exercise the said religion in their houses. . . .

IX. We also permit those of the said religion to make and continue the exercise of the same in all villages and places of our dominion where it was established by them and publicly enjoyed several and divers times in the year 1597, up to the end of the month of August, notwithstanding all decrees and judgments to the contrary. . . .

XIII. We very expressly forbid to all those of the said religion its exercise, either in respect to ministry, regulation, discipline, or the public instruction of children, or otherwise, in this our kingdom and lands of our dominion, otherwise than in the places permitted and granted by the present edict.

XIV. It is forbidden as well to perform any function of the said religion in our court or retinue, or in our lands and territories beyond the mountains, or in our city of Paris, or within five leagues of the said city. . . .

XVIII. We also forbid all our subjects, of whatever quality and condition, from carrying off by force or persuasion, against the will of their parents, the children of the said religion, in order to cause them to be baptized or confirmed in the Catholic Apostolic and Roman Church; and the same is forbidden to those of the said religion called Reformed, upon penalty of being punished with special severity. . . .

XXI. Books concerning the said religion called Reformed may not be printed and publicly sold, except in cities and places where the public exercise of the said religion is permitted.

XXII. We ordain that there shall be no difference or distinction made in respect to the said religion, in receiving subjects to be instructed in universities, colleges, and schools; and in receiving the sick and poor into hospitals, retreats, and public charities.

V

The Struggle for Parliamentary Government in England

V

The Struggle for Parliamentary Government in England

Out of the middle ages there emerged in Germany feudal anarchy, in France absolute monarchy, and in England constitutional government. It is not easy to determine why Germany, France and England took different roads into the modern era. In France and Germany, the monarchy and the nobility struggled bitterly to destroy each other. In both cases, one triumphed by leaving the other in ruins. Why, then, were the king and the nobles in England satisfied to share political power with each other? Why did they settle for compromise rather than press forward toward total victory? The answer to these questions is elusive. What matters is that the compromise was achieved and in it is the seed of much that remains today an essential component of Western civilization. The development of the English constitution represents the flowering of the idea of political freedom and responsibility. Western man has been deeply influenced by the English success in achieving individual liberty within a framework of effective government.

Magna Carta, 1215

Had the English monarch at the turn of the thirteenth century not been the unattractive, incompetent and luckless King John, the English system of government might have developed quite differently. But in the early part of his reign King John (1199–1216) managed to lose much of his continental holdings to the French and in the latter part much of his esteem to the Pope. For a time he succeeded in maintaining his authority at home by resorting to great cruelty and hired mercenaries, but it was clear that his arbitrary rule could not survive a serious crisis. The crisis came in 1214 after John, having renewed his war against the French, suffered in concert with his German allies a decisive defeat at Bouvines. When he returned home, his purse empty and his legions destroyed, he came face to face with the irate barons, who had vowed to end the royal despotism.

In January, 1215, the barons presented the king with a series of demands for reform. John delayed his answer, thrashing about in a vain search for supporters to deliver him from his adversaries. He found none. Aware that he was lost, he met the barons in a field at Runnymede on June 15, 1215, and affixed his seal to their terms. The petition of the nobles was then redrafted and issued as the Great Charter. Because it was written in Latin it is usually called by its Latin name, *Magna Carta*. It is one of the central documents in the history of Western civilization.

Magna Carta is not a statement of abstract principles or general rules. It is a commitment to effect concrete remedies to correct specific abuses. It did not claim to break new constitutional ground. On the contrary, its objective was to require the king to observe what the nobles regarded as his feudal obligations, as well as the standing laws of the realm. It rested on the feudal principle that king and nobles had mutual contractual obligations. *Magna Carta* was essentially a feudal document. It limited the power of the crown in an age when the principle of royal absolutism was growing elsewhere. *Magna Carta* planted firmly in the English constitution the principle that the king, like other Englishmen, is subject to law.

Magna Carta is significant because it survived. In both France and Germany seeds of liberty sprouted from time to time and died. John himself, after Runnymede, tried faithlessly to trample *Magna Carta* but the nobles rebelled and civil war ensued, which ended with the king's death a year later. His successor to the throne, to heal the breach in the realm, voluntarily reissued the Charter. Throughout the remainder of the Middle Ages the Great Charter was reissued again and again. It outlived its feudal origins to become the symbol of political liberty, not only for the nobles but for the English people as a whole. *Magna Carta*, medieval England's blow against tyranny, became the foundation of modern constitutional government.

The Great Charter is a lengthy document, repetitious, dated and highly technical in many of its provisions. But it is still the heart of the English political system. The most significant chapters are given below.

Chapter one guarantees the independence of the English Church, whose leaders, it must be remembered, were part of the nobility.

Chapter two limited the amount of money the king could demand when a fief passed from father to son. This payment or "relief," according to the third chapter, was waived by the king if the son was a minor, since the throne took the profits for the fief anyway during the period of the son's minority.

Chapter twelve limited the king's right to levy "scutage," a tax paid by the nobles in lieu of military service. To wage his fruitless wars, John had been excessive in levying scutage. The powers here assigned to the "general council," a body of nobles called to advise the king, anticipate the principle won later by Parliament of no taxation without representation.

Chapter fourteen set the composition of the general council, along with the procedures for summoning it.

Chapter fifteen is significant in that the barons imposed upon themselves limitations in exacting feudal dues from their vassals.

Chapter thirty-six guarantees what today is called *habeas corpus* by requiring the king to issue writs without fees. John had treated the writs as a source of revenue by charging high fees.

Chapter thirty-nine, frequently cited as the cornerstone of the English common law, guarantees what is now called "due process of law," not merely to nobles but to all freemen. It does not guarantee a jury trial as such. It is, however, a safeguard against capricious royal action.

Chapter forty affirms the right of all men, without regard to rank or wealth, to resort to the judicial process.

Chapter forty-one is aimed at encouraging commerce.

Chapter forty-two asserts the freedom to travel.

Chapter fifty-one required John to banish his mercenaries or "stipendiaries" from England.

Chapter sixty repeats the responsibility of the barons to observe toward their "dependents" the same obligations that the king must observe toward them.

Chapter sixty-one provided a means of enforcing the Great Charter. It was not effective. Though the principles of *Magna Carta* were rarely seriously challenged, much of the history of England during the succeeding centuries focuses on the struggle to enforce those principles.

Document 34

John, by the grace of God, king of England, lord of Ireland, duke of Normandy, Aquitaine, and count of Anjou, to his archbishops, bishops, abbots, earls, barons, justiciaries, foresters, sheriffs, governors, officers, and to all bailiffs, and his faithful subjects, greeting. Know ye, that we, in the presence of God, and for the salvation of our soul, and the souls of all our ancestors and heirs, and unto the honor of God and the advancement of Holy Church, and amendment of our Realm, . . . have, in the first place, granted to God, and by this our present Charter confirmed, for us and our heirs forever:

1. That the English church shall be free, and shall have her rights

entire, and her liberties inviolate; and we will that it be thus observed; which is apparent from this that the freedom of elections, which is reckoned most important and very essential to the English church, we, of our pure and unconstrained will, did grant, and did by our Charter confirm and did obtain the ratification of the same from our lord, Pope Innocent III, before the quarrel arose between us and our barons: and this we will observe, and our will is that it be observed in good faith by our heirs forever.

2. We also have granted to all the freemen of our kingdom, for us and for our heirs forever, all the underwritten liberties, to be had and holden by them and their heirs, of us and our heirs forever. If any of our earls, or barons, or others who hold of us in chief by military service, shall die, and at the time of his death his heir shall be of full age, and owe a relief, he shall have his inheritance by the ancient relief—that is to say, the heir or heirs of an earl, for a whole earldom, by a hundred pounds; the heir or heirs of a knight, for a whole knight's fee, by a hundred shillings at most; and whoever oweth less shall give less, according to the ancient custom of fees.

3. But if the heir of any such shall be under age, and shall be in ward, when he comes of age he shall have his inheritance without relief and without fine.

12. No scutage or aid shall be imposed in our kingdom, unless by the general council of our kingdom; except for ransoming our person, making our eldest son a knight and once for marrying our eldest daughter; and for these there shall be paid no more than a reasonable aid. In like manner it shall be concerning the aids of the City of London.

14. And for holding the general council of the kingdom concerning the assessment of aids, except in the three cases aforesaid, and for the assessing of scutage, we shall cause to be summoned the archbishops, bishops, abbots, earls, and greater barons of the realm, singly by our letters. And furthermore, we shall cause to be summoned generally, by our sheriffs and bailiffs, all others who hold of us in chief, for a certain day, that is to say, forty days before their meeting at least, and to a certain place. And in all letters of such summons we will declare the cause of such summons. And summons being thus made, the business shall proceed on the day appointed, according to the advice of such as shall be present, although all that were summoned come not.

15. We will not in the future grant to any one that he may take aid of his own free tenants, except to ransom his body, and to make his eldest

son a knight, and once to marry his eldest daughter; and for this there shall be paid only a reasonable aid. . . .

36. Nothing from henceforth shall be given or taken for a writ of inquisition of life or limb, but it shall be granted freely, and not denied. . . .

39. No freeman shall be taken or imprisoned, or disseised, or outlawed, or banished, or in any way destroyed, nor will we pass upon him, nor will we send upon him, unless by the lawful judgment of his peers, or by the law of the land.

40. We will sell to no man, we will not deny to any man, either justice or right.

41. All merchants shall have safe and secure conduct to go out of, and to come into, England, and to stay there and to pass as well by land as by water, for buying and selling by the ancient and allowed customs, without any unjust tolls, except in time of war, or when they are of any nation at war with us. And if there be found any such in our land, in the beginning of the war, they shall be detained, without damage to their bodies or goods, until it be known to us, or to our chief justiciary, how our merchants be treated in the nation at war with us; and if ours be safe there, the others shall be safe in our dominions.

42. It shall be lawful, for the time to come, for any one to go out of our kingdom and return safely and securely by land or by water, saving his allegiance to us (unless in time of war, by some short space, for the common benefit of the realm), except prisoners and outlaws, according to the law of the land, and people in war with us, and merchants who shall be treated as is above mentioned. . . .

51. As soon as peace is restored, we will send out of the kingdom all foreign knights, cross-bowmen, and stipendiaries, who are come with horses and arms to the molestation of our people. . . .

60. All the aforesaid customs and liberties, which we have granted to be holden in our kingdom, as much as it belongs to us, all people of our kingdom, as well clergy as laity, shall observe, as far as they are concerned, towards their dependents.

61. And whereas, for the honor of God and the amendment of our kingdom, and for the better quieting the discord that has arisen between us and our barons, we have granted all these things aforesaid. Willing to render them firm and lasting, we do give and grant our subjects the underwritten security, namely, that the barons may choose five and twenty barons of the kingdom, whom they think convenient, who shall

take care, with all their might, to hold and observe, and cause to be observed, the peace and liberties we have granted them, and by this our present Charter confirmed. . . .

63. . . . It is also sworn, as well on our part as on the part of the barons, that all the things aforesaid shall be observed in good faith, and without evil duplicity. Given under our hand, in the presence of the witnesses above named, and many others, in the meadow called Runnymede, between Windsor and Staines, the 15th day of June, in the 17th year of our reign.

James I's Claim of Divine Right, 1609

Parliamentary government had a more promising beginning on the continent than in England. As the medieval world drew to a close, the idea spread throughout Europe that the king should obtain the consent of the country for unusual expenditures or extremely hazardous enterprises. The clergy, the nobility and the rising urban middle-class began to feel they ought to be consulted on major decisions of policy. Beginning in the twelfth century, kings began to summon representative assemblies of these groups. The *Cortes* were established in the kingdoms of Spain, the *États-généraux* in Paris and the provinces, the *Landtage* and the *diet* in the Germanies, the *diet* in Poland and Bohemia. Yet these institutions withered away on the continent, where they began. It was only in England that the Parliament became a permanent instrument of state, limiting the prerogatives of the monarchy. Ultimately, it was the English Parliament that became the guide and standard for political organization, not only in the West but in other civilizations as well.

The powers of the English Parliament were forged out of conflict with the monarchy. As the king's council, Parliament began primarily as a judicial body. Its supervision of the finances of the realm began when kings went to war and needed money. To the French, wars were invariably wars of liberation, which strengthened the hand of the monarchy. To the English, they were luxuries, for which the king had to pay by the redress of grievances. During the Hundred Years War (1337–1453), the English Parliament won, step by step, increasing powers over the budget, the authority to impeach offending royal officials and general legislative prerogatives. Finally, in 1399 Parliament maneuvered to depose a king, the tyrannical Richard III, whom it replaced with King Henry IV of the House of Lancaster. Thus by the year 1400 Parliament had exercised the power to choose the king and England could be accurately described as a parliamentary monarchy.

Parliament's abrupt change of dynasty, however, was probably a premature exercise of powers. It was widely challenged and led directly to civil war, the celebrated War of the Roses, which ended with the accession of Henry VII (1485–1509), the first Tudor king. The Tudors had a taste for absolutism but they were wise enough to satisfy it obliquely. They did not challenge *Magna Carta* and its principles. Instead they exercised their tyranny by ignoring or packing Parliaments or by intimidating them into compliance. The Tudors treated Parliament as a royal agency and the country, fearful of invasion by a strong and hostile Spain, raised few objections. By the end of the sixteenth century the Tudors had succeeded in repairing the internal damage suffered during the civil war and, by defeating the Spanish Armada, in eliminating the threat from abroad. The restoration of peaceful conditions was less propitious than disorder to the growth of absolutism. When, on the death of Queen Elizabeth in 1603, the crown passed from the Tudor to the Stuart family, Parliament was once again ready to assert its claims to govern.

King James I, who reigned in Scotland before assuming the English throne, shared the Tudor taste for absolutism but not its discretion in exercising it. James I was devoted to the theory of divine right monarchy, which royalists on the continent were promoting. Persuaded that he was accountable in his actions to God alone, he was indifferent both to public opinion and to Parliament. James I flaunted the theory of divine right before Parliament, which had never accepted it coming from the Tudors during times of danger and had no reason whatever to agree to it now, James I's attitude predestined him to a bitter constitutional struggle.

James I's speech before Parliament in 1609, excerpts of which are presented below, was an open declaration of his divine right convictions. It was a clear challenge to the principles of the *Magna Carta*. Refusing to consider a redress of grievances in return for an appropriation, James I rejected the traditional bargain between Parliament and throne. He affirmed unhesitatingly that he regarded the king as above the law. James I's concept of the monarchy hastened England toward civil war.

DOCUMENT 35

The state of monarchy is the supremest thing upon earth; for kings are not only God's lieutenants upon earth, and sit upon God's throne, but even by God himself they are called gods. There be three principal similitudes that illustrate the state of monarchy: one taken out of the word of God; and the two other out of the grounds of policy and philosophy. In the Scriptures kings are called gods, and so their power after a certain relation compared to the divine power. Kings are also compared to fathers of families; for a king is truly *parens patriae*, the politic father of his people. And lastly, kings are compared to the head of this microcosm of the body of man.

Kings are justly called gods, for that they exercise a manner or resemblance of divine power upon earth; for if you consider the attributes to God, you shall see how they agree in the person of a king. God hath power to create or destroy, make or unmake at his pleasure, to give life or send death, to judge all and to be judged nor accountable to none, to raise low things and to make high things low at his pleasure, and to God are both soul and body due. And the like power have kings: they make and unmake their subjects, they have power of raising and casting down, of life and of death, judges over all their subjects and in all causes and yet accountable to none but God only. They have power to exalt low things and abase high things, and make of their subjects, like men at the chess,—a pawn to take a bishop or a knight,—and to cry up or down any of their subjects, as they do their money. And to the king is due both the affection of the soul and the service of the body of his subjects. . . .

I would wish you to be careful to avoid three things in the matter of grievances:

First, that you do not meddle with the main points of government; that is my craft: *tractent fabrilia fabri*,—to meddle with that were to lessen me. I am now an old king; for six and thirty years have I governed in Scotland personally, and now have I accomplished my apprenticeship of seven years here; and seven years is a great time for a king's experience in government; therefore there should not be too many Phormios to teach Hannibal: I must not be taught my office.

Secondly, I would not have you meddle with such ancient rights of mine as I have received from my predecessors, possessing them, *more majorum;* such things I would be sorry should be accounted for grievances. All novelties are dangerous as well in a politic as in a natural body, and therefore I would be loath to be quarreled in my ancient rights and possessions; for that were to judge me unworthy of that which my predecessors had and left me.

And, lastly, I pray you beware to exhibit for grievance anything that is established by settled law, and whereunto (as you have already had a proof) you know I will never give a plausible answer; for it is an undutiful part in subjects to press their King, wherein they know beforehand he will refuse them.

Petition of Right, 1628

King Charles I (1625–49), son of James I, was no less devoted than his father to the principle of divine right monarchy. Popular on his accession to the throne, he quickly ran afoul of Parliament and the people through the financial demands of war. King Charles took the position that it was the duty of Parliament to grant him money, but he rejected the notion that Parliament had commensurate rights. On the mistaken assumption that the people would support him, he prorogued hostile Parliaments in 1625 and 1626. But the people did not come forth with the voluntary gifts he had expected and the judges, to his dismay, declared his forced loans illegal. Riding roughshod over rights in force since *Magna Carta*, Charles—because he had no money for billets—committed the ultimate outrage of quartering troops by force in the homes of free Englishmen. When Charles convoked his third Parliament in 1628 to end his impoverishment, he found that opinion overwhelmingly opposed him. The Parliament disregarded its peripheral grievances against the king and focused directly on the violation of established English rights.

Parliament drew up the famous Petition of Right, which called upon the king to honor four specific constitutional principles: no taxation without parliamentary consent, no imprisonment without cause, no forced billeting of soldiers and no martial law in time of peace. By accepting the terms of the Petition, Charles I admitted by implication that he had acted unconstitutionally. The Petition of Right of 1628, extracts of which appear below, is second in importance only to *Magna Carta* in English constitutional history. It reaffirmed Parliament's powers after a century and a half of attack from Tudor and Stuart absolutists. It was Parliament's rejection of the theory of divine right at a time when kings and princes were growing stronger throughout the continent of Europe.

Document 36

To the King's Most Excellent Majesty:

We humbly show unto our sovereign lord the king, the lords spiritual and temporal, and commons in Parliament assembled, that whereas it is declared and enacted by a statute made in the time of the reign of King Edward I, commonly called "*Statuium de Tallagio non Concedendo*," that no tallage or aid shall be laid or levied by the king or his heirs in this realm without the good will and assent of the archbishops, bishops, earls, barons, knights, burgesses, and other the freemen of the commonality of this realm: and by authority of Parliament holden in the five and twentieth year of the reign of King Edward III, it is declared and enacted, that from thenceforth no person should be compelled to make any loans to the king against his will, because such loans were against reason and the franchise of the land; and by other laws of this realm it is provided, that none should be charged by any charge or imposition called a benevolence, nor by any such like charge; by which statutes before mentioned, and other good laws and statutes of this realm, your subjects have inherited this freedom, that they should not be compelled to contribute to any tax, tallage, aid, or other like charge not set by common consent in Parliament.

II. Yet nevertheless of late divers commissions, directed to sundry commissioners in several counties with instructions, have issued; by means whereof your people have been in divers places assembled and required to lend certain sums of money unto your Majesty, and many of them upon their refusal so to do . . . have been constrained to make appearance before your privy council and in other places, and others of them have been therefore imprisoned, confined, and sundry other ways molested and disquieted. . . .

III. And whereas also, by the statute called "The Great Charter of the liberties of England," it is declared and enacted that no freeman may be taken or imprisoned or be dispossessed of his freehold or liberties, or his free customs, or be outlawed or exiled, or in any manner destroyed but by the lawful judgment of his peers, or by the law of the land. . . .

V. Nevertheless, against the tenor of the said statutes, and other the good laws and statutes of your realm, to that end provided, divers of your subjects have of late been imprisoned without any cause showed; . . . and whereas of late great companies of soldiers and mariners have been dispersed into divers counties of this realm, and the inhabitants, against their will, have been compelled to receive them into their houses, and there to suffer them to sojourn against the laws and customs of this realm, and to the great grievance and vexation of the people. . . .

X. They (Parliament) do therefore humbly pray your most excellent Majesty that no man hereafter be compelled to make or yield any loan, gift, benevolence, tax, or such like charge, without common consent by act of Parliament; and that none be called to make answer, or take such oath, or to give attendance, or be confined, or otherwise molested or disquieted concerning the same, or for refusal thereof; and that no freeman, in any such manner as is before mentioned, be imprisoned or detained; and that your Majesty would be pleased to remove the said soldiers and mariners, and that your people may not be so burdened in time to come; and that the aforesaid commissions for proceeding by martial law may be revoked and annulled; and that hereafter no commissions of like nature may issue forth to any person or persons whatsoever, to be executed as aforesaid lest by color of them any of your Majesty's subjects be destroyed or put to death, contrary to the laws and franchise of the land. . . .

Death Warrant of Charles I, 1649

The Petition of Right proved to be barely more than a truce in the contest between Charles I and Parliament. Both sides were too dedicated to their beliefs for any permanent peace. Parliament insisted that the king dismiss the unpopular Buckingham, his favorite advisor; that he end illegal customs duties, on which the solvency of his government depended; that he pursue a more rigorously anti-Catholic policy, when he sympathized with the Catholic Church. Charles, in reply, dismissed Parliament once again and for eleven years, from 1629 to 1640, ruled without it. To raise funds, he revived old taxing systems and devised new ones. He further embarked on what appeared almost a conscious policy to provoke England's Puritans, the radical Protestants who had grown extraordinarily powerful. Inevitably a crisis had to arise in which king and Parliament would once again confront each other.

In 1639 the Scots rose up, provoking the crisis that was to lead to civil war. To suppress them, Charles once more summoned a Parliament but, after three weeks of wrangling, he dissolved it. This Parliament went down in history as the Short Parliament. Its successor, called to meet the threat of a Scottish invasion, sat officially from 1640 to 1660 and was known as the Long Parliament. In control from the outset were Charles's bitterest enemies. They first purged the royal advisors, causing several heads to fall. They then passed a series of statutes to prevent the king from ruling despotically. Having no alternative, Charles ratified the statutes. But as the reform movement rumbled on, it was clear that a substantial segment of the Parliament had had enough of disciplining the king. Before a year was out, the Long Parliament's anti-monarchical unity had disintegrated.

The showdown came in December, 1641, when the radicals proposed enactment of the Grand Remonstrance, a severe censure of the king. Though it passed by a small margin, the vote demonstrated that Charles I had found an important source of support. Nobles, high-church Anglicans, Catholics, many country squires and a variety of traditionalists proved loyal to the crown. Leading the array against them were the Puritans, who favored a minimum of royal power. Their close-cropped hair won them the nickname "Roundheads," in contrast to their opponents, the "Cavaliers." Both sides proceeded to assemble armies. Within a few months, civil war had begun.

After several years of desultory fighting, the Parliamentary army in 1645 crushed the major royalist force at the Battle of Naseby. While the victors argued over the peace terms, King Charles sought to profit from their dissension but succeeded only in making himself more distrusted. Emerging dominant from the disputes was the army and its Puritan leader, Oliver Cromwell, who represented the most radical parliamentary faction. After attempting unsuccessfully to impose severe terms on the king, Cromwell purged the remaining moderates in Parliament and began to govern with a "rump" Parliament of some fifty members. It was the Rump that voted to bring the king to justice on a charge of treason, justifying the action with the revolutionary constitutional doctrine that Commons alone, as representative of the people, was empowered to make law. Charles was tried before a special court and sentenced to death. On January 30, 1649, he was beheaded at Whitehall.

The execution of the king shocked the public and foredoomed the republican experiment. Ironically, Charles, by his dignity before the court as well as by his martyrdom, did more in death than in life to assure the perpetuation of the monarchy. Presented below is the death warrant of Charles I. Among the signators is Oliver Cromwell, the great rebel leader and head of England's only republican regime.

Document 37

Whereas Charles Stuart, king of England, is, and standeth convicted, attainted, and condemned of high treason, and other high crimes; and sentence upon Saturday last was pronounced against him by this Court, to be put to death by the severing of his head from his body; of which sentence, execution yet remaineth to be done; these [presents] are therefore to will and require you to see the said sentence executed in the open street before Whitehall, upon the morrow, being the thirtieth day of this instant month of January, between the hours of ten in the morning and five in the afternoon of the same day, with full effect. And for so doing this shall be your sufficient warrant. And these are to require all officers, soldiers, and others, the good people of this nation of England, to be assisting unto you in this service.

To Colonel Francis Hacker, Colonel Huncks, and Lieutenant Colonel Phayre, and to every of them.

Given under our hands and seals.

JOHN BRADSHAW.
THOMAS GREY.
OLIVER CROMWELL.
Etc., etc.

Declaration of Rights, 1689

Cromwell's republican experiment did not survive his death in 1658. Amid a royalist and religious reaction, political confusion grew. It soon became evident that only a restoration of the Stuart monarchy could reunite the country. In April, 1660, Charles II, son of the late king, issued a statement promising to observe English liberties if restored to the throne. A new Parliament was quickly elected and Charles invited to return. With all signs favorable to a successful reign, Charles II mounted the throne of England.

The reign, in fact, was a grievous disappointment. Charles, along with his younger brother and heir, Prince James, had been reared in the court of Louis XIV in France, where he had developed an appetite not only for absolutism but also for Catholicism. Before long, Parliament and he were again engaged in battle over the old financial and religious questions. When Prince James converted to Catholicism, much of Britain feared the monarchy had sold out to the Pope and the Catholic kings on the continent. That Charles II was able to retain the throne for twenty-five years and die a natural death was more the consequence of his lethargy and good nature than any strength of character that might have provoked open opposition.

Parliament was apprehensive when James II became king but preferred to accept him rather than to risk another civil war. James, however, was far more offensive than his older brother. Not only did he challenge Parliament but he frightened the nation as a whole by his indulgence of Catholicism. Parliament stood by patiently as long as James II's heir-apparent was a Protestant. In 1688, however, James's second wife, a Catholic, gave birth to a son and a Catholic succession seemed a likely prospect. Even the Tories, the monarchical party, were now ready to challenge the Stuart dynasty. Parliament was united.

On July 7, 1688, seven Parliamentary leaders addressed a petition to William of Orange, ruler of the Netherlands, and his wife Mary, James's

Protestant daughter by his first wife and nearest Protestant in the line of succession. They were invited to lead a popular uprising in England in behalf of the traditional liberties. James, abandoned by much of his army, gave up the chance to fight and fled to France. William and Mary arrived in England in December. While the Lords conducted a provisional government, the Commons declared: "That King James II, having endeavored to subvert the constitution of the kingdom by breaking the original contract between king and people, and by the advice of Jesuits and other wicked persons having violated the fundamental laws, and having withdrawn himself out of the kingdom, has abdicated the government, and that the throne is vacant." After much debate over constitutionality, the majority in Parliament, composed of both Tories and Whigs, agreed to offer the crown officially to William and Mary. Their acceptance settled the question of monarchical succession.

The events of 1688 are known as the Glorious Revolution. It demonstrated, once and for all, the superiority of Parliament to king. Parliament had given William and Mary the crown and what it had given it could take away. Henceforth no king could hope to retain his throne against the determined opposition of his subjects. The theory of divine right in England was dead.

Parliament conditioned the offer of the crown on William and Mary's acceptance of the Declaration of Rights, which for the first time codified English liberties and which was passed in February, 1689. The Declaration of Rights, like most English constitutional documents, was not intended to make new law but to reaffirm old law. The sovereign is even referred to as the King of France, though England had long before lost its French provinces. The Declaration was subsequently reenacted and became the Bill of Rights, a fundamental part of the English constitution. Many of its provisions were adopted verbatim into the American constitution, written a century later. The Declaration of Rights is presented here in its entirety.

Document 38

AN ACT FOR DECLARING THE RIGHTS AND LIBERTIES OF THE SUBJECT, AND SETTLING THE SUCCESSION OF THE CROWN

WHEREAS the lords spiritual and temporal, and commons, assembled at Westminster, lawfully, fully, and freely representing all the estates of the people of this realm, did upon the thirteenth day of February in the year of our Lord one thousand six hundred eighty eight, present unto their Majesties, then called and known by the names and stile of William and Mary, prince and princess of Orange, being present in their proper persons, a certain declaration in writing, made by the said lords and commons, in the words following; viz.*

* 1689 under the current calendar.

WHEREAS the late King James the Second, by the assistance of divers evil counsellors, judges, and ministers employed by him, did endeavour to subvert and extirpate the protestant religion, and the laws and liberties of this kingdom.

1. By assuming and exercising a power of dispensing with and suspending of laws, and the execution of laws, without consent of parliament.

2. By committing and prosecuting divers worthy prelates, for humbly petitioning to be excused from concurring to the said assumed power.

3. By issuing and causing to be executed a commission under the great seal for erecting a court called, The court of commissioners for ecclesiastical causes.

4. By levying money for and to the use of the crown, by pretence of prerogative, for another time, and in other manner, than the same was granted by parliament.

5. By raising and keeping a standing army within this kingdom in time of peace, without consent of parliament, and quartering soldiers contrary to law.

6. By causing several good subjects, being protestants, to be disarmed, at the same time when papists were both armed and employed, contrary to law.

7. By violating the freedom of election of members to serve in parliament.

8. By prosecutions in the court of King's bench, for matters and causes cognizable only in parliament, and by divers other arbitrary and illegal courses.

9. And whereas of late years, partial, corrupt, and unqualified persons have been returned and served on juries in trials, and particularly divers jurors in trials for high treason, which were not freeholders.

10. And excessive bail hath been required of persons committed in criminal cases, to elude the benefit of the laws made for the liberty of the subjects.

11. And excessive fines have been imposed; and illegal and cruel punishments inflicted.

12. And several grants and promises made of fines and forfeitures, before any conviction or judgment against the persons, upon whom the same were to be levied.

All which are utterly and directly contrary to the known laws and statutes, and freedom of this realm.

And whereas the said late King James the Second having abdicated the government, and the throne being thereby vacant, his highness the prince of Orange (whom it hath pleased Almighty God to make the glorious instrument of delivering this kingdom from popery and arbitrary power) did (by the advice of the lords spiritual and temporal, and divers principal persons of the commons) cause letters to be written to the lords spiritual and temporal, being protestants; and other letters to the several counties, cities, universities, boroughs, and cinque-ports, for the choosing of such persons to represent them, as were of right to be sent to parliament, to meet and sit at Westminster upon the two and twentieth day of January, in this year one thousand six hundred eighty and eight, in order to such an establishment, as that their religion, laws, and liberties might not again be in danger of being subverted: upon which letters, elections have been accordingly made,

And thereupon the said lords spiritual and temporal, and commons, pursuant to their respective letters and elections, being now assembled in a full and free representative of this nation, taking into their most serious consideration the best means for attaining the ends aforesaid; do in the first place (as their ancestors in like case have usually done) for the vindicating and asserting their ancient rights and liberties, declare:

1. That the pretended power of suspending of laws, or the execution of laws, by regal authority, without consent of parliament, is illegal.

2. That the pretended power of dispensing with laws, or the execution of laws, by regal authority, as it hath been assumed and exercised of late, is illegal.

3. That the commission for erecting the late court of commissioners for ecclesiastical causes, and all other commissions and courts of like nature are illegal and pernicious.

4. That levying money for or to the use of the crown, by pretence of prerogative, without grant of parliament, for longer time, or in other manner than the same is or shall be granted, is illegal.

5. That it is the right of the subjects to petition the King, and all committments and prosecutions for such petitioning are illegal.

6. That the raising or keeping a standing army within the kingdom in time of peace, unless it be with consent of parliament, is against law.

7. That the subjects which are protestants, may have arms for their defence suitable to their conditions, and as allowed by law.

8. That election of members of parliament ought to be free.

9. That the freedom of speech, and debates or proceedings in parlia-

ment, ought not to be impeached or questioned in any court or place out of parliament.

10. That excessive bail ought not to be required, nor excessive fines imposed; nor cruel and unusual punishments inflicted.

11. That jurors ought to be duly impanelled and returned, and jurors which pass upon men in trials for high treason ought to be freeholders.

12. That all grants and promises of fines and forfeitures of particular persons before conviction, are illegal and void.

13. And that for redress of all grievances, and for the amending, strengthening, and preserving of the laws, parliaments ought to be held frequently.

And they do claim, demand, and insist upon all and singular the premisses, as their undoubted rights and liberties; and that no declarations, judgments, doings or proceedings, to the prejudice of the people in any of the said premisses, ought in any wise to be drawn hereafter into consequence or example.

To which demand of their rights they are particularly encouraged by the declaration of his highness the prince of Orange, as being the only means for obtaining a full redress and remedy therein.

Having therefore an entire confidence, That his said highness the prince of Orange will perfect the deliverance so far advanced by him, and will still preserve them from the violation of their rights, which they have here asserted, and from all other attempts upon their religion, rights, and liberties.

II. The said lords spiritual and temporal, and commons, assembled at Westminster, do resolve, That William and Mary prince and princess of Orange be, and be declared, King and Queen of England, France and Ireland, and the dominions thereunto belonging, to hold the crown and royal dignity of the said kingdoms and dominions to them the said prince and princess during their lives, and the life of the survivor of them; and that the sole and full exercise of the regal power be only in, and executed by the said prince of Orange, in the names of the said prince and princess, during their joint lives; and after their deceases, the said crown and royal dignity of the said kingdoms and dominions to be to the heirs of the body of the said princess; and for default of such issue to the princess Anne of Denmark, and the heirs of her body; and for default of such issue to the heirs of the body of the said prince of Orange. And the lords spiritual and temporal, and commons, do pray the said prince and princess to accept the same accordingly.

III. And that the oaths hereafter mentioned be taken by all persons of whom the oaths of allegiance and supremacy might be required by law, instead of them; and that the said oaths of allegiance and supremacy be abrogated.

"I A. B. do sincerely promise and swear, That I will be faithful and bear true allegiance, to their Majesties King William and Queen Mary:

So help me God."

"I A. B. do swear, That I do from my heart abhor, detest, and abjure as impious and heretical, that damnable doctrine and position, That princes excommunicated or deprived by the pope, or any authority of the see of Rome, may be deposed or murdered by their subjects, or any other whatsoever. And I do declare, That no foreign prince, person, prelate, state or potentate hath, or ought to have any jurisdiction, power, superiority, pre-eminence, or authority ecclesiastical or spiritual, within this realm:

So help me God."

IV. *Upon which their said Majesties did accept the crown and royal dignity of the kingdoms of England, France, and Ireland, and the dominions thereunto belonging, according to the resolution and desire of the said Lords and commons contained in the said declaration.*

V. *And thereupon their Majesties were pleased, That the said lords spiritual and temporal and commons, being the two houses of parliament, should continue to sit, and with their Majesties' royal concurrence make effectual provision for the settlement of the religion, laws and liberties of this kingdom, so that the same for the future might not be in danger again of being subverted; to which the said lords spiritual and temporal, and commons, did agree and proceed to act accordingly.*

VI. Now in pursuance of the premisses, the said lords spiritual and temporal, and commons, in parliament assembled, for the ratifying, confirming and establishing the said declaration, and the articles, clauses, matters, and things therein contained, by the force of a law made in due form by authority of parliament, do pray that it may be declared and enacted, That all and singular the rights and liberties asserted and claimed in the said declaration, are the true, ancient, and indubitable rights and liberties of the people of this kingdom, and so shall be esteemed, allowed, adjudged, deemed, and taken to be, and that all and every the particulars aforesaid shall be firmly and strictly holden and observed, as they are expressed in the said declaration; and all officers and ministers whatsoever shall serve their Majesties and their successors according to the same in all times to come.

VII. And the said lords spiritual and temporal, and commons, seriously considering how it hath pleased Almighty God in his marvellous providence, and merciful goodness to this nation, to provide and preserve their said Majesties' royal persons most happily to reign over us upon the throne of their ancestors, for which they render unto him from the bottom of their hearts their humblest thanks and praises, do truly, firmly, assuredly, and in the sincerity of their hearts think, and do hereby recognize, acknowledge and declare, That King James the Second having abdicated the government, and their Majesties having accepted the crown and royal dignity as aforesaid, their said Majesties did become, were, are, and of right ought to be, by the laws of this realm, our sovereign liege lord and lady, King and Queen of England, France, and Ireland, and the dominions thereunto belonging, in and to whose princely persons the royal state, crown, and dignity of the said realms, with all honours, stiles, titles, regalities, prerogatives, powers, jurisdictions and authorities to the same belonging and appertaining, are most fully, rightfully, and intirely invested and incorporated, united and annexed.

VIII. And for preventing all questions and divisions in this realm, by reason of any pretended titles to the crown, and for preserving a certainty in the succession thereof, in and upon which the unity, peace, tranquillity, and safety of this nation doth, under God, wholly consist and depend, The said lords spiritual and temporal, and commons, do beseech their Majesties that it may be enacted, established and declared, That the crown and regal government of the said kingdoms and dominions, with all and singular the premisses thereunto belonging and appertaining, shall be and continue to their said Majesties, and the survivor of them, during their lives, and the life of the survivor of them: And that the entire, perfect, and full exercise of the regal power and government be only in, and executed by his Majesty, in the names of both their Majesties during their joint lives; and after their deceases the said crown and premisses shall be and remain to the heirs of the body of her Majesty; and for default of such issue, to her royal highness the princess Anne of Denmark, and the heirs of her body; and for default of such issue, to the heirs of the body of his said Majesty: And thereunto the said lords spiritual and temporal, and commons, do, in the name of all the people aforesaid, most humbly and faithfully submit themselves, their heirs and posterities for ever; and do faithfully promise, That they will stand to, maintain, and defend their said Majesties, and also the limitation and succession of the crown herein specified and contained to the utmost of their powers, with their lives and estates, against all persons whatsoever, that shall attempt any thing to the contrary.

IX. And whereas it hath been found by experience, that it is inconsistent with the safety and welfare of this protestant kingdom, to be governed by a papist prince, or by any King or Queen marrying a papist; the said lords spiritual and temporal, and commons, do further pray that it may be enacted, That all and every person and persons that is, are or shall be reconciled to, or shall profess the popish religion, or shall marry a papist, shall be excluded, and be for ever incapable to inherit, possess, or enjoy the crown and government of this realm, and Ireland, and the dominions thereunto belonging, or any part of the same, or to have, use, or exercise any regal power, authority, or jurisdiction within the same; and in all and every such case or cases the people of these realms shall be, and are hereby absolved of their allegiance; and the said crown and government shall from time to time descend to, and be enjoyed by such person or persons, being protestants, as should have inherited and enjoyed the same, in case the said person or persons so reconciled, holding communion, or professsing, or marrying as aforesaid, were naturally dead.

X. And that every King and Queen of this realm, who at any time hereafter shall come to and succeed in the imperial crown of this kingdom, shall on the first day of the meeting of the first parliament, next after his or her coming to the crown, sitting in his or her throne in the house of peers, in the presence of the lords and commons therein assembled, or at his or her coronation, before such person or persons who shall administer the coronation oath to him or her, at the time of his or her taking the said oath (which shall first happen) make, subscribe, and audibly repeat the declaration mentioned in the statute made in the thirtieth year of the reign of King Charles the Second, intituled, An act for the more effectual preserving the King's person and government, by disabling papists from sitting in either house of parliament. But if it shall happen, that such King or Queen, upon his or her succession to the crown of this realm, shall be under the age of twelve years, then every such King or Queen shall make, subscribe, and audibly repeat the said declaration at his or her coronation, on the first day of the meeting of the first parliament as aforesaid, which shall first happen after such King or Queen shall have attained the said age of twelve years.

XI. All which their Majesties are contented and pleased shall be declared, enacted, and established by authority of this present parliament, and shall stand, remain, and be the law of this realm for ever; and the same are by their said Majesties, by and with the advice and consent of the lords spiritual and temporal, and commons, in parliament assembled, and by the authority of the same, declared, enacted, and established accordingly.

XII. And be it further declared and enacted by the authority aforesaid, That from and after this present session of parliament, no dispensation by non obstante of or to any statute, or any part thereof, shall be allowed, but that the same shall be held void and of no effect. . . .

VI

The Monarchical State during France's *grand siècle*

VI

The Monarchical State during France's *grand siècle*

During the reign of Henri IV (1589–1610), France recovered from the depradations of the Wars of Religion. With patience and good sense, Henri brought about the pacification of the country. Though Catholics and Protestants remained bitter rivals, he reconciled each to the existence of the other. Relying heavily on the efficient Duke of Sully as his principal advisor, he restored the economy of the nation and the finances of the state. Henri IV gave the French the respite they needed to regain their strength and their confidence. When a mad assassin ended his rule in 1610, the foundation had been laid for a resurgence of French power and French absolutism.

Richelieu's Political Testament, 1624

King Louis XIII was only nine years old when he succeeded Henri IV to the throne. Under the regency of his mother, Marie de Medici, affairs in France degenerated once again. Marie reversed Henri IV's policy of opposition to the Hapsburg kings of Spain and Austria, which upset the Protestants who feared a Catholic alliance and failed to satisfy the Catholics who recognized the Hapsburgs as the chief threat to France. The instability of Marie's rule encouraged both Huguenots and nobles to provoke disorder, while the provincial governors, appointed to assert the royal presence in the countryside, in many cases became defiant of Paris. The *parlements*, the higher courts of law, showed an independence that was reminiscent of the English, without showing the equally English sense of responsibility. Even after Louis XIII himself assumed authority, France continued to disintegrate. It was not until the remarkable Cardinal Richelieu became the king's first minister in 1624 that order and stability were restored.

Richelieu, a frail and sickly prelate, was one of the great statesmen of modern times. He was completely devoted to enhancing the majesty of the king and the grandeur of the realm. Richelieu was no tyrant and preferred to pursue his goals by moderate means, but he could be ruthless with those who were obstacles to his ambition. Few first ministers exercised more power, but none ever served his sovereign more single-mindedly or more faithfully than did he.

In addition to being a brilliant statesman, Richelieu was a magnificent writer and political commentator. He helped make his own place in history by his ability to turn his fine perceptions into eloquent literature. A section of Richelieu's *Political Testament* here describes the conditions he found in France when he became minister in 1624.

Document 39

At the time when your Majesty resolved to admit me both to your council and to an important place in your confidence for the direction of your affairs, I may say that the Huguenots shared the state with you; that the nobles conducted themselves as if they were not your subjects, and the most powerful governors of the provinces as if they were sovereign in their offices.

I may say that the bad example of all of these was so injurious to this realm that even the best regulated *parlements* were affected by it, and endeavored, in certain cases, to diminish your royal authority as far as they were able in order to stretch their own powers beyond the limits of reason.

I may say that every one measured his own merit by his audacity, that in place of estimating the benefits which they received from your Majesty at their proper worth, all valued them only in so far as they satisfied the extravagant demands of their imagination; that the most arrogant were held to be the wisest, and found themselves the most prosperous.

I may also say that the foreign alliances were unfortunate, individual interests being preferred to those of the public; in a word, the dignity of the royal majesty was so disparaged, and so different from what it should be, owing to the malfeasance of those who conducted your affairs, that it was almost impossible to perceive its existence.

It was impossible, without losing all, to tolerate longer the conduct of those to whom your Majesty had intrusted the helm of state; and, on the other hand, everything could not be changed at once without violating the laws of prudence, which do not permit the abrupt passing from one extreme to another.

The sad state of your affairs seemed to force you to hasty decisions, without permitting a choice of time or of means; and yet it was necessary to make a choice of both, in order to profit by the change which necessity demanded from your prudence.

Thoughtful observers did not think that it would be possible to escape all the rocks in so tempestuous a period; the court was full of people who censured the temerity of those who wished to undertake a reform; all well knew that princes are quick to impute to those who are near them the bad outcome of the undertakings upon which they have been well advised; few people consequently expected good results from the change which it was announced that I wished to make, and many believed my fall assured even before your Majesty had elevated me.

Notwithstanding these difficulties which I represented to your Majesty, knowing how much kings may do when they make good use of their power, I ventured to promise you, with confidence, that you would soon get control of your state, and that in a short time your prudence, your courage, and the benediction of God would give a new aspect to the realm.

I promised your Majesty to employ all my industry and all the authority which it should please you to give me to ruin the Huguenot party, to abase the pride of the nobles, to bring back all your subjects to their duty, and to elevate your name among foreign nations to the point where it belongs.

Edict Ordering the Demolition of Feudal Castles, 1626

The French nobility never emerged as an important political force after the decline of feudalism. The monarchy wisely chose the policy of summoning the nobles to court, where their actions could be supervised and their energies harmlessly dissipated. When the nobility met with the clergy and the commoners in the Estates-General, its principal objective was not to win political power from the king, but to preserve its special privileges over the other classes in society. Unlike its English counterpart, the French nobility failed to develop a sense of responsibility toward the nation as a whole. When the kings ignored the Estates-General, the nobility simply let it fall into disuse. While the English nobility was making a constitution, the French nobility competed for royal favor at the court and wasted away its strength in frivolity.

Richelieu accelerated the demise of the nobility as a potential rival to the throne. In the past, rebellious or disorderly nobles had used their old feudal castles as fortresses, from which they could operate to make trouble. In 1626, he ordered the demolition of the feudal castles in France. The peasants, to whom the castles were a symbol of oppression, gladly helped execute the order. The nobility, already a hollow force, meekly submitted to Richelieu's will. The ruins of medieval *châteaux* throughout France testify to the enforcement of the law. The nobles thereby moved another step toward becoming royal lap dogs.

The Edict of 1626 ordering the demolition of the castles is presented below.

Document 40

Whereas formerly the assemblies of the estates of this realm and those of notable persons chosen to give advice to ourselves, and to the late king, our very honorable lord and father, on important affairs of this realm, and likewise the assembly of the estates of the province of Brittany held by us in the year 1614, have repeatedly requested and very humbly supplicated our said lord and father and ourselves to cause the demolition of many strongholds in divers places of this realm, which, being neither on hostile frontiers nor in important passes or places, only serve to augment our expenses by the maintenance of useless garrisons, and also serve as retreats for divers persons who on the least provocation disturb the provinces where they are located; . . .

For these reasons, we announce, declare, ordain, and will that all the strongholds, either towns or castles, which are in the interior of our realm or provinces of the same, not situated in places of importance either for frontier defense or other considerations of weight, shall be razed and demolished; even ancient walls shall be destroyed so far as it shall be deemed necessary for the well-being and repose of our subjects and the security of this state, so that our said subjects henceforth need not fear that the said places will cause them any inconvenience, and so that we shall be freed from the expense of supporting garrisons in them.

Colbert on Mercantilism, 1664

Richelieu died in 1642 and Louis XIII a year later. During the minority of Louis XIV, France was ruled by the king's mother, Anne of Austria, and Richelieu's chosen successor, the unpopular but efficient Mazarin. It was the moment for the enemies of absolutism to strike. From 1648 to 1653, a series of anti-monarchical coalitions challenged the throne. Among the participants were the *Parlements*, nobles, the Paris populace and a variety of malcontents and hangers-on at court. Their uprisings were mockingly called the *Fronde* (sling). Invariably, they were too disorganized, too disunited and too foolishly executed to have any prospect of success. In retrospect, though seeds of the 1789 revolution can be detected in them, they seem more occasions for expressing discontent than attempts to overthrow the state. By demonstrating the irresponsibility of the participants, they strengthened rather than weakened the monarchy. While the English were learning to mistrust the crown, the *Fronde* taught the French that the crown was the only national institution that could be trusted. The absolutist convictions of Louis XIV were strengthened by these petty revolts, for he retained the memory of Frondists bursting into his bedroom. After Mazarin's death in 1661, the long era of Louis XIV's personal rule began, during which he tolerated no check on his authority. Under Louis, *Le Roi Soleil*, absolutism attained its historical apogee.

Louis XIV was, in the beginning at least, a fine king. He was intelligent, hard-working, exquisitely polite, deeply interested in France and endowed with an abundance of good sense. His failing was a passionate yearning for adulation and glory. His monuments enriched the beauty of France and his conquests made France the dominant force in Europe. But these achievements were expensive and they left the state constantly burdened with debt. Louis' weakness was that he would not let even money stand in the way of his absolutism.

Louis XIV's chief finance officer and economic consultant was Colbert, worthy successor to Sully, Richelieu and Mazarin but much less an influence on the monarch than they had been. Faced with the king's indifference to solvency, as well as with a nobility exempt from taxes, an evil collection system called "tax-farming," and a tax structure that weighed most heavily on the poor, Colbert made commendable progress in putting the state on a sound financial basis. Most remarkable was the impetus he gave to French industry and commerce. Colbert was a champion of the dominant economic thinking of the age, the theory of mercantilism. Its aim was to enhance the power of the state, its means the careful management of the economy. Colbert subsidized manufacturing and shipping. He glorified hard work and protected hitherto defenseless peasants against the depradations of the idle nobility. He built roads and canals, established state industries and set enforceable standards for private production. It was he who encouraged Frenchmen to compete for colonial empire. If his efforts failed to make the French state financially stable it was because Louis XIV refused to acknowledge the dependence of a strong monarchy on a sound economy. Colbert died before he reached his goal, and subsequent ministers of Louis XIV did not bother to pursue it.

The following document, written by Colbert in 1664 over the name of Louis XIV, is a letter to the town officials and people of Marseilles, urging them to accelerate their economic activity and informing them of the assistance the state was willing to provide. It illustrates Colbert's aggressive economic thinking, based on the theory of mercantilism.

Document 41

Very dear and well beloved:

Considering how advantageous it would be to this realm to reestablish its foreign and domestic commerce, . . . we have resolved to establish a council particularly devoted to commerce, to be held every fortnight in our presence, in which all the interest of merchants and the means conducive to the revival of commerce shall be considered and determined upon, as well as all that which concerns manufactures.

We also inform you that we are setting apart, in the expenses of our state, a million livres each year for the encouragement of manufactures and the increase of navigation, to say nothing of the considerable sums which we cause to be raised to supply the companies of the East and West Indies;

That we are working constantly to abolish all the tolls which are collected on the navigable rivers;

That there has already been expended more than a million livres for the repair of the public highways, to which we shall also devote our constant attention;

That we will assist by money from our royal treasury all those who wish to reestablish old manufactures or to undertake new ones;

That we are giving orders to all our ambassadors or residents at the courts of the princes, our allies, to make, in our name, all proper efforts to cause justice to be rendered in all cases involving our merchants, and to assure for them entire commercial freedom;

That we will comfortably lodge at our court each and every merchant who has business there during all the time that he shall be obliged to remain there, having given orders to the grand marshal of our palace to indicate a proper place for that purpose, which shall be called the House of Commerce; . . .

That all the merchants and traders by sea who purchase vessels, or who build new ones, for traffic or commerce shall receive from us subsidies for each ton of merchandise which they export or import on the said voyages.

We desire, in this present letter, not only to inform you concerning all these things, but to require you, as soon as you have received it, to cause to be assembled all the merchants and traders of your town of Marseilles, and explain to them very particularly our intentions in all matters mentioned above, in order that being informed of the favorable treatment which we desire to give them, they may be the more desirous of applying themselves to commerce. Let them understand that for everything that concerns the welfare and advantage of the same they are to address themselves to Sieur Colbert. . . .

Louis XIV's Acquisition of Strasbourg, 1681

Louis XIV's military efforts, like his economic policies, at first yielded excellent results, with the promise of more to come. Louvois conducted the king's martial enterprises as efficiently as Colbert managed his finances. Louvois created for France the first organized standing army of modern times. His deputy, Vauban, a great military engineer and architect, covered France's exposed northern frontier with virtually impregnable fortresses. With Spain declining in power, Germany and Italy hopelessly divided and England wracked by revolution, France was by far the most powerful country in Europe. The temptation to expand at the expense of his neighbors was more than Louis XIV could resist. The early years of his reign brought him substantial territorial gain and much military glory.

France's principal rival on the European continent was the Hapsburg dynasty, which held the crown of the Holy Roman Empire and exercised sovereignty over Austria and part of the Balkans, Spain, northern Italy, the Low Countries and much of the Rhineland. Though its holdings largely surrounded France, the dynasty was divided into Spanish and Austrian branches, was relatively weak and posed no genuine threat to French security. Louis XIV, however, insisted that France had to expand to its "natural boundaries" in order to be safe. In three wars he tried to reach the Rhine, each time moving a little closer by acquiring some coveted territory. The Hapsburgs, by themselves, clearly lacked the capacity to thwart Louis XIV's ambitions.

So feared was the might of the French king that he was even able to annex some territories to France without fighting for them. To give a semblance of legality to his actions, he had set up "chambers of reunion" to investigate whether he could justify certain claims on the basis of ancient feudal usage. Not surprisingly, the chambers frequently rendered decisions favorable to France. With his army constantly on a war footing, Louis was always capable of enforcing these judgments. In 1681, he thus snatched Strasbourg from the moribund Holy Roman Empire. Vauban proceeded to make the city the chief French fortress on the Rhine.

The following document is a communication from the leading men of Strasbourg to the Holy Roman Emperor, describing the predicament they faced when M. de Montclair, Louis XIV's representative, presented them with an ultimatum, while a French army waited at their gates. Though nominally a part of the Empire, Strasbourg had in fact been all but independent. Its bloodless fall demonstrates the impotence of the Empire and the strength of the French under Louis XIV.

Document 42

. . . M. de Montclair informed us on the evening of the 28th, that he desired us to send to him one of our deputies to learn the intentions of His Most Christian Majesty, which are that the Sovereign Chamber of Reunion at Brisach having adjudged to the King his master the sovereignty of all Alsace, of which our city is a member, he wished in virtue of the said decree that we would recognize his said Majesty as our sovereign lord, receive a garrison, and thus merit his protection, — that the King had contemplated this step all the more seriously since he was well informed that your Imperial Majesty had sought for some time every means to secure the entry of a garrison into the city. . . .

M. the baron de Montclair gave us to understand at the same time, that if we should accede to his demands graciously and quickly, we could depend upon the preservation of our rights and privileges; but that if we should obstinately refuse, or commit the slightest act of hostility, the King had at present enough troops, artillery, and other necessary things to force us to our duty; and that as the Marquis de Louvois was to arrive to-day, he desired us to take favorable resolutions promptly in order that he might be able to inform him of them on his arrival, which was to be followed by that of the most Christian King within six days.

As we feel ourselves too weak to hold out against so great and dreadful a power as that of His Most Christian Majesty, and moreover as we do not see how we can be aided by any relief or counsel that would enable us to resist it, we have no other recource but to place ourselves in the hands of God and accept the conditions which His Most Christian Majesty shall see fit to prescribe for us.

Strasbourg, September 29, 1681

Revocation of the Edict of Nantes, 1685

As Louis XIV grew older he drew away from such judicious advisors as Colbert and Louvois who had served him so well and, vaingloriously, focused the state more and more upon himself. He spent most of his time at his sumptuous palace in Versailles, surrounded by crowds of aristocratic sycophants, rarely going out to visit the country over which he reigned. As he centralized the administration of his realm, the persons qualified to administer it became fewer. With time, Louis XIV lost his concern for the needs of the nation, became more capricious in his rule. He governed as if to demonstrate that France, no matter what the circumstances, must unquestioningly bow to his will.

Louis became increasingly autocratic in ecclesiastical as well as political matters. Intolerant of dissent, he not only suppressed Catholic heretics but persecuted Protestants. He was convinced that his absolutist state needed ideological conformity. In 1685, Louis XIV committed one of his greatest mistakes, recklessly squandering a great national asset. He reversed the century-old policy of religious toleration to revoke the Edict of Nantes.

The Edict of Nantes, issued by Henri IV in 1598, had not functioned faultlessly. The Huguenots had been granted certain privileges, among them the retention of fortified towns and castles, which isolated them from the rest of the country and encouraged them to conspire against the state, often with English Protestants. Finally Richelieu destroyed their political power in the ruthless suppression of one of their periodic uprisings. In 1629 he deprived them of their fortifications and their political organizations. After that the Huguenots behaved themselves and thrived. Their number remained relatively stable at about 1,200,000 but, thanks in large measure to a dogma favorable to capitalism, they were exceedingly prominent in business, industry and the crafts. It was a matter of indifference to Louis that the Huguenots were among the most economically useful members of his realm.

Lowis argued that the Edict of Nantes and its amendment, the Edict of Nîmes (sometimes called the Edict of Alès, a small town near Nîmes), were merely political expedients adopted by the kings of France to facilitate conversion of the heretics. Louis's persecutions, it is true, had driven away many Huguenots and converted others, so it is possible, living in his narrow world at Versailles, that he actually believed his claim that the Edict of Nantes was no longer relevant. The Revocation closed all Protestant churches, banned all worship, exiled all ministers, closed all schools and forbade all emigration. It excluded Protestants from all services of the state. By barring Protestants from overseas France, Louis ignored the precedent of the English, who sent their religious dissenters to colonize America. He thus deprived Canada and other territories of many loyal and valuable, however unwanted, Frenchmen. The Revocation of the Edict of Nantes sent hundreds of thousands of Huguenots into exile in England, Holland, Germany and America, where they established respected and useful colonies. France never quite recovered from the loss of these valuable citizens.

The initials R.P.R. in the text of the Revocation, presented below, stand for *religion prétendue réformée*, which was a mildly disparaging Catholic sobriquet for Protestantism. It means the religion which "claims" or "alleges" to be reformed.

Document 43

Louis, by the grace of God king of France and Navarre, to all present and to come, greeting:

King Henry the Great, our grandfather of glorious memory, being desirous that the peace which he had procured for his subjects after the grievous losses they had sustained in the course of domestic and foreign wars, should not be troubled on account of the R.P.R., as had happened in the reigns of the kings, his predecessors, by his edict, granted at Nantes in the month of April, 1598, regulated the procedure to be adopted with regard to those of the said religion, and the places in which they might meet for public worship, established extraordinary judges to administer justice to them, and, in fine, provided in particular articles for whatever could be thought necessary for maintaining the tranquillity of his kingdom and for diminishing mutual aversion between the members of the two religions, so as to put himself in a better position to labor, as he had resolved to do, for the reunion to the Church of those who had so lightly withdrawn from it.

As the intention of the king, our grandfather, was frustrated by his sudden death, and as the execution of the said edict was interrupted during the minority of the late king, our most honored lord and father of glorious memory, by new encroachments on the part of the adherents of the said R.P.R., which gave occasion for their being deprived of divers advantages accorded to them by the said edict, nevertheless the king, our late lord and father, in the exercise of his usual clemency, granted them yet another edict at Nîmes, in July, 1629, by means of which, tranquillity being established anew, the said late king, animated by the same spirit and the same zeal for religion as the king, the said grandfather, had resolved to take advantage of the repose to attempt to put his said pious design into execution. But foreign wars having supervened soon after, so that the kingdom was seldom tranquil from 1635 to the truce concluded in 1684 with the powers of Europe, nothing more could be done for the advantage of religion beyond diminishing the number of places for the public exercise of the R.P.R., interdicting such places as were found established to the prejudice of the dispositions made by the edicts, and suppressing of the bi-partisan courts, these having been appointed provisionally only.

God having at last permitted that our people should enjoy perfect peace, we, no longer absorbed in protecting them from our enemies, are able to profit by this truce (which we have ourselves facilitated), and devote our whole attention to the means of accomplishing the designs of our said grandfather and father, which we have consistently kept before us since our succession to the crown.

And now we perceive, with thankful acknowledgment of God's aid, that our endeavors have attained their proposed end, inasmuch as the better and the greater part of our subjects of the said R.P.R. have embraced the Catholic faith. And since by this fact the execution of the Edict of Nantes, and of all that has ever been ordained in favor of the said R.P.R. has been rendered nugatory, we have determined that we can do nothing better, in order wholly to obliterate the memory of the troubles, the confusion, and the events which the progress of this false religion has caused in the Kingdom, and which furnished occasion for the said edict and for so many previous and subsequent edicts and declarations, than entirely to revoke the said Edict of Nantes, with the special articles granted as a sequel to it, as well as all that has since been done in favor of the said religion.

I. Be it known that for these causes and others us herewith moving, and of our certain knowledge, full power, and royal authority, we have, by this present perpetual and irrevocable edict, suppressed and revoked, and do suppress and revoke, the edict of our said grandfather, given at Nantes in April, 1598, in its whole extent, together with the particular articles agreed upon in the month of May following and the letters patent issued upon the same date; and also the edict given at Nîmes in July, 1629; we declare them null and void, together with all concessions, of whatever notice they may be, made by them as well as by other edicts, declarations, and orders, in favor of the said persons of the R.P.R., the which shall remain in like manner as if they had never been granted; and in consequence we desire, and it is our pleasure, that all the temples of those of the said R.P.R. situate in our kingdom, countries, territories, and the lordships under our crown, shall be demolished without delay.

II. We forbid our subjecs of the R.P.R. to meet any more for the exercise of the said religion in any place or private house, under any pretext whatever, . . .

III. We likewise forbid all noblemen, of what condition so ever, to hold such religious exercises in their houses or fiefs, under penalty to be inflicted upon all our said subjects who shall engage in the said exercises, of imprisonment and confiscation.

IV. We enjoin all ministers of the said R.P.R., who do not choose to become converts and to embrace the Catholic, apostolic, and Roman religion, to leave our kingdom and the territories subject to us within a fortnight of the publication of our present edict, without leave to reside therein beyond that period, or, during the said fortnight, to engage in any preaching, exhortation, or any other function, on pain of being sent to the galleys. . . .

VII. We forbid private schools for the instruction of children of the said R.P.R., and in general all things whatever which can be regarded as a concession of any kind in favor of the said religion.

VIII. As for children who may be born of persons of the said R.P.R., we desire that from henceforth they be baptized by the parish priests. We enjoin parents to send them to the churches for that purpose, under penalty of five hundred livres fine, to be increased as circumstances may demand, and thereafter the children shall be brought up in the Catholic, apostolic, and Roman religion, which we expressly enjoin the local magistrates to see done.

IX. And in the exercise of our clemency towards our subjects of the said R.P.R. who have emigrated from our kingdom, lands, and territories subject to us, previous to the publication of our present edict, it is our will and pleasure that in case of their returning within the period of four months from the day of the said publication, they may, and it shall be lawful for them to, again take possession of their property, and to enjoy the same as if they had all along remained there: on the contrary, the property abandoned by those who, during the specified period of four months, shall not have returned into our kingdom, lands, and territories subject to us, shall remain and be confiscated in consequence of our declaration of the 20th of August last.

X. We repeat our most express prohibition to all our subjects of the said R.P.R., together with their wives and children, against leaving our kingdom, lands, and territories subject to us, or transporting their goods and effects there from under penalty, as respects the men, of being sent to the galleys, and as respects the women, of imprisonment and confiscation.

XI. It is our will and intention that the declarations rendered against the relapsed shall be executed according to their form and tenor.

XII. As for the rest, liberty is granted to the said persons of the R.P.R., pending the time when it shall please God to enlighten them as well as others, to remain in the cities and places of our kingdom, lands, and territories subject to us, and there to continue their commerce, and to enjoy their possessions, without being subjected to molestation or hindrance on account of the said R.P.R., on condition of not engaging in the exercise of the said religion, or of meeting under pretext of prayers or religious services, of whatever nature these may be, under the penalties above mentioned of imprisonment and confiscation. This do we give in charge to our trusty and well-beloved counselors, etc.

Given at Fontainebleau in the month of October, in the year of grace 1685, and of our reign the forty-third.

Louis XIV Accepts the Spanish Succession, 1700

Louis XIV, whatever his mistakes at home, debilitated France and the Bourbon dynasty most seriously by the senseless foreign wars in which he constantly engaged. None was more foreseeable nor more clearly portended disaster than the War of the Spanish Succession. King Charles II of Spain, who was old and feeble, had no direct heir. Though he was a Hapsburg, he was related to the Bourbon family in such a way that Louis XIV could legitimately lay claim to the succession. If a Hapsburg won the Spanish crown it would for the first time unite the family holdings under a single monarch, whose realm—the Holy Roman Empire—would surround France. If a Bourbon won it Europe's most powerful state would thereby become virtually invincible. Clearly neither Hapsburg nor Bourbon could risk letting the other acquire the prize. Nor could the other European states watch supinely the devastation of the continental balance of power. England and Holland, being maritime and colonial powers, had additional interest in keeping France out of Spain's enormous overseas empire. As the last years of the seventeenth century slipped by, Europe followed the health reports of the ailing Spanish king and recognized impending doom.

Louis XIV seemed prepared at first to head off the conflict by compromising the heritage. As early as 1668 he approved a plan to partition the Spanish holdings. In 1698, he reached an agreement with England and Holland to relinquish the Spanish crown to a Bavarian prince. But the prince died and the agreement collapsed. Shortly afterward, Louis negotiated another compromise with Austria that would have split the Spanish territories between them. But a factional fight around the Spanish throne became an obstacle to the settlement.

Perhaps Louis was not sincere in seeking to avoid war. It is known that Frenchmen at the Spanish court were scheming to have the dying king will his crown to the Bourbons, although the Louis XIV's personal role in the intrigue is unclear. King Charles II of Spain finally willed his entire inheritance to the Duke of Anjou, grandson of Louis XIV, on the grounds that France was better able to preserve the unity of the Spanish empire. But so close was the victory of the Francophiles at the Spanish court that the royal will provided for the crown to go to the Archduke Charles, the Hapsburg heir, in the event of a Bourbon refusal to reign over Spain. The dying Spanish king thus appeared to rule out the chance of compromise. It was either one rival or the other. The powerful states of Europe were on a collision course.

When the news reached France that the Spanish king had died and willed the crown to a Bourbon, Louis XIV hesitated, aware that he would have to fight to take possession of the heritage for his grandson. However, if Louis had refused the crown, war would not necessarily have been avoided, for the Hapsburg acquisition of the Spanish throne was tolerable neither to France nor to the other powers. It was tragic that Louis did not seek to negotiate a settlement which would have assured Europe that the Bourbons would not create a super-state aimed at dominating the Western world. On November 12, 1700, Louis XIV sent his answer to Spain. Far from pledging that France and Spain would not be united, which was a condition of the heritage, Louis XIV wrote ominously: "We shall exhort him (the Duke of Anjou) to remember his birth, to preserve the love of his country, . . ." Louis's letter accepting the crown on his grandson's behalf, presented here, confirmed Europe's worst fears. The powers prepared for war.

Document 44

Well-beloved Cousins and Chief Counselors, established for the universal governments of the States depending on the crown of Spain. We have received the letter signed by Your Majesty and yourselves written the first of this month, delivered to us by the Marquis De Castel dos Rios, ambassador of the most High and Mighty, and most Excellent Prince, our most dear and most beloved good Brother and Cousin, Charles the Second, king of Spain, of glorious memory; and the same ambassador remitted to us at the same time the copy of the Will made by the deceased king his master, containing the order of the heirs which he calls to the succession of his kingdoms and States, and the prudent provision he has made for the administration of the government of the kingdom till the arrival, and during the minority, of his successor.

The sensible grief which we feel for the loss of a prince, whom his excellent qualities and the strict ties of blood rendered most dear to us, is infinitely increased by the proofs which he gave us at his death, of his justice and love for his faithful subjects, and the desire he showed to maintain, after his death, the general quiet of all Europe, and the happiness of his kingdoms. We will on our part contribute to the one and the other, answering the entire confidence he always reposed in us, conforming ourselves entirely to his intentions expressed in the articles of the Will which Your Majesty and you have sent us. All our care henceforth will be to raise, by an inviolable and most strict correspondence, the Spanish Monarchy to the highest pitch of grandeur it has ever arrived at. We accept, in favor of our Grandson, the Duke of Anjou, the Will of the deceased Catholic king; our only son the Dauphin accepts it also, quitting, without any reluctance, the just rights of the deceased queen, his Mother, and our dear spouse, as well as those of the deceased queen, our most honored lady and mother, indisputably acknowledged by the opinion of the several ministers of State and Justice, consulted by the deceased king of Spain. Far from reserving to himself any part of the monarchy, he sacrifices his own interest to the desire of reëstablishing the ancient luster of a crown, which the Will of the deceased Catholic king and the voice of his people have unanimously given to our Grandson.

We will cause the Duke of Anjou immediately to depart, in order that he may the sooner give his subjects the satisfaction of receiving a king, since they are so well persuaded that God has called him to your throne. His first duty ought to be, to cause Virtue, Justice, and Religion to reign with him, and wholly to apply himself to the happiness of his people, to raise and maintain the grandeur of so mighty a monarchy, to choose always, and reward those whom he shall find in a nation so strong and wise, capable of serving him in his councils, in his armies, and in the different employments of the Church and State. We will instruct him farther in what he owes to his subjects so inviolably devoted to their king, and what to his own proper glory. We shall exhort him to remember his birth, to preserve the love of his country but, above all, to maintain forever that peace and perfect good understanding so necessary to the common happiness of our subjects and his own, which has always been the principal object of our wishes: and if the misfortunes of past conjunctures have hindered us from making it appear, we are persuaded that this great event will alter the state of things in such a way, that each day will produce hereafter new occasions to show our great esteem and particular good will to the whole Spanish nation.

In the meantime, most High and Mighty, and most Excellent Princess, our dear and entirely beloved good Sister and Cousin, We pray God, the Author of all Consolation, to give Your Majesty needful Comfort in Your just Affliction. And we assure You, most Dear and Well-beloved Cousins and prime Counselors, appointed for the Regency of Spain, of the particular Regard and Affection We have for You.

Fontainebleau, November 12, 1700

Preamble to the Grand Alliance, 1701

Louis XIV, who claimed that he wanted peace, pursued a policy after accepting the Spanish succession that appeared deliberately calculated to provoke war. His army seized the forts of the "Barrier," a buffer zone between France and Holland garrisoned under treaty by Dutch troops. He recognized the Stuart pretender as the legitimate British king, a move that could hardly have infuriated the English more. He stirred the anxiety of all Europe by reaffirming, in direct violation of the will of the late Charles II, that his grandson remained in line for the French succession. He irritated the maritime powers by declaring his intent to monopolize Spanish-American trade. Though the reaction of England and Holland to the Spanish succession was at first cautious, Louis accelerated the formation of a coalition of forces against him. In 1701, the English and the Dutch joined with Prussia, Hesse, and The Hapsburg Emperor to form the Grand Alliance against France.

The Preamble to the Grand Alliance clearly illustrates Europe's grievances against France. The three signators were the English king, the Holy Roman Emperor, and a representative of Holland, which was then a republic governed by a States-General and known as the United Provinces. The Allies, while pointing to their provocations, evidently had war aims that considerably surpassed the redress of immediate complaints.

Document 45

Whereas Charles II King of Spain, of most glorious memory, being not long since dead without issue, his sacred Imperial Majesty has claimed the succession in the kingdoms and provinces of the deceased king as lawfully belonging to his august family, but the Most Christian King, aiming at the same succession for his grandson, the Duke of Anjou, and pretending that a right did accrue to him by a certain Will of the deceased king, has usurped the possession of the entire inheritance or Spanish monarchy for the aforesaid Duke of Anjou and invaded by his arms the provinces of the Spanish Low Countries and the duchy of Milan, has a fleet ready fitted in the port of Cadiz, has sent several ships of war to the Spanish West Indies, and by this and many other ways the kingdoms of France and Spain are so closely united and cemented that they may seem henceforward not to be otherwise considered than as one and the same kingdom.

So that it sufficiently appears, unless timely care be taken, that his Imperial Majesty will be destitute of all hopes of ever receiving satisfaction in his pretension; the Holy Roman Empire will lose its rights in the fiefs belonging to it in Italy and the Spanish Netherlands; the free intercourse of Navigation and Commerce which the English and Dutch have in the Mediterranean, the Indies, and other places will be utterly destroyed; and the United Provinces will be deprived of the security which they enjoyed in the provinces of Spanish Netherlands lying between them and the French, which is commonly called a Barrier; lastly, that the French and Spaniards, being thus united, will within a short time become so formidable to all that they may easily assume to themselves the dominion over all Europe.

And therefore by this way of proceeding of the Most Christian King, his Imperial Majesty was brought under a necessity of sending an army for the preservation as well of his own private interests as the fiefs of the empire; the king of Great Britain has thought it requisite to send his forces to the assistance of the States-General, whose affairs are in the same condition as if they were actually invaded; and the said States, whose frontiers lie in a manner exposed on all sides by the breaking and taking away of that fence commonly called a Barrier, which screened them from the neighborhood of the French, are forced to do all those things for the safety and defense of their commonwealth which they should and could do if they were in a war. And whereas so dubious a posture of their affairs is more dangerous than a war itself, and that France and Spain take advantage of this state of their affairs to make a stronger and firmer union between themselves for oppressing the liberty of Europe and taking away freedom of commerce:

These reasons inducing his sacred Imperial Majesty, his sacred Royal Majesty of Great Britain, and the High and Mighty Lords of the States-General of the United Provinces to obviate so great evils as might arise from thence, and, desiring so much as lies within their power to apply remedies thereto, have thought a strict conjunction and alliance between themselves necessary for repelling the greatness of the common danger.

The Treaty of Utrecht, 1713

The War of the Spanish Succession lasted for more than ten years. Bloody battles were fought not only throughout Europe but also in America, where, taking the name of the English monarch, it became known as Queen Anne's War. In one encounter after another the French were defeated. By 1709 France, having suffered a crop failure, appeared too exhausted to defend its frontiers against impending invasion. Louis opened negotiations to end hostilities but the terms the Allies submitted to him were so harsh that he succeeded in rallying the country for another round of fighting. Events proved that the Allies had missed the opportunity for a victors' peace. In short order, the British government fell and the Holy Roman Emperor died, completely changing the situation. Since the new Emperor also claimed the Spanish throne, the English, having achieved their objectives, found no point in pursuing the war. Tired of fighting, the powers negotiated a compromise peace at Utrecht in Holland in 1713. In satisfying the interests of each of the participants, the Treaty of Utrecht cast the mold in which contemporary Europe took its form.

Though nominally the loser, France salvaged a great deal from the treaty. It confirmed the right of the Bourbon dynasty to hold the Spanish crown, which was the issue over which the war had broken out, although the French and Spanish branches—in keeping with the stipulation of Charles II's unfortunate will—became pledged to remain eternally separate. The French frontier remained essentially as Louis XIV had made it, following generally France's "natural boundaries" other than the Rhine. The treaty, however, deprived France of most of its vast colonial empire and ended French expansion in the New World.

England, by obtaining Gibraltar and most of France's American possessions, became the world's foremost maritime and colonial power.

Austria took title to most of the former holdings of the Spanish Hapsburgs in the Low Countries and Italy. These territories soon proved troublesome to an already unstable imperial throne, which was not destined to hold them long.

Savoy, elevated from a duchy to a kingdom, was given from Spain the island of Sicily, which it subsequently exchanged for Sardinia. The new territory, added to its substantial holdings in Piedmont, enabled the House of Savoy to lay the foundation for its fundamental contribution a century later to Italian unification.

The Elector of Brandenburg was recognized under his new title of King of Prussia. It marked a step in the rise of a vigorous new state in the north which would change the face of Germany.

The following document is Queen Anne's message to Parliament in 1712 on the progress of the negotiations proceeding at Utrecht. She recites the essential provisions of the forthcoming treaty, in which she takes considerable satisfaction. The Queen's own interest was well served at Utrecht, where all of Europe recognized the legitimacy of her Protestant dynasty and Louis XIV promised to banish the Stuart pretender from France.

Document 46

My Lords and Gentlemen:

The making Peace and War is the undoubted Prerogative of the Crown; yet such is the just Confidence I place in you, that at the Opening of this Session I acquainted you, That a Negotiation for a General Peace was begun; and afterwards, by Messages, I promised to communicate to you the Terms of Peace, before the same should be concluded.

In pursuance of that Promise, I now come to let you know upon what Terms a General Peace may be made.

I need not mention the Difficulties which arise from the very Nature of this Affair; and it is but too apparent that these Difficulties have been increased by other Obstructions, artfully contrived to hinder this great and good Work.

Nothing, however, has moved me from steadily pursuing, in the first Place, the true Interest of my own Kingdoms; and I have not omitted anything which might procure to our Allies what is due to them by Treaties, and what is necessary for their Security.

The Assuring of the Protestant Succession, as by Law established, in the House of Hanover, to these Kingdoms, being what I have nearest at Heart, particular Care is taken, not only to have that acknowledged in the strongest Terms, but to have an additional Security, by the Removal of that Person out of the Dominions of France, who has pretended to disturb this Settlement.

The Apprehension that Spain and the West Indies might be united to France was the chief Inducement to begin this War; and the effectual Preventing of such an Union was the Principle I laid down at the Commencement of this Treaty.

Former Examples, and the Late Negotiations, sufficiently show how difficult it is to find Means to accomplish this Work. I would not content myself with such as are speculative, or depend on Treaties only; I insisted on what is solid, and to have at Hand the Power of executing what should be agreed.

I can, therefore, now tell you, That France at last is brought to offer, that the Duke of Anjou shall, for himself and his Descendants, renounce forever all Claim to the Crown of France. And that this important Article may be exposed to no Hazard, the Performance is to accompany the Promise. . . .

France and Spain are now more effectually divided than ever. And thus, by the Blessing of God, will a real Balance of Power be fixed in Europe, and remain liable to as few Accidents as Human Affairs can be exempted from. . . .

Our Interest is so deeply concerned in the Trade of North America, that I have used my utmost Endeavours to adjust that Article in the most beneficial Manner. France consents to restore to us the whole Bay and Streights of Hudson; to deliver up the Island of Newfoundland, with Placentia, and to make an absolute Cession of Annapolis, with the rest of Nova Scotia or Acadia.

The Safety of our Home Trade will be better provided for by the Demolition of Dunkirk.

Our Mediterranean Trade, and the British Interest and Influence in those Parts, will be secured by the Possession of Gibraltar and Port Mahon, with the whole Island of Minorca, which are offered to remain in my Hands.

The Trade to Spain and to the West Indies may in general be settled, as it was in the Time of the late King of Spain, Charles II, and a particular Provision be made, That all Advantages, Rights, or Privileges which have been granted, or which may hereafter be granted, by Spain to any other Nation, shall be in like manner granted to the Subjects of Great Britain.

But the Part which we have borne in the Prosecution of this War, intitling us to some Distinction in the Terms of Peace, I have insisted and obtained, That the Asiento, or Contract for furnishing the Spanish West-Indies with Negroes, shall be made with us for the Term of Thirty Years, in the same Manner as it has been enjoyed by the French for these Ten Years past.

I have not taken upon me to determine the Interest of our Confederates; these must be adjusted in the Congress at Utrecht, where my best Endeavours shall be employed, as they have hitherto been, to procure to every one of them all just and reasonable Satisfaction. In the mean time, I think it proper to acquaint you, that France offers to make the Rhine the Barrier of the Empire; to yield Brisac, the Fort of Kehl and Landau;

and to raze all Fortresses, both of the other side of the Rhine, and in that River. . . .

As to the Protestant Interest in Germany, there will be, on the Part of France, no Objection to the Resettling thereof on the Foot of the Treaty of Westphalia.

The Spanish Low Countries may go to His Imperial Majesty; the Kingdoms of Naples and Sardinia, the Duchy of Milan, and the Places belonging to Spain on the Coast of Tuscany, may likewise be yielded by the Treaty of Peace to the Emperor.

As to the Kingdom of Sicily, tho' there remains no Dispute concerning the Cession of it by the Duke of Anjou, yet the Disposition thereof is not yet determined.

The Interests of the States General, with respect to Commerce, are agreed to, as they have been demanded by their own Ministers, with the Exception only of some very few Species of Merchandize. . . .

Those of the king of Prussia are such as, I hope, will admit of little difficulty on the part of France; and my Endeavours shall not be wanting to procure all I am able to so good an ally. . . .

France has consented that the Elector Palatine shall continue his present rank among the Electors, and remain in possession of the Upper Palatinate.

The Electoral dignity is likewise acknowledged in the House of Hanover, according to the articles inserted, at that prince's desire and my demands.

And as to the rest of the Allies, I make no doubt of being able to secure their several Interests.

VII

Western Civilization Moves to the New World

VII

Western Civilization Moves to the New World

Prior to the sixteenth century, Western civilization was limited to a relatively small area in western Europe. Its members knew little of other peoples and societies, while other peoples were only dimly aware of the character of the West. Inherent within it, however, were the seeds of expansion, which first showed signs of germinating during the Crusades of the twelfth century. During the later Middle Ages, adventurous traders—most spectacularly, the Venetian discoverer of China, Marco Polo—voyaged eastward. Though they made little impact on the countries they visited, they stimulated the curiosity of the countries to which they returned.

But why Western civilization, unlike others, spilled beyond its borders onto new continents and profoundly influenced the development of societies throughout the world is not easy to determine. Some of the explanation is certainly in its religion. Christianity, the spiritual inspiration of the West, was always deeply missionary, constantly pressing outward its frontiers. In addition, Europe, because it was not economically self-sufficient, was forever in search of such commodities as spices and cotton which were unavailable at home. By the sixteenth century, the commercial revolution had confirmed Europe in the quest for wealth. Strong national states could concentrate enough funds to invest in voyages of discovery. New navigational instruments made them technically feasible. As the medieval age gave way to the modern, inspiration and incentive united with technique to convey Western civilization around the world.

Journal of the First Voyage of Columbus, 1492

It was inevitable that, with the eastern Mediterranean dominated by hostile Turks, some daring mariner would seek to rediscover

Marco Polo's Cathay by another route. The Portuguese were devoting all their energy to going around the cape of Africa. The Spaniards, once science had established that the world was round, were willing to listen to a proposal for exploring a course to the west. None thought so much of finding a new land as of seeking the legendary wealth of ancient China.

An adventurous mariner named Christopher Columbus proposed a westward voyage to the Spanish monarchs, after Venice and his native Genoa had turned the idea down. Columbus, who also made an overture to England, was willing to sell his services to the highest bidder. Ferdinand and Isabella, the crowned heads of Castile, were sympathetic but hesitated at first to take the gamble. Finally, against the advice of their more cautious counselors, they consented to make the investment. With three small ships and eighty-seven men, Columbus set out on August 3, 1492, in quest of glory and Cathay.

The journal Columbus kept of his voyage to America is a remarkable revelation of his own motives and conceptions, as well as those of the Spanish sovereigns. He carried with him a letter of introduction to the Gran Can, whom he believed was the ruler of China. He discloses that he had been made a nobleman, given a fine title and endowed with the right to govern, as well as to profit from, his discoveries. He reveals that even then the Spanish recognized that the year 1492 loomed large in their history, for that was the year they expelled not only the invading Moors but the loyal Jews. On October 12, it became the year that a Spanish expedition discovered America, though Columbus believed until the day he died that he had found China.

In his diary entry of November 12, Columbus had already begun to reflect on the prospects of conquest. He reveals that he took several prisoners to bring back to Spain—all of whom died. He speaks of Spain's apostolic mission among the heathen natives. But he does not fail to point out that conversion would be accompanied by "the acquisition of great lordships (territories), peoples, and riches for Spain." As early as the first voyage to the New World, Columbus set the tone for the campaign of exploitation and depredation that Spain later undertook in America.

The following selections are from the journal of the first voyage of Christopher Columbus.

Document 47

Prologue: to the King and Queen of Spain

Because, O most Christian, and very high, very excellent, and puissant Princes, King and Queen of the Spains and of the islands of the Sea, our Lords, in this present year of 1492, after your Highnesses had given an end to the war with the Moors who reigned in Europe, and had finished it in the very great city of Granada, where in this present year, on the second day of the month of January, by force of arms, I saw the royal banners of your Highnesses placed on the towers of Alhambra, which is the fortress of that city, and I saw the Moorish King come forth from the gates of the city and kiss the royal hands of your Highnesses, and of the Prince my Lord, and presently in that same month, acting on the information that I had given to your Highnesses touching the lands of India, and respecting a Prince who is called *Gran Can*, which means in our language King of Kings, how he and his ancestors had sent to Rome many times to ask for learned men of our holy faith to teach him, and how the Holy Father had never complied, insomuch that many people believing in idolatries were lost by receiving doctrine of perdition: *Your Highnesses*, as Catholic Christians and Princes who love the holy Christian faith, and the propagation of it and who are enemies to the sect of Mohama and to all idolatries and heresies, resolved to send me, Cristobal Colon [Christopher Columbus], to the said Parts of India to see the said princes, and the cities and lands, and their disposition, with a view that they might be converted to our holy faith; and ordered that I should not go by land to the eastward, as had been customary, but that I should go by way of the west, whither up to this day, we do not know for certain that any one has gone.

Thus, after having turned out all the Jews from all your kingdoms and lordships, in the same month of January, your Highnesses gave orders to me that with a sufficient fleet I should go to the said parts of India, and for this they made great concessions to me, and ennobled me, so that henceforward I should be called Don, and should be Chief Admiral of the Ocean Sea, perpetual Viceroy and Governor of all the islands and continents that I should discover and gain, and that I might hereafter discover and gain in the Ocean Sea, and that my eldest son should succeed and so on from generation to generation for ever.

I left the city of Granada on the 12th of May, in the same year of 1492, being Saturday, and came to the town of Palos, which is a seaport; where I equipped three vessels well suited for such service; and departed from that port, well supplied with provisions and with many sailors, on the 3d day of August of the same year, being Friday, half an hour before sunrise, taking the route to the islands of Canaria, belonging to your Highnesses, which are in the said Ocean Sea, that I might thence take my departure for navigating until I should arrive at the Indies, and give the letters of your Highnesses to those princes, so as to comply with my orders. As part of my duty I thought it well to write an account of all the voyage very punctually, noting from day to day all that I should do and see, and that should happen, as will be seen further on. Also, Lords Princes, I resolved to describe each night what passed in the day, and to note each day how I navigated at night. I propose to construct a new chart for navigating, on which I shall delineate all the sea and lands of the Ocean in their proper positions under their bearings; and further, I propose to prepare a book, and to put down all as it were in a picture, by latitude from the equator, and western longitude. Above all, I shall have accomplished much, for I shall forget sleep, and shall work at the business of navigation, that so the service may be performed; all of which will entail great labour.

Monday, 12th of November. . . . The Admiral says that, on the previous Sunday, the 11th of November, it seemed good to take some persons from amongst those at Rio de Mares to bring to the Sovereigns, that they might learn our language, so as to be able to tell us what there is in their lands. Returning, they would be the mouthpiece of the Christians, and would adopt our customs and the things of the faith. I saw and knew (says the Admiral) that these people are without any religion, not idolaters, but very gentle, not knowing what is evil, nor the sins of murder and theft, being without arms, and so timid that a hundred would fly before one Spaniard, although they joke with them. They, however, believe and know that there is a God in heaven, and say that we have come from heaven. At any prayer that we say, they repeat, and make the sign of the cross. Thus your Highnesses should resolve to make them Christians, for I believe that, if the work was begun, in a little time a multitude of nations would be converted to our faith, with the acquisition of great lordships, peoples, and riches for Spain. Without doubt, there is in these lands a vast quantity of gold, and the Indians I have on board do not speak without reason when they say that in these islands there are places where they dig out gold, and wear it on their necks, ears, arms, and legs, the rings being very large. There are also precious stones, pearls, and an infinity of spices. . . .

Here also there is a great quantity of cotton, and I believe it would have a good sale here without sending it to Spain, but to the great cities of the Gran Can, which will be discovered without doubt, and many others ruled over by other lords, who will be pleased to serve your Highnesses, and whither will be brought other commodities of Spain and of the Eastern lands; but these are to the west as regards us. . . .

Tuesday, 27th of November. . . . The Admiral also says:—"How great the benefit that is to be derived from this country would be, I cannot say. It is certain that where there are such lands there must be an infinite number of things that would be profitable. But I did not remain long in one port, because I wished to see as much of the country as possible, in order to make a report upon it to your Highnesses, and besides, I do not know the language, and these people neither understand me nor any other in my company, while the Indians I have on board often misunderstand. Moreover, I have not been able to see much of the natives, because they often take to flight. But now, if our Lord pleases, I will see as much as possible, and will proceed by little and little, learning and comprehending; and I will make some of my followers learn the language. For I have perceived that there is only one language up to this point. After they understand the advantages, I shall labour to make all these people Christians. They will become so readily, because they have no religion or idolatry, and your Highnesses will send orders to build a city and fortress, and to convert the people. I assure your Highnesses that it does not appear to me that there can be a more fertile country nor a better climate under the sun, with abundant supplies of water. . . . If it will please God that your Highnesses should send learned men out here, they will see the truth of all I have said. I have related already how good a place *Rio de Mares* would be for a town and fortress, and this is perfectly true; but it bears no comparison with this place, nor with the *Mar de Nuestra Señora*. For here there must be a large population, and very valuable productions, which I hope to discover before I return to Castille. I say that if Christendom will find profit among these people, how much more will Spain, to whom the whole country should be subject. Your Highnesses ought not to consent that any stranger should trade here, or put his foot in the country, except Catholic Christians, for this was the beginning and end of the undertaking; namely, the increase and glory of the Christian religion, and that no other should come to these parts who was not a good Christian."

The Mayflower Compact, 1620

The Spanish acted with dispatch to take advantage of Columbus's discoveries. They were followed by the English, the French, the Portuguese and the Dutch, each of whom laid claim to land and contributed to a great era of discovery. But the sixteenth century was preeminently Spain's. After conquering the Carribean, the Spanish reduced Mexico and almost all of South America to their rule. Though their methods were barbarous, the Spanish in the name of civilization and God performed remarkable feats of exploration and exploitation. By the beginning of the seventeenth century Spain's star was falling rapidly. But before any other country placed a single permanent settler in the New World, the Spanish had converted millions to their faith and organized more territory than Rome conquered in five centuries.

The English began a serious effort at settling America in 1606, when a colony was founded in Virginia by one of two private companies incorporated by the crown. The Virginia settlers, after a poor start, discovered the virtues of tobacco cultivation, which inaugurated a flourishing trade with the mother country. In contrast to Spain's tyrannical administration to the south, Virginia imported English law and liberty. By 1619, Virginians had established the first representative government in the New World. When the Virginia Company, the chartering corporation, was dissolved because of financial difficulties, Virginia lost its autonomy and became a crown colony. It did not seem important at the time but the political change was pregnant with trouble for a later generation that would seek to assert its liberties.

New England was the other early center of English colonization in America. It was first settled by a group of Puritans, the extremist Protestants who had proved so troublesome at home. Seeking escape from Stuart oppression to live and worship freely, they went first to Holland, then decided to move to America. Mostly city-folk, the Puritans seemed ill-fitted to cope with the wilderness but, thanks to a reputation for industriousness and grit, the Virginia Company gave them a grant of land and a syndicate of English merchants agreed to finance their voyage. They arrived at Cape Cod in their tiny ship, the Mayflower, on November 11, 1620. Since they were outside the Virginia Company's jurisdiction, they decided to forestall internal political disputes by drawing up their own constitutional document. The Pilgrims—as they are known to American history—thus signed a compact which established in Plymouth, the colony they founded, a government by will of the majority. They avowed their loyalty to the crown, whose persecution they sought to escape, but they took the English idea of self-government and transplanted it in America. The Mayflower Compact became the model for the government of the New England colonies and the inspiration for the government of what ultimately became a new nation.

The Mayflower Compact of 1620 appears here in its original form, as it was prepared at Plymouth Rock.

Document 48

In the name of God, Amen. We whose names are underwritten, the loyall subjects of our dread soveraigne Lord, King James, by the grace

of God, of Great Britaine, France, & Ireland king, defender of the faith, &c., haveing undertaken, for the glorie of God, and advancemente of the Christian faith, and honour of our king & countrie, a voyage to plant the first colonie in the Northerne parts of Virginia, doe by these presents solemnly & mutualy in the presence of God, and one of another, covenant & combine our selves togeather into a civill body politick, for our better ordering & preservation & furtherance of the ends aforesaid; and by vertue hereof to enacte, constitute, and frame such just & equall lawes, ordinances, acts, constitutions, & offices, from time to time, as shall be thought most meete & convenient for the generall good of the Colonie, unto which we promise all due submission and obedience. In witness whereof we have hereunder subscribed our names at Cap-Codd the 11. of November, in the year of the raigne of our soveraigne lord, King James, of England, France, & Ireland the eighteenth, and of Scotland the fiftie fourth.
Anno: Dom. 1620.

The Declaration of Independence, 1776

Though the English colonists in America thought of themselves as Englishmen, deeply rooted to the ideas and values of Western civilization, it was inevitable that out of the peculiar conditions of colonial living they would create a society that, within the English and Western tradition, would be peculiarly their own. It was equally inevitable that the conceptions of self-government that they inherited from England would lead them, sooner or later, to question their continued status as dependents. The colonists were spiritually too English not to think of becoming American.

The king and his government in London provided them with ample pretext for such thinking. British colonial policy during the seventeenth and eighteenth centuries took its inspiration from the same mercantilist theories as Colbert's nationalist economics. The English shared the general European view of colonial empire as a source of wealth and power for the mother country. Under the Navigation and Trade Acts, the British harried American commerce and industry. New England and the neighboring colonies, heavily dependent on shipping and manufactures, were more embittered by this treatment than the south, to which such staple crops as tobacco and cotton brought a steady income. But by the late eighteenth century, north and south were united in their opposition to English economic exploitation and its companion, political oppression.

The rebelliousness of the American colonists was quickened in the eighteenth century by the movement called the Enlightenment, which spread through Western civilization new ideas exalting natural rights and the sanctity of reason. American leaders read the Englishman, John Locke, and the Frenchmen, Rousseau, Voltaire and Montesquieu, and found in them vindication of their outrage against the English king and Parliament. The Enlightenment provided the colonists with a fresh doctrine at the very moment that the rigors imposed by London were becoming most harsh.

From 1764 to 1774, the British enacted a succession of new laws taxing and regulating the colonial economy, accompanying them with increased restrictions on self-government. Americans, particularly New Englanders, began to organize to resist the English measures. In 1770, popular resentment was enflamed when British soldiers fired into a jeering crowd in Boston, center of the resistance movement. Defiance of the British grew bolder and more determined. Finally, in April, 1775, rebellion began when a band of colonists standing on the Concord Bridge in Massachusetts fired at approaching British soldiers "the shot heard round the world."

It took more than a year for the colonists to bring themselves to break irrevocably from England. But on July 4, 1776, the Second Continental Congress formally adopted Thomas Jefferson's draft of The Declaration of Independence. It is a document that derives directly from the political tradition of England and the philosophy of the European enlightenment. Though righteously indignant, it relies on reason in denouncing the deprivation of self-government and natural rights. The Declaration of Independence, presented below, was the new nation's defiant proclamation to the world of an individual destiny within the community of Western civilization.

Document 49

When in the course of human events, it becomes necessary for one people to dissolve the political bands which have connected them with another, and to assume among the powers of the earth, the separate and equal station to which the Laws of Nature and of Nature's God entitle them, a decent respect to the opinions of mankind requires that they should declare the causes which impel them to the separation.

We hold these truths to be self-evident, that all men are created equal, that they are endowed by their Creator with certain unalienable Rights, that among these are Life, Liberty and the pursuit of Happiness. That to secure these rights, Governments are instituted among Men, deriving their just powers from the consent of the governed. That whenever any Form of Government becomes destructive of these ends, it is the Right of the People to alter or to abolish it, and to institute new Government, laying its foundation on such principles and organizing its powers in such form, as to them shall seem most likely to effect their Safety and Happiness. Prudence, indeed will dictate that Governments long established should not be changed for light and transient causes; and accordingly all experience hath shewn, that mankind are more disposed to suffer, while evils are sufferable, than to right themselves by abolishing the forms to which they are accustomed. But when a long train of abuses and usurpations, pursuing invariably the same object, evinces a design to reduce them under absolute Despotism, it is their right, it is their duty, to throw off such Government, and to provide new Guards for their future security. Such has been the patient sufferance of these Colonies; and such is now the necessity which constrains them to alter their former Systems of Government. The history of the present King of Great Britain is a history of repeated injuries and usurpations, all having in direct object the establishment of an absolute Tyranny over these States. To prove this, let Facts be submitted to a candid world.

He has refused his assent to laws, the most wholesome and necessary for the public good. He has forbidden his Governors to pass Laws of immediate and pressing importance unless suspended in their operation till his Assent should be obtained, and when so suspended, he has utterly neglected to attend them.

He has refused to pass other Laws for the accommodation of large districts of people, unless those people would relinquish the right of Representation in the Legislature, a right inestimable to them and formidable to tyrants only.

He has called together legislative bodies at places, unusual, uncomfortable, and distant from the depository of their public Records, for the sole purpose of fatiguing them into compliance with his measures.

He has dissolved Representative Houses repeatedly, for opposing with manly firmness his invasions on the rights of the people.

He has refused for a long time, after such dissolutions, to cause others to be elected; whereby the Legislative powers, incapable of Annihilation, have returned to the People at large for their exercise; the State remaining in the meantime exposed to all the dangers of invasion from without, and convulsions within.

He has endeavored to prevent the population of these States; for that purpose obstructing the Laws for Naturalization of Foreigners: refusing to pass others to encourage their migration hither, and raising the conditions of new Appropriations of Lands.

He has obstructed the Administration of Justice, by refusing his Assent to Laws for establishing Judiciary powers.

He has made Judges dependent on his Will alone, for the tenure of their offices, and the amount and payment of their salaries.

He has erected a multitude of New Offices, and sent hither swarms of Officers to harass our people, and eat out their substance.

He has kept among us, in times of peace, Standing Armies, without the Consent of our legislatures.

He has affected to render the Military independent of and superior to the Civil power.

He has combined with others to subject us to a jurisdiction foreign to our constitution and unacknowledged by our laws; giving his Assent to their Acts of pretended Legislation: For quartering large bodies of armed troops among us: For protecting them by a mock Trial from punishment for any Murders which they should commit on the Inhabitants of these States: For cutting off our Trade with all parts of the world: For imposing Taxes on us without our Consent: For depriving us in many cases of the benefits of Trial by Jury: For transporting us beyond Seas to be tried for pretended offenses: For abolishing the free System of English Laws in a neighbouring Province, establishing therein an Arbitrary government, and enlarging its Boundaries so as to render it at once an example and fit instrument for introducing the same absolute rule into these Colonies: For taking away our Charters, abolishing our most valuable Laws and altering fundamentally the Forms of our Governments: For suspending our own Legislatures and declaring themselves invested with power to legislate for us in all cases whatsoever.

He has abdicated government here by declaring us out of his Protection and waging War against us.

He has plundered our seas, ravished our Coasts, burnt our towns, and destroyed the lives of our people.

He is at this time transporting large Armies of foreign Mercenaries to complete the works of death, desolation and tyranny, already begun with circumstances of cruelty and perfidy scarcely paralleled in the most barbarous ages, and totally unworthy the Head of a civilized nation.

He has constrained our fellow Citizens taken Captive on the high Seas to bear Arms against their Country, to become the executioners of their friends and Brethren, or to fall themselves by their Hands.

He has excited domestic insurrections amongst us, and has endeavoured to bring on the inhabitants of our frontiers, the merciless Indian

Savages, whose known rule of warfare is an undistinguished destruction of all ages, sexes and conditions. In every stage of these Oppressions We have Petitioned for Redress in the most humble terms. Our repeated Petitions have been answered only by repeated injury. A Prince, whose character is thus marked by every act which may define a Tyrant, is unfit to be the ruler of a free people. Nor have We been wanting in attention to our British brethren. We have warned them from time to time of attempts by their legislature to extend an unwarrantable jurisdiction over us. We have reminded them of the circumstances of our emigration and settlement here. We have appealed to their native justice and magnanimity, and we have conjured them by the ties of our common kindred to disavow these usurpations, which would inevitably interrupt our connections and correspondence. They too have been deaf to the voice of justice and of consanguinity. We must, therefore, acquiesce in the necessity, which denounces our Separation, and hold them, as we hold the rest of mankind, Enemies in War, in Peace Friends.

We, therefore, the Representatives of the United States of America, in General Congress, Assembled, appealing to the Supreme Judge of the world for the rectitude of our intentions do, in the Name, and by authority of the good People of these Colonies, solemnly publish and declare, That these United Colonies are, and of Right ought to be, Free and Independent States; that they are Absolved from all Allegiance to the British Crown, and that all political connection between them and the State of Great Britain is and ought to be totally dissolved; and that as Free and Independent States, they have full Power to levy War, conclude Peace, contract Alliances, establish Commerce, and to do all other Acts and Things which Independent States may of right do. And for the support of this Declaration, with a firm reliance on the protection of Divine Providence, we mutually pledge to each other our Lives, our Fortunes, and our sacred Honor.

Bolivar's Address at Angostura, 1819

Latin America, the vast area colonized and ruled by Spain, did not remain immune from the influences of the Enlightenment and the American Revolution, nor later from the French Revolution and the Napoleonic disruptions. The Latin colonies possessed an elite not only at home with European culture but also familiar with the ideas then sweeping through the Western world.

Latin America, however, was not as well prepared as was North America for revolution and its consequences. The tyranny of Spain, in addition to being harsher than England's, had deprived the Latins of the traditions and experiences of self-government that had readied the English colonies for independence. The Latin lands, furthermore, were ethnically, economically and geographically far more divided than the United States. Their social structure was rigid. The Church was powerful and pro-Spanish. Their masses were woefully ignorant. They lacked the means and the organization to fight a sustained war. Nonetheless, Latin America did rise up. When Bonaparte toppled the Spanish monarchy, the wars of independence began. They lasted from 1809 to 1824. They ended three hundred years of Spanish colonial rule.

The dominant figure of the Latin American wars of independence was Simon Bolivar, scion of a wealthy Caracas family. From his tutors he imbibed the liberal doctrines of the Enlightenment, particularly the egalitarian ideals of Jean-Jacques Rousseau. He traveled widely in Europe. When summoned to leadership, he proved brave and brilliant, adept both at the arts of war and in the political arena. Bolivar, called the Liberator even in his own day, was a sincere idealist but no one understood better than he the burden of Latin America's Spanish heritage. Though a man of the Enlightenment, he could not share the optimism of, say, a Jefferson about the future of his people. Bolivar recognized that when the Spanish were driven out, Latin America's quest for freedom would just begin.

Venezuela declared its independence of Spain in 1811 and established a federal constitution on the model of the United States. But the fight against the Spanish still had to be won. Bolivar was given almost unlimited military and political powers and, against a stubborn foe, waged a bitter war. In 1819, after a series of victories in Venezuela's Orinoco Basin, he convoked a congress at Angostura (later Ciudad Bolivar) to refashion the Venezuelan constitution for use by a group of newly liberated colonies that planned to unite into a nation to be called Great Colombia. In turning over his powers to the congress, Bolivar related his fears, as well as his hopes, for the political development of the new nation, of which he was soon named President. His penetrating observations reveal his deep involvement in the main currents of Western civilization and his apprehension that Latin America would be unable to navigate in them. His is a compassionate commentary on a people only half-introduced to Western ideas and to whom, as a consequence, the full benefits of Western civilization would long be denied.

Excerpts of Bolivar's remarkable speech, delivered on February 15, 1819, are presented here.

Document 50

Gentlemen:

Fortunate is the citizen, who, under the emblem of his command, has convoked this assembly of the national sovereignty so that it may exercise its absolute will! I, therefore, place myself among those most favored by Divine Providence, for I have had the honor of uniting the representatives of the people of Venezuela in this august Congress, the source of legitimate authority, the custodian of the sovereign will, and the arbiter of the Nation's destiny. . . .

Allow me, Gentlemen, to expound, with the frankness of a true republican, my respectful opinion on a *Plan of a Constitution*, which I take the liberty of submitting to you as testimony of the candor and sincerity of my sentiments. As this plan concerns the welfare of all, I venture to assume that I have the right to be heard by the representatives of the people. I well know that your wisdom needs no counsel, and I know also that my plan may perhaps appear to be mistaken and impracticable. But I implore you, Gentlemen, receive this work with benevolence, for it is more a tribute of my sincere deference to the Congress than an act of presumption. Moreover, as your function is to create a body politic, or, it might be said, to create an entire society while surrounded by every obstacle that a most peculiar and difficult situation can present, perhaps the voice of one citizen may reveal the presence of a hidden or unknown danger.

Let us review the past to discover the base upon which the Republic of Venezuela is founded.

America, in separating from the Spanish monarchy, found herself in a situation similar to that of the Roman Empire when its enormous framework fell to pieces in the midst of the ancient world. Each Roman division then formed an independent nation in keeping with its location or interests; but this situation differed from America's in that those members proceeded to reestablish their former associations. We, on the contrary, do not even retain the vestiges of our original being. We are not Europeans, we are not Indians; we are but a mixed species of aborigines and Spaniards. Americans by birth and Europeans by law, we find ourselves engaged in a dual conflict: we are disputing with the natives for titles of ownership, and at the same time we are struggling to maintain ourselves in the country that gave us birth against the opposition of the invaders. Thus our position is most extraordinary and complicated. But there is more. As our role has always been strictly passive and our political existence nil, we find that our quest for liberty is now even more difficult of accomplishment; for we, having been placed in a state lower than slavery, had been robbed not only of our freedom but also of the right to exercise an active domestic tyranny. Permit me to explain this paradox.

In absolute systems, the central power is unlimited. The will of the despot is the supreme law, arbitrarily enforced by subordinates who take part in the organized oppression in proportion to the authority that they wield. They are charged with civil, political, military, and religious functions; but, in the final analysis, the satraps of Persia are Persian, the pashas of the Grand Turk are Turks, and the sultans of Tartary are Tartars. China does not seek her mandarins in the homeland of Genghis Khan, her conqueror.

America, on the contrary, received everything from Spain, who, in effect, deprived her of the experience that she would have gained from the exercise of an active tyranny by not allowing her to take part in her own domestic affairs and administration. This exclusion made it impossible for us to acquaint ourselves with the management of public affairs; nor did we enjoy that personal consideration, of such great value in major revolutions, that the brilliance of power inspires in the eyes of the multitude. In brief, Gentlemen, we were deliberately kept in ignorance and cut off from the world in all matters relating to the science of government.

Subject to the threefold yoke of ignorance, tyranny, and vice, the American people have been unable to acquire knowledge, power, or [civic] virtue. The lessons we received and the models we studied, as pupils of such pernicious teachers, were most destructive. We have been ruled more by deceit than by force, and we have been degraded more by vice than by superstition. Slavery is the daughter of Darkness: an ignorant people is a blind instrument of its own destruction. Ambition and intrigue abuse the credulity and experience of men lacking all political, economic, and civic knowledge; they adopt pure illusion as reality; they take license for liberty, treachery for patriotism, and vengeance for justice. This situation is similar to that of the robust blind man who, beguiled by his strength, strides forward with all the assurance of one who can see, but, upon hitting every variety of obstacle, finds himself unable to retrace his steps.

If a people, perverted by their training, succeed in achieving their liberty, they will soon lose it, for it would be of no avail to endeavor to explain to them that happiness consists in the practice of virtue; that the rule of law is more powerful than the rule of tyrants, because, as the laws are more inflexible, everyone should submit to their beneficent austerity; that proper morals, and not force, are the bases of law; and that to practice justice is to practice liberty. Therefore, Legislators, your work is so much the more arduous, inasmuch as you have to reëducate men who have been corrupted by erroneous illusions and false incentives. Liberty, says Rousseau, is a succulent morsel, but one difficult to digest. Our weak fellow-citizens will have to strengthen their spirit greatly before they can digest the wholesome nutriment of freedom. Their limbs benumbed by chains, their sight dimmed by the darkness of dungeons, and their strength sapped by the pestilence of servitude, are they capable of marching toward the august temple of Liberty without faltering? Can they come near enough to bask in its brilliant rays and to breathe freely the pure air which reigns therein?

Legislators, meditate well before you choose. Forget not that you are to lay the political foundation for a newly born nation which can rise to the heights of greatness that Nature has marked out for it if you but proportion this foundation in keeping with the high plane that it aspires to attain. Unless your choice is based upon the peculiar tutelary experience of the Venezuelan people—a factor that should guide you in determining the nature and form of government you are about to adopt for the well-being of the people—and, I repeat, unless you happen upon the right type of government, the result of our reforms will again be slavery. . . .

Despite these bitter reflections, I experience a surge of joy when I witness the great advances that our Republic has made since it began its noble career. Loving what is most useful, animated by what is most just, and aspiring to what is most perfect, Venezuela, on breaking away from Spain has recovered her independence, her freedom, her equality, and her national sovereignty. By establishing a democratic republic, she has proscribed monarchy, distinctions, nobility, prerogatives, and privileges. She has declared for the rights of man and freedom of action, thought, speech, and press. These eminently liberal acts, because of the sincerity that has inspired them, will never cease to be admired. The first Congress of Venezuela has indelibly stamped upon the annals of our laws the majesty of the people, and, in placing its seal upon the social document best calculated to develop the well-being of the nation, that Congress has fittingly given expression to this thought. . . .

The more I admire the excellence of the federal Constitution of Venezuela, the more I am convinced of the impossibility of its application to our state. And, to my way of thinking it is a marvel that its prototype in North America endures so successfully and has not been overthrown at the first sign of adversity or danger. Although the people of North America are a singular model of political virtue and moral rectitude; although that nation was cradled in liberty, reared on freedom, and maintained by liberty alone; and—I must reveal everything—although those people, so lacking in many respects, are unique in the history of mankind, it is a marvel, I repeat, that so weak and complicated a government as the federal system has managed to govern them in the difficult and trying circumstances of their past. But, regardless of the effectiveness of this form of government with respect to North America, I must say that it has never for a moment entered my mind to compare the position and character of two states as dissimilar as the English-American and the Spanish-American. Would it not be most difficult to apply to Spain the English system of political, civil, and religious liberty? Hence, it would be even more difficult to adapt to Venezuela the laws of North America. Does not *L'Esprit des lois* state that laws should be suited to the people for whom they are made; that it would be a major coincidence if those of one nation could be adapted to another; that laws must take into account the physical conditions of the country, climate, character of the land, location, size, and mode of living of the people; that they should be in keeping with the degree of liberty that the Constitution can sanction respecting the religion of the inhabitants, their inclinations, resources, number, commerce, habits, and customs? This is the code we must consult, not the code of Washington! . . .

The Monroe Doctrine, 1823

The United States government watched closely as the Latins fought for their independence but made no effort to aid them. The policy of the fledgling nation of North America contained no element of crusade on behalf of freedom and democracy elsewhere. Instead, the United States applied to the Southern hemisphere the principle of non-involvement that guided its relations with Europe. Any temptation to abet republicanism among its New World neighbors succumbed to an unwillingness to become involved in foreign wars. America's foreign policy had been since its founding and was long to remain isolation from the concerns of others.

Nonetheless, the United States could not ignore European designs on the Americas. In the 1820s, the European powers were reacting severely to the liberal doctrines generated by the French Revolution and disseminated by Napoleon. Russia and France both appeared ready to aid Spain in repressing the Latin American revolutions. The United States was apprehensive that substantial European armies might soon be crossing the seas.

Britain, ostensibly, was a party to the reactionary objectives of the continental monarchs but, fortunately for the United States, shared the determination that no new European empire be established in South America. Britain still feared a resumption of its old colonial rivalry with France. In 1823, the British proposed to the United States that a joint warning be issued to keep the continental countries from interfering with the Latin American uprisings. The United States contemplated the British overture for a time, then decided to act on its own.

By 1823, the United States was a half-century old and feeling the satisfactions of strength and maturity. It had survived two foreign wars, one official and one undeclared, and had steadily expanded its frontiers. It had begun to think of itself in terms of a great destiny. The Americans, while loyal to their foreign policy principles, were ready to give them an aggressive interpretation. The result was the Monroe Doctrine.

President James Monroe expressed the new doctrine unobtrusively in his annual message to Congress on December 2, 1823. It was a warning to the European powers that the United States, while respecting the status quo, would not tolerate further intrusion by them into the affairs of the Americas. The United States thus assumed a proprietary responsibility for the Western hemisphere. The Monroe Doctrine was not an expression of political idealism but a strategy for national security. Despite the pretentions of the assertive new nation, it was the British Navy and not the United States that, for more than a century, enforced the Monroe Doctrine. Nonetheless, the Monroe Doctrine was the signal that the New World had come of age. After three centuries as child and dependent, the New World was now giving orders to the Old. Western civilization had shifted some of its weight toward America.

The following excerpts of the President's message of 1823 contain the expression of national policy known as the Monroe Doctrine.

Document 51

With the movements in this hemisphere we are of necessity more immediately connected, and by causes which must be obvious to all enlightened and impartial observers.

The political system of the allied powers is essentially different in this respect from that of America. This difference proceeds from that which exists in their respective governments; and to the defense of our own which has been achieved by the loss of so much blood and treasure, and matured by the wisdom of their most enlightened citizens and under which we have enjoyed unexampled felicity, this whole nation is devoted. We owe it, therefore, to candor and to the amicable relations existing between the United States and those powers, to declare that we should consider any attempt on their part to extend their system to any portion of this hemisphere as dangerous to our peace and safety.

With the existing colonies or dependencies of any European power we have not interfered and shall not interfere. But with the governments who have declared their independence and maintained it, and whose independence we have, on great consideration and on just principles, acknowledged, we could not view any interposition for the purpose of oppressing them, or controlling in any other manner their destiny, by any European power in any other light than as the manifestation of an unfriendly disposition towards the United States.

In the war between those new governments and Spain we declared our neutrality at the time of their recognition, and to this we have adhered, and shall continue to adhere, provided no change shall occur which, in the judgment of the competent authorities of this government shall make a corresponding change on the part of the United States indispensable to their security.

The late events in Spain and Portugal show that Europe is still unsettled. Of this important fact no stronger proof can be adduced than that the allied powers should have thought it proper, on any principle satisfactory to themselves, to have interposed by force in the internal concerns of Spain.

To what extent such interposition may be carried, on the same principle, is a question in which all independent powers whose governments differ from theirs are interested, even those most remote, and surely none more so than the United States. Our policy in regard to Europe, which was adopted at an early stage of the wars which have so long agitated that quarter of the globe, nevertheless remains the same, which is, not to interfere in the internal concerns of any of its powers; to consider the government *de facto* as the legitimate government for us; to cultivate friendly relations with it, and to preserve those relations by a frank, firm, and manly policy, meeting in all instances the just claims of every power, submitting to injuries from none.

But in regard to these continents, circumstances are eminently and conspicuously different. It is impossible that the allied powers should extend their political system to any portion of either continent without endangering our peace and happiness; nor can any one believe that our southern brethren, if left to themselves, would adopt it of their own accord. It is equally impossible, therefore, that we should behold such interposition in any form with indifference. If we look to the comparative strength and resources of Spain and those new governments, and their distance from each other, it must be obvious that she can never subdue them.

It is still the true policy of the United States to leave the parties to themselves, in the hope that other powers will pursue the same course.

VIII

The French Revolution

VIII

The French Revolution

The French monarchical state, having reached a peak of efficiency and prestige in the early years of Louis XIV's reign, disintegrated steadily as the great king grew older. His incessant wars and his luxurious living imposed on the nation an enormous burden. Had they been accompanied by equitable and responsible financial policies, the condition of the state might have remained sound, for France was a rich country and its people were industrious. But after Colbert died, Louis showed no further interest in fiscal matters and the government, in order to survive, resorted to a variety of financial expedients. New and heavier taxes were imposed, which fell—because the nobility remained exempt—on the middle-class and an already overburdened peasantry. Such old abuses as the creation of useless offices and hereditary ranks were revived. Expenditures were cut not for the extravagant court but in the construction of roads, in subsidies to commerce and industry and in developing the colonies, all of which further weakened the economy. Louis XIV's financial policies alienated the bourgeoisie and the peasantry from the crown, as his religious policies had alienated the Huguenots. Only the nobility, whose privileges the state preserved intact, remained beholden to the monarchy, but the nobility was now useless and impotent. By the time of Louis XIV's death in 1715, the exhausting quest for *grandeur* had seriously mortgaged the monarchy's future.

Louis XV, successor to the throne, did nothing to retard the disintegration. During his reign, France fought unproductive continental wars and managed to lose most of its remaining American empire to the English. Louis XV's government could barely perform the most commonplace administrative functions.

Turgot's Letter to Louis XVI, 1774

Louis XVI came to the throne in 1774 amid much hope. Though he was young, he had already established a reputation as a humanitarian. Like most members of the French elite of the mid-eighteenth century, he seemed committed to the rationalist philosophy of the Enlightenment. This philosophy, far from being antimonarchical, preached the application of reason to the traditional institutions of government. In some European countries, monarchs prided themselves on their philosophical dedication to "Enlightened Despotism." Louis XVI, who certainly thought of himself as an Enlightenment king, chose as his finance minister the upright Turgot, himself a member of the *philosophe* group of thinkers who gave the movement direction and drive. Turgot, regarded by Voltaire as the last hope of France, vowed both his devotion and his determination to Louis XVI. But aware that the king, for all his warm qualities, was irresolute and weak, he was frankly skeptical of the prospects for success.

On August 24, 1774, Turgot wrote the king a letter outlining the program he proposed to pursue, along with the apprehensions he felt about his grant of authority to pursue them. Turgot's apprehensions proved justified. The more rigorously he applied his policies, the more opposition he stirred up. Louis XVI encountered complaints from his wife, the prodigal Marie Antoinette; from the bankers and tax-collectors, who preferred the loose old ways; and from the masses, who objected to Turgot's austerity. The king dismissed Turgot after twenty-one months in office. The adventure in Enlightenment government, the experiment in fiscal responsibility, came to naught. After Turgot the slide toward disaster became even steeper.

Turgot's letter to the King, with its ray of hope and its ring of doom, is reproduced here.

Document 52

Compiegne, August 24, 1774

Sire:

Having just come from the private interview with which your Majesty has honored me, still full of the anxiety produced by the immensity of the duties now imposed upon me, agitated by all the feelings excited by the touching kindness with which you have encouraged me, I hasten to convey to you my respectful gratitude and the devotion of my whole life.

Your Majesty has been good enough to permit me to place on record the engagement you have taken upon you to sustain me in the execution of those plans of economy which are at all times, and to-day more than ever, an indispensable necessity. . . . At this moment, sire, I confine myself to recalling to you these three items:

No bankruptcy.

No increase of taxes.

No loans.

No *bankruptcy*, either avowed or disguised by illegal seductions.

No *increase of taxes;* the reason for this lying in the condition of your people, and, still more, in that of your Majesty's own generous heart.

No *loans;* because every loan always diminishes the free revenue and necessitates, at the end of a certain time, either bankruptcy or the increase of taxes. In times of peace it is permissible to borrow only in order to liquidate old debts, or in order to redeem other loans contracted on less advantageous terms.

To meet these three points there is but one means. It is to reduce expenditure below the revenue, and sufficiently below it to insure each year a saving of twenty millions, to be applied to redemption of the old debts. Without that, the first gunshot will force the state into bankruptcy.

The question will be asked incredulously, "On what can we retrench?" and each one, speaking for his own department, will maintain that nearly every particular item of expense is indispensable. They will be able to allege very good reasons, but these must all yield to the absolute necessity of economy. . . .

These are the matters which I have been permitted to recall to your Majesty. You will not forget that in accepting the place of comptroller general I have felt the full value of the confidence with which you honor me; I have felt that you intrust to me the happiness of your people, and, if it be permitted to me to say so, the care of promoting among your people the love of your person and of your authority.

At the same time I feel all the danger to which I expose myself. I foresee that I shall be alone in fighting against abuses of every kind, against the power of those who profit by these abuses, against the crowd of prejudiced people who oppose themselves to all reform, and who are such powerful instruments in the hands of interested parties for perpetuating the disorder. I shall have to struggle even against the natural goodness and generosity of your Majesty, and of the persons who are most dear to you. I shall be feared, hated even, by nearly all the court, by all who solicit favors. They will impute to me all the refusals; they will describe me as a hard man because I shall have advised your Majesty that you ought not to enrich even those that you love at the expense of your people's subsistence.

And this people, for whom I shall sacrifice myself, are so easily deceived that perhaps I shall encounter their hatred by the very measures I take to defend them against exactions. I shall be calumniated (having, perhaps, appearances against me) in order to deprive me of your Majesty's confidence. I shall not regret losing a place which I never solicited. I am ready to resign it to your Majesty as soon as I can no longer hope to be useful in it. . . .

Your Majesty will remember that it is upon the faith of your promises made to me that I charge myself with a burden perhaps beyond my strength, and it is to yourself personally, to the upright man, the just and good man, rather than to the king, that I give myself.

I venture to repeat here what you have already been kind enough to hear and approve of. The affecting kindness with which you condescended to press my hands within your own, as if sealing my devotion, will never be effaced from my memory. It will sustain my courage. It has forever united my personal happiness with the interest, the glory, and the happiness of your Majesty. It is with these sentiments that I am, sire, etc.

Decree to Abolish the Feudal System, 1789

The French Revolution was not directed against the monarchical state, as such. It was the collapse of the state that released the fury of the Revolution. Once the state ceased to act as a barrier, angry Frenchmen turned their attention to the real source of their grievances—the feudal system. Fundamentally, the French Revolution was a revolt against feudalism.

For three centuries or more, feudal institutions had survived in France without serving the purpose for which they were devised, without in fact serving any useful purpose at all. In the Middle Ages, the nobility had acquired such rights as the dispensing of justice and such privileges as the exemption from taxation, in return for which it provided military service. But the nobles no longer protected the realm and their justice had been replaced by ever growing injustice. Similarly the Church no longer fulfilled the responsibilities acquired for its privileges and, like the nobility, had become a social parasite. France, in 1789, was not aggrieved at the institution of monarchy, which retained its image as protector against aristocratic and clerical abuses. The monarchy, however, stood between the Revolution and its objectives. When it collapsed, the Revolution simply trampled over it.

Louis XVI and his inept ministers had brought the *ancien régime* to the point of bankruptcy. To escape its consequences, they decided to resurrect the decrepit *États généraux*, the Estates-General, medieval France's unsuccessful experiment with representative government. An assembly of France's noble, clerical and middle classes, the Estates-General had not been summoned since 1614, but the monarchy, in its desperation, decided to turn to it, though uncertain what precisely it was supposed to achieve.

Amid much pomp and considerable hope, but without any advance planning on the part of the king, the Estates-General opened in Versailles in May, 1789. Clearly the men of the dynamic middle-class, the Third Estate, dominated the gathering by their vigor and determination. Their interest was governmental reform, drastic enough to give them a share of the power but moderate enough to assure peace and stability. Louis XVI might have become their champion. By sanctioning a shift in power from aristocracy to middle-class, he would have given France a constitutional and moderate revolution, of which he would have been the leader. For a moment, in fact, Louis XVI seemed ready to be a revolutionary. But too dim-witted to recognize his dilemma and too irresolute to assume any initiative, he sided with the nobility and the clergy in defense of the feudal structure. He thus forced the Third Estate to choose between surrender and insurrection.

While the Third Estate tarried, mobs of Paris, too hungry and downtrodden for any loyalty to existing institutions, shattered the deadlock at Versailles and loosed the cascade. On July 14, prowling in search of arms and trouble, a surly Paris crowd stormed the Bastille, an old royal fortress where cannon were stored and political foes of the regime imprisoned. Here the first blood of the Revolution was shed. From the Bastille, symbol of royal despotism, violence quickly spread about the country. France was soon aflame. The moment for moderation had been lost.

On the night of August 4, 1789, the Viscount de Nouailles, once a fighter in America's war of independence, declared before the Estates-General—now reconstituted as the National Assembly—that feudal abuses were the sole source of France's passion. In an atmosphere charged with emotion, he pleaded with his fellow nobles to surrender the vestiges of their feudal power and restore justice in the country. Rapturously the Assembly applauded him. Responding like penitants, in bizarre fashion, nobles and clergy began vying with each other in sacrificing privileges. It seemed as if the feudal structure could not fall fast enough to suit them. For days resolutions of divestiture were passed. On August 11, the National Assembly enacted into law all of the fervid gestures of the preceding week. In this one great and strange episode, feudalism in France was dead.

The National Assembly's decree abolishing feudalism, though deeply revolutionary, is in many respects restrained. Its tone toward the king is deferential. It respects the rights of private property, including indemnification for seizure. It makes careful provision for a period of transition between old institutions and new. In its references to dovecotes and pigeon houses, which today sound so odd, it reveals how pervasive were the antiquated feudal abuses at which it was directed. The decree abolishing feudalism, presented below, is a middle-class document, meant for the modern world.

Document 53

Article I. The National Assembly hereby completely abolishes the feudal system. It decrees that, among the existing rights and dues, both feudal and *censuel*, all those originating in or representing real or personal serfdom shall be abolished without indemnification. All other dues are declared redeemable, the terms and mode of redemption to be fixed by the National Assembly. Those of the said dues which are not extinguished by this decree shall continue to be collected until indemnification shall take place.

II. The exclusive right to maintain pigeon houses and dovecotes is abolished. The pigeons shall be confined during the seasons fixed by the community. During such periods they shall be looked upon as game, and every one shall have the right to kill them upon his own land.

III. The exclusive right to hunt and to maintain uninclosed warrens is likewise abolished, and every landowner shall have the right to kill, or to have destroyed on his own land, all kinds of game, observing, however, such police regulations as may be established with a view to the safety of the public.

All hunting *capitaineries* [preserves], including the royal forests, and all hunting rights under whatever denomination, are likewise abolished. Provision shall be made, however, in a manner compatible with the regard due to property and liberty, for maintaining the personal pleasures of the king.

The president of the Assembly shall be commissioned to ask of the king the recall of those sent to the galleys or exiled, simply for violations of the hunting regulations, as well as for the release of those at present imprisoned for offenses of this kind, and the dismissal of such cases as are now pending.

IV. All manorial courts are hereby suppressed without indemnification. But the magistrates of these courts shall continue to perform their functions until such time as the National Assembly shall provide for the establishment of a new judicial system.

V. Tithes of every description, as well as the dues which have been substituted for them, under whatever denomination they are known or collected (even when compounded for), possessed by secular or regular congregations, by holders of benefices, members of corporations (including the Order of Malta and other religious and military orders), as well as those devoted to the maintenance of churches, those impropriated to lay persons, and those substituted for the *portion congrue*, are abolished, on condition, however, that some other method be devised to provide for the expenses of divine worship, the support of the officiating clergy, for the assistance of the poor, for repairs and rebuilding of churches and parsonages, and for the maintenance of all institutions, seminaries, schools, academies, asylums, and organizations to which the present funds are devoted. Until such provision shall be made and the former possessors shall enter upon the enjoyment of an income on the new system, the National Assembly decrees that the said tithes shall continue to be collected according to law and in the customary manner.

Other tithes, of whatever nature they may be, shall be redeemable in such manner as the Assembly shall determine. Until this matter is adjusted, the National Assembly decrees that these, too, shall continue to be collected.

VI. All perpetual ground rents, payable either in money or in kind, of whatever nature they may be, whatever their origin and to whomsoever they may be due, . . . shall be redeemable at a rate fixed by the Assembly. No due shall in the future be created which is not redeemable.

VII. The sale of judicial and municipal offices shall be abolished forthwith. Justice shall be dispensed *gratis*. Nevertheless the magistrates at present holding such offices shall continue to exercise their functions and to receive their emoluments until the Assembly shall have made provision for indemnifying them.

VIII. The fees of the country priests are abolished, and shall be discontinued so soon as provision shall be made for increasing the minimum salary (*portion congrue*) of the parish priests and the payment to the curates. A regulation shall be drawn up to determine the status of the priests in the towns.

IX. Pecuniary privileges, personal or real, in the payment of taxes are abolished forever. Taxes shall be collected from all the citizens, and from all property, in the same manner and in the same form. Plans shall be considered by which the taxes shall be paid proportionally by all, even for the last six months of the current year.

X. Inasmuch as a national constitution and public liberty are of more advantage to the provinces than the privileges which some of these enjoy, and inasmuch as the surrender of such privileges is essential to the intimate union of all parts of the realm, it is decreed that all the peculiar privileges, pecuniary or otherwise, of the provinces, principalities, districts, cantons, cities, and communes, are once for all abolished and are absorbed into the law common to all Frenchmen.

XI. All citizens, without distinction of birth, are eligible to any office or dignity, whether ecclesiastical, civil, or military and no profession shall imply any derogation.

XII. Hereafter no remittances shall be made for annates or for any other purpose to the court of Rome, the vice legation at Avignon, or to the nunciature at Lucerne. The clergy of the diocese shall apply to their bishops in regard to the filling of benefices and dispensations, the which shall be granted *gratis* without regard to reservations, expectancies, and papal months, all the churches of France enjoying the same freedom.

XIII. (This article abolishes various ecclesiastical dues.)

XIV. Pluralities shall not be permitted hereafter in cases where the revenue from the benefice or benefices held shall exceed the sum of three thousand livres. Nor shall any individual be allowed to enjoy several pensions from benefices, or a pension and a benefice, if the revenue which he already enjoys from such sources exceeds the same sum of three thousand livres.

XV. The National Assembly shall consider, in conjunction with the king, the report which is to be submitted to it relating to pensions, favors, and salaries, with a view to suppressing all such as are not deserved, and reducing those which shall prove excessive; and the amount shall be fixed which the king may in the future disburse for this purpose.

XVI. The National Assembly decrees that a medal shall be struck in memory of the recent grave and important deliberations for the welfare of France, and that a Te Deum shall be chanted in gratitude in all the parishes and churches of France.

XVII. The National Assembly solemnly proclaims the king, Louis XVI, the *Restorer of French Liberty.*

XVIII. The National Assembly shall present itself in a body before the king, in order to submit to him the decrees which have just been passed, to tender to him the tokens of its most respectful gratitude, and to pray him to permit the Te Deum to be chanted in his chapel, and to be present himself at this service.

XIX. The National Assembly shall consider, immediately after the constitution, the drawing up of the laws necessary for the development of the principles which it has laid down in the present decree. The latter shall be transmitted by the deputies without delay to all the provinces, together with the decree of the 10th of this month, in order that it may be printed, published, read from the parish pulpits and posted up wherever it shall be deemed necessary.

Declaration of the Rights of Man and of the Citizen, 1789

The French Revolution quickly took on momentum. The Assembly was flooded with demands for a declaration of rights, on the model of the British Bill of Rights and the American Declaration of Independence. Members enthusiastically went to work on such a document. They frequently consulted with Thomas Jefferson, author of the American Declaration of Independence, who was then serving as United States Minister to France. On August 26, the National Assembly approved the Declaration of the Rights of Man and of the Citizen. It became, with the decree abolishing feudalism, the foundation of the Revolution.

The Declaration of the Rights of Man and of the Citizen is the apotheosis of eighteenth century political idealism. It was meant to be universal, applicable not just to Frenchmen but to all men. More than any other document, it established the ideal of freedom for Western civilization. The Declaration was republican in character, claiming political sovereignty for the people, though the Revolution still did not plan to shed the monarchy. It was also bourgeois in the esteem it expressed for property and order. It was defiantly anti-feudal, denouncing feudal vestiges as evil. It was full of hopes and dreams, like the Revolution itself in 1789.

The Declaration remained the gospel of revolutionaries for most of a century, until a new doctrine came along to challenge it. But it continues today to be a goal toward which many peoples aspire. The Declaration of the Rights of Man and of the Citizen, which follows below, is one of the lasting triumphs of the French Revolution.

Document 54

The representatives of the French people, organized as a National Assembly, believing that the ignorance, neglect, or contempt of the rights of man are the sole cause of public calamities and of the corruption of governments, have determined to set forth in a solemn declaration the natural, unalienable, and sacred rights of man, in order that this declaration, being constantly before all the members of the Social body, shall remind them continually of their rights and duties; in order that the acts of the legislative power, as well as those of the executive power, may be compared at any moment with the objects and purposes of all political institutions and may thus be more respected, and, lastly, in order that the grievances of the citizens, based hereafter upon simple and incontestable principles, shall tend to the maintenance of the constitution and redound to the happiness of all. Therefore the National Assembly recognizes and proclaims, in the presence and under the auspices of the Supreme Being, the following rights of man and of the citizen:

Article 1. Men are born and remain free and equal in rights. Social distinctions may be founded only upon the general good.

2. The aim of all political association is the preservation of the natural and imprescriptible rights of man. These rights are liberty, property, security, and resistance to oppression.

3. The principle of all sovereignty resides essentially in the nation. No body nor individual may exercise any authority which does not proceed directly from the nation.

4. Liberty consists in the freedom to do everything which injures no one else; hence the exercise of the natural rights of each man has no limits except those which assure to the other members of the society the enjoyment of the same rights. These limits can only be determined by law.

5. Law can only prohibit such actions as are hurtful to society. Nothing may be prevented which is not forbidden by law, and no one may be forced to do anything not provided for by law.

6. Law is the expression of the general will. Every citizen has a right to participate personally, or through his representative, in its foundation. It must be the same for all, whether it protects or punishes. All citizens, being equal in the eyes of the law, are equally eligible to all dignities and to all public positions and occupations, according to their abilities, and without distinction except that of their virtues and talents.

7. No person shall be accused, arrested, or imprisoned except in the cases and according to the forms prescribed by law. Any one soliciting, transmitting, executing, or causing to be executed, any arbitrary order, shall be punished. But any citizen summoned or arrested in virtue of the law shall submit without delay, as resistance constitutes an offense.

8. The law shall provide for such punishments only as are strictly and obviously necessary, and no one shall suffer punishment except it be legally inflicted in virtue of a law passed and promulgated before the commission of the offense.

9. As all persons are held innocent until they shall have been declared guilty, if arrest shall be deemed indispensable, all harshness not essential to the securing of the prisoner's person shall be severely repressed by law.

10. No one shall be disquieted on account of his opinions, including his religious views, provided their manifestation does not disturb the public order established by law.

11. The free communication of ideas and opinions is one of the most precious of the rights of man. Every citizen may, accordingly, speak, write, and print with freedom, but shall be responsible for such abuses of this freedom as shall be defined by law.

12. The security of the rights of man and of the citizen requires public military forces. These forces are, therefore, established for the good of all and not for the personal advantage of those to whom they shall be intrusted.

13. A common contribution is essential for the maintenance of the public forces and for the cost of administration. This should be equitably distributed among all the citizens in proportion to their means.

14. All the citizens have a right to decide, either personally or by their representatives, as to the necessity of the public contribution; to grant this freely; to know to what uses it is put; and to fix the proportion, the mode of assessment and of collection and the duration of the taxes.

15. Society has the right to require of every public agent an account of his administration.

16. A society in which the observance of the law is not assured, nor the separation of powers defined, has no constitution at all.

17. Since property is an inviolable and sacred right, no one shall be deprived thereof except where public necessity, legally determined, shall clearly demand it, and then only on condition that the owner shall have been previously and equitably indemnified.

Civil Constitution of the Clergy, 1790

The National Assembly, having established itself as the government of France under a system of constitutional monarchy, continued to face the bankruptcy produced by the *ancien régime*. In its desperate search for funds to run the country, the Assembly found conveniently available the wealth of the Church. Unlike the monarchy, the Revolution did not depend on the Church for support. It was painless for the Assembly to expropriate the clerical wealth. On April 10, 1790, ecclesiastical possessions were declared the property of the nation.

Since the Assembly did not intend to abolish the Church, the confiscation compelled the creation of a civil budget for the conduct of religious worship. Having acknowledged its responsibility for financing the Church, the Assembly then proceeded to draw up rules to govern the Church's operations. The Civil Constitution of the Clergy, the third of the basic documents of the Revolution, made the Church, in effect, an agency of the government. The Assembly completely reorganized ecclesiastical administration, as it had recently done with civil administration, applying the logical standards so exalted by the Enlightenment. The Assembly abolished the old dioceses and made the new ones coincide with the *départements*, the new units of civil administration. It provided for popular election of the clergy and virtual independence from Rome. Most controversially, the Assembly required the clergy to swear an oath of loyalty to the king and to the new constitution of the state. The Civil Constitution of the Clergy swept away the feudal organization of the Church and extended the Revolution into the field of religion.

The Civil Constitution of the Clergy ended the virtual unanimity with which France had received the Revolution's changes. The required oath was the Revolution's first major divisive act. All but a few bishops refused to swear. The parish clergy, which was heavily sympathetic to the Revolution, split into sworn and refractory priests. The Pope condemned the Civil Constitution of the Clergy and thereby persuaded Louis XVI to change his attitude toward the Revolution. The king, a devout Catholic, began to think less of cooperating with the Revolution and more about overturning it. The Civil Constitution introduced the first note of ugliness into the heady Revolutionary spirit.

Whatever its political repercussions, the Civil Constitution of the Clergy effected lasting ecclesiastical reforms. In the Church, as in state and social organization, feudalism was formally erased forever. The chief articles, presented below, illustrate the Revolution's pursuit of logic, order, symmetry and uniformity.

Document 55

The National Assembly, after having heard the report of the ecclesiastical committee, has decreed and do decree the following as constitutional articles:

Title I

Article I. Each department shall form a single diocese, and each diocese shall have the same extent and the same limits as the department.

II. The seat of the bishoprics of the eighty-three departments of the kingdom shall be established as follows: that of the department of the Lower Seine at Rouen; that of the department of Calvados at Bayeux; . . .

All other bishoprics in the eighty-three departments of the kingdom, which are not included by name in the present article, are, and forever shall be, abolished. . . .

IV. No church or parish of France nor any French citizen may acknowledge upon any occasion, or upon any pretext whatsoever, the authority of an ordinary bishop or of an archbishop whose see shall be under the supremacy of a foreign power, nor that of his representatives residing in France or elsewhere; without prejudice, however, to the unity of the faith and the intercourse which shall be maintained with the visible head of the universal Church, as hereafter provided. . . .

XX. All titles and offices other than those mentioned in the present constitution, dignities, canonries, prebends, half prebends, chapels, chaplainships, both in cathedral and collegiate churches, all regular and secular chapters for either sex, abbacies and priorships, both regular and *in commendam*, for either sex, as well as all other benefices and prestimonies in general, of whatever kind or denomination, are from the day of this decree extinguished and abolished and shall never be reestablished in any form.

Title II

Article I. Beginning with the day of publication of the present decree, there shall be but one mode of choosing bishops and parish priests, namely that of election.

II. All elections shall be by ballot and shall be decided by the absolute majority of the votes.

III. The election of bishops shall take place according to the forms and by the electoral body designated in the decree of December 22, 1789, for the election of members of the departmental assembly. . . .

VI. The election of a bishop can only take place or be undertaken upon Sunday, in the principal church of the chief town of the department, at the close of the parish mass, at which all the electors are required to be present. . . .

XIX. The new bishop may not apply to the pope for any form of confirmation, but shall write to him, as to the visible head of the universal Church, as a testimony to the unity of faith and communion maintained with him. . . .

XXI. Before the ceremony of consecration begins, the bishop elect shall take a solemn oath, in the presence of the municipal officers, of the people, and of the clergy, to guard with care the faithful of his diocese who are confided to him, to be loyal to the nation, the law, and the king, and to support with all his power the constitution decreed by the National Assembly and accepted by the king. . . .

XXV. The election of the parish priests shall take place according to the forms and by the electors designated in the decree of December 22, 1789, for the election of members of the administrative assembly of the district. . . .

XL. Bishoprics and parishes shall be looked upon as vacant until those elected to fill them shall have taken the oath above mentioned.

Title III

Article I. The ministers of religion, performing as they do the first and most important functions of society and forced to live continuously in the place where they discharge the offices to which they have been called by the confidence of the people, shall be supported by the nation.

II. Every bishop, priest, and officiating clergyman in a chapel of ease shall be furnished with a suitable dwelling, on condition, however, that the occupant shall make all the necessary current repairs. This shall not affect at present, in any way, those parishes where the priest now receives a money equivalent instead of his dwelling. The departments shall, moreover, have cognizance of suits arising in this connection, brought by the parishes and by the priests. Salaries shall be assigned to each, as indicated below.

III. The bishop of Paris shall receive fifty thousand livres; the bishops of the cities having a population of fifty thousand or more, twenty thousand livres; other bishops, twelve thousand livres. . . .

V. The salaries of the parish priests shall be as follows: in Paris, six thousand livres; in cities having a population of fifty thousand or over, four thousand livres; in those having a population of less than fifty thousand and more than ten thousand, three thousand livres; in cities and towns of which the population is below ten thousand and more than three thousand, twenty-four hundred livres. . . .

VII. The salaries *in money* of the ministers of religion shall be paid every three months, in advance, by the treasurer of the district. . . .

XII. In view of the salary which is assured to them by the present constitution, the bishops, parish priests, and curates, shall perform the episcopal and priestly functions *gratis*.

Title IV

Article I. The law requiring the residence of ecclesiastics in the districts under their charge shall be strictly observed. All vested with an ecclesiastical office or function shall be subject to this, without distinction or exception. . . .

VI. Bishops, parish priests, and curates may, as active citizens, be present at the primary and electoral assemblies; they may be chosen electors, or as deputies to the legislative body, or as members of the general council of the communes or of the administrative councils of their districts or departments.

Louis XVI's Letter to the King of Prussia, 1791

Louis XVI finally decided to break with the Revolution by fleeing Paris. On the night of June 20, 1791, he crowded the royal family into a coach and headed for the frontier, where a French army presumably loyal to him was waiting. At Varennes, not far from the border, the royal family was recognized and apprehended, then brought back to the capital as prisoners. The spell which united the Revolution and the throne was broken. France's long love affair with the monarchy had given way openly to mutual loathing. A republic was now inevitable.

The Paris mobs were ready to depose the king at once. But the bourgeoisie, which retained a majority in the Assembly, still hesitated to form any government more radical than a constitutional monarchy. The two forces physically clashed at the Champ de Mars on July 17, 1791, when soldiers under the Assembly's command fired on a large crowd demonstrating against the crown. The "Massacre of the Champ de Mars" became a symbol of class warfare, a fresh element in the Revolution. After the Champ de Mars, the Assembly continued its work of writing a constitution for a limited monarchy, which it finished in September. In an illusion of national reconciliation, King Louis XVI himself appeared before the Assembly to receive it and to pledge himself to its execution.

But the Assembly elected under the new constitution, called the Legislative, was far more radical than its predecessor. Though it did not strike out immediately against the monarchy, its membership and its debate, as well as its early decrees, suggested that it intended to oust the royal family. The king began to look for help outside France's borders, where powerful dynasties and disaffected emigrés waited for an opportunity to overthrow the Revolution they detested and feared. It was no secret in Paris at the end of 1791 that Louis XVI would welcome foreign intervention on his behalf.

In 1792, Revolutionary France went to war against the principal crowned heads of Europe, largely on its own initiative. That the king and the court were secretly assisting the enemy was widely suspected but not substantiated. On July 25, 1792, the Duke of Brunswick, commander of the enemy armies, openly declared himself an ally of the French king. Nothing could more certainly have sealed the king's doom. France became aroused, both against the king and the invaders, now regarded virtually as one. In the passion of national danger, the extreme radicals of the Legislative seized power and, burning their bridges behind them, determined to execute the king. In the king's records they found evidence sufficient to incriminate him as a conspirator with foreign powers. On January 16, 1793, the Legislative by a small margin voted the death penalty for Louis XVI. Five days later he was executed. In the heat of war, over the body of the king, the republic was founded.

Louis XVI's letter to the King of Prussia, dated December 3, 1791, was not found until after the execution. But it was most conclusive proof that Louis had conspired with the enemies of the state. The text of the letter has been looked upon as the Revolution's vindication for regicide.

Document 56

Paris, December 3, 1791

My Brother;

I have learned through M. du Moustier of the interest which your Majesty has expressed not only in my person but also in the welfare of my kingdom. In giving me these proofs, the attitude of your Majesty has, in all cases where your interest might prove advantageous to my people, excited my lively appreciation. I confidently take advantage of it at this time when, in spite of the fact that I have accepted the new constitution, seditious leaders are openly exhibiting their purpose of entirely destroying the remnants of the monarchy. I have just addressed myself to the emperor, the empress of Russia, and to the kings of Spain and Sweden; I am suggesting to them the idea of a congress of the chief powers of Europe, supported by an armed force, as the best means of checking seditious parties, of establishing a more desirable order of things, and of preventing the evil which afflicts us from reaching the other states of Europe.

I trust that your Majesty will approve my ideas, and that you will maintain the most absolute secrecy about the proposition I am making to you. You will easily understand that the circumstances in which I find myself force me to observe the greatest caution. That is why no one but the Baron of Breteuil is informed of my plans, and your Majesty may therefore communicate to him anything you wish. . . .

Your good brother,
LOUIS.

Proclamation on Spreading the Revolution, 1792

The armies of the Revolution defeated the Duke of Brunswick and his invading force at Valmy on September 20, 1792. The immediate threat was overcome and French columns began a pursuit of the retreating enemy into Belgium and Germany. In their baggage, France's triumphant soldiers carried the intoxicating ideas of the Revolution.

Though the Revolution had at first pledged an end to wars of conquest, France—even in revolutionary exultation—could not resist the temptation to drive to its "natural boundaries." Clearly Paris was perplexed at the problem of justifying its aggression. Finally, the Revolutionary government announced a policy of building a ring of independent countries on France's frontiers, to which would be introduced the blessings of the Revolution. Thus military and spiritual goals were made to coincide.

The Republican government went a step further on December 15, 1792, when it issued a proclamation designating the armies of France the vehicle for disseminating liberty and reform throughout Europe. The proclamation, presented below, was intended for the inhabitants of countries occupied by French soldiers. Though it was, to be sure, an excuse for an aggressive foreign policy, it also reflects the sincere belief in the universality of revolutionary doctrine that undoubtedly animated most Frenchmen. Nonetheless, the proclamation put Europe on notice that Revolutionary France was determined to upset the traditional balance of continental power. The Revolution's dynamism would lead to decades of war.

Document 57

The French people to the people of ; brothers and friends:

We have conquered our liberty and we shall maintain it. We offer to bring this inestimable blessing to you, for it has always been rightly ours, and only by a crime have our oppressors robbed us of it. We have driven out your tyrants. Show yourselves free men and we will protect you from their vengeance, their machinations, or their return.

From this moment, the French nation proclaims the sovereignty of the people, the suppression of all civil and military authorities which have hitherto governed you and of all the taxes which you bear, under whatever form, the abolition of the tithe, of feudalism, of seigniorial rights and monopolies of every kind, of serfdom, whether real or personal, of hunting and fishing privileges, of the *corvée,* the salt tax, the tolls and local imposts, and, in general, of all the various kinds of taxes with which you have been loaded by your usurpers; it also proclaims the abolition among you of all noble and ecclesiastical corporations and of all prerogatives and privileges opposed to equality. You are, from this moment, brothers and friends; all are citizens, equal in rights, and all are alike called to govern, to serve, and to defend your country.

IX

Napoleon and the Reaction

IX

Napoleon and the Reaction

The Revolution, after the execution of the king, rolled on to greater and greater excess, as if men were no longer able to bring to bear the force of reason to control its direction. Involvement in foreign wars provided pretext for the Terror, when the most radical of the elected representatives invoked virtue to do away with the more moderate, and blood flowed freely over the cobblestones of Paris. After the Terror ran its course and devoured its own leaders, the inevitable revulsion set in, known historically as the Thermidorian Reaction. In 1795, the survivors of the Convention, the representative assembly which had sanctioned the excesses of Robespierre, became the target of royalist counter-revolutionaries. It was saved by an armed force under the command of a young brigadier general named Napoleon Bonaparte, who acquired the reputation of a defender of the Revolution by firing into a royalist mob. But under the Convention, the Revolution in effect came to an end. It remained to be determined whether the Revolution's achievements would be wiped away or preserved.

The Coup d'état of 18 Brumaire, 1799

Successor to the Convention in 1795 was a Directory of five members, which acted as executive, and two chambers, the Five Hundred and the Elders, which served as the legislature. It was, however, an ineffective and corrupt regime in which rivals competed for power and problems went unresolved. The Directory failed to deal with poverty and hunger, while the people in Paris and in the provinces became more discontent and unruly. Though its armies continued to win victories abroad, the Directory generated increasing contempt. France seemed anxious to rescue the essentials from the Revolution, then put an end to bitterness, disorder and instability.

Bonaparte, son of a poor Corsican patriot, perceived these yearnings and decided that from them he could satisfy his own aspirations for power. In 1799, having won glory in Italy and in Egypt, he was the most popular man in France, though he was still not 30 years old. When the Abbé Sieyès, a shrewd intriguer inside the Directory, proposed to use Bonaparte as his sword in a *coup d'état*, the young general agreed to cooperate, scheming all the time to turn events to his own advantage. Napoleon was determined to make the *coup* the vehicle for his own designs.

The plan, presumably, was for Napoleon to appear before the Council of Five Hundred, overwhelm the members by his presence, then simply announce he was taking over the government. He would have the help of his brother Lucien, who was acting president of the body, which met in the relatively isolated suburb of Saint-Cloud to escape the pressure of the Paris mobs. On November 9, 1799—18 Brumaire by the Revolutionary calendar—Napoleon marched into the Council chamber and, before the hostile audience of parliamentarians, suddenly lost his composure. Cool a thousand times under fire, he almost fainted under the stares of politicians and would certainly have ruined the *coup* had not Lucien called upon the grenadiers to clear the hall. Acting according to plan, Lucien then summoned a handful of sympathetic members of the Council to serve as a rump body. They voted into power three consuls to succeed the Directory. One was Sieyès, who expected to rule. Another was a certain Roger-Ducos, who quickly disappeared from the scene. The third was Bonaparte, who emerged with little delay as the dominant member and dictator. Few disputed the legality of the new Consulate. France, wanting nothing more than domestic tranquillity, thus gave way to the Napoleonic regime.

On 19 Brumaire, Bonaparte issued a statement to the people of France giving his version of the *coup d'état*. That statement follows below. It is a highly colored version, resorting at times to outright fabrication. There was, for example, no genuine attempt at assassination. Certainly Napoleon's own role was far less heroic than he pretends. The statement succeeded, however, in persuading Frenchmen that he was the strong leader they needed. As a "soldier of liberty and a citizen devoted to the republic," Napoleon offered France the Revolution's virtues without its faults. France, which needed little persuasion, gratefully accepted the offer.

Document 58

19th Brumaire, 11 o'clock P.M.

To the People:

Frenchmen, on my return to France I found division reigning among all the authorities. They agreed only on this single point, that the constitution was half destroyed and was unable to protect liberty.

Each party in turn came to me, confided to me their designs, imparted their secrets, and requested my support. But I refused to be the man of a party.

The Council of Elders appealed to me. I answered their appeal. A plan of general restoration had been concerted by men whom the nation has been accustomed to regard as the defenders of liberty, equality, and property. This plan required calm deliberation, free from all influence and all fear. The Elders therefore resolved upon the removal of the legislative bodies to Saint-Cloud. They placed at my disposal the force necessary to secure their independence. I was bound, in duty to my fellow-citizens, to the soldiers perishing in our armies, and to the national glory acquired at the cost of so much blood, to accept the command.

The Council assembled at Saint-Cloud. Republican troops guaranteed their safety from without, but assassins created terror within. Many deputies in the Council of Five Hundred, armed with stilettos and pistols, spread the menace of death around them.

The plans which ought to have been developed were withheld. The majority of the Council was disorganized, the boldest orators were disconcerted, and the futility of submitting any salutary proposition was quite evident.

I proceeded, filled with indignation and chagrin, to the Council of the Elders. I besought them to carry their noble designs into execution. I directed their attention to the evils of the nation, which were their motives for conceiving those designs. They concurred in giving me new proofs of their unanimous good will.

I presented myself before the Council of the Five Hundred alone, unarmed, my head uncovered, just as the Elders had received and applauded me. My object was to restore to the majority the expression of its will and to secure to it its power.

The stilettos which had menaced the deputies were instantly raised against their deliverer. Twenty assassins rushed upon me and aimed at my breast. The grenadiers of the Legislative Body, whom I had left at the door of the hall, ran forward and placed themselves between me and the assassins. One of these brave grenadiers had his clothes pierced by a stiletto. They bore me out.

At the same moment cries of "Outlaw him!" were raised against the defender of the law. It was the horrid cry of assassins against the power destined to repress them. They crowded around the president [Lucien Bonaparte] uttering threats. With arms in their hands, they commanded him to declare me outlawed. I was informed of this. I ordered him to be rescued from their fury, and six grenadiers of the legislative body brought him out. Immediately afterwards some grenadiers of the legislative body charged the hall and cleared it.

The seditious, thus intimidated, dispersed and fled. The majority, freed from their assailants, returned freely and peaceably into the hall, listened to the propositions for the public safety, deliberated, and drew up the salutary resolution which will become the new and provisional law of the republic.

Frenchmen, you will doubtless recognize in this conduct the zeal of a soldier of liberty, of a citizen devoted to the republic. Conservative, judicial, and liberal ideas resumed their sway upon the dispersion of those seditious persons who had domineered in the councils and who proved themselves the most odious and contemptible of men.

BONAPARTE

Napoleon's Proclamation at Austerlitz, 1805

Napoleon's goal was to mold the Revolution to suit his own image. He was not anti-Revolutionary. He simply selected those facets of the Revolution that pleased him and rejected those that did not. Napoleon established a military dictatorship, thereby depriving Frenchmen of their liberty, but he retained the Revolution's social changes, which assured them of their equality. Napoleon's financial, ecclesiastical, judicial and educational innovations were brilliant and Revolutionary—in that they were anti-feudal—but they were also dictatorial. His enlightened administration won him the support of the business interests, the peasantry and the Catholics whom the Revolution had once alienated. Napoleon's firm hand restored the tranquillity that existed before 1789 without restoring the *ancien régime.*

In 1802, Napoleon appointed himself Consul for life. His decision was overwhelmingly confirmed in a popular plebiscite. But Napoleon was still not satisfied. His objective seemed to be not simply the acquisition of new titles but a kind of impregnation of himself and his family inside the traditions of France, so that Bonapartes would be what Bourbons had been. On December 2, 1804, Napoleon Bonaparte, in the presence of Pope Pius

VII in Paris's Church of Notre Dame, placed a crown upon his head and declared himself Napoleon I, Emperor of the French. He seemed to have confirmed thereby that he was, as he himself believed, France's "man of destiny."

Until he became Emperor, Napoleon's reign was characterized by peace, interrupted by a few easy victories on the battlefield. As first Consul, he showed more interest in consolidating himself at home than in adventures abroad. His spectacular victories were against the Austrians, who surrendered to France undisputed dominance of the continent. If Britain had been content to have France rule the land and France to have Britain rule the seas, the prospects after 1802 for an extended period of peace would have been good. Unfortunately, both were restless. France concentrated an army on the Channel coast, waiting for the opportunity to invade Britain. The British worked feverishly to rebuild the old continental coalition against France. In 1805, Britain put together the alliance known as the Third Coalition. Uniting Austria, Russia and Sweden, Britain's avowed purpose was to overthrow the Napoleonic regime.

Before the troops of the Third Coalition could menace the frontiers of France, Napoleon abandoned his plans to invade England, faced his army about and, after a long march, turned his finely trained troops on the Austrians near the town of Ulm in the Tyrols. Virtually without a fight, an Austrian army estimated at 100,000 men surrendered on October 20, 1805. Though Lord Nelson the next day sank the French fleet off Trafalgar and ended the French threat to the British Isles, Napoleon wasted no time on remorse. He seized Vienna, then pivoted to the north to meet an army of Austrians and Russians at Austerlitz. In a brilliant display of his military genius, Napoleon—on the first anniversary of his coronation—overwhelmed his adversaries. The Third Coalition was broken.

Napoleon's victory proclamation at Austerlitz, issued on December 3, 1805, flashed with the Emperor's confidence in himself and in France. He was exultant in his triumph and so were his soldiers. The proclamation, presented below, celebrated the Empire's finest moment.

Document 59

Soldiers, I am satisfied with you. In the battle of Austerlitz you have justified what I expected from your intrepidity. You have covered yourselves with eternal glory. An army of one hundred thousand men which was commanded by the emperors of Russia and Austria has been in less than four hours either cut off or dispersed. Those that escaped your swords have thrown themselves into the lakes. Forty stands of colors, the stands of the Russian imperial guard, one hundred and twenty pieces of cannon, twenty generals, and above thirty thousand prisoners are the fruits of this ever-memorable battle. Their infantry, so celebrated and so superior to you in numbers, has proved unable to resist your charge, and henceforth you have no rivals to fear.

Thus in less than two months the third coalition is conquered and dissolved. Peace cannot be far off; but, as I promised my people before crossing the Rhine, I will conclude it only upon terms consistent with my pledge, which shall secure not only the indemnification, but the reward, of my allies.

Soldiers, when the French people placed the imperial crown upon my head I trusted to you to enable me to maintain it in that splendor of glory which could alone give it value in my estimation. But at that moment our enemies entertained the design of tarnishing and degrading it; and the iron crown, which was gained by the blood of so many Frenchmen, they would have compelled me to place on the head of my bitterest foe,—an extravagant and foolish proposal, which you have brought to naught on the anniversary of your emperor's coronation. You have taught them that it is easier for them to defy and to threaten than to subdue us.

Soldiers, when everything necessary to the security, the happiness, and the prosperity of our country has been achieved, I will return you my thanks in France. Then will you be the objects of my tenderest care. My people will receive you with rapture and joy. To say to me, "I was in the battle of Austerlitz," will be enough to authorize the reply, "That is a brave man."

NAPOLEON

Headquarters at Austerlitz December 3, 1805.

The Berlin Decree, 1806

Napoleon's glittering triumph at Austerlitz concealed the fact that the seeds of his collapse had already been sown. He had created an empire that was too grandiose for a single man to supervise. He himself was losing the fine physical and intellectual edge that had given him such an advantage over his adversaries. He faced now all over Europe the fiery patriotism and the techniques of national mobilization that the French Revolution had spawned, then exported. He faced a Europe that no longer looked on Frenchmen as revolutionaries and liberators but as conquerors.

Napoleon's control of the continent began to slip away at the very moment his ambitions became most grandiose.

After Austerlitz, Napoleon—without a fleet—thought he had discovered the means of defeating England. He reasoned that he could overcome this "nation of shopkeepers," whose survival depended so heavily on foreign trade, by blockading it into poverty. Napoleon determined to close the ports of Europe to Britain's ships. Though he was aware that Europe wanted Britain's products as much as Britain wanted to deliver them, he was confident he could impose the blockade on Europe and enforce it with French arms.

Napoleon chose to announce his "continental system" for defeating Britain after a great victory. In October, 1806, he met the Prussian army at Jena, defeated it thoroughly and entered Berlin in triumph. On November 21, he issued the fateful proclamation. The Berlin Decree, extracts of which are presented below, seeks to justify France's action by citing British provocations. But Napoleon was not to win sympathy for the French. The continental system, which was barely enforceable at best, encountered resistance all over Europe. It proved far more damaging to Napoleon than to the British.

Document 60

From our Imperial Camp at Berlin
November 21, 1806

NAPOLEON, *emperor of the French and king of Italy, in consideration of the facts:*

1. That England does not recognize the system of international law universally observed by all civilized nations.

2. That she regards as an enemy every individual belonging to the enemy's state, and consequently makes prisoners of war not only of the crews of armed ships of war but of the crews of ships of commerce and merchantmen, and even of commercial agents and of merchants traveling on business.

3. That she extends to the vessels and commercial wares, and to the property of individuals, the right of conquest which is applicable only to the possessions of the belligerent power.

4. That she extends to unfortified towns and commercial ports, to harbors and the mouths of rivers, the right of blockade, which, in accordance with reason and the customs of all civilized nations, is applicable only to strong places. . . . That she has declared districts in a state of blockade which all her united forces would be unable to blockade, such as entire coasts and the whole of an empire.

5. That this monstrous abuse of the right of blockade has no other aim than to prevent communication among the nations and to raise the commerce and the industry of England upon the ruins of that of the continent. . . .

8. That it is a natural right to employ such arms against an enemy as he himself makes use of, and to combat in the same way as he combats. Since England has disregarded all ideas of justice and every high sentiment implied by civilization among mankind, we have resolved to apply to her the usages which she has ratified in her maritime legislation.

The provisions of the present decree shall continue to be looked upon as embodying the fundamental principles of the empire until England shall recognize that the law of war is one and the same on land and on sea, and that the rights of war cannot be extended so as to include private property of any kind or the persons of individuals unconnected with the profession of arms, and that the right of blockade shall be restricted to fortified places actually invested by sufficient forces.

We have consequently decreed and do decree that which follows:

Article I. The British Isles are declared to be in a state of blockade.

II. All commerce and all correspondence with the British Isles is forbidden. Consequently, letters or packages directed to England, or to an Englishman, or written in the English language, shall not pass through the mails and shall be seized.

III. Every individual who is an English subject, of whatever state or condition he may be, who shall be discovered in any country occupied by our troops or by those of our allies, shall be made a prisoner of war.

IV. All warehouses, merchandise, or property of whatever kind belonging to a subject of England shall be respected as a lawful prize.

V. Trade in English goods is prohibited, and all goods belonging to England or coming from her factories or her colonies are declared a lawful prize. . . .

VII. No vessel coming directly from England or from the English colonies, or which shall have visited these since the publication of the present decree, shall be received in any port.

VIII. Any vessel contravening the above provision by a false declaration shall be seized, and the vessel and cargo shall be confiscated as if it were English property. . . .

X. The present decree shall be communicated by our minister of foreign affairs to the kings of Spain, of Naples, of Holland, and of

Etruria, and to our other allies whose subjects like ours, are the victims of the unjust and barbarous maritime legislation of England.

(Signed)

NAPOLEON

Treaty of Fontainebleau, 1814

The continental system provoked the rupture between Napoleon and Tsar Alexander of Russia which, in turn, precipitated the downfall of the French Empire. Relations between the Emperor and the Tsar had never been better than after their meeting at Tilsit in 1807, when Alexander acquired the impression that he and Napoleon were to share hegemony of the continent. Instead he found that Napoleon regarded him as a French auxiliary, functioning only to bring western and central Europe under French domination. The Emperor and the Tsar would probably have settled their differences had Napoleon not insisted that Russia apply the continental system rigorously. The drop in trade with Britain, however, had been damaging to the Russian economy and agitated the populace. The Tsar's decision to abandon the continental system convinced Napoleon of the need for war.

In June, 1812, Napoleon led an army of 600,000 Frenchmen and satellite peoples across the Neimen into Russia. The Russians, whose forces were inferior in numbers and equipment, declined to fight. Their withdrawal enticed the invaders deeper and deeper into hostile country. In September Napoleon entered Moscow, only to have it burned to the ground within a day. At the end of October, frustrated that the victory he believed he had earned continued to elude him, he began the long march back to the frontier. The retreat from Moscow, one of the high tragedies of history, destroyed Napoleon's *grande armée*. Under constant attack from the severities of winter and Russia's guerillas, Napoleon's army faded away until, when it recrossed the Niemen on December 13, 1812, fewer than 100,000 men were left.

From that time, Europe generated growing momentum against Napoleon. Russia negotiated an alliance with Prussia. Gradually all of Germany was in arms against the French. In October, 1813, Napoleon lost the fateful Battle of Nations at Leipzig against Austrian, Russian and Prussian forces. It marked the collapse of Napoleonic power outside France. Henceforth Napoleon could fight only a holding action within France against armies pressing in from all sides. In the desperate months of February and March,

1814, Napoleon skillfully led his badly decimated forces in a defensive war but he was unable to hold off the invaders. Paris surrendered on March 31, 1814. On April 11, Napoleon abdicated.

At Fontainebleau, Napoleon concluded his personal treaty with the sovereigns of Europe. The tribute of the conquerors to the man who had threatened them for fifteen years is itself remarkable. Napoleon renounced for himself and his family the thrones he had acquired in France and elsewhere. But the victors, far from treating the vanquished as a criminal of war, gave him the pleasant island of Elba in the Mediterranean as a place of exile and even assigned him sovereignty over it. The Treaty of Fontainebleau, the principal sections of which are presented below, is a tribute to the esteem Europe accorded to an extraordinary man. It is dated April 11, 1814, the date of Napoleon's abdication.

Document 61

His Majesty the Emperor Napoleon, on the one hand, and, on the other, their Majesties the emperor of Austria, the king of Prussia, and the emperor of all the Russias, both in their own names and those of their allies. . . .

1. His Majesty the Emperor Napoleon renounces for himself, his successors, and descendants, as well as for all the members of his family, all right of sovereignty and dominion as well in the French empire as in the kingdom of Italy and in every other country.

2. Their Majesties the Emperor Napoleon and the Empress Maria Louisa shall retain their titles and rank, to be enjoyed during their lifetime. The mother, brothers, sisters, nephews, and nieces of the emperor shall retain, wherever they may be, the titles of princes of his family.

3. The island of Elba, adopted by his Majesty the Emperor Napoleon as the place of his residence, shall form during his life a separate principality, which shall be possessed by him in full sovereignty and proprietorship.

There shall be given to the Emperor Napoleon, besides full proprietorship of the island of Elba, an annual revenue of two million francs. . . .

5. The duchies of Parma, Piacenza, and Guastalla shall be given in full proprietorship and sovereignty to her Majesty the Empress Maria Louisa. They shall pass to her son and to his descendants in the direct line. The prince, her son, shall assume from this moment the title of Prince of Parma, Piacenza, and Guastalla. . . .

Louis XVIII's Charter of 1814

After Napoleon's fall, France turned back almost reflexively to the Bourbon monarchy. It was not simply that the great powers, France's conquerors, wanted a Bourbon restoration. The French themselves, weary of war and adventure, were willing to return to the Bourbons as the symbol of stability and peace. Talleyrand, who emerged from the Napoleonic debacle as France's most powerful political figure, leaned heavily on the principle of "legitimacy," not only to bring back the royal family but to bargain in behalf of French territorial integrity. Talleyrand understood, however, that restoring the Bourbon monarchy did not mean restoring the *ancien régime*. After twenty-five years of revolution, even the sovereigns of Europe conceded that French absolutism was dead. Both victors and vanquished agreed that France was to be governed by a constitutional monarchy, under the direction of the heir of the late king Louis XVI. Thus the Bourbons returned to Paris.

Louis XVIII (1814–1824); the heir, was a brother of the late king. Though fat and prosaic, he was not unintelligent. Despite an affection for royal prerogatives, he realized he could not push France backward to another age. He insisted on reckoning his reign from the death of Louis XVII—who had never ruled—and on replacing the Revolutionary tricolor with the Bourbon family's *fleur-de-lis*. But he consented to rule under a Charter, though he chose to grant it on his own authority rather than negotiate it with representatives of the country. While he acknowledged responsibility for the execution of its provisions, Louis thereby retained a flimsy argument on behalf of his own dynastic legitimacy. The Charter setting the terms of his reign ended with: "*Given* at Paris, in the year of Grace 1814, and of our reign the nineteenth." But notwithstanding the condescending tone, Louis XVIII renounced any pretention to royal absolutism.

The Charter did not really please anyone. It was too royalist for the revolutionaries and too revolutionary for the royalists. Still, it became the constitution of France, serving as a bridge between old regime and new. It lasted, through a series of crises, as France's basic constitutional document until 1848.

Louis XVIII's Charter, of which excerpts are given below, begins with the king's interpretation of the history leading to it. The Public Rights of the French, which follow, are astonishingly reminiscent of the Declaration of the Rights of Man of 1789. The succeeding section establishes the governing institutions of the constitutional monarchy. Though conceived in reaction, the Charter demonstrates how thoroughly the French Revolution obliterated the feudal world that had existed before it.

Document 62

Louis, by the grace of God king of France and Navarre, to all those to whom these presents come, salutation:

Divine Providence, in recalling us to our estates after a long absence, has imposed grave responsibilities upon us. Peace was the first necessity of our subjects, and with this we have unceasingly occupied ourselves. That peace so essential to France and to the rest of Europe has been signed.

A Constitutional Charter was demanded by the existing condition of the kingdom; we promised this and now publish it. We have taken into consideration the fact that, although the whole authority in France resides in the person of the king, our predecessors have not hesitated to modify the exercise of this in accordance with the differences of the times. It was thus that the communes owed their enfranchisement to Louis the Fat, the confirmation and extension of their rights to St. Louis and Philip the Fair, and that the judicial system was established and developed by the laws of Louis XI, Henry II, and Charles IX. It was in this way, finally, that Louis XIV regulated almost every portion of the public administration by various ordinances which have never been surpassed in wisdom.

We, like the kings our predecessors, have had to consider the effects of the ever-increasing progress of knowledge, the new relations which this progress has introduced into society, the direction given to the public mind during half a century, and the serious troubles resulting therefrom. We have perceived that the wish of our subjects for a Constitutional Charter was the expression of a real need; but in yielding to this wish we have taken every precaution that this charter should be worthy of us and of the people whom we are proud to rule. Able men taken from the highest official bodies of the state were added to the commissioners of our council to elaborate this important work. While we recognize that the expectations of enlightened Europe ought to be gratified by a free monarchical constitution, we have had to remember that our first duty toward our people was to preserve, for their own interest, the rights and prerogatives of our crown.

We hope that, taught by experience, they may be convinced that the Supreme authority alone can give to institutions which it establishes the power, permanence, and dignity with which it is itself clothed; that, consequently, when the wisdom of kings freely harmonizes with the wish of the people, a Constitutional Charter may long endure, but that when concessions are snatched with violence from a weak government, public liberty is not less endangered than the throne itself.

We have sought the principles of the Constitutional Charter in the French character and in the venerable monuments of past centuries. Thus we perceived in the revival of the peerage a truly national institution which binds memories to hope by uniting ancient and modern times. We have replaced by the Chamber of Deputies those ancient assemblies of the March Field and May Field, and those chambers of the third estate which so often exhibited at once proof of their zeal for the interests of the people and fidelity and respect for the authority of kings.

In thus endeavoring to renew the chain of time which fatal excesses had broken, we effaced from our memory, as we would we might blot out from history, all the evils which have afflicted the country during our absence. Happy to find ourselves again in the bosom of our great family, we could only respond to the love of which we receive so many testimonies by uttering words of peace and consolation. The dearest wish of our heart is that all Frenchmen may live like brothers, and that no bitter memory should ever trouble the tranquillity which should follow the solemn decree which we grant them today.

Confident in our intentions, strong in our conscience, we engage ourselves, before the assembly which listens to us, to be faithful to this Constitutional Charter; with the intention, moreover, of swearing to maintain it with added solemnity before the altars of Him who weighs in the same balance kings and nations.

For these reasons we have voluntarily, and by the free exercise of our royal authority, granted and do grant, concede, and accord, as well for us as for our successors forever the Constitutional Charter, as follows.

Public Rights of the French

Article 1. All Frenchmen are equal before the law, whatever may be their title or rank.

2. They contribute without distinction to the impositions of the state in proportion to their fortune.

3. They are all equally eligible to civil and military positions.

4. Their personal liberty is likewise guaranteed; no one can be prose-

cuted or arrested except in the cases and in the manner prescribed by law.

5. All may with equal liberty make profession of their religion and enjoy the same protection for their worship.

6. Nevertheless the Roman Catholic and apostolic religion is the religion of the state.

7. The ministers of the Roman Catholic and apostolic religion, and those of other Christian forms of worship only, shall receive subsidies from the royal treasury.

8. All Frenchmen have the right to publish and cause their opinions to be printed, if they conform to the laws destined to check the abuse of this liberty.

9. All property is inviolable; that known as *national* property forms no exception, since the law recognizes no difference between that and other property.

10. The state may demand the surrender of property in the interest of the public when this is legally certified, but only with previous indemnification.

11. All investigation of opinions expressed or of votes cast previous to the Restoration is prohibited; oblivion of these is imposed upon the courts and upon citizens alike.

12. The conscription is abolished; the method of recruiting both for the army and the navy shall be determined by law.

Form of the Government of the King

13. The person of the king is inviolable and sacred; his ministers are responsible. In the king alone is vested the executive power.

14. The king is the supreme head of the state; he has command of the land and naval forces, declares war, concludes treaties of peace, alliance, and commerce, appoints all the officials of the public administration, and issues the regulations and ordinances necessary for the execution of the laws and the safety of the state.

15. The legislative power is exercised jointly by the king, the Chamber of Peers and the Chamber of Deputies of the departments.

16. The right of initiating legislation belongs to the king.

17. Proposed laws are submitted, at the option of the king, either to the Chamber of Peers or to the Chamber of Deputies, except laws for raising taxes, which must be submitted to the Chamber of Deputies first.

18. Every law must be discussed and passed freely by a majority of each of the two houses.

19. The chambers have the right to petition the king to submit a law relating to any subject and to indicate what they deem the law should contain. . . .

The Holy Alliance, 1815

The Congress of Vienna, called to restore stability to Europe after a quarter-century of disruption, was suddenly interrupted in March, 1815, when Napoleon escaped from Elba and returned to France to regain his power. Acclaimed by his people, Napoleon promised Europe that he would make war no more. But the allies chose not to believe him, reloaded their cannon and marched on France. Napoleon met them at Waterloo in Belgium and was decisively defeated. For the second time he abdicated but, on this occasion, was far less generously treated. The British sent him off to exile at St. Helena, a barren island in the South Atlantic, where he died in 1821. After Napoleon's "hundred days" of liberty were over, the Congress of Vienna resumed its work.

Amid pomp and glitter, the titled heads of Europe and their principal ministers labored to put together a continent that would be both conservative and stable. Dominating the deliberations was Prince Metternich, the most powerful man in Austria, an enlightened and intelligent reactionary. The wily Talleyrand represented France and succeeded, despite France's bad repute, in making the French voice heard. The Congress of Vienna was hostile to revolution, not simply because its members were deeply angered at the French experience and deeply attached to traditional values, but because they were also dedicated to peace, which in their view revolution inevitably threatened. The Congress of Vienna aimed at making a settlement equitable to all the major powers of Europe and at maintaining it in order to preserve European tranquillity.

At Metternich's suggestion, the four powers which had brought Napoleon to his knees—Austria, Russia, Prussia and Britain—agreed to the establishment of a Concert of Europe, an organization pledged to enforce the status quo created at Vienna. At the same time Russia's sentimental Tsar Alexander proposed to endow Metternich's aims with spiritual qualities by making the Concert into a Christian union. The Tsar persuaded the Prussian king and the Austrian emperor to join with him in forming a Holy Alliance for the application of justice and Christian charity. Though the British king declined membership, all but a few European rulers subscribed officially to the Holy Alliance. Most recognized it as a bit of superfluous mysticism but the Holy

Alliance and the Concert of Europe soon became all but indistinguishable. Ultimately it came to be understood as a royal pact against the liberties of the people. It was, in fact, true that the Concert of Europe and the Holy Alliance before long became instruments of reaction. The sovereigns of Europe chose to use them not so much to keep the peace as to repress popular uprisings. For even the spirit of the Holy Alliance could not overcome the spirit of 1789, which continued to generate change. Nonetheless, the balance of power devised at Vienna was so equitable that for a hundred years it saved Europe from a general war.

The following document is the full text of the Holy Alliance, signed at Paris in September, 1815, by Emperor Francis I of Austria, King Frederick William of Prussia and Tsar Alexander of Russia.

Document 63

In the name of the Most Holy and Indivisible Trinity.

Their Majesties the Emperor of Austria, the King of Prussia, and the Emperor of Russia, having, in consequence of the great events which have marked the course of the three last years in Europe, and especially of the blessings which it has pleased Divine Providence to shower down upon those States which place their confidence and their hope on it alone, acquired the intimate conviction of the necessity of settling the rules to be observed by the Powers, in their reciprocal relations, upon the sublime truths which the Holy Religion of our Saviour teaches:

They solemly declare that the present Act has no other object than to publish, in the face of the whole world, their fixed resolution, both in the administration of their respective States and in their political relations with every other Government, to take for their sole guide the precepts of that Holy Religion, namely, the precepts of Justice, Christian Charity, and Peace, which, far from being applicable only to private concerns, must have an immediate influence on the councils of princes, and guide all their steps, as being the only means of consolidating human institutions and remedying their imperfections. In consequence, their Majesties have agreed on the following Articles:

Art. I. Conformably to the words of the Holy Scriptures, which command all men to consider each other as brethren, the three contracting Monarchs will remain united by the bonds of a true and indissoluble fraternity, and considering each other as fellow-countrymen, they will, on all occasions and in all places, lend each other aid and assistance; and, regarding themselves towards their subjects and armies as fathers of families, they will lead them, in the same spirit of fraternity with which they are animated, to protect Religion, Peace, and Justice.

Art. II. In consequence, the sole principle of force, whether between the said Governments or between their Subjects, shall be that of doing each other reciprocal service, and of testifying by unalterable good will the mutual affection with which they ought to be animated, to consider themselves all as members of one and the same Christian nation; the three allied Princes, looking on themselves as merely delegated by Providence to govern three branches of the one family, namely, Austria, Prussia, and Russia, thus confessing that the Christian world, of which they and their people form a part, has in reality no other Sovereign than Him, to whom alone power really belongs, because in Him alone are found all the Treasures of love, science, and infinite wisdom, that is to say, God, our Divine Saviour, the Word of the Most High, the Word of Life. Their Majesties consequently recommend to their people, with the most tender solicitude, as the sole means of enjoying that Peace which arises from a good conscience, and which alone is durable, to strengthen themselves every day more and more in the principles and exercise of the duties which the Divine Saviour has taught to mankind.

Art. III. All the Powers who shall choose solemnly to avow the sacred principles which have dictated the present Act, and shall acknowledge how important it is for the happiness of nations, too long agitated, that these truths should henceforth exercise over the destinies of mankind all the influence which belongs to them, will be received with equal ardor and affection into this Holy Alliance.

Done in triplicate and signed at Paris, the year of Grace 1815, 14-26th September.

(L.S.) FRANCIS
(L.S.) FREDERICK WILLIAM
(L.S.) ALEXANDER

Circular Note of Troppau, 1820

Metternich's plan for a Concert of Europe became the Quadruple Alliance of Austria, Russia, Prussia and England, which guaranteed by treaty for twenty years the territorial settlement reached at Vienna. The treaty also provided for periodic Congresses, the purposes of which were at first vague but which were empowered to examine "the measures which . . . shall be judged most salutary for the repose and prosperity of the peoples. . . ." Metternich intended to use these Congresses to suppress revolutionary movements wherever they might appear.

The first Congress was in Aix-la-Chapelle in 1818, when France was admitted into the Alliance. At Carlsbad in 1819 and Vienna in 1820 measures were ordered to defend the status quo in Germany and attention was directed to uprisings in Spain and Naples against corrupt and tyrannical kings. Indifferent to the injustices at its source, Metternich was determined to stop the contagion of revolution before it spread.

In 1820, a Congress was convened at Troppau in the dominions of the Austrian Empire. There the Alliance agreed formally on the policy of forcibly suppressing liberal revolutions. Britain's dissent from this Alliance policy led ultimately to the collapse of the Metternich system. But in the years following Troppau, the four continental monarchies possessed sufficient power on their own to crush rebellions and guarantee the rule of tyrants. After their revolutions were suppressed by the legions of the Alliance, both Spain and Naples lapsed into long periods of tyrannical reaction.

Metternich's explanation of the decisions made at the Congress of Troppau, which is presented below, illustrates the reactionary thinking that characterized the ruling classes during the post-Napoleonic period.

Document 64

Having been informed of the false and exaggerated rumors which have been circulated by ill-intentioned and credulous persons in regard to the results of the conferences at Troppau, the allied courts deem it necessary to transmit authentic explanations to their representatives at foreign courts, in order to enable them to refute the erroneous ideas to which these rumors have given rise. The brief report here annexed will enable them to do this. . . .

Troppau, December 8, 1820

Brief Review of the First Results of the Conferences at Troppau

The events which took place in Spain March 8 and at Naples July 2, as well as the catastrophe in Portugal, could not but arouse a feeling of the deepest indignation, apprehension, and sorrow in those who are called upon to guard the tranquillity of the nations; and, at the same time, it emphasized the necessity of uniting in order to determine in common the means of checking the misfortunes which threaten to envelop Europe. It was but natural that these sentiments should leave a deep impression upon those powers which had but lately stifled revolution and which now behold it once more raise its head.

Nor was it less natural that these powers, in encountering revolution for the third time, should have recourse to the same methods which they had employed with so much success in the memorable struggle which freed Europe from a yoke she had borne for twenty years. Everything encouraged the hope that that alliance, formed in the most critical circumstances, crowned with the most brilliant success, and strengthened by the conventions of 1814, 1815, and 1818, as it had prepared the way for, established, and assured the peace of the world, and delivered the European continent from the military representatives of revolution, so it would be able to check a new form of oppression, not less tyrannical and fearful, namely, that of revolt and crime. Such were the motives and the aim of the meeting at Troppau.

. . . The powers are exercising an incontestable right in taking common measures in respect to those States in which the overthrow of the government through a revolt, even if it be considered simply as a dangerous example, may result in a hostile attitude toward all constitutions and legitimate governments. The exercise of this right becomes an urgent necessity when those who have placed themselves in this situation seek to extend to their neighbors the ills which they have brought upon themselves and to promote revolt and confusion around them. . . .

Nothing could menace more directly the tranquillity of the neighboring States than the revolution at Naples, gaining ground as it did daily. In view of the fact that the allied courts could not be attacked so promptly and immediately as these neighboring States, it was deemed expedient to proceed, in regard to the Kingdom of the Two Sicilies, according to the principles above enunciated.

In order to prepare conciliatory measures toward this end, the monarchs convened at Troppau resolved to ask the king of the Two Sicilies to meet them at Laibach, with the single aim of freeing him from all external compulsion and placing him in the position of mediator between his erring people and the States whose tranquillity they threaten. . . .

It is needless to prove that the resolutions taken by the powers are in no way to be attributed to the idea of conquest, or to any intention of interfering with the independence of other governments in their internal administration, or, lastly, to the purpose of preventing wise improvements freely carried out and in harmony with the true interests of the people. Their only desire is to preserve and maintain peace, to deliver Europe from the scourge of revolution, and to obviate or lessen the ills which arise from the violation of the precepts of order and morality.

X

Social Unrest in the Nineteenth Century

X

Social Unrest in the Nineteenth Century

The post-Napoleonic reaction, of which the Congress of Vienna was the principal political manifestation, extended also into literature, the arts and religion. But the ideas planted by the French Revolution continued to force their way to the surface, not only in the tyrannical soil of Spain and Naples, but throughout all of the Western world.

The Decembrist Manifesto, 1825

A little shoot reached even into Russia, the darkest corner of Europe, where the eccentric Tsar Alexander dreamed of conducting a government of virtue but ran instead a black and brutal tyranny. Russian army officers who had served in the occupation of France from 1815 to 1818 returned home with new ideas about the rights of man and the responsibilities of kings. Some of them assumed the leadership of a movement to reform the Russian state. Because their societies had necessarily to remain secret, they could not disseminate their ideas to the population as a whole. This small circle of intellectual officers planted a germ of revolution in Russia but, in a soil of widespread ignorance and police oppression, it was slow to grow.

The revolutionaries saw an opportunity for action when on November 19, 1825, Tsar Alexander died childless, leaving two brothers—Nicholas and Constantine—to vie for the throne. While the two brothers debated the succession, a group of conspirators under Prince Trubetskoi prepared a manifesto declaring the old regime to be at an end and a provisional government to be established. On December 14, the day the manifesto was issued, a mass of Russians gathered in the Senate Square in St. Petersburg to protest the proclamation of Nicholas, the more reactionary of the two brothers, as Tsar. But despite their initiative the revolutionaries were ill-prepared to seize power. Nicholas brought up cannon and crushed the rebellion with much loss of life. The conspirators were subsequently tried and either shot or sent into exile in Siberia. The Decembrist Revolt, named for the month of the abortive uprising, enlarged the breach between the monarchy and the intellectual leadership of the nation. The episode created a legend on which revolutionary movements in Russia fed for almost a century.

The Decembrist Manifesto, reproduced here, offers a view of conditions in Russia in the nineteenth century and of the ideas imported from France that were meant to correct them. Article 5, for instance, strikes at the institution of serfdom, which still enslaved millions of Russian peasants. Article 10 denounces Alexander's system of quartering his soldiers in communities all over Russia.

But though the Manifesto aimed at abuses which affected everyone, probably few in Russia were well enough educated to understand it. According to a popular anecdote, when the revolutionaries, in their bitter opposition to Nicholas, cried "Long live Constantine, long live the Constitution," the masses believed they were hailing Constantine and his wife. As an expression of severe discontent in Russia, the Decembrist uprising was undoubtedly premature. Yet it was conclusive proof that the French Revolution had lit a flame and, no matter how tyrannical their government, oppressed peoples would look to the light it shed.

Document 65

The Manifesto of the Senate should proclaim:

(1) abolition of the former government;

(2) establishment of a Provisional Government until a permanent one is decided upon by representatives;

(3) freedom of the press, hence abolition of censorship;

(4) religious tolerance to all faiths;

(5) abolition of the right to own men;

(6) equality of all classes before the law and therefore abolition of military courts and all sorts of judicial commissions from which all cases proceed to civil courts;

(7) announcement of rights for every citizen to occupy himself with whatever he wishes and therefore—nobleman, merchant, middle-class man, peasant—all to have equal right to enter military, civil, or clerical

service, trade wholesale or retail, paying established taxes for such trade; to acquire all kinds of property such as land, or houses in villages and cities; make all kinds of contracts among themselves, or summon each other for trial;

(8) cancellation of poll tax and arrears;

(9) abolition of monopolies on salt and alcohol: permission for free distillation and for the procuring of salt with payment of tax according to the respective amounts of salt and alcohol produced;

(10) abolition of recruiting and military colonies;

(11) reduction of the term of military service for privates to be followed by equalization of military service of all classes;

(12) retirement without exception of all privates who have served fifteen years;

(13) the creation of Community, County, Gubernia, and Regional administrations, which are to be substituted for all civil service men appointed formerly by the government;

(14) public trials;

(15) introduction of a jury system in criminal and civil courts. There shall be created an administration of two or three persons to which all the highest officers of the government shall be subordinated, such as the Ministry, the Council, the Ministerial Committee, the Army and Navy; in a word, the entire Supreme Executive government, but not the legislative nor judicial. For the latter there remains the Ministry subordinated to the Provisional Government, but for decision of cases not passed upon by the lower courts there will remain a department of the Senate which shall handle civil and criminal cases; its members shall remain in service until a permanent administration is established.

The Provisional Government is instructed to:

(1) equalize all classes;

(2) form all local, Community, County, Gubernia, and Regional administrations;

(3) form a National Guard;

(4) form a judicial branch with a jury;

(5) equalize recruiting obligations among all classes;

(6) abolish a permanent army;

(7) establish a form of election of representatives in the Lower Chamber which will have to ratify the future form of Government.

Chartist Petition of 1838

In Britain, as on the continent, reaction characterized the years that followed Waterloo. The landed aristocracy managed the country, allowing only the great commercial class to share in the exercise of power. But the British industrial middle class and the urban working class, more highly developed than anywhere in Europe, grew progressively more aggressive in their demands for a more democratic distribution of authority. Until 1830, when Charles X's aristocratic government was overthrown in Paris, the British ruling classes remained indifferent to pleas for reform. In 1832, however, a major Reform Act was passed which admitted most of the industrial middle class into the political partnership. The British government, while remaining a tight corporation, enlarged sufficiently to satisfy industrial as well as commercial and agricultural interests. To the upper and middle classes, the arrangement was quite agreeable. Proudly the British spoke of it as the "Victorian Compromise," the ideal coalition for the exercise of responsible conservative government.

The working class was conspicuously excluded from a role in the Victorian Compromise. The Reform Act of 1832 did nothing to improve dismal wages, abominable working conditions or congested living. Still, the British working class was not of a revolutionary temperament. It wanted social reform but remained optimistic about achieving it within the going political framework. The English working class, more than any other in Europe, had confidence in the nation. It was willing to be persistent in the quest of its goals, without resorting to violence.

The Chartist movement most dramatically concentrated the passion of the working class for social reform in the mid-nineteenth century. The Chartists were convinced that they could achieve social democracy by means of political democracy. They asked for universal manhood suffrage, annual election of Parliaments, equal electoral districts, secret ballots, elimination of property qualifications for Parliamentary candidacy and payment of salaries to members of Parliament. Their objective was, to be sure, social revolution but, unlike the Russian Decembrists, they planned to achieve it through parliamentary procedure.

Chartism was one of the century's first working-class movements. It possessed the strength of mass support with the accompanying fault of untrained leadership and vulnerability to demagogy. In 1838, the Chartists presented to the Parliament a charter, from which they derive their name, and a petition containing 1,238,000 signatures. Parliament rejected the petition and prepared to fight a civil war, but Chartism lacked a capacity for violence. Its members clearly preferred talking to fighting. The movement continued to grow although, faced with solid opposition, it made no substantial gains. After the Paris uprising of 1848, a few militant Chartist leaders made a final effort to exploit discontent and organized a march on London. The Chartist "army" was scattered with ease. The movement was discredited and Britain's working class turned its attention to trade unionism to meet its needs. Ultimately, Chartism was vindicated by the enactment of many of its proposals into law. Britain became the political democracy that the Chartists sought. It came slowly, however, while the social democracy that hopefully was to accompany it remained painfully elusive.

The Chartist Petition of 1838, presented here, vividly illustrates the grievances and hopes of the British working class during the great century of industrial expansion. However downtrodden, the workingman seems full of confidence in his country and its future.

Document 66

National Petition

Unto the Honourable the Commons of the United Kingdom of Great Britain and Ireland in Parliament assembled, the Petition of the undersigned, their suffering countrymen,

Humbly Sheweth

That we, your petitioners, dwell in a land whose merchants are noted for enterprise, whose manufacturers are very skilful, and whose workmen are proverbial for their industry.

The land itself is goodly, the soil rich, and the temperature wholesome; it is abundantly furnished with the materials of commerce and trade; it has numerous and convenient harbours, in facility of internal communication it exceeds all others.

For three-and-twenty years we have enjoyed a profound peace.

Yet, with all these elements of national prosperity, and with every disposition and capacity to take advantage of them, we find ourselves overwhelmed with public and private suffering.

We are bowed down under a load of taxes; which, notwithstanding, fall greatly short of the wants of our rulers; our traders are trembling on the verge of bankruptcy; our workmen are starving; capital brings no profit and labour no remuneration; the home of the artificer is desolate, and the warehouse of the pawnbroker is full; the workhouse is crowded, and the manufactory is deserted.

We have looked on every side, we have searched diligently in order to find out the causes of a distress so sore and so long continued.

We can discover none in nature, or in Providence.

Heaven has dealt graciously by the people but the foolishness of our rulers has made the goodness of God of none effect.

The energies of a mighty kingdom have been wasted in building up the power of selfish and ignorant men, and its resources squandered for their aggrandisement.

The good of a party has been advanced to the sacrifice of the good of the nation; the few have governed for the interest of the few, while the interest of the many has been neglected, or insolently and tyrannously trampled upon.

It was the fond expectation of the people that a remedy for the greater part, if not for the whole, of their grievances would be found in the Reform Act of 1832.

They were taught to regard that Act as a wise means to a worthy end; as the machinery of an improved legislation when the will of the masses would be at length potential.

They have been bitterly and basely deceived.

The fruit which looked so fair to the eye has turned to dust and ashes when gathered.

The Reform Act has effected a transfer of power from one domineering faction to another, and left the people as helpless as before.

Our slavery has been exchanged for an apprenticeship to liberty, which has aggravated the painful feeling of our social degradation, by adding to it the sickening of still deferred hope.

We come before your Honourable House to tell you, with all humility, that this state of things must not be permitted to continue; that it cannot long continue without very seriously endangering the stability of the throne and the peace of the kingdom; and that if by God's help and all lawful and constitutional appliances, an end can be put to it, we are fully resolved that it shall speedily come to an end.

We tell your Honourable House that the capital of the master must no longer be deprived of its due reward; that the laws which make food dear, and those which by making money scarce, make labour cheap, must be abolished; that taxation must be made to fall on property, not on industry; that the good of the many, as it is the only legitimate end, so must it be the sole study of the Government.

As a preliminary essential to these and other requisite changes; as means by which alone the interests of the people can be effectually vindicated and secured, we demand that those interests be confided to the keeping of the people.

When the State calls for defenders, when it calls for money, no consideration of poverty or ignorance can be pleaded in refusal or delay of the call.

Required as we are universally, to support and obey the laws, nature and reason entitle us to demand, that in the making of the laws, the universal voice shall be implicitly listened to.

We perform the duties of freemen; we must have the privileges of freemen.

We demand universal suffrage

The suffrage, to be exempt from the corruption of the wealthy and the violence of the powerful, must be secret.

The assertion of our right necessarily involves the power of its uncontrolled exercise.

We demand the ballot

The connection between the representatives and the people, to be beneficial must be intimate.

The legislative and constituent powers, for correction and for instruction, ought to be brought into frequent contact.

Errors, which are comparatively light when susceptible of a speedy popular remedy, may produce the most disastrous effects when permitted to grow inveterate through years of compulsory endurance.

To public safety as well as public confidence, frequent elections are essential.

We demand annual parliaments

With power to choose, and freedom in choosing, the range of our choice must be unrestricted.

We are compelled, by the existing laws, to take for our representatives, men who are incapable of appreciating our difficulties, or who have little sympathy with them; merchants who have retired from trade, and no longer feel its harassings; proprietors of land who are alike ignorant of its evils and their cure; lawyers, by whom the honours of the senate are sought after only as means of obtaining notice in the courts.

The labours of a representative, who is sedulous in the discharge of his duty, are numerous and burdensome.

It is neither just, nor reasonable, nor safe, that they should continue to be gratuitously rendered.

We demand that in the future election of members of your Honourable

House, the approbation of the constituency shall be the sole equalification; and that to every representative so chosen shall be assigned, out of the public taxes, a fair and adequate remuneration for the time which he is called upon to devote to the public service.

Finally, we would most earnestly impress on your Honourable House, that this petition has not been dictated by any idle love of change; that it springs out of no inconsiderate attachement to fanciful theories; but that it is the result of much and long deliberation, and of convictions, which the events of each succeeding year tend more and more to strengthen.

The management of this mighty kingdom has hitherto been a subject for contending factions to try their selfish experiments upon.

We have felt the consequences in our sorrowful experience—short glimmerings of uncertain enjoyment swallowed up by long and dark seasons of suffering.

If the self-government of the people should not remove their distresses, it will at least remove their repining.

Universal suffrage will, and it alone can, bring true and lasting peace to the nation; we firmly believe that it will also bring prosperity.

May it therefore please your Honourable House to take this our petition into your most serious consideration; and to use your utmost endeavours, by all constitutional means, to have a law passed, granting to every male of lawful age, sane mind, and unconvicted of crime, the right of voting for members of Parliament; and directing all future elections of members of Parliament to be in the way of secret ballot; and ordaining that the duration of Parliaments so chosen shall in no case exceed one year; and abolishing all property qualifications in the members; and providing for their due remuneration while in attendance on their Parliamentary duties.

And your petitioners, etc. . . .

Decrees of French Provisional Government on Labor, 1848

Beginning with the Bourbon Restoration of 1814, France groped for a system of government that would reconcile its monarchical with its revolutionary tradition. Louis XVIII, firm yet sensible, reigned until his death in 1824. But his successor, Charles X, was autocratic and repressive and was overthrown in a brief uprising in 1830. The new king, Louis Philippe of the ruling family's Orleanist branch, claimed to rule not so much by the grace of God as by the good will of the nation. His regime, called the bourgeois monarchy, served the propertied classes almost exclusively, depriving the working class of both the responsibilities and the benefits of government. Like the Victorian Age in England, the age of Louis Philippe was characterized by great industrial advance. However, the lot of the French worker, like his English counterpart, became more dismal as the society became more productive. For the working man, at least, France had not found the government that could resolve the conflict between order and progress.

French social thinkers thus found ample provocation for devising new theories of social organization, the principal of which was socialism. Saint-Simon and Fourier preached a sort of spiritual socialism and attracted large followings. The more hard-headed Louis Blanc argued for the establishment of national workshops, which the government would finance and the workers operate. Blanc's ideas became popular in the industrial slums of Paris and other factory cities, where misery was acute. The working class in France, unlike its English counterpart, saw the redress of its grievances in profound social change, not simply in political reform.

In 1848, Louis Philippe's government, capably and conservatively conducted by Prime Minister Francois Guizot, appeared unassailable, despite its indifference to social problems. But quite unexpectedly, the king and his ministers committed a series of blunders and, during the last week in February, restless Paris rose up. When the king looked around for defenders, he found that he had virtually none. Louis Philippe was sent off to exile in England, the conservative members of Parliament fled to their homes and a small remaining group from the left proclaimed a provisional republic. The monarchy, as it happened, was forever dead.

Louis Blanc, the socialist thinker, was among the founders of the new provisional government. His sole objective was to establish the national workshops and to reorganize the utilization of property and labor. Behind him were the Paris masses, ready to man the barricades if they were offered a stirring egalitarian cause. On February 25 and 26, the provisional government issued a series of decrees to put Blanc's ideas into practice. France had, in effect, created a workingman's state.

Before long, however, the revolutionaries of 1848 broke up into republicans and socialists, the former showing no sympathy for the designs of the latter. In April a parliamentary election was held, which was won by moderate, anti-socialist republicans. While socialists were being purged from the direction of the state, the national workshops one by one collapsed, the consequence of poor conception, hasty organization, inefficient administration, political opposition and a general economic slump. When the Assembly, on June 21, shouted down Louis Blanc's protests and abolished the national workshops, the Paris masses took to the barricades. Class warfare was on.

During the "June Days" of 1848, France's moderate republican government put down in ferocious fashion the social revolution of the working class. The Parisians, by fighting, did what the British Chartists lacked the will to do, for, without the Chartists' confidence in the future, they were far more desperate. In a rain of artillery shells, the workingman's state was terminated. The embittered proletariat, disillusioned about its prospects of finding satisfaction within the established political structure, would become more and more alienated from the rest of the nation.

The following are among the decrees issued by the provisional government on February 25 and 26, 1848. They contain not so much an expression of political philosophy, as did the Chartist Petition of 1838, as a practical program for economic and social action. They represent France's experiment with social revolution—a revolution that failed.

Document 67

The provisional government of the French republic decrees that the Tuileries shall serve hereafter as a home for the veterans of labor.

The provisional government of the French republic pledges itself to guarantee the means of subsistence of the workingman by labor.

It pledges itself to guarantee labor to all citizens.

It recognizes that workingmen ought to enter into associations among themselves in order to enjoy the advantage of their labor. . . .

The provisional government of the French republic decrees that all articles pledged at the pawn shop, since the first of February, consisting of linen, garments, or clothes, etc., upon which the loan does not exceed ten francs, shall be given back to those who pledged them. The minister of finance is ordered to meet the payments incidental to the execution of the present edict.

The provisional government of the republic decrees the immediate establishment of national workshops. The minister of public works is charged with the execution of the present decree. . . .

The Communist Manifesto, 1848

Socialism, until 1848, was a vague philosophical ideal, espoused in different forms by different thinkers, who possessed in common a dedication to a benevolent society organized to permit an equitable distribution of the fruits of production. Karl Marx changed socialism into a rigorous dogma. Brilliant and erudite, he expounded the form of socialism that has passed permanently into the tradition of Western civilization. He placed socialism into the arena with such values as Christianity, individualism, parliamentarianism and liberalism as a competitor for the allegiance of Western man. Since publication of the Communist Manifesto of 1848, debate between socialists has been all but limited to interpretations of Marx. In one form or another Marxism has influenced the spirit of revolution, wherever it has been found, for more than a century.

Marx built his social philosophy on the contention that "the history of all hitherto existing society is the history of class struggles." From this premise he applied facts, using scientific methods, to develop his interpretation of history. Though guilty of straining his facts to serve his conclusions, Marx nonetheless contributed a methodology and offered a perception of history that have since changed drastically the study of the social sciences. Marx found the replacement of the aristocracy by the bourgeoisie as Western civilization's ruling class to be the dominant factor in modern history. The next step in historical evolution, a step he regarded as inevitable, would be the proletariat's seizure of power from the bourgeoisie. The Communist Manifesto was thus both a philosopher's exposition and a pamphleteer's call to action. As the foundation for Communist strategy and doctrine, it remains one of the most important documents of our age.

The Communist Manifesto was prepared for a meeting of the Communist League, which Marx helped to form in London in 1847. It was written in German, Marx's native language. It has been translated into almost every language to act as a ferment to social change far beyond the boundaries of the West. The excerpts here are from an authorized translation. The final line of this version, which is inelegantly translated, is usually rendered by the more exciting: "Workers of the world, unite!"

Document 68

A SPECTRE is haunting Europe—the spectre of Communism. All the powers of old Europe have entered into a holy alliance to exorcise this spectre; Pope and Czar, Metternich and Guizot, French Radicals and German police-spies.

Where is the party in opposition that has not been decried as communistic by its opponents in power? Where the Opposition that has not hurled back the branding reproach of Communism, against the more advanced opposition parties, as well as against its reactionary adversaries?

Two things result from this fact.

I. Communism is already acknowledged by all European Powers to be itself a Power.

II. It is high time that Communists should openly, in the face of the whole world, publish their views, their aims, their tendencies, and meet this nursery tale of the spectre of Communism with a Manifesto of the party itself.

To this end, Communists of various nationalities have assembled in London, and sketched the following manifesto, to be published in the English, French, German, Italian, Flemish and Danish languages.

. . .

The history of all hitherto existing society is the history of class struggles.

. . .

The modern bourgeois society that has sprouted from the ruins of feudal society, has not done away with class antagonisms. It has but established new classes, new conditions of oppression, new forms of struggle in place of the old ones.

Our epoch, the epoch of the bourgeoisie, possesses this distinctive feature; it has simplified the class antagonisms. Society as a whole is more and more splitting up into two great classes directly facing each other: Bourgeoisie and Proletariat.

. . .

The bourgeoisie, wherever it has got the upper hand, has put an end to all feudal, patriarchal, idyllic relations. It has pitilessly torn asunder the motley feudal ties that bound man to his "natural superiors," and has left remaining no other nexus between man and man than naked self-interest, than callous "cash payment."

. . .

In proportion as the bourgeoisie, i.e., capital, is developed, in the same proportion is the proletariat, the modern working-class, developed, a class of laborers, who live only so long as they find work, and who find work only so long as their labor increases capital. These laborers, who must sell themselves piecemeal, are a commodity, like every article of commerce, and are consequently exposed to all the vicissitudes of competition, to all the fluctuations of the market.

. . .

Modern industry has converted the little work-shop of the patriarchal master into the great factory of the industrial capitalist. Masses of laborers, crowded into the factory, are organized like soldiers. As privates of the industrial army they are placed under the command of a perfect hierarchy of officers and sergeants. Not only are they the slaves of the bourgeois class, and of the bourgeois State, they are daily and hourly enslaved by the machine, by the over-looker, and, above all, by the individual bourgeois manufacturer himself.

. . .

But with the development of industry the proletariat not only increases in number, it becomes concentrated in greater masses, its strength grows, and it feels that strength more. The various interests and conditions of life within the ranks of the proletariat are more and more equalized, in proportion as machinery obliterates all distinctions of labor, and nearly everywhere reduces wages to the same low level. The growing competition among the bourgeois, and the resulting commercial crises, make the wages of the workers ever more fluctuating. The unceasing improvement of machinery, ever more rapidly developing, makes their livelihood more and more precarious; the collisions between individual workmen and individual bourgeois take more and more the character of collisions between two classes. Thereupon the workers begin to form combinations (Trades Unions) against the bourgeois.

. . .

This organization of the proletarians into a class, and consequently into a political party, is continually being upset again by the competition between the workers themselves. But it ever rises up again, stronger, firmer, mightier.

. . .

It has become evident that the bourgeoisie is unfit any longer to be the ruling class in society, and to impose its conditions of existence upon society as an over-riding law. It is unfit to rule, because it is incompetent to assure an existence to its slave within his slavery, because it cannot help letting him sink into such a state that it has to feed him, instead of being fed by him. Society can no longer live under this bourgeoisie, in other words, its existence is no longer compatible with society.

The essential condition for the existence, and for the sway of the bourgeois class, is the formation and augmentation of capital; the condition for capital is wage-labor. Wage-labor rests exclusively on competition between the laborers. The advance of industry, whose involuntary promoter is the bourgeoisie, replaces the isolation of the laborers, due to competition, by their involuntary combination, due to association. The development of Modern Industry, therefore, cuts from under its feet the very foundation on which the bourgeoisie produces and appropriates products. What the bourgeoisie therefore produces, above all, are its own grave-diggers. Its fall and the victory of the proletariat are equally inevitable.

. . .

The immediate aim of the Communists is the same as that of all the other proletarian parties: formation of the proletariat into a class, overthrow of the bourgeois supremacy, conquest of political power by the proletariat.

. . .

The distinguishing feature of Communism is not the abolition of property generally, but the abolition of bourgeois property. But modern bourgeois private property is the final and most complete expression of the system of producing and appropriating products, that is based on class antagonism, on the exploitation of the many by the few.

In this sense, the theory of the Communists may be summed up in the single sentence: Abolition of private property.

. . .

The Communists are reproached with desiring to abolish countries and nationalities.

The working men have no country. We cannot take from them what they have not got. Since the proletariat must first of all acquire political supremacy, must rise to be the leading class of the nation, must constitute itself the nation, it is, so far, itself national, though not in the bourgeois sense of the word.

National differences, and antagonisms between peoples, are daily more and more vanishing, owing to the development of the bourgeoisie, to freedom of commerce, to the world-market, to uniformity in the mode of production and in the conditions of life corresponding thereto.

The supremacy of the proletariat will cause them to vanish still faster. United action, of the leading civilized countries at least, is one of the first conditions for the emancipation of the proletariat.

. . .

The proletariat will use its political supremacy, to wrest, by degrees, all capital from the bourgeoisie, to centralize all instruments of production in the hands of the State, i.e., of the proletariat organized as the ruling class; and to increase the total of productive forces as rapidly as possible.

Of course, in the beginning, this cannot be effected except by means of despotic inroads on the rights of property, and on the conditions of bourgeois production; by means of measures, therefore, which appear economically insufficient and untenable, but which, in the course of the movement, outstrip themselves, necessitate further inroads upon the old social order, and are unavoidable as a means of entirely revolutionizing the mode of production.

These measures will of course be different in different countries.

Nevertheless in the most advanced countries the following will be pretty generally applicable:

1. Abolition of property in land and application of all rents of land to public purposes.

2. A heavy progressive or graduated income tax.

3. Abolition of all right of inheritance.

4. Confiscation of the property of all emigrants and rebels.

5. Centralization of credit in the hands of the State, by means of a national bank with State capital and an exclusive monopoly.

6. Centralization of the means of communication and transport in the hands of the State.

7. Extension of factories and instruments of production owned by the State; the bringing into cultivation of waste lands, and the improvement of the soil generally in accordance with a common plan.

8. Equal liability of all to labor. Establishment of industrial armies, especially for agriculture.

9. Combination of agriculture with manufacturing industries; gradual abolition of the distinction between town and country, by a more equable distribution of population over the country.

10. Free education for all children in public schools. Abolition of children's factory labor in its present form. Combination of education with industrial production, etc., etc.

When, in the course of development, class distinctions have disappeared, and all production has been concentrated in the hands of a vast association of the whole nation, the public power will lose its political character. Political power, properly so called, is merely the organized power of one class for oppressing another. If the proletariat during its contest with the bourgeoisie is compelled, by the force of circumstances, to organize itself as a class, if, by means of a revolution, it makes itself the ruling class, and, as such, sweeps away by force the old conditions of production, then it will, along with these conditions, have swept away the conditions for the existence of class antagonisms, and of classes generally, and will thereby have abolished its own supremacy as a class.

In place of the old bourgeois society, with its classes and class antagonisms, we shall have an association, in which the free development of each is the condition for the free development of all.

. . .

The Communists disdain to conceal their views and aims. They openly declare that their ends can be attained only by the forcible overthrow of all existing social conditions. Let the ruling classes tremble at a Communistic revolution. The proletarians have nothing to lose but their chains. They have a world to win.

Workingmen of all countries, unite!

The Gettysburg Address, 1863

The Thirteenth Amendment, 1865

The United States, too, went through a painful period of adjustment during the nineteenth century. Committed by its Declaration of Independence to human equality and freedom, the nation lived with the ugly paradox of human slavery in its midst. Vainly it sought to accommodate to its principles the presence of several million Negroes in bondage. But the moral dilemma, far from approaching resolution, grew in intensity.

As the years passed, the North, where climate and economic organization were not congenial to slavery, applied increasing pressure on the South to contain slavery, if not to abolish it. At the same time, the South, growing more dependent on slave labor and its cotton crop, found the challenge less and less tolerable. The issue was reducing itself into the competition between a system based on free labor and free men and a system based on slaves and masters. In the rising discord, the slave himself was virtually forgotten.

Throughout the first half of the century, North and South had maneuvered vigorously for advantage, the North determined to prevent the extension of slavery, the South convinced that it must expand to survive. By the mid-1850s, sectionalism dominated politics and the Republican Party had been founded to speak for the North. In 1860, the Republicans elected Abraham Lincoln as President on a platform that promised to halt the spread of slavery, though by no means to abolish it. Nonetheless, the states of the South saw Lincoln as a menace to their institutions and chose to secede from the Union.

The Civil War began as an effort by the North to preserve the Union. The North itself was divided on slavery as a moral question. Only as the war progressed did Lincoln guide the struggle to an ideological terrain. His motive in doing so was partly political, for he wanted to keep Europe, where slavery was looked on as uncivilized, from going to the South's aid. But it also grew out of Lincoln's deep conviction that slavery was a moral wrong and that equality was mankind's proper condition. Step by step, Lincoln shifted the North's goal from the defense of the Union, which was purely political, to the advancement of human freedom, which was deeply moral.

On January 1, 1863, Lincoln signed the Emancipation Proclamation, which set free the slaves in the rebellious states. But the Emancipation Proclamation was, in many respects, a meaningless document. It freed no slaves, for it applied only to lands over which Lincoln exercised no control. Its legality was debatable, since it was enacted without statutory authority. It largely duplicated earlier legislation passed by Congress. The Emancipation Proclamation was a military maneuver. It was still several steps away from a national commitment to equality.

Lincoln made that commitment at Gettysburg on November 19, 1863. Four and a half months before, the North had won its most important military victory on the rolling hills around the town. The North still might have lost the war but the South could not thereafter have won it. In dedicating the military cemetery at Gettysburg, Lincoln gave the Civil War a new direction. He renewed the nation's allegiance to the principles of the Declaration of Independence. It was Lincoln who saw the Civil War as part of the long struggle within Western civilization between democracy and aristocracy, between freedom and oppression, between equality and slavery. Succinct as it is, the Gettysburg Address is a summation of a nation's history and its hopes. It remains to this day the most lucid exposition of the American goal.

Document 69A

Lincoln's Gettysburg Address

Fourscore and seven years ago our fathers brought forth on this continent a new nation, conceived in liberty and dedicated to the proposition that all men are created equal.

Now we are engaged in a great civil war, testing whether that nation or any nation so conceived and so dedicated can long endure. We are met on a great battlefield of that war. We have come to dedicate a portion of that field as a final resting-place for those who here gave their lives that that nation might live. It is altogether fitting and proper that we should do this.

But, in a larger sense, we cannot dedicate, we cannot consecrate, we cannot hallow this ground. The brave men, living and dead, who struggled here have consecrated it far above our poor power to add or detract. The world will little note nor long remember what we say here, but it can never forget what they did here. It is for us the living rather to be dedicated here to the unfinished work which they who fought here have thus far so nobly advanced. It is rather for us to be here dedicated to the great task remaining before us—that from these honored dead we take increased devotion to that cause for which they gave the last full measure of devotion—that we here highly resolve that these dead shall not have died in vain, that this nation under God shall have a new birth of freedom, and that government of the people, by the people, for the people shall not perish from the earth.

Not until after the Civil War did the United States legally emancipate the Negro slave. The Thirteenth Amendment, ratification of which became a condition for the return of a rebellious state to the Union, was formally attached to the Constitution in December, 1865. It was an end unforseen in 1861, when Lincoln himself would have accepted the status quo on slavery in order to maintain the nation intact. It was a noble conclusion to the fiercest of all tests of the American nation's capacity to endure.

As the Gettysburg Address testifies, Lincoln clearly foresaw that the Thirteenth Amendment was simply a first step to a distant objective. It meant that the United States had at last resolved the contradiction of slavery in a free society—by abolishing the former, while exalting the latter. The Thirteenth Amendment was America's constitutional commitment to the vision of the Gettysburg Address. The commitment has often been violated. The vision has been elusive. But the ideas have remained a National objective.

Document 69B

Thirteenth Amendment to the Constitution of the United States

1. Neither slavery nor involuntary servitude, except as a punishment for crime whereof the party shall have been duly convicted, shall exist within the United States, or any place subject to their jurisdiction.

2. Congress shall have power by appropriate legislation to enforce the provisions of this article.

Pope Leo XIII's Rerum Novarum, 1891

As the nineteenth century closed, the Catholic Church took significant steps toward an accommodation with a world from which it had become, over the years, more and more estranged. Nationalism had made a mockery of its ancient claims to temporal sovereignty. Democratic movements regarded it as an inevitable ally of monarchy and aristocracy. Proponents of a new social order saw it as an implacable upholder of the status quo. In 1846, the reign of Pope Pius IX began with a fresh promise of papal liberalism but ended 22 years later with the Holy See more deeply dedicated than ever to social and political reaction. The Papacy, it seemed, was an anachronism, a medieval bastion crumbling before the inexorable tide of change. But in 1878 Leo XIII mounted the papal throne and the Church of Rome, venerable symbol of institutional obduracy, once again demonstrated the flexibility that has been at the source of its vigor for almost two thousand years.

Leo XIII worked constantly throughout the twenty-five years of his reign to find the areas in which the Church, without surrendering fundamental dogma, could meet the demands of modern society. He commanded Catholics to fulfill their responsibilities as citizens in democratic states, thereby repudiating the old union of churchmen and royalists in France. He put an end to the *kulturkampf* in Germany by coming to terms with Bismarck, consenting thereby to an abated role for the Church in predominantly Protestant cultures. He designated Thomism, with its exaltation of reason, as the inseparable companion of faith, as the official Catholic philosophy. In encouraging the creation of new Catholic faculties and universities, he sought to make the Church a leader in the quest for truth. If he did little to resolve the Papacy's differences with the Italian government, he at least did little to aggravate them. Leo XIII, by preaching and by example, was indefatigable in his efforts to bend Catholic attitudes to the requirements of contemporary life.

Of Leo XIII's many pronouncements none was more important than the encyclical *Rerum Novarum*, in which he delineated the modern position of the Church on basic social questions. Published in 1891, it was both an attack on Marxian socialism, which excluded religion from its system, and an exhortation to the faithful to apply the principles of social justice within the framework of the existing system. *Rerum Novarum* dealt with the responsibilities of the Church as a social organization and with the rights and duties of the state and the individual, labor and capital, rich and poor. It was a defense of private property and, at the same time, an appeal for economic and social reform. Far from revolutionary, *Rerum Novarum* declared that "Nothing is more useful than to look upon the world as it really is, . . ." But it called upon the state to promote the interests of the working class by assuring just wages and adequate conditions of labor, by encouraging the formation of unions, by safeguarding the integrity of the family, by taking responsibility for the welfare of all members of the community.

Rerum Novarum, though several times updated by succeeding Popes, retains the freshness of a contemporary statement. It remains the inspiration of Catholic social action. It is an ancient institution's brilliant, if belated, response to modern challenge.

Rerum Novarum, a rather repetitious document, consumes some forty pages of text. The following excerpts summarize its attitudes toward Marxism, its theological arguments in behalf of reforming society and the essence of its social program.

Document 70

It is not surprising that the spirit of revolutionary change, which has so long disturbed the nations of the world, should have passed beyond politics and made its influence felt in the field of political economy. The elements of a conflict are unmistakable,—the growth of industry and the surprising discoveries of science, the changed relations of masters and workmen, the enormous fortunes of individuals and the poverty of the masses, the increased self-reliance and the closer mutual combination of the working population, and, finally, a general moral deterioration. The momentous seriousness of the present state of things just now fills every mind with painful apprehension; wise men discuss it; practical men propose schemes; popular meetings, legislatures, and sovereign princes,—all are occupied with it, and there is nothing which has a deeper hold on public attention.

Therefore, Venerable Brethren, as on former occasions, when it seemed opportune to refute false teaching, we have addressed you in the interest of the Church and of the commonweal, and have issued letters on Political Power, on Human Liberty, on the Christian Constitution of the State, and on similar subjects, so now we have thought it useful to speak on the *Condition of Labor*.

All agree, and there can be no question whatever, that some remedy must be found, and quickly found, for the misery and wretchedness which press so heavily at this moment on the large majority of the very poor. The ancient workmen's guilds were destroyed in the last century, and no other organization took their place. Public institutions and the laws have repudiated the ancient religion. Hence, by degrees, it has come to pass that workingmen have been given over, isolated and defenseless, to the callousness of employers and the greed of unrestrained competition. The evil has been increased by rapacious usury, which although more than once condemned by the Church, is, nevertheless, under a different form, but with the same guilt, still practiced by avaricious and grasping men. And to this must be added the custom of working by contract, and the concentration of so many branches of trade in the hands of a few individuals, so that a small number of very rich men have been able to lay upon the masses of the poor a yoke little better than slavery itself.

To remedy these evils the socialists, working on the poor man's envy of the rich, endeavor to destroy private property, and maintain that individual possessions should become the common property of all, to be administered by the State or by municipal bodies. They hold that, by thus transferring property from private persons to the community, the present evil state of things will be set to rights, because each citizen will then have his equal share of whatever there is to enjoy. But their proposals are so clearly futile for all practical purposes, that if they were carried out the workingman himself would be among the first to suffer. Moreover, they are emphatically unjust, because they would rob the lawful possessor, bring the State into a sphere that is not its own, and cause complete confusion in the community. . . .

What is of still greater importance, however, is that the remedy they propose is manifestly opposed to justice, for every man has by nature the right to possess property as his own. This is one of the chief points of distinction between man and the animal creation. Man alone among animals possesses reason; it must therefore be within his right to have things not merely for temporary and momentary use, as other living beings have them, but in stable and permanent possession; he must have not only things which perish in the using, but also those which, though used, remain for use in the future. . . .

And to say that God has given the earth to the use and enjoyment of the whole human race is not to deny that there can be private property. For God has granted the earth to mankind in general; not in the sense that all without distinction can deal with it as they please, but rather that no part of it has been assigned to any one in particular, and that the limits of private possessions have been left to be fixed by man's own industry and the laws of individual peoples. . . .

The contention that the civil government should at its option intrude into and exercise intimate control over the family and the household is a great and pernicious error. True, if a family finds itself in exceeding distress, utterly deprived of the counsel of friends, and without any prospect of extricating itself, it is right that extreme necessity be met by public aid, since each family is part of the commonwealth. . . . Paternal authority can neither be abolished nor absorbed by the state; for it has the same source as human life itself . . . The socialists, therefore, in setting aside parent and setting up a State supervision, act against natural justice and destroy the structure of the home. . . .

Let it be laid down, in the first place, that humanity is destined to remain as it is. It is impossible to reduce human society to a level. The socialists may do their utmost, but all striving against nature is vain. There naturally exist among mankind innumerable differences of the most important kind; people differ in capability, in diligence, in health, and in strength; an unequal fortune is a necessary result of inequality in condition. Such inequality is far from being disadvantageous either to individuals or to the community; social and public life can only go on by the help of various kinds of capacity and the playing of many parts; and each man, as a rule, chooses the part which peculiarly suits his case.

As regards bodily labor, even had man never fallen from "the state of innocence," he would not have been wholly unoccupied; but that which would then have been his free choice and delight became afterwards compulsory, and the painful expiation of his sin. "Cursed be the earth in thy work; in thy labor thou shalt eat of it all the days of thy life." In like manner, the other pains and hardships of life will have no end or cessation on this earth, for the consequences of sin are bitter and hard to bear, and they must be with man as long as life lasts. To suffer and to endure, therefore, is the lot of humanity; let men try as they may, no strength and no artifice will ever succeed in banishing from human life the ills and troubles which beset it. If any there be who pretend differently,—who hold out to a hard-pressed people freedom from pain and trouble, undisturbed repose, and constant enjoyment,—they cheat the people and impose upon them; and their lying promises will only make the evil worse than before. There is nothing more useful than to look at the world as it really is,—and at the same time to look elsewhere for a remedy to its troubles.

The great mistake that is made in the matter now under consideration, is to possess one's self of the idea that class is naturally hostile to class; that rich and poor are intended by nature to live at war with one another. So irrational and so false is this view that the exact contrary is the truth. Just as the symmetry of the human body is the result of the disposition of the members of the body, so in a State it is ordained by nature that these two classes should exist in harmony and agreement, and should, as it were, fit into one another, so as to maintain the equilibrium of the body politic. Each requires the other; capital cannot do without labor, nor labor without capital. Mutual agreement results in pleasantness and good order; perpetual conflict necessarily produces confusion and violence.

Now, in preventing such strife as this, and in making it impossible, the efficacy of Christianity is marvelous and manifold. First of all, there is nothing more powerful than religion (of which the Church is the interpreter and guardian) in drawing rich and poor together, by reminding each class of its duties to the other, and especially of the duties of justice. Thus religion teaches the laboring man and the workman to carry out honestly and well all equitable agreements freely made; never to injure capital, or to attack the person of an employer; never to employ violence in representing his own cause, or to engage in riot or disorder; and to have nothing to do with men of evil principles, who work upon the people with artful promises, and raise foolish hopes which usually end in disaster and in repentance when too late. Religion teaches the owner and employer not to look upon their work people as their bondsmen but to respect in every man his dignity as a person ennobled by Christian character. They are reminded that, according to natural reason and Christian philosophy, working for gain is creditable, not shameful, to a man, since it enables him to earn an honorable livelihood; but to misuse men as though they were things in the pursuit of gain or to value them solely for their physical powers—that is truly shameful and inhuman. . . .

It must not be supposed that the solicitude of the Church is so preoccupied with the spiritual concerns of its children as to neglect their temporal and earthly interests. Her desire is that the poor, for example, should rise above poverty and wretchedness, and better their condition in life; and for this she makes a strong endeavor . . . Christian morality, when adepuately and completely practiced, leads of itself to temporal prosperity, for it merits the blessing of that God who is the source of all blessings; it powerfully restrains the greed of possession and the thirst for pleasure—twin plagues, which too often make a man who is void of self-restraint miserable in the midst of abundance; it makes men supply for the lack of means through economy, teaching them to be content with frugal living and, further, keeping them out of the reach of those vices which devour not small incomes merely but large fortunes and dissipate many a goodly inheritance. . . .

Rights must be religiously respected wherever they exist and it is the duty of the public authority to prevent and punish injury, and to protect every one in the possession of his own. Still, when there is a question of defending the rights of individuals, the poor and badly off have a claim to special consideration. The richer class have many ways of shielding themselves and stand less in need of help from the State; whereas the mass of the poor have no resources of their own to fall back upon and must chiefly depend upon the assistance of the State. And it is for this reason that wage-earners, since they mostly belong to the mass of the needy, should be specially cared for and protected by the government. . . .

If we turn now to things exterior and corporeal, the first concern of all is to save the poor workers from the cruelty of men of greed who use human beings as mere instruments for making money. It is neither justice nor humanity so to grind men down with excessive labor as to stupefy their minds and wear out their bodies. . . . Work which is suitable for a strong man cannot reasonably be required from a woman or a child. And, in regard to children, great care should be taken not to place them in workshops and factories until their bodies and minds are sufficiently mature. For just as severe weather destroys the buds of spring, so too early an experience of life's hard work blights the young promise of a child's powers and makes any real education impossible. Women, again, are not suited for certain occupations; a woman is by nature fitted for home-work, and it is that which is best adapted at once to preserve her modesty and to promote the good bringing-up of children and the well-being of the family. As a general principle it may be laid down that a workman ought to have leisure and rest proportionate to the wear and tear of his strength, for waste of strength must be repaired by cessation from hard work. . . .

We now approach a subject of very great importance, and one on which, if extremes are to be avoided, right ideas are absolutely necessary. Wages, we are told, are fixed by free consent; and therefore the employer, when he pays what was agreed upon, has done his part, and is not called upon for anything further. The only way, it is said, in which injustice could happen would be if the master refused to pay the whole of the wages, or the workman would not complete the work undertaken; when this happens the State should intervene, to see that each obtains his own,—but not under any other circumstances.

This mode of reasoning is by no means convincing to a fair-minded man, for there are important considerations which it leaves out of view altogether. To labor is to exert one's self for the sake of procuring what is necessary for the purposes of life, and, most of all, for self-preservation. "In the sweat of thy brow thou shalt eat bread." . . . The preservation of life is the bounden duty of each and all, and to fail therein is a crime. It follows that each one has a right to procure what is required in order to live; and the poor can procure it in no other way than by work and wages.

Let the working man and the employer make free agreements and, in particular, let them agree freely as to the wages; nevertheless, there underlies a dictate of natural justice more imperious and ancient than any bargain between man and man; namely, that wages ought not to be insufficient to support a frugal and well-behaved wage-earner. If through necessity or fear of a worse evil the workman accept harder conditions because an employer or contractor will afford him no better, he is made the victim of force and injustice. . . .

Employers and workmen may of themselves effect much, in the matter we are treating, by means of such organizations as afford opportune aid to those who are in distress. . . . The most important of all are workingmen's unions, for these virtually include all the rest. History attests what excellent results were brought about by the artificers' guilds of olden times. They were the means of affording not only many advantages to the workmen but, in no small degree, of promoting the advancement of art. . . . Such unions should be suited to the requirements of this our age—an age of wider education, of different habits, and of far more numerous requirements in daily life. It is gratifying to know that there are actually in existence not a few organizations of this nature, consisting either of workmen alone or of workmen and employers together, but it were greatly to be desired that they should become more numerous and more efficient. . . .

The condition of the working class is the pressing question of the hour, and nothing can be of higher interest to all classes of the State than that it should be rightly and reasonably settled. But it will be easy for Christian working men to solve it aright if they will form associations, choose wise guides, and follow on the path which with much advantage to themselves and the common weal was trodden by their fathers before them. . . .

XI

The Rise of Modern Germany

XI

The Rise of Modern Germany

GERMANY HAD FOR SO LONG BEEN DIVIDED into hundreds of sovereign principalities that unification, at the beginning of the nineteenth century, appeared inconceivable. These principalities continued to give their nominal allegiance to the Holy Roman Empire, which, as Voltaire said, was neither Holy nor Roman nor an Empire. Nonetheless, the Empire remained a unifying idea. Two German states—Austria and Prussia—exceeded all the others in power. Potentially one or the other might have taken the leadership in a unification movement. Neither, however, was as powerful as France and the French had no intention of submitting to the creation of a unified, thus menacing, Germany as their neighbor.

Napoleon's Confederation of the Rhine, 1806

Ironically, the rise of a strong and unified Germany began with triumphant Napoleon's decision to build up German challengers to Austria and Prussia. When France occupied the left bank of the Rhine, Napoleon authorized the friendly princes he had dispossessed to take compensation on the right bank. One hundred twelve principalities east of the Rhine were thus swallowed up by their larger neighbors. Bavaria, Würtemburg, Baden and Saxony became the major beneficiaries. Napoleon's scheme appeared vindicated in 1805, when all four of the strengthened principalities fought as France's allies against Prussia and Austria in the War of the Third Coalition. To reward them, Napoleon recognized Bavaria, Würtemburg and Saxony as kingdoms and Baden as a grand-duchy.

After his great victory at Austerlitz in 1805, and the Treaty of Pressburg which followed it, Napoleon, confident of having destroyed Austria's capacity as a military rival, decided to make the rest of Germany into a French satellite state. At his direction, the Kings of Bavaria and Würtemburg, the Grand Duke of Baden and a variety of ecclesiastical and temporal princes officially seceded from the Holy Roman Empire to form a new Confederation of the Rhine. Ultimately all of Germany joined the Confederation, save Austria, Prussia and a handful of petty states. Napoleon, pleased to have placed Germany under the domination of France, assumed the title of Protector of the Confederation of the Rhine.

Napoleon followed the formation of the Confederation by withdrawing his recognition of the Holy Roman Empire. He intended thereby to reduce the prestige of the Hapsburg emperor and to strengthen France. On August 1, 1806, his representative appeared before the Diet of the Holy Roman Empire to announce that the Empire was dissolved. Francis II of Austria duly complied with Napoleon's command and surrendered the crown of his ancestors, satisfying himself henceforth with the less exalted title of Hereditary Emperor of Austria. Thus the Holy Roman Empire, which from the time of Charlemagne had existed only in men's minds anyway, came to an ignominious and unlamented end.

The Confederation of the Rhine did not last beyond the period of Napoleon's glory. Most of its members abandoned him as soon as his power began to fade. But though Napoleon's puppet state disappeared, the vigorous nationalism and yearning for unification that Napoleon had generated remained. Napoleon's political consolidation in Germany also stayed intact, since hundreds of old sovereign jurisdictions were never restored.

Napoleon's order to the Imperial Diet dissolving the Holy Roman Empire is presented here.

Document 71

The undersigned, chargé d'affaires of his Majesty the emperor of the French and King of Italy, at the general diet of the German empire, has received orders from his Majesty to make the following declarations to the diet:

Their Majesties the kings of Bavaria and of Würtemberg, the sovereign princes of Ratisbon, Baden, Burg, Hesse-Darmstadt, and Nassau, as well as the other leading princes of the south and west of Germany, have resolved to form a confederation between themselves which shall secure them against future contingencies, and have thus ceased to be states of the empire.

The position in which the Treaty of Pressburg has explicitly placed the courts allied to France, and indirectly those princes whose territory they border or surround, being incompatible with the existence of an empire, it becomes a necessity for those rulers to reorganize their relations upon a new system and to remove a contradiction which could not fail to be a permanent source of agitation, disquiet, and danger.

France, on the other hand, is directly interested in the maintenance of peace in southern Germany and yet must apprehend that the moment she shall cause her troops to recross the Rhine discord, the inevitable consequence of contradictory, uncertain, and ill-defined conditions, will again disturb the peace of the people and reopen, possibly, the war on the continent. Feeling it incumbent upon her to advance the welfare of her allies and to assure them the enjoyment of all the advantages which the Treaty of Pressburg secures to them and to which she is pledged, France cannot but regard the confederation which they have formed as a natural result and a necessary sequel to that treaty.

For a long period successive changes have, from century to century, reduced the German constitution to a shadow of its former self. Time has altered all the relations, in respect to size and importance, which originally existed among the various members of the confederation, both as regards each other and the whole of which they have formed a part.

The diet has no longer a will of its own; the sentences of the superior courts can no longer be executed; everything indicates such serious weakness that the federal bond no longer offers any protection whatever and only constitutes a source of dissension and discord between the powers. The results of three coalitions have increased this weakness to the last degree. . . . The Treaty of Pressburg assures complete sovereignty to their Majesties the kings of Bavaria and of Würtemberg and to his Highness the elector of Baden. This is a prerogative which the other electors will doubtless demand, and which they are justified in demanding; but this is in harmony neither with the letter nor the spirit of the constitution of the empire.

His Majesty the emperor and king is, therefore, compelled to declare that he can no longer acknowledge the existence of the German constitution, recognizing, however, the entire and absolute sovereignty of each of the princes whose states compose Germany to-day, maintaining with them the same relations as with the other independent powers of Europe.

His Majesty the emperor and king has accepted the title of Protector of the Confederation of the Rhine. He has done this only with a view to peace and in order that by his constant mediation between the weak and the powerful he may obviate every species of dissension and disorder.

Having thus provided for the dearest interests of his people and of his neighbors, and having assured, so far as in him lay, the future peace of

Europe, and that of Germany in particular, heretofore constantly the theater of war, by removing a contradiction which placed people and princes alike under the delusive protection of a system contrary both to their political interests and to their treaties, his Majesty the emperor and king trusts that the nations of Europe will at last close their ears to the insinuations of those who would maintain an eternal war upon the continent. He trusts that the French armies which have crossed the Rhine have done so for the last time, and that the people of Germany will no longer witness, except in the annals of the past, the horrible pictures of disorder, devastation, and slaughter which war invariably brings with it.

His Majesty declared that he would never extend the limits of France beyond the Rhine and he has been faithful to his promise. At present his sole desire is so to employ the means which Providence has confided to him as to free the seas, restore the liberty of commerce, and thus assure the peace and happiness of the world.

BACHER.

Ratisbon, August 1, 1806.

Prussian Edict of Emancipation, 1807

Prussia's ambition to become a great power, which Frederick the Great (1740–86) brought close to achievement, suffered a grievous setback on the battlefield of Jena in 1806, when Napoleon's legions decimated the vaunted Prussian army. The disaster gave Prussian leaders cause for much reflection. They decided that Prussia must emulate France in reorganizing the state along modern, progressive lines. In 1807, Prussia's Hohenzollern monarchy embarked on a program of internal reform. It changed Prussia from a semi-feudal to an enlightened monarchical state, ready to resume its quest for greatness.

The Prussian reforms, as distinguished from the changes in France, were granted from above, with an eye toward increasing the central power. They were not, therefore, a step toward popular government. On the contrary, they carefully preserved the power of the feudal lords, but they shifted this power to a modern social and political structure. Before the period of reform exhausted itself, it had extended to national and local administration, the army, education, industry and agriculture. The changes demonstrated a capacity for national regeneration that was all the more remarkable for being the product of the established ruling class.

The first and probably most important of the edicts was that which emancipated Prussia's serfs and made them free men. It authorized all classes of citizens to own land and pursue the occupations of their choice. A conservative decree, it did not give to the peasant the land he tilled but, on the contrary, confirmed the ownership of the nobles. Nonetheless, it abolished the cumbersome legal distinctions between classes and, most important, freed capital and labor to flow into areas where they were needed and from which they had been arbitrarily excluded.

The Edict of Emancipation of 1807, important excerpts of which are given below, provided the impetus for a healthy surge forward by Prussian agriculture and industry.

Document 72

We, Frederick William, by the grace of God king of Prussia etc., etc., hereby make known and proclaim that: Since peace has been established we have been occupied before everything else with the care for the depressed condition of our faithful subjects and the speediest revival and greatest possible improvement in this respect. We have considered that, in face of the prevailing want, the means at our disposal would be insufficient to aid each individual and even if they were sufficient, we could not hope to accomplish our object; and that, moreover, in accordance with the imperative demands of justice and with the principles of a judicious economic policy, it behooves us to remove every obstacle which has hitherto prevented the individual from attaining such a state of prosperity as he was capable of reaching. We have further considered that the existing restrictions, both on the possession and enjoyment of landed property and on the personal condition of the agricultural laborer, especially interfere with our benevolent purpose and disable a great force which might be applied to the restoration of agriculture,—the former, by their prejudicial influence upon the value of landed property and the credit of the proprietor; the latter, by diminishing the value of labor. We desire, therefore, to reduce both kinds of restrictions as far as the common well-being demands, and we accordingly ordain the following:

1. Every inhabitant of our states is competent, without any limitation on the part of the state, to own or mortgage landed property of every kind. The noble may therefore own not only noble, but also non-noble, citizen and peasant lands of every kind, and the citizen and peasant may

possess not only citizen, peasant, and other non-noble, but also noble tracts of land without in any case needing special permission for any acquisition whatever, although henceforth as before, every change of ownership must be announced to the authorities. All privileges which are possessed by nobles over citizen inheritances are entirely abolished. . . .

2. Every noble is henceforth permitted, without any derogation from his station, to engage in citizen occupation, and every citizen or peasant is allowed to pass from the citizen into the peasant class or from the peasant into the citizen class. . . .

10. From the date of this ordinance no new relation of serfdom, whether by birth or marriage, or by assuming the position of a serf, or by contract, can be created.

11. With the publication of the present ordinance the existing relations of serfdom of those serfs, with their wives and children, who possess their peasant holdings by inheritance, or in their own right, or by perpetual leases, or of copyhold, shall cease entirely, together with all mutual rights and duties.

12. From Martinmas, one thousand eight hundred and ten (1810), all serfdom shall cease throughout our whole realm. From Martinmas, 1810, there shall be only free persons, as is already the case upon the royal domains in all our provinces,—free persons, however, still subject, as a matter of course, to all obligations which bind them, as free persons, by reason of the possession of an estate or by virtue of a special contract.

To this declaration of our supreme will every one whom it may concern, and in particular our provincial authorities and other officials, are exactly and dutifully to conform, and the present ordinance is to be universally made known.

Given authentically, under our own royal signature, at Memel, October 9, 1807.

FREDERICK WILLIAM,
Schrötter, Stein, Schrötter II.

German Act of Confederation, 1815

The Vienna Congress in 1815 faced a dilemma in dealing with Germany. Despite the principle of legitimacy and the claims of hundreds of dethroned princes, the participants had no intention of restoring the feudal anarchy that existed before Napoleon. They rejected with equal firmness proposals to revive the Holy Roman Empire. On the other hand, the Vienna Congress had no intention of creating a unified Germany, if only because unification would have provoked too many powers. Either Prussia or Austria would have had to dominate a German state. Prussia, for the moment, was too weak to assume the responsibility. Austria, which ruled over many non-Germanic lands, had its own imperial problems without taking on new ones. But neither Prussia nor Austria would tolerate a united Germany under the leadership of the other, while France would not tolerate a united Germany at all. Though a feeling of nationalism was growing in Germany, the Congress of Vienna cautiously chose to devise a compromise, which would delay a decision on unification to a later day.

Vienna created a Confederation or Bund, a loose union representing some thirty-eight states and free cities. Its legislative body was the *Bundestag* or Diet, an assembly of ambassadors which met at Frankfort-on-Main under the presidency of Austria. Curiously, among its members were the kings of England, Denmark and the Netherlands, each in his capacity as sovereign over some Germany territory but each, obviously, more devoted to his non-Germanic kingdom. The Diet was paralyzed by the requirement that decisions be approved by a two-thirds majority. Constitutional changes needed unanimous consent. Though Austria was the dominant member, both Prussia and Austria possessed enough power to check any initiative on the part of the other. Thus the Germans acquired a parliament but they still had no king, no flag, no army—no nation. What was more ominous, they had no machinery for achieving unification by constitutional methods. For unification, Germany would need revolution or war.

The following extracts contain the principal provisions of the German Act of Confederation, signed on June 8, 1815. The Peace of Paris, referred to in the opening sentence, was the first treaty negotiated with France after Napoleon's fall. The Act of Confederation is reminiscent of the American Articles of Confederation, the early constitution that established a weak alliance between the colonies and which proved quite unsatisfactory. Still, the German Confederation endured until Prussia challenged Austria in 1866 and unified Germany by force of arms.

Document 73

In the name of the Most Holy and Indivisible Trinity:

The sovereign princes and the free towns of Germany, motivated by their common desire to implement Article VI of the Peace of Paris (May 30, 1814), and convinced of the advantages which would accrue for the security and independence of Germany and for the well-being and equilibrium of Europe from a strong and lasting union, have agreed to unite themselves in a perpetual confederation, and, for this reason, have given their representatives and envoys at the Congress of Vienna full powers. . . .

Article 1. The sovereign princes and the free towns of Germany, including their Majesties, the Emperor of Austria and the Kings of Prussia, Denmark, and the Netherlands—the Emperor of Austria and the King of Prussia because of their possessions formerly belonging to the German Empire; the King of Denmark for Holstein; and the King of the Netherlands for the Grand Duchy of Luxemburg—unite in a perpetual union which shall be called the German Confederation.

Article 2. The aim of this Confederation shall be the maintenance of the external and internal security of Germany as well as the independence and inviolability of the individual German states.

Article 3. All members of the Confederation shall have equal rights. They all agree to maintain the Act of Confederation.

Article 4. The affairs of the Confederation shall be managed by a Diet of the Confederation, in which all members of the Confederation shall vote through their representatives, either individually or collectively, in the following manner, without prejudice to their rank:

	Votes		*Votes*
1. Austria	1	13. Brunswick and Nassau	1
2. Prussia	1	14. Mecklenburg-Schwerin and Mecklenburg-Strelitz	1
3. Bavaria	1	15. Holstein-Oldenburg, Anhalt, and Schwarzburg	1
4. Saxony	1	16. Hohenzollern, Liechtenstein, Reuss, Schaumburg-Lippe, Lippe, and Waldeck	1
5. Hanover	1	17. The Free Towns, Lübeck, Frankfort, Bremen, and Hamburg	1
6. Würtemberg	1		
7. Baden	1		
8. Electoral Hesse	1		
9. Grand Duchy of Hesse	1		
10. Denmark, for Holstein	1		
11. The Netherlands, for the Grand Duchy of Luxemburg	1		
12. The grand ducal and ducal houses of Saxony	1		
		Total votes	17

Article 5. Austria shall preside over the Diet of the Confederation. Each member of the confederation shall have the right to initiate and

support proposals. Austria as the presiding state is bound within a given period to bring these proposals to deliberation. . . .

Article 9. The Diet of the Confederation shall meet at Frankfort on Main. The first meeting shall take place on September 1, 1815. . . .

Article 11. All members of the Confederation pledge themselves to protect Germany as a whole, and also every single confederated state, against attack. . . . If war is declared by the Confederation, no individual member may negotiate separately with the enemy, conclude an armistice, or make peace.

Article 12. The members of the Confederation reserve to themselves the right of forming alliances of any kind. However, they pledge themselves to make no commitments that shall be directed against the security of the Confederation or any individual state within it.

Frankfort Constitution of 1849

The uprising in Paris in 1848 was the spark that ignited a holocaust of revolutionary fervor throughout Germany and all of Europe. Mobs rose up against reactionary monarchies from Italy to Scandinavia to Bohemia. In Germany the middle-class seized upon the moment as the opportunity to forge a nation under a liberal and constitutional king. The Prussian monarch, Frederick William IV, was himself overcome by the fervor and consented to abet the cause of German revolution, while in Vienna the emperor accepted the principle of a constitution and dispatched Metternich into exile. Everywhere there were public meetings, processions, demonstrations and demands for liberal reform. Under popular pressure, press restrictions and police control were suddenly dropped. The buoyant wave of optimism that originated in Paris swept over all of Germany in that deceptive spring of 1848.

The Diet of the Confederation responded to the emotion by proclaiming a national flag, then by calling a national parliament, to be elected by the universal suffrage of all Germans. Despite the haste and general inexperience of the electors, the calibre of the delegates sent to the parliament was outstanding. The parliament's weakness, in fact, turned out to be not an excess of demagogues, as might have been expected, but an excess of pompous and ponderous intellectuals, incapable of decisive action. Still, high hopes reposed in this body when it met in Frankfort for the first time in May, 1848.

The parliament's major problem was to create a state that would comfortably accommodate both Austria and Prussia. But how could the parliament include in a German state all the Slavs, Czechs, Poles, Croats, Rumanians and Magyars who were under Austrian rule? Prussia, which was Protestant and more liberal than Austria, seemed to offer more of what the parliament sought, yet Austria would not consent to a position inferior to that of Prussia. For months the Frankfort parliament deliberated, while the revolutionary ardor cooled in both Berlin and Vienna. At last, on March 28, 1849, almost a year after it opened, the parliament decided by a vote of 290 to 248 to offer the hereditary crown of Germany to the king of Prussia.

In Berlin, King Frederick William IV, a German nationalist and an early hero of the revolution, had already begun suppressing the Prussian liberal movement. He was not the man to accept such a challenge as the German crown. Though a king of generous emotions, he had little courage and few convictions. He was troubled that his dynasty lacked the esteem of the Hapsburgs, the former Holy Roman Emperors and long the natural leaders of Germany. On April 3, 1849, he refused the crown of imperial Germany, on the ground that it was worthless coming from an elected parliament. With this rejection, the movement for a liberal, democratic, united Germany collapsed.

The Frankfort Constitution of 1849 remains one of history's great lost opportunities. From a technical point of view, it was an excellent constitution, providing an admirable balance between the large and the petty states, centralism and particularism, power and liberalism. No section was more significant than the Fundamental Rights of the German People, upon the drafting of which an excessive amount of time was spent but which meant so much to a people rebelling against autocracy. It proceeded directly from the great British, French and American documents of human rights. Parts of Section VI of the Frankfort Constitution, the Fundamental Rights of the German People, are reproduced below. It indicates how narrowly Germany, which so long endured tyranny and disunion, missed the introduction of Western liberalism and democracy.

Document 74

Section VI.
The Fundamental Rights of the German People

130. The German people shall possess the following fundamental rights. These rights shall serve as a standard for the individual German states, and no constitution or legislation of a German state shall abolish or circumscribe them.

Article 1

131. The German people consists of the citizens of the states which make up the Reich.

132. Every German has the right of German Reich's citizenship. He can exercise this right in every German land. Reich's franchise legislation shall provide for the right of the individual to vote for members of the national assembly.

133. Every German has the right to live or reside in any part of the Reich's territory, to acquire and dispose of property of all kinds, to pursue his livelihood, and to win the right of communal citizenship.

The terms for living and residence shall be established by a law of settlement; trade regulations shall be established by regulations affecting trade and industry; both to be set by the Reich's administration for all of Germany.

134. No German state is permitted to make a distinction between its citizens and other Germans in civil, criminal, and litigation rights which relegates the latter to the position of foreigners.

135. Capital punishment for civil offenses shall not take place, and, in those cases where condemnation has already been made, shall not be carried out, in order not to infringe upon the hereby acquired civil law.

136. Freedom of emigration shall not be limited by any state; emigration levies shall not be established.

All matters of emigration remain under the protection and care of the Reich.

Article 2

137. There are no class differences before the law. The rank of nobility is abolished.

All special class privileges are abolished.

All Germans are equal before the law.

All titles, insofar as they are not bound with an office, are abolished and never again shall be introduced.

No citizen shall accept a decoration from a foreign state.

Public office shall be open to all men on the basis of ability.

All citizens are subject equally to military service; there shall be no draft substitutions.

Article 3

138. The freedom of man shall be inviolable.

The arrest of a person, with the exception of one caught in the act, shall take place only under a legally executed warrant. This warrant must be served on the arrested person at the moment of the arrest or within the next twenty-four hours. . . .

139. Capital punishment, with the exception of cases prescribed by military law or naval law concerning mutiny, is abolished, as are sentences to public whipping, branding, and bodily punishment.

140. The house of every German is inviolable. . . .

Any search of premises must take place, when practicable, with the assistance of the inhabitants.

The inviolability of premises shall provide no hindrance to the apprehending of a fugitive from justice.

141. The confiscation of letters and papers, except at an arrest or house search, can take place with a legally executed warrant, which must be served on the arrested person at once or within the next twenty-four hours.

142. The secrecy of letters is inviolable.

Necessary exceptions in cases of criminal investigation and in the event of war shall be established by legislation.

Article 4

143. Every German shall have the right freely to express his opinion through speech, writing, publication, and illustration.

The freedom of the press shall be suspended under no circumstances through preventive measures, namely, censorship, concessions, security orders, imposts, limitation of publication or bookselling, postal bans, or other restraints. . . .

Article 5

144. Every German has complete freedom of religion and conscience.

No one is required to reveal his religious convictions.

145. Every German possesses the unlimited right for the private or public exercise of his religion.

Any crimes or acts which prevent the exercise of freedom of religion shall be punished by law. . . .

Article 6

152. Arts and science, research and teaching, shall be free.

153. Teaching and education remain under the authority of the state, and, with the exception of religious instruction, are removed from the authority of the clergy. . . .

157. There shall be no fees for instruction in public schools and lower trade schools. . . .

158. Every person is free to choose his work or profession, and to prepare himself for it wherever and however he wishes.

Article 7

159. Every German possesses the right of written petition to the authorities, to the representatives of the people, and to the Reichstag. . . .

Article 8

161. All Germans have the right to assemble peaceably and without arms; special permission for this is not needed.

Association of people outdoors can be forbidden in the event that it endangers public order and security. . . .

Article 9

164. Property is inviolable.

Expropriation of property can take place only when necessary for the common welfare, only on a legal basis, and with legal compensation.

Ecclesiastical property shall be protected by Reich's legislation. . . .

173. Taxation shall be so regulated that favoritism for individual classes or property-holders shall cease.

Article 10

174. All jurisdiction stems from the state. There shall be no patrimonial courts.

175. Judicial power shall be exercised independently by judges. There shall be no cabinet or ministerial justice. . . .

176. Judicial judgments shall be public and oral. . . .

183. Legal judgments of German jurists shall be equally valid and ratified in all German lands.

Article 11

184. Every community shall have as fundamental rights of its constitution:

a. election of its chairman and representatives

b. independent control of its communal activities with the assistance of the local police under legal supervision of the state

c. publication of its budget

d. public consideration of its affairs. . . .

Article 12

186. Every German state shall have a constitution with representation of the people.

The ministers are responsible to the people. . . .

Article 13

188. The non-German-speaking people of Germany are guaranteed their national development, namely, equal rights for their languages, insofar as they exist in their territories, in ecclesiastical matters, in education, in administration of local affairs, and in laws.

Article 14

189. Every German citizen stands under the protection of the Reich.

Bismarck's "Blood and Iron" Speech, 1862

When the Frankfort Parliament collapsed, the leadership of the German unification movement passed from the middle-class liberals to the aristocratic militarists of Prussia, whose objective in uniting Germany was the control of the largest possible armed force. Austria to them represented not so much an enemy as an obstacle to Prussian hegemony in Germany and central Europe.

Otto von Bismarck, a landed aristocrat of extremely conservative views, was the man destined to lead the military unification movement. Bismarck was first summoned to the Prussian chancellorship when the lower house of the Parliament, a vestige of the liberal reforms of 1848, refused to vote funds that the king wanted to strengthen the army. William I, successor to the hapless Frederick William IV, gave Bismarck a free hand to deal with the Parliament. Bismarck chose to govern in defiance of the constitution, without the confidence of the Parliament or a legal budget. While the Prussian people watched indifferently, Bismarck broke the power of parliamentary rule. He proceeded then to build one of the finest armies in Europe, which he planned to use to unite Germany on Prussia's terms.

On September 30, 1862, Bismarck outlined to a parliamentary commission the policies he planned to pursue. He concluded his speech with the declaration that Prussia would decide the great questions of the day with "iron and blood." Changed, to step up the rhythm, to "blood and iron," the phrase spread quickly throughout Germany and the world, as a warning of what Europe could expect from Prussia. Bismarck's famous phrases appear below.

Document 75

. . . It is true that we can hardly escape complications in Germany, although we do not seek them. Germany does not look to Prussia's liberalism, but to her power. The south German States—Bavaria, Würtemberg, and Baden—would like to indulge in liberalism, and because of that no one will assign Prussia's role to them! Prussia must collect her forces and hold them in reserve for an opportune moment, which has already come and gone several times. Since the Treaty of Vienna, our frontiers have not been favorably designed for a healthy body politic. Not by speeches and majorities will the great questions of the day be decided—that was the mistake of 1848 and 1849—but by iron and blood.

Treaty of Prague, 1866

Bismarck, one of the shrewdest statesmen of modern times, set as his goal the elimination of Austria from influence over German affairs. Like a chess champion, he planned many moves ahead to achieve his ends. In 1864, he revived an old dispute with Denmark over the duchies of Schleswig and Holstein, which were German in character but ruled by the Danish king. On the pretext that Germans in the provinces were increasingly oppressed, Prussia and Austria jointly declared war and snatched the territories away from the Danes. Foreseeably, the two great German powers then fell out over the spoils. Austria wanted to make Schleswig-Holstein into a separate state, with membership in the German Confederation, which it dominated. Bismarck objected, but consented to a compromise under which Austria occupied Holstein while Prussia occupied Schleswig. Bismarck then readied his army for a war against Austria.

Bismarck, characteristically, left little to chance. He contracted an alliance which, in return for an Italian attack on Austria from the south, would give to Italy Austria's Italian territories. He made some vague promises to the French to keep them neutral. When all was ready, he began to foment agitation and intrigue in Holstein. This moved Austria to protest before the Diet of the German Confederation. Feigning great indignation, Bismarck ordered his troops to drive Austria out of Holstein. He then proposed a sweeping reorganization of the German Confederation, to exclude Austria. Outraged, the Austrians called on the Diet to repudiate the Prussian plan and appealed for a general mobilization of the German states to back Austrian rights. When the Diet, reflecting German anxiety over Prussia's intentions, approved the Austrian proposals, Bismarck withdrew from the Confederation and announced to the world that he was preparing to fight a "defensive" war in the interests of German unity. So astutely had he managed his diplomacy that public opinion throughout Europe was overwhelmingly favorable to Prussia.

The War of 1866 that pitted Prussia and Italy against Austria and several lesser German states lasted only seven weeks. The Hapsburgs were totally unprepared to face the mighty Prussian war machine. Though the Austrians fought successfully against the Italians, they were crushed by the Prussians at Sadowa on July 3 and immediately sued for peace.

The Treaty of Prague, signed between Prussia and Austria in August, 1866, became the foundation of German unification. The Hapsburgs ceded Holstein to Prussia, as well as Venetia to Italy. They paid the Prussians a small indemnity. Most important, however, Austria consented to the dissolution of the German Confederation and the creation of a new North German Confederation, of which it would not be a member and which Prussia would dominate. Austria, the principal power in Germany since the Middle Ages, was now excluded from Germany. Prussia, annexing a few more principalities, stretched across Germany from Russia to France, ruling two-fifths of German territory and three-fifths of Germany's population. Prussia's Hohenzollern king presided over the North German Confederation, which lacked only four south German states to encompass the entire nation. Through "blood and iron," Bismarck had all but unified his country.

The key provisions of the Treaty of Prague are given here.

Document 76

In the name of the All Highest and Indivisible Trinity!

His Majesty, the King of Prussia, and His Majesty, the Emperor of Austria, animated by the desire to bring back to their countries the benefits of peace, have agreed to transform the preliminary negotiations signed at Nikolsburg on July 26, 1866, into a definite treaty of peace. . . .

Article 2. As a means of implementing Article 6 of the peace preliminaries, . . . His Majesty, the Emperor of Austria, agrees to the Union of the Kingdom of Lombardy-Venetia and the Kingdom of Italy, without any other burdensome conditions. . . .

Article 4. His Majesty, the Emperor of Austria, recognizes the dissolution of the former German Bund and gives his assent to a new form of Germany without participation of the Austrian Empire. . . .

Article 5. His Majesty, the Emperor of Austria, assigns to His Majesty, the King of Prussia, all the rights acquired by the Vienna Peace of October 30, 1864, in the Duchies of Holstein and Schleswig, with the added understanding that the population of the northern district of Schleswig, if they have expressed the wish through a free plebiscite to enter a union with Denmark, shall be transferred to Denmark. . . .

Article 11. His Majesty, the Emperor of Austria, pledges himself, in order to help cover a part of the war costs of Prussia, to pay to His Majesty, the King of Prussia, the sum of forty million Prussian talers. From this sum there will be subtracted fifteen million Prussian talers, which Austria, according to Article 12 of the Vienna Peace of October 30, 1864, is still to receive from the Duchies of Schleswig and Holstein, and an additional five million Prussian talers, as equivalent for the costs of the Prussian army in Austria during the occupation until the conclusion of peace, so that only twenty million Prussian talers remain to be paid in cash.

Half of this sum is to be paid concurrently with the exchange of ratifications of the present treaty, and the second half to be paid in cash three weeks later. . . .

Article 14. The ratification of the present treaty shall be exchanged at Prague within the space of eight days, or sooner if possible.

In witness whereof the respective plenipotentiaries have signed the present treaty, and have affixed to it the seals of their arms.

Done at Prague, on the 23d day of the month of August, in the year of Grace, 1866.

(L.S.) BRENNER (L.S.) WERTHER

Proclamation of the German Empire, 1871

Germany's last obstacle to unification was France. Although Napoleon III, the French emperor, had stood by passively while north Germany fell under Prussian control, he was more likely to act in face of a threat to south Germany. Bismarck was convinced that if he could provoke a war against France, the south German states would enter the Prussian fold in patriotic fervor. For, though the south Germans mistrusted Prussia for its Protestantism and anti-liberalism, they distrusted Napoleon III even more. Bismarck judged that he had only to trick the French into declaring war to complete his mission of unification.

With his usual cunning, Bismarck seized his opportunity as soon as it presented itself. He took a telegram that was part of French-German diplomatic correspondence—the famous Ems Dispatch—and made it public in a form so doctored that both countries regarded it as necessary to take to the battlefield to preserve their honor. France declared war in July, 1870. As Bismarck had predicted, the south German states allied themselves with Prussia. Within a few months, the French army was decisively beaten. Napoleon III had abdicated, and the Empire was in collapse.

Though France fought on tenaciously after the emperor fled, the outcome of the war was never in doubt. Paris held out until January, 1871, when cold and starvation compelled capitulation. In February the French called for a cease-fire to permit the election of a National Assembly with authority to negotiate a peace. The treaty that was signed required France to cede Alsace and much of Lorraine to Germany and to pay an enormous indemnity. The harsh terms were not an example of Bismarck's statemanship at its best. They assured a thriving irredentist movement in France, which would become the source of much trouble for Germany.

The consummation of Bismarck's plan for German unification was, however, the most spectacular result of the Franco-Prussian War. By November, 1870, the North German Confederation and the South German states had concluded a series of treaties of union. The name of the union was changed from German Confederation to German Empire and the Prussian king's title from President of the Confederation to Emperor—or Kaiser—of Germany. The solemn ceremony inaugurating the Empire was conducted not in Germany but in Louis XIV's Hall of Mirrors in Versailles. It was, as well as the final humiliation for France, the ultimate triumph for Bismarck and Prussia.

Kaiser William I issued his imperial proclamation from Versailles on January 18, 1871, while the Germans were still besieging Paris. It announced the "restoration" of a German Empire that, in reality, had never existed. "Kaiser" was a resurrection of the old imperial title. William I placed Germany on the foundation of the historical fiction known as the Holy Roman Empire, the chief office of which, his proclamation announced, "has not been occupied for more than sixty years." The new nation, conceived by militarists for militaristic purposes, was thus dedicated to an expansionist myth. The origins of united Germany put it on a perilous path.

The Proclamation of the German Empire appears below.

Document 77

WHEREAS, The German Princes and the Free Cities have called unanimously upon us to revive and assume, with the restoration of the German Empire, the German imperial office, which has not been occupied for more than sixty years; and

WHEREAS, Adequate arrangements have been made for this purpose in the Constitution of the German Confederation;

Therefore, we, William, by the grace of God, King of Prussia, do hereby proclaim that we have considered it to be a duty to our common Fatherland to respond to the summons of the unified German Princes and cities and to accept the German imperial title. As a result, we and those who succeed us on the throne of Prussia, henceforth, shall bear the imperial title in all our relations and in all the activities of the German Empire, and we trust to God that the German nation will be granted the ability to construct a propitious future for the Fatherland under the symbol of its ancient glory.

We assume the imperial title, aware of the duty of protecting, with German loyalty, the rights of the Empire and of its members, of maintaining the peace, and of protecting the independent rulers of Germany, which, in turn, is dependent upon the united power of the people.

We assume the title in the hope that the German people will be granted the ability to enjoy the fruits of its zealous and self-sacrificing wars in eternal peace, inside boundaries that give the Fatherland a security against renewed French aggression which has been lost for centuries. May God grant that we and our successors on the imperial throne may at all times enhance the wealth of the German Empire, not through military conquests, but by the blessings and the gifts of peace, within the realm of national prosperity, freedom, and morality.

Issued at General Headquarters, Versailles, January 18, 1871.

William

XII

The Unification of Italy

XII

The Unification of Italy

In Italy, as elsewhere in Europe, Napoleon's arrival evoked nationalistic yearnings. The inspiration he transmitted from the French Revolution created a conviction among Italians, particularly the intellectuals, that their country ought, like France, to be free and united. Paradoxically these sentiments generated a feeling of resentment against Napoleon's presence in Italy. His departure was a source of joy, although in his place the Congress of Vienna restored the old Austrian, Papal and Bourbon tyrannies. On Napoleon's heels there grew up in Italy a network of secret societies called the *Carbonari* (charcoal burners), the aims of which were to provoke revolution against the oppressive princes who ruled Italian territories. For the first time in centuries—perhaps in all history—the inhabitants of the peninsula had become conscious of being not simply Roman or Tuscan or Lombardian but Italian.

Mazzini's Instructions to Young Italy

No man more embodied the *Risorgimento*, the drive for Italian unification, than Giuseppe Mazzini, prophet, romantic, apostle of action, who infused Italian nationalism with a spiritual quality and a sense of mission. Mazzini's writings stirred all of Italy, but had particular impact on the young and vigorous members of Italy's growing middle class. In 1831, Mazzini founded a secret revolutionary order called "Young Italy." Its aim was a unified and republican Italy, which conflicted with the objective of those patriots who favored unity under a constitutional monarchy or even, in the case of a few, under the Pope. But what Mazzini had in common with other patriots—his deep sense of Italian nationality— outweighed the differences. Mazzini raced indefatigably over Italy spreading his gospel, fomenting revolt. His pleas evoked great nationalist sentiment and provided the foundation for the *Risorgimento* movement.

The following excerpt is from Mazzini's instructions to the members of Young Italy. It proclaims his political objectives and describes the methods by which he proposed to achieve them.

Document 78

Young Italy is a brotherhood of Italians who believe in a law of *progress* and *duty*, and are convinced that Italy is destined to become one nation, convinced also that she possesses sufficient strength within herself to become one, and that the ill success of her former efforts is to be attributed not to the weakness, but to the misdirection of the revolutionary elements within her,—that the secret force lies in constancy and unity of effort. They join this association with the firm intention of consecrating both thought and action to the great aim of reconstituting Italy as one independent sovereign nation of free men and equals. . . .

The aim of the association is *revolution;* but its labors will be essentially educational, both before and after the day of revolution; and it therefore declares the principles upon which the national education should be conducted, and from which alone Italy may hope for safety and regeneration. . . .

Young Italy is *republican* and *unitarian,*—republican, because theoretically every nation is destined, by the law of God and humanity, to form a free and equal community of brothers; and the republican government is the only form of government that insures this future: Because all true sovereignty resides essentially in the nation, the sole progressive and continuous interpreter of the supreme moral law; . . . because the monarchical element being incapable of sustaining itself alone by the side of the popular element, it necessarily involves the existence of the intermediate element of an aristocracy,—the source of inequality and corruption to the whole nation; because both history and the nature of things teach us that elective monarchy tends to generate anarchy, and hereditary monarchy tends to generate despotism; because, when monarchy is not—as in the Middle Ages—based upon the belief, now extinct, in right divine, it becomes too weak to be a bond of unity and authority in the State; because the inevitable tendency of the series of progressive transformations taking place in Europe is toward the enthronement of the republican principle, and because the inauguration of the monarchical principle in Italy would carry along with it the necessity of a new revolution shortly after.

Our Italian tradition is essentially republican; our great memories are republican; the whole history of our national progress is republican; whereas the introduction of monarchy amongst us was coeval with our decay, and consummated our ruin by its constant servility to the foreigner and antagonism to the people as well as to the unity of the nation. . . .

Young Italy is *unitarian*, because, without unity there is no true nation; because, without unity there is no real strength; and Italy, surrounded as she is by powerful, united, and jealous nations, has need of strength above all things; because federalism, by reducing her to the political impotence of Switzerland, would necessarily place her under the influence of one of the neighboring nations; because federalism, by reviving the local rivalries now extinct, would throw Italy back upon the Middle Ages; . . . because federalism, by destroying the unity of the great Italian family, would strike at the root of the great mission Italy is destined to accomplish for humanity; because Europe is undergoing a progressive series of transformations, which are gradually and irresistibly guiding European society to form itself into vast and united masses; because the entire work of internal civilization in Italy will be seen, if rightly studied, to have been tending for ages toward unity.

The means by which Young Italy proposes to reach its aim are education and insurrection, to be adopted simultaneously and made to harmonize with each other. Education must ever be directed to teach, by example, word, and pen, the necessity of insurrection. Insurrection, whenever it can be realized, must be so conducted as to render it a means of national education. . . .

Victor Emmanuel Opens the Italian Parliament, 1860

Italians, like other Europeans, caught the revolutionary contagion of 1848 and rose up against their oppressors. The brutal repression of their efforts demonstrated that popular ardor and courage were insufficient weapons for the achievement of unification. An army was necessary and Camillo Cavour, brilliant minister of Piedmont-Sardinia, resolved to create one strong enough to defeat Austria, Italy's principal foe. Cavour's tiny kingdom, only five million in population, was the logical one to lead the *Risorgimento*. It had on the throne Victor Emmanuel of the House of Savoy, a liberal, enlightened monarch. It was free of foreign rule, well governed, industrious and ambitious. After 1848, Cavour undertook a campaign to achieve a goal parallel to Bismarck's in Germany. Cavour set out to unify Italy.

Cavour's first move was to win the sympathy of Britain and France by enlisting on their side in the Crimean War. He demonstrated in the Crimea that his army could fight. In 1858 Cavour negotiated a bargain with Napoleon III, the French emperor, which was to have great consequences for Italy. He agreed to cede to France the provinces of Nice and Savoy, Sardinia's French-speaking territories west of the Alps. In return, the emperor agreed to join him in a war of liberation against the Hapsburgs. In April, 1859, Cavour succeeded in provoking Austria into opening hostilities.

The French army that came to the aid of Piedmont-Sardinia was not very good but the Austrian army was worse. On June 4, the French and Sardinians decisively defeated the Austrians at Magenta and swept into Milan. In the provinces of Modena, Parma and Tuscany, meanwhile, the population rose up and drove their oppressive sovereigns into exile. In Romagna, a part of the Papal states, the people chased out the Pope's representatives. Cavour's agents, wherever the old government was swept away, stepped in skillfully to organize the public powers under the Sardinian king. On June 24, French and Austrian armies met again at Solferino and the Hapsburgs were once more badly beaten. Nothing now seemed to stand in the way of full national unity.

But suddenly Cavour and his king learned to their utter dismay that Napoleon III, because of difficulties at home, had decided to withdraw from the war, leaving Italy to fight on alone. Furious at the French, Cavour wanted to continue the struggle, but the king decided wisely against gambling all in another battle with the Austrians. By the Treaty of Villafranca, Sardinia received Lombardy from Austria but not Venetia, which the French had promised to redeem. The terms of the Treaty also provided for the restoration of the dukes of Modena and Tuscany, while Napoleon sheepishly agreed to relinquish his claims to Nice and Savoy.

But before the treaty took effect, constituent assemblies in Tuscany and Modena, as well as in Parma and the Romagna, voted not to receive back their old rulers and to recognize Victor Emmanuel as sovereign. Cavour, swallowing his anger, now proposed another deal to Napoleon III. He once more offered France Nice and Savoy in return for which Napoleon III would recognize and guarantee the union of the north and central Italian provinces under the Sardinian king. Napoleon accepted the bribe. Almost half of the Italian peninsula now acknowledged the rule of Victor Emmanuel. Only

Venetia, the Papal States and the Bourbon kingdom of the two Sicilies eluded Cavour's grasp.

The first Italian parliament was opened by King Victor Emmanuel in April, 1860, in his capital city of Turin. The king reviewed the exalting events which had led to the parliament, treating with graciousness the equivocal role of France. Quite openly he warned the Pope that the States of the Church was one of the objectives of his unification program. King Victor Emmanuel's speech, reproduced in part here, reflects his satisfaction with the triumphs of the *Risorgimento* but leaves no doubt that its work would go on until completed.

Document 79

The last time that I opened this parliament, in the midst of the travails of Italy and dangers to the State, faith in divine justice encouraged me to prophesy a happy issue for us. In a very short space of time an invasion has been repelled; Lombardy has been freed, thanks to the glorious exploits of our heroes, and central Italy has been delivered, thanks to the remarkable courage of its inhabitants; and to-day the representatives of right and of the hopes of the nation are assembled about me.

We owe many benefits to a magnanimous ally, to the bravery of his soldiers as well as of ours, to the self-abnegation of the volunteers, and to the harmony of the various peoples; and we render thanks to God, for without superhuman aid these enterprises, memorable not only for our own generation but for ages to come, could not have been achieved.

Out of gratitude to France for the services she has rendered to Italy, and in order to consolidate the union of the two nations, which have a community of origin, of principles, and of destiny, some sacrifice was necessary; I have made that one which costs most to my own heart. Subject to the vote of the people and the approbation of the parliament, . . . I have agreed to a treaty providing for the reunion of Savoy and of the district of Nice to France.

We still have many difficulties to overcome, but, sustained by public opinion and by the love of the people, I will not permit any right or liberty to be infringed or diminished.

Although I am as consistent in my respect toward the supreme head of our religion as the Catholic rulers, my ancestors, they have always shown themselves ready, nevertheless, should the ecclesiastical authority resort to spiritual arms in support of its temporal interests. I will, relying upon a pure conscience and the traditions of my forefathers, find strength to maintain civil liberty and my authority, for the exercise of which I owe an account only to God and to my people. . . .

Garibaldi's Account of the Taking of Naples, 1860

Giuseppe Garibaldi, one of history's most dynamic and romantic figures, wrested the south of Italy from the tyrannical Bourbon dynasty and presented it to the Italian kingdom. A free-booting republican and a veteran of the 1848 uprisings, Garibaldi set out in May, 1860, with a band of 1000 irregular troops to attack the Kingdom of Two Sicilies, whose rulers, though decadent, had demonstrated a remarkable capacity for survival. With the secret help of Cavour, who distrusted Garibaldi's republicanism while admiring his audacity, Garibaldi reached Sicily, where he faced an army that though far larger and better equipped than his was disorganized and demoralized. Using courage, bluff and tactical skill, Garibaldi defeated the Bourbon troops again and again. He swept through Sicily, then invaded the mainland. On the ancient battlefields of Campagna he won his final victories. On October 1, he entered the Bourbon capital, the great city of Naples, in triumph.

Cavour by now was apprehensive about the intentions of Garibaldi, who he feared might be tempted to establish a republic in the south and perpetuate the national rift. He feared also that Garibaldi, who was deeply anticlerical, might impetuously march on Rome and thereby incite the fury of Catholics all over Europe. Cavour decided on a daring stroke of his own. He ordered the Sardinian army of 35,000 men to fight its way across the Papal territories and block Garibaldi's path to the Eternal City. Cavour, encountering little trouble with the Pope's forces, annexed en route Umbria and the Marches, two of the Papal provinces. When his soldiers reached Naples they were, to Cavour's relief, not challenged but welcomed by Garibaldi. On November 7, 1860, King Victor Emmanuel and the remarkable freebooter paraded through Naples together. The next day Garibaldi, refusing all titles and public honors, turned over his powers to the king of Italy and retired to his home.

Garibaldi's triumphs completed the kingdom of Italy, save for Venetia, which Austria retained, and the city of Rome, which remained in the Pope's hands. The following is Garibaldi's own account of the events that sealed the union of the south with the rest of the nation.

Document 80

The first of October dawned on the plains of the ancient capital of Campagna upon a hideous tumult, a fratricidal conflict. On the side of the Bourbons, it is true, foreign mercenaries were numerous,—Bavarians, Swiss, and others belonging to the nations who for centuries had been accustomed to look upon this Italy of ours as their pleasure ground. This crew, under the guidance and with the blessings of the priest, have always been accustomed, by sheer right of the strongest, to cut the throats of the Italians, trained from childhood by the priest to bow the knee to them. But it is only too certain that the greater number of the men who fought on the slopes of Tifata were sons of this unhappy country driven to butcher one another,—one side led by a young king, the child of crime, the other fighting for the sacred cause of their country. . . .

The enemy, after an obstinate combat, were routed all along the line and retired in disorder within the walls of Capua about five P.M., their retreat being covered by the guns of that fortress. About the same time Bixio announced to me the victory of his right wing over the Bourbon troops, so that I was able to telegraph to Naples, "Victory all along the line."

[The next day] the Bourbon troops, taken unawares, offered but little resistance and were driven back almost at a run, hotly pursued by the brave Calabrians as far as Caserta Vecchia. A few of them held this village for a short time, firing from the windows and from behind the cover afforded by some ruined walls; but these were quickly surrounded and made prisoners. . . .

With the victory of Caserta Vecchia, October 2, the glorious period of our campaign of 1860 closes. The Italian army of the north, sent by Farini and Company to combat the "revolution personified" in us, found us brothers; and to this army fell the task of completing the annihilation of Bourbonism in the Two Sicilies. In order to regulate the position of our gallant fellow-soldiers, I asked for the recognition of the army of the south as a part of the national army; and it was a piece of injustice not to grant my request. They resolved to enjoy the fruits of conquest while banishing the conquerors.

When I understood that this was the case, I handed over to Victor Emmanuel the dictatorship conferred upon me by the people, and proclaimed him King of Italy. To him I recommended my gallant comrades, the thought of whom was the only painful element of my departure, eager as I was to return to my solitude.

Austro-Italian Treaty on Venetia, 1866

The Kingdom of Italy was officially proclaimed in March, 1861. Two months later Cavour died at the age of 52. Those who succeeded him, if less competent, were no less determined to complete the task of unification. The Kingdom of Italy was impatient to get on with its unfinished business.

In April, 1866, Italy signed an agreement to assist Prussia in its impending war with Austria. In return, Italy was to receive Venetia from the defeated Austrians. When the war began Italy met its commitment and hurled an army at the Austrians from the south. The Italian troops performed badly, however, and only Prussia's decisive victory in the north saved the situation. When Austria surrendered, Italy was awarded its promised share of the booty.

By the Treaty of Vienna of 1866, the principal provisions of which are presented below, Austria conceded the loss of the Hapsburg holdings in Lombardo-Venetia. The Treaty joined to the Kingdom of Italy the last parcel of territory on the peninsula—except Rome. The Eternal City remained the final target.

Document 81

Article I. There shall be from the date of the exchange of the Ratifications of the present Treaty, Peace and Friendship between His Majesty the King of Italy and His Majesty the Emperor of Austria, their heirs and successors, their States and their respective subjects in perpetuity.

Article II. The Italian and Austrian Prisoners of War shall be immediately delivered up on both sides.

Article III. His Majesty the Emperor of Austria agrees to the Union of the Lombardo-Venetian Kingdom to the Kingdom of Italy.

Article IV. The Frontier of the Ceded Territory is determined by the actual administrative confines of the Lombardo-Venetian Kingdom. . . .

Article XIV. Inhabitants or natives of the Territory ceded by the present Treaty will have for the space of a year, from the day of the date on which the Ratifications are exchanged, and conditionally on a previous declaration before the competent authorities, full and entire power to export their Movables, free of duty, and to retire with their families into the States of His Imperial and Royal Apostolic Majesty, in which case their quality of Austrian subjects will be retained by them. They will be at liberty to keep their immovable property situated on the ceded Territory. . . .

Article XV. The Lombardo-Venetian subjects in the Austrian army will be immediately discharged from military service and sent back to their homes.

It is understood that those amongst them who declare their wish to remain in the service of His Imperial and Royal Apostolic Majesty shall be free to do so, and will not be disturbed on this account, either in person or in property.

The same guarantees are assured to the Civil Employees, natives of the Lombardo-Venetian Kingdom, who manifest their intention of keeping the offices they occupy in the Austrian Service. . . .

Papal Encyclical Protesting the Seizure of Rome, 1870

Rome eluded the designs of the Kingdom of Italy throughout the 1860s. The Papal government was kept in office only by the good graces of Napoleon III, who maintained a garrison in Rome to satisfy Catholic sentiment at home. On several occasions French troops beat off attempts by irregular forces under Garibaldi to take the city. The Italian government, meeting impatiently at Turin, made no secret of its intention to declare Rome the capital of the Kingdom. It was clear that an Italian army would sweep down on the Eternal City at the first favorable opportunity.

The opportunity arose in 1870, when France called home its Roman garrison to participate in the fight against Prussia. In a final entreaty, King Victor Emmanuel pleaded with Pope Pius IX to relinquish the sovereignty over the temporal possessions and accept the protection of the Italian Kingdom. The Pope, however, insisted that his temporal sovereignty was vital to the maintenance of his spiritual independence. He announced that he would yield only to force.

On September 20, 1870, an Italian column breached the thin lines of the pontifical forces and entered the city. In an instant the temporal power—founded by the Donation of Pepin in 756 and the source of so much trouble ever since—collapsed. The black-robed autocracy, whose corruption and inefficiency had scandalized the nineteenth century, no longer blighted the spiritual mission of the Papacy. A plebiscite of Roman citizens overwhelmingly ratified union with the Kingdom of Italy.

Pope Pius IX responded to the seizure by declaring himself a prisoner and withdrawing to the recesses of the vast Vatican palace. For six decades he and his successors refused any relations with the Italian government, although Italy guaranteed them complete liberty. During this period, the loss of the temporal states proved to be an unforeseen blessing to the Papacy. No longer burdened with the pressures of Italian nationalism or the cares of temporal administration, the Popes enjoyed a resurgence as a moral force in the Western world. The end of eleven hundred years of Papal dominion permitted the development of a stronger, purer Church. In retrospect, it is clear that the temporal power had been a serious diversion from the religious mission of the Catholic Church.

In May, 1871, however, Pope Pius IX saw no happy future for a Papacy deprived of its temporal power. He sent an encyclical to the higher clergy condemning the Italian action, vowing the impossibility of reconciliation. He openly appealed to the Catholic powers to restore his sovereignty. None responded. The relations between the Papacy and the Italian Kingdom remained poisoned until 1929, when the two signed a series of agreements known as the Lateran Treaties which settled their relations. It was only then that the Popes emerged from their self-imposed imprisonment.

The Encyclical of Pope Pius IX of 1871 is, in part, presented below.

Document 82

. . . We deem it an obligation imposed upon us by our Holy Apostolic office solemnly to declare through you to the entire world that not merely the so-called "guarantees," perversely fabricated through the machinations of the Sub-alpine government, but all the titles, honors, immunities, and privileges of whatever nature which may be included under the name of securities or "guarantees" can in no way suffice to maintain the free and unrestricted exercise of the powers which God has granted us and preserve the freedom which is essential to the Church.

We, therefore, in accordance with the duty which our office imposes upon us do once more declare—as we have repeatedly declared and made known—that we cannot, without violating our most sacred pledges, agree to any form of reconciliation that shall in any degree destroy or diminish our rights, which are at the same time the rights of God of the Apostolic See. We can, accordingly, never in any manner acknowledge or accept those securities or "guarantees" devised by the Sub-alpine government, however they may be stated, nor any others, no matter how sanctioned, which may be offered us under the false pretense that they will serve as a protection for our sacred authority and our independence, and will take the place of, and compensate us for, our temporal dominion with which it has pleased Divine Providence to fortify and strengthen the Holy See,—a dominion to which our right is confirmed by an uninterrupted series of valid legal titles as well as by eleven hundred years and more of possession.

For it must be clearly evident to all that the Roman Pontiff, if he be subjected to the dominion of another prince and is no longer actually in possession of sovereign power himself, cannot escape (whether in respect to his personal conduct or the acts of his apostolic office) from the will of the ruler to whom he is subordinated, who may prove to be a heretic, a persecutor of the Church, or be involved in war with other princes. Indeed, is not this very concession of guarantees in itself a clear instance of the imposition of laws upon us,—upon us on whom God has bestowed authority to make laws relating to the moral and religious order,—on us who have been designated the expounder of natural and divine law throughout the world? And do not these laws imposed upon us by the secular government affect the entire Church, and yet under the present circumstances their enforcement depends entirely upon the will of this secular power.

Touching the relation of the Church and civil society, venerable brethren, you are well aware that we have received, through the person of St. Peter, directly from God himself all the powers and authority necessary for the government of the entire Church; nay more, that these prerogatives and rights, as well as the freedom of the Church, were won and redeemed by the blood of Jesus Christ and are to be cherished and revered in proportion to the infinite preciousness of that divine blood. Of this we should render ourselves unworthy should we consent to accept from princes of this world these our rights, diminished and dishonored in the form they are tendered us. For Christian princes are sons, not rulers, of the Church. . . .

God grant that the princes of the earth (who are vitally interested in taking measures to prevent such an act of usurpation as that from which we now suffer from being perpetrated, to the destruction of all law and order) may combine with unanimous wills and hearts and endeavor to allay the dissensions and disorder to which rebellion has given rise, and put an end to the fatal machinations of faction in order that the Holy See may be restored to its rights, the visible head of the Church once more enjoy his complete freedom, and civil society again rejoice in the peace for which it has so long yearned.

Victor Emmanuel's Speech in Rome, 1871

When the Italian Parliament, representing the entire nation, met for the first time in Rome in 1871, Italy could look back on a magnificent achievement and, at the same time, anticipate the great problems that accompany nationhood. King Victor Emmanuel, in his address to the Italian Parliament, reflects both the pride of accomplishment and recognition of the vast work that remained to be done. Excerpts of the speech of Victor Emmanuel are presented here.

Document 83

Senators and Deputies, gentlemen:

The work to which we consecrated our life is accomplished. After long trials of expiation Italy is restored to herself and to Rome. Here, where our people, after centuries of separation, find themselves for the first time solemnly reunited in the person of their representatives; here where we recognize the fatherland of our dreams, everything speaks to us of greatness; but at the same time it all reminds us of our duties. The joy that we experience must not let us forget them. . . .

We have proclaimed the separation of Church and State. Having recognized the absolute independence of the spiritual authority, we are convinced that Rome, the capital of Italy, will continue to be the peaceful and respected seat of the Pontificate. In this way we shall succeed in reassuring the consciences of men. It is thus, by the firmness of our resolutions, and by the moderation of our acts, that we have been able to hasten the national unity without altering our amicable relations with foreign powers. . . .

Economic and financial affairs, moreover, claim our most careful attention. Now that Italy is established, it is necessary to make it prosperous by putting in order its finances; we shall succeed in this only by persevering in the virtues which have been the source of our national regeneration. Good finances will be the means of reënforcing our military organization. Our most ardent desire is for peace, and nothing can make us believe that it can be troubled. But the organization of the army and the navy, the supply of arms, the works for the defense of the national territory, demand long and profound study. The future will demand a severe accounting for any negligence on our part. You will examine the measures which will be presented to you to this end by my government. . . .

Senators and deputies, a vast range of activity opens before you; the national unity which is today attained will have, I hope, the effect of rendering less bitter the struggles of parties, the rivalry of which will have henceforth no other end than the development of the productive forces of the nation.

I rejoice to see that our population already gives unequivocal proofs of its love of work. The economic awakening is closely associated with the political awakening. The banks multiply, as do the commercial institutions, the expositions of the products of art and industry, and the congresses of the learned. We ought, you and I, to favor this productive movement while giving to professional and scientific education more attention and efficiency, and opening to commerce new avenues of communication and new outlets. . . .

A brilliant future opens before us. It remains for us to respond to the blessings of Providence by showing ourselves worthy of bearing among the nations the glorious names of Italy and Rome.

XIII

Reform, Reaction and Revolution in Russia

XIII

Reform, Reaction and Revolution in Russia

Russia, suffering under an autocracy that ignorance and isolation sustained, was virtually untouched by the revolutionary wave that swept across Europe in 1848. Tsar Nicholas I, whose thirty year reign was characterized by remorseless cruelty, had successfully deprived liberalism of all but the smallest influence in his realm. Still, Russians were not insensitive to the tyranny, inefficiency and corruption of their government, which became so evident during the Crimean War of 1854–6. Russia was growing more discontent. The monarchy, as an institution, was becoming more and more alienated from the people.

Tsar Alexander II's Emancipation of the Serfs, 1861

When a new tsar, Alexander II, assumed the throne in 1855, he was convinced that Russia had to make some gesture toward liberal reform, which seemed to him to be the West's source of strength. Alexander at once relaxed press censorship and police repression, stirring up thereby the Russian appetite for significant political, economic and social change. Russia appeared ready at last to make an accommodation with the modern world.

Tsar Alexander II recognized that to transform Russia into a modern state, the first requirement was the abolition of serfdom. The principal obstacle to its realization was not so much the opposition as the enormity of the task. Russian serfs numbered some 47 million, about half of them on crown holdings. They possessed the traditional feudal rights, which included hereditary land tenure, however burdensome the obligations that accompanied them. The conditions under which the serfs lived varied considerably but in many cases, particularly on crown lands, they were quite tolerable. When they were intolerable, it was often the consequence of primitive agricultural techniques, which kept the nobles who owned the land almost as impoverished as the serfs who tilled it. Having concluded that the perpetuation of serfdom was unwise, Alexander II determined to win glory as the Tsar Liberator.

The tsar's dilemma was how to free the serfs without turning them into a landless, rootless, ignorant proletariat. At the same time, he had to find the means of compensating the nobility, the foundation of his autocracy, for its losses. The tsar chose a group of nobles to serve on a "Committee on the State of the Peasantry" to resolve the problems. While the serfs looked forward exultantly to a kind of agrarian utopia, the nobles worked first to impede emancipation, then to win the best terms possible. The resultant declaration, which satisfied neither side, was issued by the tsar on March 3, 1861.

Under its provisions, the peasant became a free subject of the tsar. He was given the right to retain his cottage and garden. The remaining land he tilled was divided between the land-owner and the local village community, the *mir*, in which he held a share and theoretically a plot of his own. The *mir*, however, managed his land and owed the state its cost. The peasant, as a consequence, paid not only his taxes but also his proportion of the *mir's* indebtedness. Without really having acquired any land of his own the peasant thus faced greater financial hardship than before. Many emancipated serfs simply joined what became an army of tramps.

The state, meanwhile, indemnified the nobles through the sale of bonds. But the nobles, untrained in the management both of money and their estates, frequently dissipated their funds and they, too, became poorer. They looked resentfully at their former serfs, while the peasants looked longingly at the remaining holdings of the nobles. However lofty its intentions, emancipation served to exacerbate bitterness against the crown and between the classes.

Alexander II's Act of Emancipation was inadequate to cure Russia's social ills. It would have achieved its goals only in the company of many other reforms, none of which were undertaken. The text of the declaration, presented below, reflects the tsar's high motives, which were its strength, as well as his excessive concern for the aristocracy, which was its weakness. The consequence of the Act was an aggravation of conditions of life in Russia.

Document 84

We, Alexander II, by the grace of God Tsar and Autocrat of all the Russias, King of Poland, Grand Duke of Finland, etc. make known to all our faithful subjects:

Summoned to the throne of our ancestors by Divine Providence and the sacred law of heredity, we have promised ourselves with heartfelt sincerity to extend our affection and imperial solicitude to all our faithful subjects, whatever their rank or condition, from the soldier who nobly bears arms in the defense of his country to the humble artisan who faithfully carries on his industry; from the functionary who occupies a high office in the State to the laborer whose plow furrows the fields.

As we consider the various classes of which the State is composed, we are convinced that the laws of our empire which have wisely provided for the upper and middle classes, and have fixed with precision their rights and obligations, have not reached the same degree of success in relation to the peasants bound to the soil, who, either through ancient laws or custom, have been hereditarily subjected to the authority of the landlords. Indeed, the rights of landowners over their serfs have hitherto been very extensive and very imperfectly defined by the laws, which have been supplemented by tradition, custom, and the good will of the landlords.

This system has at best established patriarchal relations based upon the fairness and benevolence of the landowners and an affectionate docility on the part of the peasants; but as manners have lost their simplicity, the paternal ties between the landlords and the peasants have been weakened. Furthermore, as the seigniorial authority falls into the hands of those exclusively intent on their own selfish advantage, those relations of mutual good will have tended to give way and open the door to arbitrariness, burdensome to the peasants and hostile to their prosperity. This has served to develop in them an indifference to all progress.

These facts did not fail to impress our predecessors of glorious memory, and they took measures to improve the lot of the peasants; but these measures have had little effect, since they were either dependent for their execution on the individual initiative of such landlords as might be animated by a liberal spirit or were merely local in their scope, or adopted as an experiment.

We became convinced, therefore, that the work of fundamentally ameliorating the condition of the peasant was for us a sacred heritage from our ancestors, a mission which in the course of events Divine Providence had called us to fulfill. We have commenced this work by demonstrating our imperial confidence in the nobility of Russia, who have given us so many proofs of their devotion and their constant disposition to make sacrifices for the well-being of the country. It was to the nobility themselves that, in conformity to their own wishes, we reserved the right of formulating the provisions for the new organization of the peasants—provisions which involve the necessity of limiting their own rights over the peasants, and of accepting the responsibilities of a reform which could only be accomplished with some material losses to them. Our confidence has not been deceived. We have found the nobility, united in committees in the various governments, ready to make, through agents who enjoyed their confidence, the voluntary sacrifices of their rights so far as the personal servitude of the peasants is concerned.

The propositions of the local committees of the nobility—which varied greatly, as might be expected from the nature of the problem—have been collated, compared, and reduced to a regular system, then adjusted and supplemented by a higher committee appointed for the purpose. The new provisions thus formulated relative to the peasants and the domestic serfs of the landholders have been submitted to the Council of the Empire. After having invoked divine assistance we have resolved to carry out the work according to the regulations thus drawn up.

The peasants now bound to the soil shall, within the term fixed by the law, be vested with the full rights of freemen. The landed proprietors, while they shall retain all the rights of ownership over all the lands now belonging to them, shall transfer to the peasants, in return for a rent fixed by law, the full enjoyment of their cottages, farm buildings, and gardens. Furthermore, in order to assure to the peasants their subsistence and enable them to meet their obligations toward the State, the landlords shall turn over to the peasants a quantity of arable and other land provided for in the regulations above mentioned. In return for these allotments the peasant families shall be required to pay rent to the landlords, as fixed by the provisions of the law. Under these conditions, which are temporary, the peasants shall be designated as "temporarily bound."

At the same time the peasants are granted the right of purchasing their cottages and gardens, and, with the consent of the landlords, they may acquire in complete ownership the arable lands and other lands allotted to them as a permanent holding. By the acquisition of a complete title to the land assigned them the peasants shall be freed from their obligations toward the landlords for land thus purchased, and thus enter definitively into the class of free peasants and landowners.

Since the new organization, owing to the unavoidable complexity of the changes which it involves, cannot immediately be put into execution, a lapse of time is necessary, which cannot be less than two years or thereabouts; to avoid all misunderstanding and to protect public and private interests during this interval, the system actually existing on the estates of landowners will be maintained up to the moment when the new system shall have been instituted by the completion of the required preparatory measures.

Aware of all the difficulties of the reform we have undertaken, we place our trust in the goodness of Divine Providence, who watches over the destinies of Russia. We also count upon the generous devotion of our faithful nobility, and we are happy to testify to that body the gratitude it has deserved from us, as well as from the country, for the disinterested support it has given to the accomplishment of our designs. Russia will not forget that the nobility, actuated solely by its respect for the dignity of man and its love for its neighbor, has spontaneously renounced the rights it enjoyed in virtue of the system of serfdom now abolished, and has laid the foundation of a new future for the peasants. We also entertain the firm hope that it will also direct its further efforts to carry out the new regulation by maintaining good order, in a spirit of peace and benevolence.

In order to render the transactions between the landlords and the peasants easier, so that the latter may acquire in full proprietorship their houses and the adjacent lands and buildings, the government will grant them assistance, according to a special regulation, through loans of money or a transfer of mortgages encumbering an estate.

When the first rumors of this great reform contemplated by the government spread among the country people who were scarcely prepared for it, it gave rise in some instances to misunderstandings among individuals more intent upon liberty than mindful of the duties which liberty imposes. But generally the good sense of the country has asserted itself. It has been understood that the landlords would not be deprived of rights legally acquired, except for a fit and sufficient indemnity, or by a voluntary concession on their part; that it would be contrary to all equity for the peasants to accept the enjoyment of the lands conceded by the landlords without at the same time accepting equivalent charges.

And now we confidently hope that the freed serfs, in the presence of the new future which is opened before them, will appreciate and recognize the considerable sacrifices which the nobility has made on their behalf. They will understand that the blessing of an existence based upon full ownership of their property, as well as the greater liberty in the administration of their possessions, entails upon them, with new duties towards society and themselves, the obligation of justifying the new laws by a loyal and judicious use of the rights which are now accorded them.

For if men do not themselves endeavor to insure their own well-being under the ægis of the laws, the best of those laws cannot guarantee it to them. Only by assiduous labor, a rational expenditure of their strength and resources, a strict economy, and, above all, by an upright life,—a life constantly inspired by the fear of the Lord,—can they hope for prosperity and progress.

And now, my orthodox and faithful people, make the holy sign of the cross and join thy prayers to ours, invoking the blessing of the Most High upon thy first free labors, for this alone is a sure pledge of private well-being and the public weal.

Given at St. Petersburg, the nineteenth day of February [March 3 by the conventional calendar], of the year of grace 1861 and the seventh of our reign.

ALEXANDER

Tsar Nicholas II Announces his Policy, 1894

Tsar Alexander II, to his disillusion, faced growing unrest in the years following emancipation. His troubles were aggravated by a rapid increase in population, which intensified pressure on the land and forced a general migration to the cities, where a sullen and embittered proletariat was created. At the same time, he lost all support from the intelligentsia, who became deeply involved in movements of social protest, the character of which was not Western but deeply Russian. The country spawned nihilists, anarchists and populists, all profoundly hostile to the government. In the late 1870s, terrorists came to dominate the protest movements. The tsar, no longer a reformer, responded to their acts by intensifying police repression, a policy which made assassins into heroes. Finally, in 1881, the terrorists reached the head of the state himself. While driving through the streets of St. Petersburg, Tsar Alexander II was killed by an assassin's bomb.

Alexander III, the new tsar, was temperamentally more autocratic than his father. Far from contemplating reform, he was passionately dedicated to reaction. He reduced educational opportunities. He sought to force the many peoples of his diverse empire into the Russian mold. But whatever his faults, he worked hard and possessed enough understanding of national needs to encourage industrial expansion. Having benefited from a popular revulsion to terrorism, he ruled during a period of relative calm and left Russia in sound economic condition. He seemed to demonstrate that the tsars could govern a modern country with the obsolete institutions long since abandoned by the West.

A strong, clear-headed successor to Alexander III might conceivably have saved the Russian monarchy, but Nicholas II, who became tsar in 1894, was weaker and less intelligent than his father, although no less autocratic. Nicholas II, the last of the Romanov monarchs, intended to make no compromise with liberalism or constitutionalism. His declaration on ascending the throne, presented below, is a candid statement of the attitude he brought to his responsibilities. Nicholas II was determined to defy the ideas that had come to dominate the West.

Document 85

I am glad to see here the representatives of all the different classes of the country assembled to express to me their submissive and loyal feelings. I believe in the sincerity of those feelings which are inherent in every Russian heart. But it has been brought to My knowledge that during the last months there have been heard in some zemstvos [local councils] the voices of those who indulged in . . . senseless dreams with respect to the participation of the zemstvos in the general direction of the internal affairs of the State. Let it be known by all that I shall devote my whole power to the best service of the people, but that the principle of autocracy will be maintained by me as firmly and unswervingly as by my lamented father.

The October Manifesto, 1905

The disintegration of the tsarist state accelerated during the Russo-Japanese War of 1904–5. The war revealed that the government was not only cruel and inept at home but unable to protect the national interest abroad. News of military disasters coming from the Far East became the occasion for renewed restlessness, which was no longer confined to a tiny enlightened minority. A great proletarian class, prepared to strike and to riot, was ready to give expression to deep feelings of dissatisfaction. Political awareness, growing for a century, was now acute, especially in the cities. The stage was set for the events that toppled the Romanov dynasty.

On Sunday, January 22, 1905, tens of thousands of workingmen, with their wives and children, appeared before the tsar's Winter Palace to present a petition. Their aims were modest, their attitude humble. They gave no sign of belligerency. But the tsar's soldiers fired their rifles point-blank into the unsuspecting mass, killing and wounding some 1500 persons. Bloody Sunday, as the day came to be called, ended forever any sense of unity between the tsar and his subjects.

Faced after Bloody Sunday with rising terror, Nicholas II decided to make a gesture of conciliation. In June, 1905, he promised to convene a National Assembly, but in August, when he announced his conditions, he incurred more popular wrath by making the Assembly virtually powerless. The people would no longer be diverted by meaningless concessions. In September the humiliating terms of the treaty of peace between Russia and Japan were announced. The esteem of the monarchy sank to a new low.

The revolutionary ardor of the Russian people reached a climax in mid-October, 1905, when a general strike broke out throughout the country. Led by a network of revolutionary committees, it developed—quite spontaneously—into the most successful general strike in history. For nearly two weeks transportation, industry, commerce and communications did not function. But even in the face of such massive hostility, Nicholas hesitated to grant real concessions. Finally, the general strike forced him to yield. It was clear that only a decisive act from the throne could forestall total anarchy.

On October 30, 1905, the tsar gave his people a constitution. His declaration, known as the October Manifesto, established an elected assembly called the *Duma*, which was to be chosen on a wide franchise and empowered to enact all laws for the country. The Manifesto also included an imposing list of civil liberties. For a few weeks, it looked as if Russia, thanks to the martyrs of Bloody Sunday and the general strike, had broken through to the modern world. The October Manifesto, presented here, suggested that the struggle for individual liberty and constitutional government in Russia had been won.

Document 86

The rioting and agitation in the capitals and in many localities of OUR Empire fills OUR heart with great and deep grief. The welfare of the Russian Emperor is bound up with the welfare of the people and its sorrows are HIS sorrows. The turbulence which has broken out may confound the people and threaten the integrity and unity of OUR Empire.

The great vow of service by the Tsar obligates US to endeavor, with all OUR strength, wisdom, and power, to put an end as quickly as possible to the disturbance so dangerous to the Empire. In commanding the responsible authorities to take measures to stop disorders, lawlessness, and violence, and to protect peaceful citizens in the quiet performance of their duties, WE have found it necessary to unite the activities of the Supreme Government, so as to insure the successful carrying out of the general measures laid down by US for the peaceful life of the state.

WE lay upon the Government the execution of OUR unchangeable will:

1. To grant to the population the inviolable right of free citizenship, based on the principles of the freedom of person, conscience, speech, assembly, and union.

2. Without postponing the intended elections for the State Duma and in so far as possible, in view of the short time that remains before the assembling of that body, to include in the participation of the work of the Duma those classes of the population that have been until now entirely deprived of the right to vote, and to extend in the future, by the newly created legislative way, the principles of the general right of election.

3. To establish as an unbreakable rule that no law shall go into force without its confirmation by the State Duma and that the persons elected by the people shall have the opportunity for actual participation in supervising the legality of the acts of authorities appointed by US.

We call on all the true sons of Russia to remember their duties toward their country, to assist in combating these unheard-of disturbances, and to join US with all their might in reëstablishing quiet and peace in the country.

Given in Peterhof, on the seventeenth (thirtieth) day of October in the year of our Lord 1905, and the eleventh year of OUR reign.

NICHOLAS

Nicholas Dismisses the First Duma, 1906

The liberal democratic reforms promised in the October Manifesto came too late to satisfy the proletarian masses of Moscow and St. Petersburg. Like the Parisian working class, they no longer saw their salvation in parliamentary democracy but demanded instead a socialist revolution. In November, 1906, their leaders called a second, and in December, a third general strike. Both failed. In Moscow a few weeks later, armed workingmen rose up but the army, still loyal to the throne, brutally put them down. Middle-class liberals were by now horrified at the disorder and at the prospect of a socialist state. Opposition to the throne had thus split and reaction had set in. The tsar's ministers made their preparations to capitalize on the rift between the bourgeois reformers and the working class revolutionaries.

In May, 1906, the first Duma, duly elected according to the tsar's pledge, met amid much pomp and hope. Nicholas made a friendly speech of welcome. Within a short time, however, the new parliament and the old bureaucracy were locked in combat, while the parliament itself was bitterly divided on how to deal with the throne. The strongest party in the Duma was the Constitutional Democrats, known as the Cadets, that advocated a British-type monarchy. To their right were the Octobrists, well-disposed to the crown and in favor of an autocratic constitution like that in the Kaiser's Germany. To the left was a large amorphous group of radicals, profoundly separated on matters of doctrine. The Social Democrats had their majority wing, or *bolsheviki*, which favored instant and forceful action in behalf of socialism, and their minority wing, or *mensheviki*, which preferred a gradual approach. The Social Revolutionary Party, which shared the Social Democrats' radical outlook, rejected the industrial emphasis of the Social Democratic doctrine in favor of the goals of land reform. This divided and inexperienced body, devoted to a multiplicity of political and social objectives, tried to emulate the Western practice of bringing the tsar's ministers to account. But the tsar, despite the exalted pretentions of the October Manifesto, had no intention of submitting.

The tsar understood that in the Duma he had created a body he could not control. On July 21, 1906, after quietly moving reliable troops into St. Petersburg, he declared the first Duma dissolved. With unusual efficiency his police—resorting to arrests, executions, bribery and intimidation—suppressed dissent. Though two more Dumas were called, on a progressively narrower franchise and subject to increasing supervision, the parliamentary experiment was over. The tsar's government executed certain reforms of its own in the succeeding years but none solved the basic social and political problems that faced Russia and the dynasty. By suppressing the Duma, the tsar demonstrated beyond doubt that he would tolerate no constitutional limitation to his absolutism.

The tsar's decree of July 21, 1906, deprived the Russian people of any share in the power of the state. It was a superb expression of paternalism. Significantly, it dwelt on the problems of the peasant, revealing an indifference to the lot of the proletariat, which presented the real threat to the regime. The declaration, reproduced below, was a major step in the fall of the Romanov dynasty and the Russian monarchical system.

Document 87

We summoned the representatives of the nation by our will to the work of productive legislation. Confiding firmly in divine clemency and believing in the great and brilliant future of our people, we confidently anticipated benefits for the country from their labors. We proposed great reforms in all departments of the national life. We have always devoted our greatest care to the removal of the ignorance of the people by the light of instruction, and to the removal of their burdens by improving the conditions of agricultural work.

A cruel disappointment has befallen our expectations. The representatives of the nation, instead of applying themselves to the work of productive legislation, have strayed into spheres beyond their competence, and have been making inquiries into the acts of local authorities established by ourselves, and have been making comments upon the imperfections of the fundamental laws, which can only be modified by our imperial will. In short, the representatives of the nation have undertaken really illegal acts, such as the appeal by the Duma to the nation.

The peasants, disturbed by such anomalies, and seeing no hope of the amelioration of their lot, have resorted in a number of districts to open pillage and the destruction of other people's property, and to disobedience of the law and of the legal authorities. But our subjects ought to remember that an improvement in the lot of the people is only possible under conditions of perfect order and tranquillity. We shall not permit arbitrary or illegal acts, and we shall impose our imperial will on the disobedient by all the power of the State.

We appeal to all well-disposed Russians to combine for the maintenance of legal authority and the restoration of peace in our dear fatherland. May calm be reëstablished once more in Russia, and may God help us to accomplish the chiefest of our tasks, the improvement of the lot of the peasant. Our will on this point is unalterable. The Russian husbandman, in case his land is too small to maintain him, shall be supplied, without prejudice to the property of others, with legitimate and honest means for enlarging his holdings. The representatives of the other classes will, at our request, devote all their efforts to the promotion of this great undertaking which will be given a definitely legal form by a future Duma.

In dissolving the Duma we confirm our immutable intention of maintaining this institution, and in conformity with this intention we fix March 5, 1907, as the date of the convocation of a new Duma by a ukase addressed to the Senate. With unshakable faith in divine clemency and in the good sense of the Russian people, we shall expect from the new Duma the realization of our efforts and their promotion of legislation in accordance with the requirements of a regenerated Russia.

Faithful sons of Russia, your Tsar calls upon you as a father upon his children to unite with him for the regeneration of our holy fatherland. We believe that giants in thought and action will appear, and that, thanks to their assiduous efforts the glory of Russia will continue to shine.

NICHOLAS

Proclamation Establishing a Provisional Government, 1917

Though Russia entered World War I poorly prepared, its army was large, brave and reasonably well led. From 1914 to 1916 the Russians won some brilliant successes, particularly against the Austrians, and though they suffered some grievous defeats against the Germans, they remained a constant threat to Germany from the east. By 1917, however, Russia's ammunition was virtually exhausted. Russian industry could not replenish stocks and the Allies, with Russian ports closed during cold weather, could not deliver enough to keep the army fighting. Had the British attack on Gallipoli succeeded, the Allies would have opened a year-round route into Russia through the Black Sea. When it failed, Russia—and the tsardom—were doomed to defeat.

In Petrograd—the new name given to the capital—the government had degenerated into a state of sheer madness, unique even for the Romanov dynasty. The tsar, under the influence of the tsarina, repeatedly dismissed qualified ministers and replaced them with sycophants and mediocrities. By far the most influential man in the Russian capital was the charlatan Rasputin, a religious mystic and libertine who thoroughly dominated the tsarina and campaigned against even the slightest reform. Meanwhile, mismanagement and corruption were everywhere, in the army, navy, industry, the railways, food supply, finance. Finally a group of nobles assassinated Rasputin but Nicholas II had by now become obsessed with the need to change nothing. He dismissed all who differed with him or who pleaded with him to replace chaos with responsible government. Nicholas II, with unbelievable smugness, marched grandly forward toward dynastic suicide.

When bread riots broke out in Petrograd and Moscow in March, 1917, army and police units for the first time refused to fire on the crowds. In the face of growing disorder, the Duma—which had been elected from the richest classes—delivered a final plea to the tsar to establish a popular government. The tsar's ministers replied by dismissing the Duma for insubordination. The Duma, however, refused to be dispersed. The revolution was on.

Over the succeeding days rioting increased while the soldiers, defying their commanders, joined the mobs to seize public buildings. The Duma was now the only government left in Russia. It elected a twelve-man executive committee to exercise power, then dispatched two delegates to meet the tsar at the front and to inform him that he must abdicate in favor of his son. Nicholas chose, instead, to abdicate in favor of his brother, the Grand Duke Michael. It was the last act of the Russian monarchy. Michael declared that he would accept the throne only at the request of the Constituent Assembly, elected by plebiscite. In the meantime Russia was being ruled by a provisional government responsible to the Duma.

Head of the Provisional Government was Prince Lvov, who chose a cabinet of prominent liberals. The cabinet was dominated by Alexander Kerenski, Minister of Justice and member of the Social Revolutionary Party. But in another part of Petrograd, the government's authority was threatened by a Soviet of Workers and Soldiers Deputies, a body far more radical. For the moment the Soviet issued no challenge, while the army and the provincial governments pledged their loyalty to Lvov. The tsar and his family, comfortable in captivity, simply faded from the picture. The Provisional Government vowed to continue the war and planned for the transformation of Russia into an efficient democratic state.

The following proclamation was issued on March 16, 1917, to announce the establishment of the Provisional Government. It marks the definitive end of the Romanov tsardom. The principles that the Cabinet pledges to guide its action herald the beginning of a liberal democratic regime. The proclamation was received with enthusiasm throughout the democratic countries of the Western world.

Document 88

Citizens, the Provisional Executive Committee of the members of the Duma, with the aid and support of the garrison of the capital and its inhabitants, has triumphed over the dark forces of the Old Régime to such an extent as to enable it to organize a more stable executive power. With this idea in mind, the Provisional Committee has appointed, as ministers of the first Cabinet representing the public, men whose past political and public life assures them the confidence of the country.

PRINCE GEORGE E. LVOV, Prime Minister and Minister of the interior.

P. N. MILIUKOV, Minister of Foreign Affairs
A. I. GUCHKOV, Minister of War and Marine
M. I. TERESCHENKO, Minister of Finance
A. A. MANUILOV, Minister of Education
A. I. SHINGAREV, Minister of Agriculture
N. V. NEKRASOV, Minister of Transportation
A. I. KONOVALOV, Minister of Commerce and Industry
A. F. KERENSKI, Minister of Justice
VL. LVOV, Holy Synod

The Cabinet will be guided in its actions by the following principles:

1. An immediate general amnesty for all political and religious offenses, including terrorist acts, military revolts, agrarian offenses, etc.

2. Freedom of speech and press; freedom to form labor unions and to strike. These political liberties should be extended to the army in so far as war conditions permit.

3. The abolition of all social, religious and national restrictions.

4. Immediate preparation for the calling of a Constituent Assembly, elected by universal and secret vote, which shall determine the form of government and draw up the Constitution for the country.

5. In place of the police, to organize a national militia with elective officers, and subject to the local self-governing body.

6. Elections to be carried out on the basis of universal, direct, equal, and secret suffrage.

7. The troops that have taken part in the revolutionary movement shall not be disarmed or removed from Petrograd.

8. On duty and in war service, strict military discipline should be maintained, but when off duty, soldiers should have the same public rights as are enjoyed by other citizens.

The Provisional Government wishes to add that it has no intention of taking advantage of the existence of war conditions to delay the realization of the above-mentioned measures of reform.

President of the Duma, M. RODZIANKO
President of the Council of Ministers, PRINCE LVOV
Ministers MILIUKOV, NEKRASOV, MANUILOV,
KONOVALOV, TERESCHENKO, VL. LVOV,
SHINGAREV, KERENSKI.

Proclamation of the October Revolution, 1917

The provisional Government, unlike the French Legislative Assembly in 1792, was unable simultaneously to conduct a revolution and fight a foreign war. The difference between them was that France in 1792 was united, while Russia in 1917 was hopelessly divided. The departure of the tsar had removed Russia's symbol of authority. The Provisional Government almost from the beginning had to compete with the Petrograd Soviet, which, under the domination of the dynamic Vladimir Lenin, worked assiduously to undermine the government's power. It importuned the soldiers to leave the front and return home. It encouraged the peasants to seize the fields of the aristocracy. It stirred the workers to further agitation and rioting. The Provisional Government worked valiantly to overcome the forces of disruption and anarchy but failed to command discipline either at the front or in the rear.

Alexander Kerenski, who emerged as leader of the Provisional Government, was actually a radical among democrats but he was detested by Lenin and his Bolshevik followers. On July 14 Kerenski succeeded in suppressing an uprising of the Petrograd Soviet but his power was declining. His fall came on November 17, 1917 (October 25 by the Russian calendar), when the Petrograd military garrison recognized the authority of the Revolutionary Committee of the Soviet. With comparatively little fighting, the forces loyal to Lenin took over the city. Kerenski's efforts to rally support failed, in Moscow as well as in the capital. The Petrograd Soviet of Workers and Soldiers Deputies assumed the power of the state. The socialist revolution had been accomplished.

The following document is the proclamation of the Petrograd Soviet announcing the fall of the Provisional Government and the victory of what we now know as Communism.

Document 89

The Provisional Government is deposed. The State Power has passed into the hands of the organ of the Petrograd Soviet of Workers and Soldiers Deputies, the Military Revolutionary Committee, which stands at the head of the Petrograd proletariat and garrison.

The cause for which the people were fighting: immediate proposal of a democratic peace, abolition of landlord property-rights over the land, labor control over production, creation of a Soviet Government—that cause is securely achieved.

LONG LIVE THE REVOLUTION OF WORKMEN, SOLDIERS AND PEASANTS!

MILITARY REVOLUTIONARY COMMITTEE

Petrograd Soviet of Workers and Soldiers Deputies.

25 October, 1917, 10 A.M.

XIV

The Great War

XIV

The Great War

The First World War was the horrible, if coldly logical, consequence of a development that began during the Middle Ages and accelerated rapidly after the French Revolution. The apogee was the dynamic, proud, assertive national state.

By the late years of the nineteenth century, Europe was crowded with such states. Each was sovereign, a law unto itself. None recognized an obligation to a higher authority which might have regulated relations between them. Every one was convinced that it possessed the right to seek political aggrandizement at the expense of any other.

Europe, at the end of the nineteenth century, was rich and full of restless energy. Its states raced for wealth and glory to Asia and Africa, where they sought to colonize territories and subjugate other civilizations. They competed vigorously for the spoils of the disintegrating Ottoman Empire in the east. They spent vast sums on new and lethal weapons to menace one another on land and sea. After a century of relative peace, the European states seemed ready to take a chance on war.

The anarchy of the states of Europe jostling rudely against one another made a motive for war—like Italy's in 1860 or Germany's in 1870—almost unnecessary. The nation states did not necessarily want war. They certainly had no idea what new technology would make of war. But by their passivity to the prospect of war, they let events take the initiative and lead them to it. By the end of the century, the states of Europe had created conditions that made war all but inevitable.

The leaders of the European states were not unaware of the danger, yet in their quest for national security, they spurned peace and made war more likely. Their technique, in addition to expanding their armies, was to contract alliances, many of them secret. In the past, alliances had sometimes deterred a potential enemy. The alliances contracted before the First World War served only to assure irresponsible nations that their irresponsibility would be redeemed by others. Under the system of entangling alliances, one nation offered its fate as the guarantee to another. Together the states of

Europe made certain that no war could be a small war and that no country, whether innocent or guilty, could be secure.

Austro-German Treaty of Alliance, 1879

Bismarck initiated the alliance system after the War of 1870 in an effort to discourage the French from contemplating revenge. He organized the *Dreikaiserbund* or Three Emperors League, a loose arrangement by which Germany, Russia and Austria agreed to preserve the *status quo* on the continent. But in 1878, Bismarck was forced to choose between Russia and Austria, who were competing for morsels of the Ottoman Empire in Eastern Europe. When Bismarck chose to support Austria, Russia withdrew from the League. In 1879 Bismarck went to Vienna, where he signed a treaty which committed Germany and Austria to assist each other in case either became involved in a war against Russia. The treaty established the celebrated Dual Alliance, the nucleus of what became a vast and complex network of relations between European states. The Treaty of Alliance, the key passages of which are given below, in a sense repaired the breach in German unity that Bismarck had created in 1866. It consolidated the two German empires in Central Europe into a single diplomatic entity. The unity of the two Empires remained the foundation of German foreign policy until 1918.

Document 90

Article I.

Should, contrary to their hope, and against the loyal desire of the two High Contracting Parties, one of the two Empires be attacked by Russia, the High Contracting Parties are bound to come to the assistance one of the other with the whole war strength of their Empires, and accordingly only to conclude peace together and upon mutual agreement.

Article II.

Should one of the High Contracting Parties be attacked by another Power, the other High Contracting Party binds itself hereby, not only not to support the aggressor against its high Ally, but to observe at least a benevolent neutral attitude towards its fellow Contracting Party.

Should, however, the attacking party in such a case be supported by Russia, either by an active cooperation or by military measures which constitute a menace to the Party attacked, then the obligation stipulated in Article I of this Treaty for reciprocal assistance with the whole fighting force, becomes equally operative, and the conduct of the war by the two High Contracting Parties shall in this case also be in common until the conclusion of a common peace.

Franco-Russian Alliance, 1892

Bismarck concluded his brilliant career as German Chancellor by tempting Russia back into his alliance system and by enlarging it to embrace Italy. Since his objective remained the isolation of France, it mattered little that the Russian treaty was both temporary and limited, for it could have been renewed. The Italian treaty was the consequence of a typical Bismarckian trick. Both France and Italy coveted Tunisia. It made no difference to Germany which one had it. Bismarck, to divert French attention from the Rhine, persuaded Paris to seize it. The Italians then became furious at France and applied for membership in the alliance of the German powers. A new treaty was signed, linking Germany, Austria and Italy in the Triple Alliance. Thus all of Europe, save France, was Germany's friend when Bismarck retired in 1890.

Young Kaiser William II, who assumed the throne in 1888 and shortly thereafter eased Bismarck out of power, was vain, impetuous and unintelligent. He proceeded almost at once to dismantle the diplomatic structure that Bismarck had so painstakingly built. When, in 1890, he refused to renew the treaty with Russia, he became the broker for the Franco-Russian understanding that Bismarck had always dreaded. France and Russia, both apprehensive of Germany, were natural allies. Russia needed French money. France needed Russian manpower. That Bismarck had kept them apart for so long testified eloquently to his diplomatic genius. By bringing France and Russia together, Kaiser William II ended France's isolation and acquired for Germany hostile powers on both eastern and western frontiers.

French and Russian military authorities signed a convention in August, 1892, the text of which follows. It aimed specifically at trapping Germany into two-front war. Instead of France, it was Germany now that was surrounded. In January, 1894, an exchange of notes between Paris and Petrograd elevated the military convention into a formal treaty. Its terms, however, remained secret until 1918, when World War I was over.

Document 91

France and Russia, animated by a common desire to preserve peace and having no other purpose than to prepare for the necessities of a defensive war, provoked by an attack of the forces of the Triple Alliance against either of them, have agreed on the following provisions:

1. If France is attacked by Germany, or by Italy supported by Germany, Russia shall employ all her available forces to fight Germany.

If Russia is attacked by Germany, or by Austria supported by Germany, France shall employ all her available forces to fight Germany.

2. In case the forces of the Triple Alliance or of any one of the Powers belonging to it, should be mobilized, France and Russia, at the first word of this event, and without need of a previous agreement, shall mobilize immediately and simultaneously all their forces, and shall transport them as near as possible to their frontiers.

3. The forces available which must be employed against Germany shall be, for France 1,300,000 men, for Russia, 700,000 to 800,000 men.

These forces shall be brought into action so completely and with such speed that Germany will have to fight simultaneously in the East and in the West.

4. The Staffs of the armies of the two countries shall constantly take council together to prepare for and to facilitate the execution of the above-mentioned measures.

They shall communicate to each other, in time of peace, all the information in regard to the armies of the Triple Alliance which is already in their possession or which shall come into their possession.

The ways and means of corresponding in time of war shall be studied and worked out in advance.

5. France and Russia shall not conclude peace separately.

6. The present Agreement shall have the same duration as the Triple Alliance.

7. All the clauses enumerated above shall be kept absolutely secret.

Entente Cordiale, 1903

Though France, by the treaty with Russia, had emerged from diplomatic isolation, the potential enemies that faced her were still formidable. In addition to the Central Powers and Italy, there was England, for centuries France's traditional foe. In the last decades of the nineteenth century, France and England had competed bitterly for colonial territories and, at Fashoda in 1898, had almost gone to war. But England, like France, possessed a fear of German aggression intensified by the Kaiser's decision to challenge Britain's mastery of the seas. As the new century opened, France and England simultaneously came to the conclusion that it was time to re-examine their long-standing hostility. England's King Edward VIII was friendly toward France. France's foreign minister, Delcassé, was shrewd enough to defy conventional diplomacy. Both countries were ready to embark on a diplomatic revolution.

In July, 1903, Delcassé dispatched an emissary, a M. Étienne, to London to feel out the British Foreign Office on the possibility of a *rapprochement.* Over the course of the next nine months, the British and the French bargained to settle outstanding colonial differences. Though France made greater concessions, both countries reasoned they could give up some colonial objectives in return for enhanced security at home. When they reached an agreement, it ostensibly covered only the outstanding colonial problems, but, in reality, its meaning was far greater. The *Entente Cordiale*—the Friendly Understanding—which emerged from the discussions was not a hard and fast alliance. It was nothing more than a mutual acknowledgement of common interest. The extent to which it bound the two countries to each other was never quite clear. It did, however, mean the end of Britain's historic aversion to peacetime continental commitments. It meant recognition by both countries that Germany was their principal threat. Not until the eve of the war, when the two general staffs met for discussion, did it take on a positive military character. When the war itself came, it proved as binding as the German-Austrian Alliance.

The documentation on the *Entente Cordiale* consists of a few diplomatic notes and a declaration concerning Egypt and Morocco. Nothing more formal was ever negotiated. These papers contain barely a hint of diplomatic revolution or of national commitment. The first three notes from the British Foreign Office describe generally the formation of the *Entente Cordiale*. The fourth selection is an extract of the treaty concerning Egypt and Morocco. It is dated April 8, 1904, which is usually reckoned as the beginning of the *Entente*.

DOCUMENT 92

(The Marquess of Lansdowne [Secretary of State for Foreign Affairs] to Sir E. Monson [British Ambassador at Paris].)

Foreign Office, July 2, 1903

M. Étienne called upon me at the Foreign Office to-day, and spoke to me at some length and with great freedom in regard to the political relations of France and Great Britain.

He told me that he was paying a short visit to this country in the hopes of promoting a good understanding between the two Governments. There seemed to him to be no really serious points of divergence between them, and the moment appeared to be particularly propitious for such a *rapprochement* as he suggested.

He passed in review of the various political questions which have lately occupied the joint attention of the British and French Foreign Offices.

. . .

At the conclusion of the conversation, M. Étienne expressed his belief that the most serious menace to the peace of Europe lay in Germany, that a good understanding between France and England was the only means of holding German designs in check, and that if such an understanding could be arrived at, England would find that France would be able to exercise a salutary influence over Russia and thereby relieve us from many of our troubles with that country.

* * *

(The Marquess of Lansdowne to Sir E. Monson.)

Foreign Office, July 7, 1903

The French Ambassador mentioned to me some days before the President's arrival that it would be agreeable to M. Delcassé to meet me during his stay in London, and to discuss with me some of the points with regard to which his Excellency and I had at various times had conversations.

M. Delcassé called upon me this morning, and we exchanged ideas at some length in regard to these questions.

After expressing the pleasure which it gave me to have this opportunity of learning his views at first hand, I said that, as he was aware, I had on several occasions discussed with M. Cambon the position of our two countries in Newfoundland, Morocco, Siam, the New Hebrides, and other parts of the world. Those discussions had, up to the present, not led to any definite results. They had, however, I thought, been useful in clearing the ground, and they certainly had led me to the conclusion that the points at issue between the two Governments were few in number, and by no means incapable of adjustment.

M. Delcassé expressed his entire agreement, and added that this view now prevailed in the French Chamber, which was inclined to take a reasonable, not to say friendly, line in regard to all such questions. As for the French Government, they had ceased to desire a wide extension of their Colonial possessions, and were intent, not upon adding to them, but upon consolidating them, and removing all sources of future trouble within them and upon their borders.

I replied that His Majesty's Government were influenced by very similar sentiments, and that I certainly thought the opportunity was in every way propitious for a frank exchange of opinions between the two Governments.

. . .

(The Earl of Cromer [British Consul-General and Agent in Egypt], to the Marquess of Lansdowne, Cairo, July 17, 1903.)

The main question is manifestly Morocco.

My own opinion, which is one I have entertained for a long time, is distinctly in favour of making concessions in Morocco in return for counter-concessions in Egypt and elsewhere, but if we are to adopt this policy we ought to do so with our eyes open to what it means.

I observe that M. Étienne, in his conversation with you, stated that "the Sultan of Morocco's Government appeared to be on the point of falling to pieces," to which you replied that "these Eastern Monarchies often managed to survive in spite of apparent decay and seemingly unsurmountable difficulties." This is perfectly true, but the reason is also obvious. It is that the agony of these decadent Oriental States, such as Turkey and Persia, is prolonged owing to the dissensions and rivalries amongst the possible heirs to the succession. I think it would be found, in practice, that if once the French succession were secured, the agony of Morocco would not be of long duration. Some opportunity would speedily occur for putting an end to it. Hence, in spite of M. Delcassé's statement, of which I do not doubt the sincerity, that the French Government has no desire to "*brusquer les choses*," I have very little doubt that, when once the French are assured that they can make good their rights to the succession, without any risk of serious interference on our part, Morocco will, to all intents and purposes, become before long a French province.

The question, therefore, to my mind is this: have we any objection to Morocco becoming a French province? Personally, I see none, provided always (1) that we get an adequate *quid pro quo* in Egypt and elsewhere and (2) that the French comply with your three conditions, as regards Morocco. These, if I understand rightly, are (1) the seaboard is to be neutralised; (2) a proper regard is to be shown to Spanish interests and susceptibilities; and (3) a guarantee is to be obtained that British trade and enterprise will not be placed at any legal disadvantage in Morocco.

. . .

(Declaration between the United Kingdom and France respecting Egypt and Morocco. Signed at London, April 8, 1904.)

Article I.

His Britannic Majesty's Government declare that they have no intention of altering the political status of Egypt.

The Government of the French Republic, for their part, declare that they will not obstruct the action of Great Britain in that country by asking that a limit of time be fixed for the British occupation or in any other manner, and that they give their assent to the draft Khedivial Decree annexed to the present Arrangement, containing the guarantees considered necessary for the protection of the interests of the Egyptian bondholders, on the condition that, after its promulgation, it cannot be modified in any way without the consent of the Powers Signatory of the Convention of London of 1885.

It is agreed that the post of Director-General of Antiquities in Egypt shall continue, as in the past, to be entrusted to a French *savant.*

The French schools in Egypt shall continue to enjoy the same liberty as in the past.

Article II.

The Government of the French Republic declare that they have no intention of altering the political status of Morocco.

His Britannic Majesty's Government, for their part, recognise that it appertains to France, more particularly as a Power whose dominions are conterminous for a great distance with those of Morocco, to preserve order in that country, and to provide assistance for the purpose of all administrative, economic, financial, and military reforms which it may require.

They declare that they will not obstruct the action taken by France for this purpose, provided that such action shall leave intact the rights which Great Britain, in virtue of Treaties, Conventions, and usage, enjoys in Morocco, including the right of coasting trade between the ports of Morocco, enjoyed by British vessels since 1903.

Article III.

His Britannic Majesty's Government, for their part, will respect the rights which France, in virtue of Treaties, Conventions, and usage, enjoys in Egypt, including the right of coasting trade between Egyptian ports accorded to French vessels. . . .

Austrian Ultimatum to Serbia, 1914

Somehow Europe avoided a general war in the early years of the twentieth century. Although crisis followed crisis, the major powers resolved them without hostilities. From 1911 to 1913, the Balkan nations fought among themselves but the big powers, while meddling in the conflict, refrained from taking up arms. In the summer of 1914, conditions appeared no more dangerous than they had been throughout the previous decade. Austria, France and Russia were rattling their sabers a little louder than usual but Germany and England seemed to be doing more to quiet them. The volatile Balkans, for the moment, appeared to be in a state of equilibrium. Then, on June 28, 1914, the Archduke Francis Ferdinand, heir to the Austrian throne, was assassinated. Within five weeks all of Europe was plunged into a holocaust.

Francis Ferdinand symbolized the contention not between the Alliance and the Entente powers but between Austria-Hungary and Serbia, rivals for hegemony in the Balkans. Austria was greedy for Balkan territory and, to the dismay of Serbia and Russia, had recently snatched the contested Slavic provinces of Bosnia and Hercegovina from the crumbling Turkish empire. Serbia dreamed of leading a great Balkan unification movement, in the style of Piedmont-Sardinia in Italy and Prussia in Germany. Since it served as a check on Austrian ambitions, Serbia had the support of Russia. The ill-fated Archduke Francis Ferdinand, a champion of Austria's policy of Slavic expansion, represented a threat to Serbian aims.

By visiting Bosnia, Francis Ferdinand knew he was provoking the Serbs. He knew also that his life was in danger. In Sarajevo, the Bosnian capital, he was gunned down by a young Slavic conspirator and patriot named Gavrilo Princip. Serbia's involvement was suspected but only later was it learned how deeply the Serbian government was implicated in the assassination plot. During the month that passed before Austria acted, the world did not suspect that it was on the threshold of the greatest war in history.

On July 23, the Austrian ambassador delivered an ultimatum at Belgrade, the Serbian capital. The apologies and pledges it called for were reasonable enough. But it stipulated that Austrian officials supervise the execution of its terms. It demanded further that Austria have the right to select Serbs for dismissal from the army and the civil service. Obviously, given the nationalistic temperament of the day, these last conditions were unacceptable. The Serbian reply was nonetheless polite, almost submissive. To some of the Austrian demands Serbia yielded and to none did it offer a categorical refusal. Austria, however, demanded all or nothing. A half hour after he received the Serbian note, the Austrian ambassador left Belgrade for Vienna. His departure meant war.

In retrospect, it is clear that Austria was determined to use the murder of Francis Ferdinand as the pretext for ending the Serbian challenge in the Balkans. Austria did not want satisfaction from its ultimatum. It wanted to destroy Serbian independence. But for the reckless alliance system, Austria might have conducted its aggression and Europe would have come to live with the results. Because of the alliances, the major powers leaned on one another, as friends or enemies, and when one fell the others, like dominoes, tumbled afterwards into the inferno.

After the assassination, Austria notified Germany that it was preparing for war. Germany made only a feeble effort to impose restraint. Russia, having urged defiance of Vienna, was committed to come to Serbia's aid. On July 28, Austria declared war on Serbia. The next day Russia mobilized its army. Germany, under its treaty obligations, declared war against Russia on August 1. When France mobilized to aid the Russians, Germany declared war on France. On August 4, Germany invaded Belgium. England then declared war on Germany. What had so long appeared inevitable had at last come to pass. The Great War was on.

Presented below is the Austrian ultimatum to Serbia of July 23, 1914. It is the act that ignited World War I. The four years of deadly struggle that followed it ended a stage of Western history. After the Great War, the world would never be the same.

Document 93

On the 31st of March, 1909, the Serbian Minister in Vienna, on the instructions of the Serbian Government, made the following declaration to the Imperial and Royal Government:

"Serbia recognizes that the *fait accompli* regarding Bosnia has not affected her rights, and consequently she will conform to the decisions that the Powers may take in conformity with Article 25 of the Treaty of Berlin. In deference to the advice of the Great Powers, Serbia undertakes to renounce from now onwards the attitude of protest and opposition which she has adopted with regard to the annexation since last autumn. She undertakes, moreover, to modify the direction of her policy with regard to Austria-Hungary and to live in future on good neighborly terms with the latter."

The history of recent years, and in particular the painful events of the 28th June last, have shown the existence of a subversive movement with the object of detaching a part of the territories of Austria-Hungary from the Monarchy. The movement which had its birth under the eye of the Serbian Government has gone so far as to make itself manifest on both sides of the Serbian frontier in the shape of acts of terrorism and a series of outrages and murders.

Far from carrying out the formal undertakings contained in the declaration of the 31st March, 1909, the Royal Serbian Government has done nothing to repress these movements. It has permitted the criminal machinations of various societies and associations directed against the Monarchy, and has tolerated unrestrained language on the part of the press, the glorification of the perpetrators of outrages, and the participation of officers and functionaries in subversive agitation. It has permitted an unwholesome propaganda in public instruction, in short, it has permitted all manifestations of a nature to incite the Serbian population to hatred of the Monarchy and contempt of its institutions.

This culpable tolerance of the Royal Serbian Government had not ceased at the moment when the events of the 28th June last proved its fatal consequences to the whole world.

It results from the depositions and confessions of the criminal perpetrators of the outrage of the 28th June, that the Sarajevo assassinations were planned in Belgrade; that the arms and explosives with which the murderers were provided had been given to them by Serbian officers and functionaries belonging to the Narodna Odbrana; and finally that the passage into Bosnia of the criminals and their arms was organized and effected by the chiefs of the Serbian frontier service.

The above-mentioned results of the magisterial investigation do not permit the Austro-Hungarian Government to pursue any longer the attitude of expectant forbearance which they have maintained for years in the face of the machinations hatched in Belgrade, and thence propagated in the territories of the Monarchy. The results, on the contrary, impose on them the duty of putting an end to the intrigues which form a perpetual menace to the tranquillity of the Monarchy.

To achieve this end the Imperial and Royal Government see themselves compelled to demand from the Royal Serbian Government a formal assurance that they condemn this dangerous propaganda against the Monarchy; in other words, the whole series of tendencies, the ultimate aim of which is to detach from the Monarchy territories belonging to it, and that they undertake to suppress by every means this criminal and terrorist propaganda.

In order to give a formal character to this undertaking the Royal Serbian Government shall publish on the front page of their Official Journal of the 13/26 July the following declaration:

"The Royal Government of Serbia condemn the propaganda directed against Austria-Hungary—i.e., the general tendency of which the final aim is to detach from the Austro-Hungarian Monarchy territories belonging to it, and they sincerely deplore the fatal consequences of these criminal proceedings.

"The Royal Government regret that Serbian officers and functionaries participated in the above-mentioned propaganda and thus compromised the good neighborly relations to which the Royal Government were solemnly pledged by their declaration of March 31, 1909.

"The Royal Government, who disapprove and repudiate all idea of interfering or attempting to interfere with the destinies of the inhabitants of any part whatsoever of Austria-Hungary, consider it their duty formally to warn officers and functionaries and the whole population of the kingdom, that henceforward they will proceed with the utmost rigor against persons who may be guilty of such machinations, which they will use all their efforts to anticipate and suppress."

This declaration shall simultaneously be communicated to the Royal Army as an order of the day by His Majesty the King and shall be published in the Official Bulletin of the Army.

The Royal Serbian Government further undertake:

1. To suppress any publication which incites to hatred and contempt of the Austro-Hungarian Monarchy and the general tendency of which is directed against its territorial integrity;

2. To dissolve immediately the society styled "Narodna Odbrana," to confiscate all its means of propaganda, and to proceed in the same manner against other societies and their branches in Serbia which engage in propaganda against the Austro-Hungarian Monarchy. The Royal Government shall take the necessary measures to prevent the societies dissolved from continuing their activities under another name and form;

3. To eliminate without delay from public instruction in Serbia, both as regards the teaching body and also as regards the methods of instruction, everything that serves, or might serve, to foment the propaganda against Austria-Hungary;

4. To remove from the military service, and from the administration

in general, all officers and functionaries guilty of propaganda against the Austro-Hungarian Monarchy whose names and deeds the Austro-Hungarian Government reserve to themselves the right of communicating to the Royal Government;

5. To accept the collaboration in Serbia of representatives of the Austro-Hungarian Government for the suppression of the subversive movement directed against the territorial integrity of the Monarchy;

6. To take judicial proceedings against accessories to the plot of the 28th June who are on Serbian territory; delegates of the Austro-Hungarian Government will take part in the investigation relating thereto;

7. To proceed without delay to the arrest of Major Voija Tankositch and of the individual named Milan Ciganovitch, a Serbian State employee, who have been compromised by the results of the magisterial inquiry at Sarajevo;

8. To prevent by effective measures the cooperation of the Serbian authorities in the illicit traffic in arms and explosives across the frontier, to dismiss and punish severely the officials of the frontier service at Schabatz and Loznica guilty of having assisted the perpetrators of the Sarajevo crime by facilitating their passage across the frontier.

9. To furnish the Imperial and Royal Government with explanations regarding the unjustifiable utterances of high Serbian officials, both in Serbia and abroad, who, notwithstanding their official position, have not hesitated since the crime of 28th June to express themselves in interviews in terms of hostility to the Austro-Hungarian Government; and, finally,

10. To notify the Imperial and Royal Government without delay of the execution of the measures comprised under the preceding heads.

The Austro-Hungarian Government expect the reply of the Royal Government by 6 o'clock on Saturday evening the 25th July.

Wilson Proposes Declaration of War, 1917

After two and a half years of furious fighting, the war was still at a deadlock. Brutally, massively, the killing went on, with neither side capable of forcing a decision. What was worse, neither side seemed to know for what it was fighting, which gave the killing a quality of senselessness. Still, men died bravely, to a purpose or not, while their leaders sought desperately for strategies to break the deadlock. Germany, inferior in men and material to the Allies, was most tempted to gamble to win. As 1917 opened, Berlin thought it had discovered the key to victory, if only it acted with daring and dispatch.

Germany was aware that the Allied war effort depended heavily on materiel shipped across the Atlantic from the United States. Technically, American war goods were sold to whoever would buy them. In reality, the British naval blockade made it impossible for ships to reach Germany, so the Allies were America's only belligerent customer. The arrangement satisfied the United States, where sentiment overwhelmingly favored an Allied victory. It roiled Germany. Germany's only weapon against the Allied supply line from America was the submarine, an instrument of war so new that no rules governed its use. Deadly but fragile, the submarine could not risk surfacing to permit passengers and crews to take to lifeboats before their ships were sent to the bottom. Throughout the war the United States and Germany argued constantly over the rights of the German U-boat against shipping destined for Allied ports. In 1915, the United States contemplated war when a submarine sank the British liner *Lusitania* with the loss of 128 American lives. After several more brushes with war, the German government pledged in 1916 to sink no more liners or merchant vessels without ample warning. But in 1917, the German general staff decided that the Central Powers faced ultimate defeat if American shipments to the Allies did not stop. Though the Germans knew that resumption of submarine warfare would provoke the United States into war, the German admiralty was confident it would starve Britain into submission before America's presence could make a difference. In January, 1917, Germany announced a policy of unlimited submarine warfare.

President Woodrow Wilson severed diplomatic relations with Germany at once, then began to prepare the nation for involvement in hostilities. Wilson attempted to transform the conflict from a contest for dubious national goals to a great moral crusade on behalf of freedom and democracy. Wilson, who had earlier sought to arbitrate a peace without victory, now saw the war as a righteous instrument for advancing the cause of free government. The Russian Revolution of March, 1917, seemed to remove the last contradiction to his premise. On April 2, 1917, after several sinkings by German submarines, Wilson appeared before Congress to present his war message. He outlined carefully the German provocations and offered his own conception of what the war meant. To the weary Allies, Wilson's idealism was admirable but mattered less than Wilson's divisions. While finding his ideals thrilling, Europe was not prepared to accept them. What seemed more important was that the United States had reached maturity and was ready to play a responsible role in determining the destiny of Western civilization. The New World, in 1917, was coming to the rescue of the Old.

The following excerpts are from Wilson's address to Congress on April 2, 1917, recommending a declaration of war against Germany. Four days later, America was a belligerent power.

Document 94

Gentlemen of the Congress:

I have called the Congress into extraordinary session because there are serious, very serious, choices of policy to be made, and made immediately, which it was neither right nor constitutionally permissible that I should assume the responsibility of making.

On the third of February last I officially laid before you the extraordinary announcement of the Imperial German Government that on and after the first day of February it was its purpose to put aside all restraints of law or of humanity and use its submarines to sink every vessel that sought to approach either the ports of Great Britain and Ireland or the western coasts of Europe or any of the ports controlled by the enemies of Germany within the Mediterranean. That had seemed to be the object of the German submarine warfare earlier in the war, but since April of last year the Imperial Government had somewhat restrained the commanders of its undersea craft in conformity with its promise then given to us that passenger boats should not be sunk, and that due warning would be given to all other vessels which its submarines might seek to destroy, when no resistance was offered or escape attempted, and care taken that their crews were given at least a fair chance to save their lives in their open boats. The precautions taken were meagre and haphazard enough, as was proved in distressing instance after instance in the progress of the cruel and unmanly business, but a certain degree of restraint was observed. The new policy has swept every restriction aside. Vessels of every kind, whatever their flag, their character, their cargo, their destination, their errand, have been ruthlessly sent to the bottom without warning and without thought of help or mercy of those on board, the vessels of friendly neutrals along with those of belligerents. Even hospital ships and ships carrying relief to the sorely bereaved and stricken people of Belgium, though the latter were provided with safe conduct through the proscribed areas by the German Government itself and were distinguished by unmistakable marks of identity, have been sunk with the same reckless lack of compassion or of principle.

I was for a little while unable to believe that such things would in fact be done by any government that had hitherto subscribed to the humane practices of civilized nations. International law had its origin in the attempt to set up some law which would be respected and observed upon the seas, where no nation had right of dominion and where lay the free highways of the world. By painful stage after stage has that law been built up, with meagre enough results, indeed, after all was accomplished that could be accomplished, but always with a clear view, at least, of what the heart and conscience of mankind demanded. This minimum of right the German Government has swept aside under the plea of retaliation and necessity and because it has no weapons which it could use at sea except these which it is impossible to employ as it is employing them without throwing to the winds all scruples of humanity or of respect for the understandings that were supposed to underlie the intercourse of the world. I am not now thinking of the loss of property involved, immense and serious as that is, but only of the wanton and wholesale destruction of the lives of non-combatants, men, women, and children engaged in pursuits which have always, even in the darkest periods of modern history, been deemed innocent and legitimate. Property can be paid for; the lives of peaceful and innocent people cannot be. The present German submarine warfare against commerce is a warfare against mankind.

It is a war against all nations. American ships have been sunk, American lives taken, in ways which it has stirred us very deeply to learn of, but the ships and people of other neutral and friendly nations have been sunk and overwhelmed in the waters in the same way. There has been no discrimination. The challenge is to all mankind. Each nation must decide for itself how it will meet it. The choice we make for ourselves must be made with a moderation of counsel and a temperateness of judgment befitting our character and our motives as a nation. We must put excited feeling away. Our motive will not be revenge or the victorious assertion of the physical might of the nation, but only the vindication of right, of human right, of which we are only a single champion. . . .

With a profound sense of the solemn and even tragical character of the step I am taking and of the grave responsibilities which it involves, but in unhesitating obedience to what I deem my constitutional duty, I advise that the Congress declare the recent course of the Imperial German Government to be in fact nothing less than war against the government and people of the United States; that it formally accept the status of belligerent which has thus been thrust upon it; and that it take immediate steps not only to put the country in a more thorough state of defense but also to exert all its power and employ all its resources to bring the Government of the German Empire to terms and end the war. . . .

We have no quarrel with the German people. We have no feeling towards them but one of sympathy and friendship. It was not upon their impulse that their government acted in entering this war. It was not with their previous knowledge or approval. It was a war determined upon as wars used to be determined upon in the old, unhappy days when peoples were nowhere consulted by their rulers and wars were provoked and waged in the interest of dynasties or of little groups of ambitious men who were accustomed to use their fellow men as pawns and tools. Self-governed nations do not fill their neighbour states with spies or set the course of intrigue to bring about some critical posture of affairs which will give them an opportunity to strike and make conquest. Such designs can be successfully worked out only under cover and where no one has the right to ask questions. Cunningly contrived plans of deception or aggression, carried, it may be, from generation to generation, can be worked out and kept from the light only within the privacy of courts or behind the carefully guarded confidences of a narrow and privileged class. They are happily impossible where public opinion commands and insists upon full information concerning all the nation's affairs.

A steadfast concert for peace can never be maintained except by a partnership of democratic nations. No autocratic government could be trusted to keep faith within it or observe its covenants. It must be a league of honour, a partnership of opinion. Intrigue would eat its vitals away; the plottings of inner circles who could plan what they would and render account to no one would be a corruption seated at its very heart. Only free peoples can hold their purpose and their honour steady to a common end and prefer the interests of mankind to any narrow interest of their own. . . .

We are now about to accept gauge of battle with this natural foe to liberty and shall, if necessary, spend the whole force of the nation to check and nullify its pretensions and its power. We are glad, now that we see the facts with no veil of false pretence about them, to fight thus for the ultimate peace of the world and for the liberation of its peoples, the German peoples included: for the rights of nations great and small and the privilege of men everywhere to choose their way of life and of obedience. The world must be made safe for democracy. Its peace must be planted upon the tested foundations of political liberty. We have no selfish ends to serve. We desire no conquest, no dominion. We seek no indemnities for ourselves, no material compensation for the sacrifices we shall freely make. We are but one of the champions of the rights of mankind. We shall be satisfied when those rights have been made as secure as the faith and the freedom of nations can make them.

Just because we fight without rancour and without selfish object, seeking nothing for ourselves but what we shall wish to share with all free peoples, we shall, I feel confident, conduct our operations as belligerents without passion and ourselves observe with proud punctilio the principles of right and of fair play we profess to be fighting for. . . .

It is a distressing and oppressive duty, Gentlemen of the Congress, which I have performed in thus addressing you. There are, it may be, many months of fiery trial and sacrifice ahead of us. It is a fearful thing to lead this great peaceful people into war, into the most terrible and disastrous of all wars, civilization itself seeming to be in the balance. But the right is more precious than peace, and we shall fight for the things which we have always carried nearest our hearts, for democracy, for the right of those who submit to authority to have a voice in their own governments, for the rights and liberties of small nations, for a universal dominion of right by such a concert of free peoples as shall bring peace and safety to all nations and make the world itself at last free. To such a task we can dedicate our lives and our fortunes, everything that we are and everything that we have; with the pride of those who know that the day has come when America is privileged to spend her blood and her might for the principles that gave her birth and happiness and the peace which she has treasured. God helping her, she can do no other.

Treaty of Versailles, 1919

America's presence was sufficient to tip the scales in favor of the Allies. In November, 1918, Germany, exhausted and divided, consented to an armistice. Two months later, the representatives of twenty-seven victorious nations met in Louis XIV's sumptuous palace at Versailles to draw up the treaty of peace.

Woodrow Wilson, determined to impose his ideals on the settlement, represented the United States. But if his popularity in Europe was at a peak, his objectives were received at best with indulgence. David Lloyd-George, the British Prime Minister, had pledged to his electorate that he would extract from Germany every possible penny to repay the expenses of the war. Georges Clemenceau, the French premier, vowed to guarantee the future security of France by annexing German territory and depriving Germany of the means to recuperate from the war. Germany, which had not signed a surrender but a cease-fire based on Wilson's lenient Fourteen Points, was not even represented at Versailles. Neither were Russia or Austria, important as was their influence in Europe. The United States, France and Britain, with some small help from Italy and Japan, had decided to set the terms of the peace.

The liberal, democratic victors of World War I had failed to learn a lesson from the reactionaries of the Congress of Vienna who, a century before, understood, at least, that peace could not be assured without the participation of those who would be responsible for keeping it. Versailles was a negotiation between victors, not between victors and vanquished. Though World War I, thanks largely to Wilson, had ended on a note of hope, these victors did not have the wisdom or the vision to conclude a just peace. The Versailles Conference was designed for disillusionment.

Though Wilson's ideals received much homage at Versailles, they were followed only when they suited the purposes of the dominating powers. The delegates cited the principle of self-determination, for instance, to justify the dismemberment of the German and Austrian empires, but they overlooked it when the Italians claimed rights over Slavs, when it conflicted with secret promises made during the war, when Austria sought union with Germany in order to retain its economic viability. In the end, Wilson himself adopted the petty, vindictive spirit that characterized the conference.

A century before, Europe could reasonably blame Napoleon for an epoch of carnage, but the delegates at Vienna were wise enough to understand that vengeance was not the way to peace. Virtually all of Europe shared the blame for World War I, yet the delegates at Versailles had the audacity not only to make Germany and its allies concede exclusive guilt for the war but also to punish them for it. By the time the conference convened, Germany had of its own volition banished the Kaiser's autocracy in favor of a democratic government. But Versaille saw to it that the democratic regime got its start under the most inauspicious circumstances. The loss of German territories was the least of the burdens. Reparations were set at a figure far in excess of Germany's ability to pay, as well as in excess of Germany's responsibility. Despite Wilson's lofty declarations on general disarmament, Germany alone was deprived of a large army. Inexplicably, while the Versailles negotiations were underway, the Allies maintained their wartime blockade, so that Germans continued to die of starvation. But most outrageous, Germany's new democratic government had to live under the dishonor of Article 231, the war guilt clause, which made Germans seethe with anger. Whatever its aims, the result of the Versailles Conference was to create conditions fertile for another round of war.

The Versailles Treaty was a ponderously long document. The following are its more important provisions.

Document 95

Article 42

Germany is forbidden to maintain or construct any fortifications either on the left bank of the Rhine or on the right bank to the west of a line drawn 50 kilometres to the East of the Rhine. . . .

Article 45

As compensation for the destruction of the coal mines in the north of France and as part payment towards the total reparation due from Germany for the damage resulting from the war, Germany cedes to France in full and absolute possession, with exclusive rights of exploitation, unencumbered and free from all debts and charges of any kind, the coal mines situated in the Saar Basin. . . .

Article 49

Germany renounces in favour of the League of Nations, in the capacity of trustee, the government of the territory defined above.

At the end of fifteen years from the coming into force of the present Treaty the inhabitants of the said territory shall be called upon to indicate the sovereignty under which they desire to be placed. . . .

Section V

Alsace Lorraine

The High Contracting Parties, recognising the moral obligations to redress the wrong done by Germany in 1871 both to the rights of France and to the wishes of the population of Alsace and Lorraine, which were separated from their country in spite of the solemn protest of their representatives at the Assembly of Bordeaux.

Agree upon the following Articles:

Article 51

The territories which were ceded to Germany in accordance with the Preliminaries of Peace signed at Versailles on February 26, 1871, and the

Treaty of Frankfort of May 10, 1871, are restored to French sovereignty as from the date of the Armistice of November 11, 1918.

The provisions of the Treaties establishing the delimitation of the frontiers before 1871 shall be restored. . . .

Article 80

Germany acknowledges and will respect strictly the independence of Austria, within the frontiers which may be fixed in a Treaty between that State and the Principal Allied and Associated Powers; she agrees that this independence shall be unalienable, except with the consent of the Council of the League of Nations.

Article 81

Germany, in conformity with the action already taken by the Allied and Associated Powers, recognises the complete independence of the Czecho-Slovak State which will include the autonomous territory of the Ruthenians to the south of the Carpathians. Germany hereby recognises the frontiers of this State as determined by the Principal Allied and Associated Powers and the other interested States. . . .

Article 87

Germany, in conformity with the action already taken by the Allied and Associated Powers, recognises the complete independence of Poland. . . .

Article 89

Poland undertakes to accord freedom of transit to persons, goods, vessels, carriages, wagons and mails in transit between East Prussia and the rest of Germany over Polish territory, including territorial waters, and to treat them at least as favourably as the persons, goods, vessels, carriages, wagons and mails respectively of Polish or of any other more favoured nationality, origin, importation, starting-point, or ownership as regards facilities, restrictions and all other matters. . . .

Article 102

The Principal Allied and Associated Powers undertake to establish the town of Danzig, together with the rest of the territory described in Article 100, as a Free City. It will be placed under the protection of the League of Nations. . . .

Article 116

Germany acknowledges and agrees to respect as permanent and inalienable the independence of all the territories which were part of the former Russian Empire on August 1, 1914.

In accordance with the provisions of Article 259 of Part IX (Financial Clauses) and Article 292 of Part X (Economic Clauses) Germany accepts definitely the abrogation of the Brest-Litovsk Treaties and of all other treaties, conventions and agreements entered into by her with the Maximalist Government in Russia.

The Allied and Associated Powers formally reserve the rights of Russia to obtain from Germany restitution and reparation based on the principles of the present Treaty. . . .

Article 119

Germany renounces in favour of the Principal Allied and Associated Powers all her rights and titles over her oversea possessions. . . .

Article 159

The German military forces shall be demobilised and reduced as prescribed hereinafter. . . .

Article 160

(1) By a date which must not be later than March 31, 1920, the German Army must not comprise more than seven divisions of infantry and three divisions of cavalry.

After that date the total number of effectives in the Army of the States constituting Germany must not exceed one hundred thousand men, including officers and establishments of depots. The Army shall be devoted exclusively to the maintenance of order within the territory and to the control of the frontiers.

The total effective strength of officers, including the personnel of staffs, whatever their composition, must not exceed four thousand.

Article 181

After the expiration of a period of two months from the coming into force of the present Treaty the German naval forces in commission must not exceed:

6 battleships of the *Deutschland* or *Lothringen* type,
6 light cruisers,
12 destroyers,
12 torpedo boats,

or an equal number of ships constructed to replace them as provided in Article 190.

No submarines are to be included.

All other warships, except where there is provision to the contrary in the present Treaty, must be placed in reserve or devoted to commercial purposes. . . .

Article 198

The armed forces of Germany must not include any military or naval air forces. . . .

Article 231

The Allied and Associated Governments affirm and Germany accepts the responsibility of Germany and her allies for causing all the loss and damage to which the Allied and Associated Governments and their nationals have been subjected as a consequence of the war imposed upon them by the aggression of Germany and her allies.

Article 232

The Allied and Associated Governments recognise that the resources of Germany are not adequate after taking into account permanent diminutions of such resources which will result from other provisions of the present Treaty, to make complete reparation for all such loss and damage.

The Allied and Associated Governments, however, require, and Germany undertakes, that she will make compensation for all damage done to the civilian population of the Allied and Associated Powers and to their property during the period of the belligerency of each as an Allied or Associated Power against Germany by such aggression by land, by sea and from the air, and in general all damage as defined in Annex I hereto. . . .

Article 233

The amount of the above damage for which compensation is to be made by Germany shall be determined by an Inter-Allied Commission, to be called the *Reparation Commission* and constituted in the form and with the powers set forth hereunder and in Annexes II and VII inclusive hereto.

This Commission shall consider the claims and give to the German Government a just opportunity to be heard.

The findings of the Commission as to the amount of damage defined as above shall be concluded and notified to the German Government on or before May 1, 1921, as representing the extent of that Government's obligations. . . .

Covenant of the League of Nations, 1919

Wilson endured the sacrifice of many of his principles at Versailles because he believed that the League of Nations would provide the machinery for rectifying international injustice and preserving peace. He pressed tirelessly for establishment of the League. To him, it represented vindication of America's entry into the war and the culmination of his own high ideals. England shared his enthusiasm for it. France, still afraid of Germany, looked upon it as a means of enforcing the provisions of the Versailles Treaty. Japan wanted—vainly—to make it into a vehicle for promoting the concept of racial equality. Other countries accepted the League for a variety of reasons but, at the least, it was looked upon as a source of hope. It seemed the best promise for a stable future.

The League of Nations Covenant provided for an Assembly representing all countries and a Council of nine members, of which the United States, Great Britain, France, Italy and Japan were to be permanent and the rest elected at regular intervals. Headquarters were to be at Geneva, which would also be the seat of the League secretariat, a sort of international civil service. Attached to the League were a World Court to adjudicate disputes and an International Labor Office to elevate working conditions. All League members were required to submit their international quarrels either to arbitration or to the Council. Decisions of the Council, however, had to be unanimous, which made them difficult to reach, and could not readily be enforced, since the Council possessed no police powers. Therein lay the basic weakness of the League organization.

The League failed, however, for many reasons. Not the least of them, ironically, was the refusal of the United States to accept membership, despite Wilson's role of leadership. But despite its failure, many of the ideals which were at its source remained unimpaired, to be put to use after the next great international conflict.

Though membership was global, the League reflected the prejudice of its founders that Europe was still the focus of the world. The Covenant of the League of Nations is essentially a Western document, based on a Western idea. Non-Western nations were invited to subscribe to this Western idea. In a way, the League of Nations was an effort to renew the unity of Western civilization.

Presented here are the principal articles of the Covenant of the League of Nations dealing with organization and the maintenance of peace. The Covenant formed an integral part of the Treaty of Versailles of 1919.

Document 96

The High Contracting Parties,

In order to promote international co-operation and to achieve international peace and security

by the acceptance of obligations not to resort to war,

by the prescription of open, just and honourable relations between nations,

by the firm establishment of the understandings of international law as the actual rule of conduct among Governments, and

by the maintenance of justice and a scrupulous respect for all treaty obligations in the dealings of organised peoples with one another,

Agree to this Covenant of the League of Nations:

Article 1.

The original Members of the League of Nations shall be those of the Signatories which are named in the Annex to this Covenant and also such of those other States named in the Annex as shall accede without reservation to this Covenant. Such accession shall be effected by a declaration deposited with the Secretariat within two months of the coming into force of the Covenant. Notice thereof shall be sent to all other Members of the League.

Any fully self-governing State, Dominion or Colony not named in the Annex may become a Member of the League if its admission is agreed to by two-thirds of the Assembly, provided that it shall give effective guarantees of its sincere intention to observe its international obligations, and shall accept such regulations as may be prescribed by the League in regard to its military, naval and air forces and armaments.

Any member of the League may, after two years' notice of its intention so to do, withdraw from the League, provided that all its international obligations and all its obligations under this Covenant shall have been fulfilled at the time of its withdrawal.

Article 2.

The action of the League under this Covenant shall be effected through the instrumentality of an Assembly and of a Council, with a permanent Secretariat. . . .

Article 3.

The Assembly shall consist of Representatives of the Members of the League.

The Assembly shall meet at stated intervals and from time to time as occasion may require at the Seat of the League or at such other place as may be decided upon.

The Assembly may deal at its meetings with any matter within the sphere of action of the League or affecting the peace of the world.

At meetings of the Assembly each Member of the League shall have one vote, and may have not more than three Representatives.

Article 4.

The Council shall consist of Representatives of the Principal Allied and Associated Powers, together with Representatives of four other Members of the League. These four Members of the League shall be selected by the Assembly from time to time in its discretion. Until the appointment of the Representatives of the four Members of the League first selected by the Assembly, Representatives of Belgium, Brazil, Spain and Greece shall be members of the Council.

With the approval of the majority of the Assembly, the Council may name additional Members of the League whose Representatives shall always be members of the Council; the Council with like approval may increase the number of Members of the League to be selected by the Assembly for representation on the Council.

The Assembly shall fix by a two-thirds majority the rules dealing with the election of the non-permanent members of the Council, and particularly such regulations as relate to their term of office and the conditions of re-eligibility.

The Council shall meet from time to time as occasion may require, and at least once a year, at the Seat of the League, or at such other place as may be decided upon.

The Council may deal at its meetings with any matter within the sphere of action of the League or affecting the peace of the world.

Any Member of the League not represented on the Council shall be invited to send a Representative to sit as a member at any meeting of the Council during the consideration of matters specially affecting the interests of that Member of the League.

At meetings of the Council, each Member of the League represented in the Council shall have one vote, and may have not more than one Representative.

Article 5.

Except where otherwise expressly provided in this Covenant or by terms of the present Treaty, decisions at any meeting of the Assembly or of the Council shall require the agreement of all the Members of the League represented at the meeting.

All matters of procedure at meetings of the Assembly or of the Council, including the appointment of Committees to investigate particular matters, shall be regulated by the Assembly or by the Council and may be decided by a majority of the Members of the League represented at the meeting.

The first meeting of the Assembly and the first meeting of the Council shall be summoned by the President of the United States of America.

Article 6.

The permanent Secretariat shall be established at the Seat of the League. The Secretariat shall comprise a Secretary General and such secretaries and staff as may be required.

The first Secretary General shall be the person named in the Annex; thereafter the Secretary General shall be appointed by the Council with the approval of the majority of the Assembly.

The secretaries and staff of the Secretariat shall be appointed by the Secretary General with the approval of the Council.

The Secretary General shall act in that capacity at all meetings of the Assembly and of the Council.

The expenses of the League shall be borne by the Members of the League in the proportion decided by the Assembly.

Article 7.

The Seat of the League is established at Geneva.

The Council may at any time decide that the Seat of the League shall be established elsewhere.

All positions under or in connection with the League, including the Secretariat, shall be open equally to men and women.

Representatives of the Members of the League and officials of the League when engaged on the business of the League shall enjoy diplomatic privileges and immunities.

The buildings and other property occupied by the League or its officials or by Representatives attending its meetings shall be inviolable.

Article 8.

The Members of the League recognise that the maintenance of peace requires the reduction of national armaments to the lowest point consistent with national safety and the enforcement by common action of international obligations.

The Council, taking account of the geographical situation and circumstances of each State, shall formulate plans for such reduction for the consideration and action of the several Governments.

Such plans shall be subject to reconsideration and revision at least every ten years.

After these plans shall have been adopted by the several Governments, the limits of armaments therein fixed shall not be exceeded without the concurrence of the Council.

The Members of the League agree that the manufacture by private enterprise of munitions and implements of war is open to grave objections. The Council shall advise how the evil effects attendant upon such manufacture can be prevented, due regard being had to the necessities of those Members of the League which are not able to manufacture the munitions and implements of war necessary for their safety.

The Members of the League undertake to interchange full and frank information as to the scale of their armaments, their military, naval and air programmes and the condition of such of their industries as are adaptable to warlike purposes.

Article 9.

A permanent Commission shall be constituted to advise the Council on the execution of the provisions of Articles 1 and 8, and on military, naval and air questions generally.

Article 10.

The Members of the League undertake to respect and preserve as against external aggression the territorial integrity and existing political independence of all Members of the League. In case of any such aggression or in case of any threat or danger of such aggression the Council shall advise upon the means by which this obligation shall be fulfilled.

Article 11.

Any war or threat of war, whether immediately affecting any of the Members of the League or not, is hereby declared a matter of concern to the whole League, and the League shall take any action that may be deemed wise and effectual to safeguard the peace of nations. In case any such emergency should arise the Secretary General shall on the request of any Member of the League forthwith summon a meeting of the Council.

It is also declared to be the friendly right of each Member of the League to bring to the attention of the Assembly or of the Council any circumstance whatever affecting international relations which threatens to disturb international peace or the good understanding between nations upon which peace depends.

Article 12.

The Members of the League agree that if there should arise between them any dispute likely to lead to a rupture, they will submit the matter either to arbitration *or judicial settlement* or to inquiry by the Council, and they agree in no case to resort to war until three months after the award by the arbitrators or *the judicial decision* or the report by the Council.

In any case under this Article the award of the arbitrators or *the judicial decision* shall be made within a reasonable time, and the report of the Council shall be made within six months after the submission of the dispute.

Article 13.

The Members of the League agree that whenever any dispute shall arise between them which they recognize to be suitable for submission to arbitration *or judicial settlement* and which cannot be satisfactorily settled by diplomacy, they will submit the whole subject-matter to arbitration *or judicial settlement.*

Disputes as to the interpretation of a treaty, as to any question of international law, as to the existence of any fact which if established would constitute a breach of any international obligation, or as to the extent and nature of the reparation to be made for any such breach, are declared to be among those which are generally suitable for submission to arbitration *or judicial settlement.*

For the consideration of any such dispute the court to which the case is referred shall be the Permanent Court of International Justice or any tribunal agreed on by the parties to the dispute or stipulated in any convention existing between them.

The Members of the League agree that they will carry out in full good faith any award or decision that may be rendered, and that they will not resort to war against a Member of the League which complies therewith. In the event of any failure to carry out such an award or decision, the Council shall propose what steps should be taken to give effect thereto.

Article 14.

The Council shall formulate and submit to the Members of the League for adoption plans for the establishment of a Permanent Court of International Justice. The Court shall be competent to hear and determine any dispute of an international character which the parties thereto submit to it. The Court may also give an advisory opinion upon any dispute or question referred to it by the Council or by the Assembly.

Article 15.

If there should arise between Members of the League any dispute likely to lead to a rupture, which is not submitted to arbitration or *judicial settlement* in accordance with Article 13, the Members of the League agree that they will submit the matter to the Council. Any party to the dispute may effect such submission by giving notice of the existence of the dispute to the Secretary General, who will make all necessary arrangements for a full investigation and consideration thereof.

For this purpose the parties to the dispute will communicate to the Secretary General, as promptly as possible, statements of their case, with all the relevant facts and papers, and the Council may forthwith direct the publication thereof.

The Council shall endeavor to effect a settlement of the dispute, and if such efforts are successful, a statement shall be made public giving such facts and explanations regarding the dispute and the terms of settlement thereof as the Council may deem appropriate.

If the dispute is not thus settled, the Council either unanimously or by a majority vote shall make and publish a report containing a statement of the facts of the dispute and the recommendations which are deemed just and proper in regard thereto.

Any Member of the League represented on the Council may make public a statement of the facts of the dispute and of its conclusions regarding the same.

If a report by the Council is unanimously agreed to by the members thereof other than the Representatives of one or more of the parties to the dispute, the Members of the League agree that they will not go to war with any party to the dispute which complies with the recommendations of the report.

If the Council fails to reach a report which is unanimously agreed to by the members thereof, other than the Representatives of one or more of the parties to the dispute, the Members of the League reserve to themselves the right to take such action as they shall consider necessary for the maintenance of right and justice.

If the dispute between the parties is claimed by one of them, and is found by the Council, to arise out of a matter which by international law is solely within the domestic jurisdiction of that party, the Council shall so report, and shall make no recommendation as to its settlement.

The Council may in any case under this Article refer the dispute to the Assembly. The dispute shall be so referred at the request of either party to the dispute, provided that such request be made within fourteen days after the submission of the dispute to the Council.

In any case referred to the Assembly, all the provisions of this Article and of Article 12 relating to the action and powers of the Council shall apply to the action and powers of the Assembly, provided that a report made by the Assembly, if concurred in by the Representatives of those Members of the League represented on the Council and of a majority of the other Members of the League, exclusive in each case of the Representatives of the parties to the dispute, shall have the same force as a report by the Council concurred in by all the members thereof other than the Representatives of one or more of the parties to the dispute.

Article 16.

Should any Member of the League resort to war in disregard of its covenants under Articles 12, 13 or 15, it shall *ipso facto* be deemed to have committed an act of war against all other Members of the League, which hereby undertake immediately to subject it to the severance of all trade or financial relations, the prohibition of all intercourse between their nationals and the nationals of the covenant-breaking State, and the prevention of all financial, commercial or personal intercourse between the nationals of the covenant-breaking State and the nationals of any other State, whether a Member of the League or not.

It shall be the duty of the Council in such case to recommend to the several Governments concerned what effective military, naval or air force the Members of the League shall severally contribute to the armed forces to be used to protect the covenants of the League.

The Members of the League agree, further, that they will mutually support one another in the financial and economic measures which are taken under this Article, in order to minimise the loss and inconvenience resulting from the above measures, and that they will mutually support one another in resisting any special measures aimed at one of their number by the covenant-breaking State, and that they will take the necessary steps to afford passage through their territory to the forces of any of the Members of the League which are co-operating to protect the covenants of the League.

Any Member of the League which has violated any covenant of the League may be declared to be no longer a Member of the League by a vote of the Council concurred in by Representatives of all the other Members of the League represented thereon. . . .

Article 20.

The Members of the League severally agree that this Covenant is accepted as abrogating all obligations or understandings *inter se* which are inconsistent with the terms thereof, and solemnly undertake that they will not hereafter enter into any engagements inconsistent with the terms thereof.

In case any Member of the League shall, before becoming a Member of the League, have undertaken any obligations inconsistent with the terms of this Covenant, it shall be the duty of such Member to take immediate steps to procure its release from such obligations.

Article 21.

Nothing in this Covenant shall be deemed to affect the validity of international engagements, such as treaties of arbitration or regional understandings like the Monroe doctrine, for securing the maintenance of peace.

XV

World War II and the Nuclear Age

XV

World War II and the Nuclear Age

The Versailles Treaty proved indigestible to the Western world. The victors in the war declined to enforce it. The vanquished were determined to change it. Scarcely a participant, on either side, believed he had been treated justly by it or felt any stake in defending it. The League of Nations, its most hopeful creation, disintegrated before a swarm of destructive forces. Despite Wilson's idealism and the bloody lessons of the battlefield, Versailles had created anarchy in Europe that was worse than before Sarajevo.

The Munich Agreement, 1938

France, presumably, was the strongest continental power after World War I, protected not only by a substantial army but by devoted allies, Czechoslovakia and Poland, on Germany's flanks. But France, which had suffered most heavily among the major belligerents, was drained of vitality. When Germany, under the banner of Nazism, began to regain its strength in the early 1930s, France lacked the energy to react. In 1934, Hitler violated the Versailles Treaty by vastly enlarging Germany's armed forces. In 1936 he occupied the Rhineland and, in 1938 he annexed Austria. The French could have stopped Nazism cold on each occasion, particularly if they had called for help on the willing Czechs or Poles. But Britain, having retreated from the problems of the continent, offered neither encouragement nor assistance, while the United States, in isolation across the sea, acknowledged no responsibility whatever for maintaining the European peace it had helped to design. Alone, the French were paralyzed, while Fascism—not only in Germany but in Italy—became more pugnacious. In one crisis after another, the democracies revealed a bankruptcy of moral resources. By the late 1930s, Germany was once again the strongest power in Europe, with ambition that was both ruthless and boundless.

After his Austrian aggression, Hitler set as his next objective Czechoslovakia, claiming as his pretext the Wilsonian principle of self-determination for the clamorous German minority known as *Sudetendeutch.* In May, 1938, he rushed his troops to the Czech border but a threat from the French, who appeared to be waking from their lethargy, persuaded him to retreat. In September, however, the democracies once again lost their nerve. When Hitler announced his intention of annexing the Sudetenland even at the price of war, the British and the French—without consulting the Czechs—consented to let him do it. Yet when Hitler, having won such an easy victory, enlarged his demand to include non-Germanic areas, the French and British prepared for war. Hitler declared that his troops would march on October 1, then peremptorily moved the date up to September 28. On the eve of his self-imposed deadline, he announced a postponement of action for 24 hours and invited to a conference in Munich—the third international meeting on the Czech crisis—Prime Minister Neville Chamberlain of Britain, Premier Edouard Daladier of France and Dictator Benito Mussolini of Italy. At Munich the democracies gave Hitler all he wanted: the most highly industrialized segment of Czechoslovakia, containing not only Sudeten Germans but 750,000 Czechs as well. Chamberlain flew back to London to speak the words that would stick in his throat. "I return from Germany bringing peace and honor," he said. In fact, he had neither. He had alienated the Russians and sold out the Czechs. He did not even save the rump of Czechoslovakia, which Hitler swallowed up a few months later. Within less than a year, France and England, weaker for having lost their friends, were once again at war with Germany.

"Munich" has passed into the lexicon of diplomacy as a synonym for craven appeasement. Chamberlain, author of the message presented below, became its symbol. The Munich Agreement—the text of which follows—symbolizes more vividly than any other act the moribund condition of Western democracy on the eve of World War II. Its effect, of course, was not to satisfy but to stimulate the appetite of the dictators. It was thus an unmistakable step toward war, not toward peace. The democracies learned a painful lesson at Munich. It has ever since put them on their guard.

Document 97

A. Personal Message Sent by the Prime Minister (Neville Chamberlain) to the Reichschancellor on September 28, 1938.

After reading your letter I feel certain that you can get all essentials without war and without delay.

I am ready to come to Berlin myself at once to discuss arrangements for transfer with you and representatives of Czech Government, together with representatives of France and Italy if you desire.

I feel convinced we could reach agreement in a week. However much you distrust Prague Government's intentions, you cannot doubt power of British and French Governments to see that promises are carried out fairly and fully and forthwith. As you know I have stated publicly that we are prepared to undertake that they shall be so carried out.

I cannot believe that you will take responsibility of starting a world war which may end civilisation for the sake of a few days' delay in settling this long-standing problem.

B. Agreement Concluded at Munich on September 29, 1938.

Germany, the United Kingdom, France, and Italy, taking into consideration the agreement, which has been already reached in principle for the cession to Germany of the Sudeten German territory, have agreed on the following terms and conditions governing the said cession and the measures consequent thereon, and by this agreement they each hold themselves responsible for the steps necessary to secure its fulfilment:—

1. The evacuation will begin on the 1st October.

2. The United Kingdom, France, and Italy agree that the evacuation of the territory shall be completed by the 10th October, without any existing installations having been destroyed and that the Czechoslovak Government will be held responsible for carrying out the evacuation without damage to the said installations.

3. The conditions governing the evacuation will be laid down in detail by an international commission composed of representatives of Germany, the United Kingdom, France, Italy, and Czechoslovakia.

4. The occupation by stages of the predominantly German territory by German troops will begin on the 1st October. The four territories marked on the attached map will be occupied by German troops in the following order: the territory marked No. I on the 1st and 2nd of October, the territory marked No. II on the 2nd and 3rd of October, the territory marked No. III on the 3rd, 4th, and 5th of October, the territory marked No. IV on the 6th and 7th of October. The remaining territory of preponderantly German character will be ascertained by the aforesaid international commission forthwith and be occupied by German troops by the 10th of October.

5. The international commission referred to in paragraph 3 will

determine the territories in which a plebiscite is to be held. These territories will be occupied by international bodies until the plebiscite has been completed. The same commission will fix the conditions in which the plebiscite is to be held, taking as a basis the conditions of the Saar plebiscite. The commission will also fix a date, not later than the end of November, on which the plebiscite will be held.

6. The final determination of the frontiers will be carried out by the international commission. This commission will also be entitled to recommend to the four Powers, Germany, the United Kingdom, France and Italy, in certain exceptional cases minor modifications in the strictly ethnographical determination of the zones which are to be transferred without plebiscite.

7. There will be a right of option into and out of the transferred territories, the option to be exercised within six months from the date of this agreement. A German-Czechoslovak commission shall determine the details of the option, consider ways of facilitating the transfer of population and settle questions of principle arising out of the said transfer.

8. The Czechoslovak Government will within a period of four weeks from the date of this agreement release from their military and police forces any Sudeten Germans who may wish to be released, and the Czechoslovak Government will within the same period release Sudeten German prisoners who are serving terms of imprisonment for political offences.

ADOLF HITLER
NEVILLE CHAMBERLAIN
EDOUARD DALADIER
BENITO MUSSOLINI

Munich,
September 29, 1938

British Declaration of War, 1939

Having found the principle of self-determination insufficient to justify his ambitions, Hitler now demanded *lebensraum*, a living space for crowded Germany. With such a doctrine, there were no bounds to the claims he could make. The democracies no longer retained their illusions about Hitler's intentions and prepared to fight. Still, they could not summon the energy to act with decision. In a disastrous diplomatic failure, they let Hitler outmaneuver them and conclude a non-aggression pact with the Soviet Union. They were thus deprived of the ally in the east that had done so much to salvage victory in World War I. In Italy, Germany had at France's flank another ally it had lacked in World War I. Only Poland, weak and vulnerable, remained committed to the Allies. As war approached, France and England—the victors just two decades before in what had been said to be the war to end wars—were practically isolated and menaced with calamitous defeat.

Hitler's agreement with the Russians left him free to turn next to Poland, which was linked to the democracies by treaties of mutual assistance. Having learned their lesson at Munich, Britain and France were prepared to honor their commitment to the Poles. But Hitler was not even contemplating peace. He wanted war. On August 31, he presented the British ambassador with an ultimatum containing his demands on Poland. Before the British could consider them, the invasion of Poland was underway. On September 3, 1939, the two Western democracies declared war on Nazi Germany and World War II began.

The following document is the statement of Prime Minister Chamberlain to the House of Commons on the inauguration of hostilities. The final, poignant paragraph sums up Chamberlain's realization that the policy of appeasement had led straight to disaster.

Document 98

When I spoke last night to the House, I could not but be aware that in some parts of the House there were doubts and some bewilderment as to whether there had been any weakening, hesitation or vacillation on the part of His Majesty's Government. In the circumstances, I make no reproach, for if I had been in the same position as hon. members not sitting on this Bench and not in possession of all the information which we have, I should very likely have felt the same. The statement which I have to make this morning will show that there were no grounds for doubt. We were in consultation all day yesterday with the French Government, and we felt that the intensified action which the Germans were taking against Poland allowed no delay in making our own position clear. Accordingly, we decided to send to our Ambassador in Berlin instructions which he was to hand at nine o'clock this morning to the German Foreign Secretary and which read as follows:

"Sir,

In the communication which I had the honour to make to you on 1st September, I informed you, on the instructions of His Majesty's

Principal Secretary of State for Foreign Affairs, that unless the German Government were prepared to give His Majesty's Government in the United Kingdom satisfactory assurances that the German Government had suspended all aggressive action against Poland and were prepared promptly to withdraw their forces from Polish territory, His Majesty's Government in the United Kingdom would, without hesitation, fulfil their obligations to Poland.

"Although this communication was made more than 24 hours ago, no reply has been received, but German attacks upon Poland have been continued and intensified. I have, accordingly, the honour to inform you that unless not later than 11 A.M., British Summer Time, today September 3rd, satisfactory assurances to the above effect have been given by the German Government and have reached His Majesty's Government in London, a state of war will exist between the two countries as from that hour."

That was the final Note. No such undertaking was received by the time stipulated, and, consequently, this country is at war with Germany. I am in a position to inform the House that, according to arrangements made between the British and French Governments, the French Ambassador in Berlin is at this moment making a similar demarche, accompanied also by a definite time limit. The House has already been made aware of our plans. As I said the other day, we are ready.

This is a sad day for all of us, and to none is it sadder than to me. Everything that I have worked for, everything that I have hoped for, everything that I have believed in during my public life, has crashed into ruins. There is only one thing left for me to do; that is, to devote what strength and powers I have to forwarding the victory of the cause for which we have to sacrifice so much. I cannot tell what part I may be allowed to play myself; I trust I may live to see the day when Hitlerism has been destroyed and a liberated Europe has been re-established.

Churchill's Speech after Dunkirk, 1940

Allied arms were totally inadequate to match the German onslaught. Poland fell in a month, before a single British or French soldier was able to come to its aid. Throughout the winter of 1939–40, there was a lull in the fighting, during which the Allies not only failed to overcome their substantial military deficiencies but even began to think that Germany might be interested in a return to peace. They learned differently, however, in the spring. In April, the Nazis simultaneously attacked Denmark and Norway, overrunning the former in a day, the latter in a few weeks. Even Britain's vaunted sea power was unable to thwart the German amphibious effort into Scandinavia. The string of Allied defeats led to the resignation of the indecisive governments of Chamberlain in Britain and Daladier in France. Their determination bulwarked, the Allies now waited for the next Nazi blow to fall.

On May 10, the German army struck at France through Belgium, the Netherlands and Luxembourg, all neutral countries. Sweeping aside the tiny armies of the Low Countries, the German Panzer divisions quickly pierced the French defensive lines and swarmed over the countryside. Instead of driving toward Paris as they had in 1914, the German columns wheeled toward the sea in a strategy designed to cut off most of the British, French and Belgian armies from reinforcements coming from the south. Unable to stop the Germans from closing their great pincer, the Allies could only surrender or attempt an evacuation by sea. The Belgian king surrendered, leaving an important gap in the Allied lines. The French and British, tired and disorganized, fought on desperately to protect a salvage operation being undertaken from the tiny Channel port of Dunkirk. It was a military marvel that more than 335,000 soldiers were evacuated under tremendous pressure from Dunkirk's docks and beaches. The evacuation meant that the British had an army intact, even if all its equipment had been left in France. Dunkirk was a brilliant feat of arms and courage. But it was not victory.

Winston Churchill, the new British prime minister, knew that defeat on the continent was imminent. The French, fighting virtually alone, could not stop the German juggernaut. Not only their armies but their morale was broken. The French had already begun to speak of capitulation. Churchill, however, was defiant. On June 4, 1940, he described to the House of Commons the recent miracle of Dunkirk and its terrible significance. His message was somber but he conveyed an unmistakable confidence that Britain would survive and win. Churchill told the British that the French would fight on and that ultimately the New World, as it had in 1917, would come to rescue the old. He was wrong about the French, right about the United States. Right or wrong, however, he inspired the British to continue the struggle gallantly against what, at the time, appeared to be insuperable odds. Churchill's speech after Dunkirk, and others like it, undoubtedly made a major contribution toward saving the great libertarian tradition in Western civilization from destruction by the foulest political regime known to Western history. The excerpts of Churchill's speech presented here represent a landmark of World War II and a pinnacle of the Western spirit.

Document 99

. . . The German eruption swept like a sharp scythe around the right and rear of the Armies of the north. Eight or nine armored divisions, each of about four hundred armored vehicles of different kinds, but carefully assorted to be complementary and divisible into small self-contained units, cut off all communications between us and the main French Armies. It severed our own communications for food and ammunition, which ran first to Amiens and afterwards through Abbeville, and it shore its way up the coast to Boulogne and Calais, and almost to Dunkirk. Behind this armored and mechanized onslaught came a number of German divisions in lorries, and behind them again there plodded comparatively slowly the dull brute mass of the ordinary German Army and German people, always so ready to be led to the trampling down in other lands of liberties and comforts which they have never known in their own.

I have said this armored scythe-stroke almost reached Dunkirk—almost but not quite. Boulogne and Calais were the scenes of desperate fighting. The Guards defended Boulogne for a while and were then withdrawn by orders from this country. The Rifle Brigade, the 60th Rifles, and the Queen Victoria's Rifles, with a battalion of British tanks and 1,000 Frenchmen, in all about four thousand strong, defended Calais to the last. The British Brigadier was given an hour to surrender. He spurned the offer, and four days of intense street fighting passed before silence reigned over Calais, which marked the end of a memorable resistance. Only 30 unwounded survivors were brought off by the Navy, and we do not know the fate of their comrades. Their sacrifice, however, was not in vain. At least two armored divisions, which otherwise would have been turned against the British Expeditionary Force, had to be sent to overcome them. They have added another page to the glories of the light divisions, and the time gained enabled the Graveline water lines to be flooded and to be held by the French troops.

Thus it was that the port of Dunkirk was kept open. When it was found impossible for the Armies of the north to reopen their communications to Amiens with the main French Armies, only one choice remained. It seemed, indeed, forlorn. The Belgian, British and French Armies were almost surrounded. Their sole line of retreat was to a single port and to its neighboring beaches. They were pressed on every side by heavy attacks and far outnumbered in the air.

When, a week ago today, I asked the House to fix this afternoon as the occasion for a statement, I feared it would be my hard lot to announce the greatest military disaster in our long history. I thought—and some good judges agreed with me—that perhaps 20,000 or 30,000 men might be re-embarked. But it certainly seemed that the whole of the French First Army and the whole of the British Expeditionary Force north of the Amiens-Abbeville gap would be broken up in the open field or else would have to capitulate for lack of food and ammunition. These were the hard and heavy tidings for which I called upon the House and the nation to prepare themselves a week ago. The whole root and core and brain of the British Army, on which and around which we were to build, and are to build, the great British Armies in the later years of the war, seemed about to perish upon the field or to be led into an ignominious and starving captivity.

That was the prospect a week ago. But another blow which might well have proved final was yet to fall upon us. The King of the Belgians had called upon us to come to his aid. Had not this Ruler and his Government severed themselves from the Allies, who rescued their country from extinction in the late war, and had they not sought refuge in what has proved to be a fatal neutrality, the French and British Armies might well at the outset have saved not only Belgium but perhaps even Poland. Yet at the last moment, when Belgium was already invaded, King Leopold called upon us to come to his aid, and even at the last moment we came. He and his brave, efficient Army, nearly half a million strong, guarded our left flank and thus kept open our only line of retreat to the sea. Suddenly, without prior consultation, with the least possible notice, without the advice of his Ministers and upon his own personal act, he sent a plenipotentiary to the German Command, surrendered his Army, and exposed our whole flank and means of retreat. . . .

The enemy attacked on all sides with great strength and fierceness, and their main power, the power of their far more numerous Air Force, was thrown into the battle or else concentrated upon Dunkirk and the beaches Pressing in upon the narrow exit, both from the east and from the west, the enemy began to fire with cannon upon the beaches by which alone the shipping could approach or depart. They sowed magnetic mines in the channels and seas; they sent repeated waves of hostile aircraft, sometimes more than a hundred strong in one formation, to cast their bombs upon the single pier that remained, and upon the sand dunes upon which the troops had their eyes for shelter. Their U-boats, one of which was sunk, and their motor launches took their toll of the vast traffic which now began. For four or five days an intense struggle reigned. All their armored divisions—or what was left of them—together with great masses of infantry and artillery, hurled themselves in vain upon the ever-narrowing, ever-contracting appendix within which the British and French Armies fought.

Meanwhile, the Royal Navy, with the willing help of countless merchant seamen, strained every nerve to embark the British and Allied troops; 220 light warships and 650 other vessels were engaged. They had to operate upon the difficult coast, often in adverse weather, under an almost ceaseless hail of bombs and an increasing concentration of artillery fire. Nor were the seas, as I have said, themselves free from mines and torpedoes. It was in conditions such as these that our men carried on with little or no rest, for days and nights on end, making trip after trip across the dangerous waters, bringing with them always men whom they had rescued. The numbers they have brought back are the measure of their devotion and their courage. The hospital ships, which brought off many thousands of British and French wounded, being so plainly marked were a special target for Nazi bombs; but the men and women on board them never faltered in their duty.

Meanwhile, the Royal Air Force, which had already been intervening in the battle, so far as its range would allow, from home bases, now used part of its main metropolitan fighter strength, and struck at the German bombers and at the fighters which in large numbers protected them. This struggle was protracted and fierce. Suddenly the scene has cleared, the crash and thunder has for the moment—but only for the moment—died away. A miracle of deliverance, achieved by valor, by perseverance, by perfect discipline, by faultless service, by resource, by skill, by unconquerable fidelity, is manifest to us all. The enemy was hurled back by the retreating British and French troops. He was so roughly handled that he did not hurry their departure seriously. The Royal Air Force engaged the main strength of the German Air Force, and inflicted upon them losses of at least four to one; and the Navy, using nearly 1,000 ships of all kinds, carried over 335,000 men, French and British, out of the jaws of death and shame, to their native land and to the tasks which lie immediately ahead. We must be very careful not to assign to this deliverance the attributes of a victory. Wars are not won by evacuations. But there was a victory inside this deliverance, which should be noted. It was gained by the Air Force. Many of our soldiers coming back have not seen the Air Force at work; they saw only the bombers which escaped its protective attack. They underrate its achievements. I have heard much talk of this; that is why I go out of my way to say this. I will tell you about it.

This was a great trial of strength between the British and German Air Forces. Can you conceive a greater objective for the Germans in the air than to make evacuation from these beaches impossible, and to sink all these ships which were displayed, almost to the extent of thousands? Could there have been an objective of greater military importance and significance for the whole purpose of the war than this? They tried hard, and they were beaten back; they were frustrated in their task. We got the Army away; and they have paid fourfold for any losses which they have inflicted. Very large formations of German aeroplanes—and we know that they are a very brave race—have turned on several occasions from the attack of one-quarter of their number of the Royal Air Force, and have dispersed in different directions. Twelve aeroplanes have been hunted by two. One aeroplane was driven into the water and cast away by the mere charge of a British aeroplane, which had no more ammunition. All of our types—the Hurricane, the Spitfire and the new Defiant—and all our pilots have been vindicated as superior to what they have at present to face. . . .

I return to the Army. In the long series of very fierce battles, now on this front, now on that, fighting on three fronts at once, battles fought by two or three divisions against an equal or somewhat larger number of the enemy, and fought fiercely on some of the old grounds that so many of us knew so well—in these battles our losses in men have exceeded 30,000 killed, wounded and missing. I take occasion to express the sympathy of the House to all who have suffered bereavement or who are still anxious. The President of the Board of Trade is not here today. His son has been killed, and many in the House have felt the pangs of affliction in the sharpest form. But I will say this about the missing: We have had a large number of wounded come home safely to this country, but I would say about the missing that there may be very many reported missing who will come back home, some day, in one way or another. In the confusion of this fight it is inevitable that many have been left in positions where honor required no further resistance from them.

Against this loss of over 30,000 men, we can set a far heavier loss certainly inflicted upon the enemy. But our losses in material are enormous. We have perhaps lost one-third of the men we lost in the opening days of the battle of 21st March, 1918, but we have lost nearly as many guns—nearly one thousand—and all our transport, all the armored vehicles that were with the Army in the north. This loss will impose a further delay on the expansion of our military strength. That expansion had not been proceeding as fast as we had hoped. The best of all we had to give had gone to the British Expeditionary Force, and although they had not the numbers of tanks and some articles of equipment which were desirable, they were a very well and finely equipped Army. They had the first-fruits of all that our industry had to give, and that is gone. And now here is this further delay. How long it will be, how long it will last, depends upon the exertions which we make in this Island. An effort the like of which has never been seen in our records is now being made. Work is proceeding everywhere, night and day, Sundays and week days. Capital and Labor have cast aside their interests, rights, and customs and put them into the common stock. Already the flow of munitions has leaped forward. There is no reason why we should not in a few months overtake the sudden and serious loss that has come upon us, without retarding the development of our general program.

Nevertheless, our thankfulness at the escape of our Army and so many men, whose loved ones have passed through an agonizing week, must not blind us to the fact that what has happened in France and Belgium is a colossal military disaster. The French Army has been weakened, the Belgian Army has been lost, a large part of those fortified lines upon which so much faith had been reposed is gone, many valuable mining districts and factories have passed into the enemy's possession, the whole of the Channel ports are in his hands, with all the tragic consequences that follow from that, and we must expect another blow to be struck almost immediately at us or at France. We are told that Herr Hitler has a plan for invading the British Isles. This has often been thought of before. When Napoleon lay at Boulogne for a year with his flat-bottomed boats and his Grand Army, he was told by someone, "There are bitter weeds in England." There are certainly a great many more of them since the British Expeditionary Force returned.

The whole question of home defense against invasion is, of course, powerfully affected by the fact that we have for the time being in this Island incomparably more powerful military forces than we have ever had at any moment in this war or the last. But this will not continue. We shall not be content with a defensive war. We have our duty to our Ally. We have to reconstitute and build up the British Expeditionary Force once again, under its gallant Commander-in-Chief, Lord Gort. All this is in train; but in the interval we must put our defenses in this Island into such a high state of organization that the fewest possible numbers will be required to give effective security and that the largest possible potential of offensive effort may be realized. On this we are now engaged. . . .

Turning once again, and this time more generally, to the question of invasion, I would observe that there has never been a period in all these long centuries of which we boast when an absolute guarantee against invasion, still less against serious raids, could have been given to our people. In the days of Napoleon the same wind which would have carried his transports across the Channel might have driven away the blockading fleet. There was always the chance, and it is that chance which has excited and befooled the imaginations of many Continental tyrants. Many are the tales that are told. We are assured that novel methods will be adopted, and when we see the originality of malice, the ingenuity of aggression, which our enemy displays, we may certainly prepare ourselves for every kind of novel stratagem and every kind of brutal and treacherous maneuver. I think that no idea is so outlandish that it should not be considered and viewed with a searching, but at the same time, I hope, with a steady eye. We must never forget the solid assurances of sea power and those which belong to air power if it can be locally exercised.

I have, myself, full confidence that if all do their duty, if nothing is neglected, and if the best arrangements are made, as they are being made, we shall prove ourselves once again able to defend our Island home, to ride out the storm of war, and to outlive the menace of tyranny, if necessary for years, if necessary alone. At any rate, that is what we are going to try to do. That is the resolve of His Majesty's Government—every man of them. That is the will of Parliament and the nation. The British Empire and the French Republic, linked together in their cause and in their need, will defend to the death their native soil, aiding each other like good comrades to the utmost of their strength. Even though large tracts of Europe and many old and famous States have fallen or may fall into the grip of the Gestapo and all the odious apparatus of Nazi rule, we shall not flag or fail. We shall go on to the end, we shall fight in France, we shall fight on the seas and oceans, we shall fight with growing confidence and growing strength in the air, we shall defend our Island, whatever the cost may be, we shall fight on the beaches, we shall fight on the landing grounds, we shall fight in the fields and in the streets, we shall fight in the hills; we shall never surrender, and even if, which I do not for a moment believe, this Island or a large part of it were subjugated and starving, then our Empire beyond the seas, armed and guarded by the British Fleet, would carry on the struggle, until, in God's good time, the New World, with all its power and might, steps forth to the rescue and the liberation of the old.

Hitler's Proclamation on Invading Russia, 1941

Like Napoleon, Hitler was militarily and temperamentally unable to invade the British Isles, so he turned to indirect methods of conquering them. He bombarded English cities from the air unmercifully. He tried to starve the population by a vicious U-boat blockade. He raved and he blustered, but the British would not go down. They behaved, in fact, as if they expected to win, thrashing the Italians in Africa and sinking some of Germany's best ships. In frustration, Hitler turned elsewhere for booty. By the spring of 1941, the Nazis had taken over the Balkans and had rescued the Italians in Africa. They then struck out in the direction of Suez and India, hopeful of beating Britain by shutting off vital supplies from the East. Still the British held on.

Hitler, again emulating Napoleon, finally decided to turn his attention to Russia. It was not a decision lightly reached. Despite the Russian-German treaty of friendship, Hitler had to compete with the Soviet Union in Poland and in the Balkans. The Communist state represented, by its presence, a constant threat to the Nazi state. Hitler deeply aspired to reduce Soviet Russia to Nazi control. Convinced he could avoid the pitfalls that destroyed Napoleon, he expected to defeat Russia quickly, then return to finish his assault on the stubborn British.

Hitler's proclamation of June 22, 1941, announced the Russian invasion to the German people. Typically Hitlerian, it is composed of truths, half-truths and outright lies. It is a madman's distortion of history and justice. Characteristically, Hitler presents himself as long suffering and forbearing, put upon not only by Britain and Russia but by democrats, reactionaries and Jews. No one but Hitler, the supreme liar, could have declared after violating such an array of solemn agreements that, "When the German Reich gives a guarantee, that means it also abides by it. We are neither Englishmen nor Jews." It is also significant that Hitler could have referred to himself as "the representative of European culture and civilization," when he was so intent on wrecking European culture and civilization. His decision to invade Russia was his costliest mistake. It was the turning point of the war. The proclamation, of which excerpts are given here, marks a moment of salvation in Western history.

Document 100

German People!
National Socialists!

Weighted down with heavy cares, condemned to months-long silence, the hour has now come when at last I can speak frankly.

When on September 3, 1939, the German Reich received the English declaration of war there was repeated anew a British attempt to render impossible every beginning of a consolidation and thereby of Europe's rise, by fighting whatever power on the Continent was strongest at any given time.

That is how of yore England ruined Spain in many wars. That is how she conducted her wars against Holland. That is how later she fought France with the aid of all Europe and that is how at the turn of the century she began the encirclement of the then German Reich and in 1914 the World War. Only on account of its internal dissension was Germany defeated in 1918. The consequences were terrible.

After hypocritical declarations that the fight was solely against the Kaiser and his regime, the annihilation of the German Reich began according to plan after the German Army had laid down its arms.

While the prophecies of the French statement, that there were 20,000,000 Germans too many—in other words, that this number would have to be exterminated by hunger, disease or emigration—were apparently being fulfilled to the letter, the National Socialist movement began its work of unifying the German people and thereby initiating resurgence of the Reich. This rise of our people from distress, misery and shameful disregard bore all the signs of a purely internal renaissance. Britain especially was not in any way affected or threatened thereby.

Nevertheless, a new policy of encirclement against Germany, born as it was of hatred, recommenced immediately. Internally and externally there resulted that plot familiar to us all between Jews and democrats, Bolshevists and reactionaries, with the sole aim of inhibiting the establishment of the new German people's State, and of plunging the Reich anew into impotence and misery.

Apart from us the hatred of this international world conspiracy was directed against those peoples which like ourselves were neglected by fortune and were obliged to earn their daily bread in the hardest struggle for existence.

Above all, the right of Italy and Japan to share in the goods of this world was contested just as much as that of Germany and in fact was formally denied.

The coalition of these nations was, therefore, only an act of self-protection in the face of the egoistic world combination of wealth and power threatening them. As early as 1936 Prime Minister Churchill, according to statements by the American General Wood before a committee of the American House of Representatives, declared Germany was once again becoming too powerful and must therefore be destroyed. In the summer of 1939 the time seemed to have come for England to begin to realize its intended annihilation by repetition of a comprehensive policy of encirclement of Germany.

The plan of the campaign of lies staged for this purpose consisted in declaring that other people were threatened, in tricking them with British promises of guarantees and assistance, and of making them march against Germany just as it did preceding the Great War. Thus Britain from May to August, 1939, succeeded in broadcasting to the world that Lithuania, Estonia, Latvia, Finland and Bessarabia as well as the Ukraine were being directly threatened by Germany.

A number of these States allowed themselves to be misled into accepting the promise of guarantee proffered with these assertions, thus joining the new encirclement front against Germany. Under these circumstances I considered myself entitled to assume responsibility before my own conscience and before the history of the German people not only of assuring these countries or their governments of the falseness of British assertions, but also of setting the strongest power in the east, by especially solemn declarations, at rest concerning the limits of our interests.

National Socialists! At that time you probably all felt that this step was bitter and difficult for me. Never did the German people harbor hostile feeling against the peoples of Russia. However, for over ten years Jewish Bolshevist rulers had been endeavoring from Moscow to set not only Germany but all Europe aflame. At no time ever did Germany attempt to carry her National Socialist *Weltanschauung* into Russia, but on the contrary Jewish Bolshevist rulers in Moscow unswervingly endeavored to foist their domination upon us and other European peoples, not only by ideological means but above all with military force.

The consequences of the activity of this regime were nothing but chaos, misery and starvation in all countries. I, on the other hand, have been striving for twenty years with a minimum of intervention and without destroying our production, to arrive at a new socialist order in Germany which not only eliminates unemployment but also permits the worker to receive an ever greater share of the fruits of his labor.

The success of this policy of economic and social reconstruction of our people, consisting of systematically eliminating differences of rank and class, has a true people's community as the final aim of the world.

It was therefore only with extreme difficulty that I brought myself in August, 1939, to send my foreign minister to Moscow in an endeavor there to oppose the British encirclement policy against Germany. I did this only from a sense of all responsibility toward the German people, but above all in the hope after all of achieving permanent relief of tension and of being able to reduce sacrifices which might otherwise have been demanded of us. . . .

Victory in Poland which was won by German troops exclusively caused me to address yet another peace offer to the Western Powers. It was refused owing to efforts of international and Jewish warmongers.

At that time already the reason for such refusal lay in the fact that Britain still had hopes of being able to mobilize a European coalition against Germany which was to include the Balkans and Soviet Russia. It was therefore decided in London to send Mr. Cripps as ambassador to Moscow. He received clear instructions under all circumstances to resume relations between the English and Soviet Russia and develop them in a pro-British direction. The British press reported on the progress of this mission as long as tactical reasons did not impose silence.

In the autumn of 1939 and spring of 1940 the first results actually made themselves felt. As Russia undertook to subjugate by armed force not only Finland but also the Baltic States she suddenly motivated this action by the assertion, as ridiculous as it was false, that she must protect these countries from an outside menace or forestall it. This could only be meant to apply to Germany, for no other power could even gain entrance into the Baltic area, let alone go to war there. Still I had to be silent. However, those in power in the Kremlin immediately went further.

Whereas in the spring of 1940 Germany, in accordance with the so-called pact of friendship, withdrew her forces from the Far Eastern frontier and, in fact, for the most part cleared these areas entirely of German troops, a concentration of Russian forces at that time was already beginning in a measure which could only be regarded as a deliberate threat to Germany. . . .

While our soldiers from May 5, 1940, on had been breaking Franco-British power in the west, Russian military deployment on our eastern frontier was being continued to a more and more menacing extent. From August, 1940, on I therefore considered it to be in the interest of the Reich no longer to permit our eastern provinces, which moreover had already been laid waste so often, to remain unprotected in the face of this tremendous concentration of Bolshevist divisions.

Thus there resulted British-Soviet Russian co-operation intended mainly at the tying up of such powerful forces in the east that radical conclusion of the war in the west, particularly as regards aircraft, could no longer be vouched for by the German High Command. This, however, was in line with the objects not only of the British but also of the Soviet Russian policy, for both England and Soviet Russia intended to let this war go on for as long as possible in order to weaken all Europe and render it progressively more impotent.

Russia's threatened attack on Rumania was in the last analysis equally intended to gain possession of an important base, not only of Germany's but also of Europe's, economic life, or at least destroy it. The Reich, especially since 1933, sought with unending patience to gain States in Southeast Europe as trading partners. We therefore also had the greatest interest in their internal constitutional consolidation and organization. Russia's advance into Rumania and Greece's tie-up with England threatened to turn these regions, too, within a short time into a general theater of war.

Contrary to our principles and customs, and at the urgent request of the then Rumanian Government, which was itself responsible for this development, I advised acquiescence to the Soviet Russian demands for the sake of peace and the cession of Bessarabia. The Rumanian Government believed, however, that it could answer for this before its own people only if Germany and Italy in compensation would at least guarantee the integrity of what still remained of Rumania. I did so with heavy heart, principally because when the German Reich gives a guarantee, that means it also abides by it. We are neither Englishmen nor Jews. . . .

I adopted the only attitude that I could adopt as the responsible leader of the German Reich but also as the representative of European culture and civilization and conscious of my responsibility. The consequence was to increase in Soviet Russia the activity directed against the Reich, above all, however, the immediate commencement of undermining the new Rumanian state from within and an attempt to remove the Bulgarian Government by propaganda. . . .

If any final proof was required for the coalition meanwhile formed between England and Soviet Russia despite all diversion and camouflage, the Yugoslav conflict provided it. While I made every effort to undertake a final attempt to pacify the Balkans and in sympathetic co-operation with Il Duce invited Yugoslavia to join the Tripartite Pact, England and Soviet Russia in a joint conspiracy organized that coup d'état which in one night removed the then government which had been ready to come to agreement. . . .

Since even now I still believed it better not to speak, those in power in the Kremlin went still further: The Government of the German Reich today possesses documentary evidence which proves that Russia, in order finally to bring Serbia into the war, gave her a promise to supply her via Salonika with arms, aircraft, munitions and other war materials against Germany. And this happened almost at the very moment when I myself advised Japanese Foreign Minister Matsuoka that eased tension with Russia always was in hope, thereby to serve the cause of peace.

Only the rapid advance of our incomparable divisions to Skoplje as well as the capture of Salonika itself frustrated the aims of this Soviet Russian-Anglo-Saxon plot. Officers of the Serb air force, however, fled to Russia and were there immediately received as allies.

The victory of the Axis Powers in the Balkans in the first instance thwarted the plan to involve Germany this Summer in months-long battles in Southeastern Europe while meantime steadily completing the alignment of Soviet Russian armies and increasing their readiness for war in order, finally, together with England and supported by American supplies anticipated, to crush the German Reich and Italy.

Thus Moscow not only broke but miserably betrayed the stipulations of our friendly agreement. All this was done while the rulers in the Kremlin, exactly as in the case of Finland and Rumania, up to the last moment pretended peace and friendship and drew up an ostensibly innocent démenti.

Although until now I was forced by circumstances to keep silent again and again, the moment has now come when to continue as a mere observer would not only be a sin of omission but a crime against the German people—yes, even against the whole of Europe.

Today something like 160 Russian divisions are standing at our frontiers. For weeks constant violations of this frontier have taken place, not only affecting us but from the far north down to Rumania. Russian airmen consider it sport nonchalantly to overlook these frontiers, presumably to prove to us that they already feel themselves masters of these territories. During the night of June 17 to June 18 Russian patrols again penetrated into the Reich's territory and could only be driven back after prolonged firing. This has brought us to the hour when it is necessary for us to take steps against this plot devised by the Jewish–Anglo-Saxon warmongers and equally the Jewish rulers of the Bolshevist center in Moscow.

German people! At this moment a march is taking place that, as regards extent, compares with the greatest the world hitherto has seen. United with their Finnish comrades, the fighters of the victory of Narvik are standing in the Northern Arctic. German divisions commanded by the conqueror of Norway, in co-operation with the heroes of Finnish freedom, under their marshal, are protecting Finnish soil. Formations of the German eastern front extend from East Prussia to the Carpathians. German and Rumanian soldiers are united under Chief of State Antonescu from the banks of the Pruth along the lower reaches of the Danube to the shores of the Black Sea. The task of this front, therefore, no longer is the protection of single countries, but the safeguarding of Europe and thereby the salvation of all.

I therefore decided today again to lay the fate and future of the German Reich and our people in the hands of our soldiers.

May God help us especially in this fight!

The Atlantic Charter, 1941

The United States looked on in stupefaction while France fell. Like most Americans, President Roosevelt had not realized how fragile was European democracy. Aware that America's first lines of defense were in Europe, he determined not to let Britain go down the way France did. But because American public opinion was hostile to intervention, he had to tread perilously between commitments to Britain's survival and keeping

America out of war. It was predictable that the commitment to Britain would ultimately overwhelm the commitment to peace. As the months passed, the United States became more and more directly engaged in defeating Fascism.

In August, 1941, Roosevelt met Chuchill aboard an American warship anchored off the coast of Newfoundland. He proposed to the Prime Minister that they subscribe jointly to a set of war aims, although only one of their countries was at war. To make sure that he would not be trapped as Wilson had been by a host of secret agreements, Roosevelt first assured himself that his war aims had not long before been mortgaged away. He then produced the draft of a document he had prepared, which he and Churchill later signed. It became known as the Atlantic Charter. Over the course of the war, the Soviet Union, China and dozens of other nations who were fighting Germany subscribed to the Charter. Although it was not until December 7, 1941, that the Japanese forced the United States into open belligerency by attacking Pearl Harbor, in fact the United States had been a major participant in the war since 1940 and the Atlantic Charter had publicly committed it to Fascism's defeat.

Roosevelt, in conjunction with Churchill, issued the Atlantic Charter in the form of a communiqué on August 14, 1941. It is Wilsonian both in its principles and its ideals. Its section eight foreshadows the formation of the United Nations, though the United States was still strongly isolationist. It reaffirmed the Wilsonian pledge of desistance from territorial aggrandizement and the Wilsonian dedication to self-determination for all peoples. The Charter is the embellishment of Roosevelt's earlier Declaration of the Four Freedoms—freedom of religion and speech, freedom from want and fear. It revealed how closely united were the democratic communities within Western civilization. The text of the Atlantic Charter is presented below.

Document 101

The President of the United States of America and the Prime Minister, Mr. Churchill, representing His Majesty's Government in the United Kingdom, being met together, deem it right to make known certain common principles in the national policies of their respective countries on which they base their hopes for a better future of the world.

"First, their countries seek no aggrandizement, territorial or other;

"Second, they desire to see no territorial changes that do not accord with the freely expressed wishes of the peoples concerned;

"Third, they respect the right of all peoples to choose the form of government under which they will live; and they wish to see sovereign rights and self-government restored to those who have been forcibly deprived of them;

"Fourth, they will endeavor, with due respect for their existing obligations, to further the enjoyment by all states, great or small, victor or vanquished, of access, on equal terms, to the trade and to the raw materials of the world which are needed for their economic prosperity;

"Fifth, they desire to bring about the fullest collaboration between all nations in the economic field with the object of securing, for all, improved labor standards, economic advancement, and social security;

"Sixth, after the final destruction of the Nazi tyranny, they hope to see established a peace which will afford to all nations the means of dwelling in safety within their own boundaries, and which will afford assurance that all the men in all the lands may live out their lives in freedom from fear and want;

"Seventh, such a peace should enable all men to traverse the high seas and oceans without hindrance;

"Eighth, they believe that all of the nations of the world, for realistic as well as spiritual reasons, must come to the abandonment of the use of force. Since no future peace can be maintained if land, sea, or air armaments continue to be employed by nations which threaten, or may threaten, aggression outside of their frontiers, they believe, pending the establishment of a wider and permanent system of general security, that the disarmament of such nations is essential. They will likewise aid and encourage all other practicable measures which will lighten for peace-loving peoples the crushing burden of armaments."

FRANKLIN D. ROOSEVELT
WINSTON S. CHURCHILL

Truman Introduces the Atomic Age, 1945

In the summer of 1945, Japan, fighting alone, was mortally wounded. Italy had surrendered almost two years before and Germany the previous May. Japan had lost its empire. Its cities had been reduced to rubble, its fleet was at the bottom, its population was on the point of starvation. Had the United States and Britain offered reasonable terms, Japan would probably have capitulated. But the policy of the Allies was unconditional surrender, which persuaded the Japanese—with their brave and fanatical army—to fight on to defend their homeland and emperor.

Though Japan could not win, it appeared that thousands more American casualties were to be the price of Allied victory.

Then on August 6, 1945, an American plane dropped an atomic bomb on Hiroshima, a city of 350,000 inhabitants. More than 90 per cent of the city was leveled and 130,000 persons were killed. The Nuclear Age had begun.

The atomic bomb was the culmination of a mammoth research program undertaken in 1940 at the instigation of the physicist Albert Einstein, who feared that Germany would be first with nuclear arms. Ironically, the Nazis had given up their atomic research program to concentrate on rockets, which they developed into weapons that were excellent but insufficient to change the course of the war. American research produced a weapon that was far deadlier. The first atomic bomb was tested on July 16, 1945, on the desert near Alamagordo, New Mexico. The bomb that fell on Hiroshima, tiny compared to its successors, equalled 20,000 tons of TNT. Three days later, a more powerful bomb was dropped on the city of Nagasaki. On the following day, the fourth of the Nuclear Age, Japan agreed to capitulate. But for the right to retain their emperor, the Japanese surrendered unconditionally. Though the war was over, a chapter of history that was potentially far more terrifying had been introduced.

The nuclear bomb—acquired by Russia in 1949, Britain in 1952, France in 1960, Communist China in 1964—has since dominated international relations. A product of Western technology, it has been developed to the point that it can wipe out the civilization of the entire world in an hour. Since Nagasaki, nuclear weapons have not been used to kill, but history does not encourage the conviction that man will demonstrate such self-restraint for long. Western civilization can rise to the challenge. If it fails to do so, it will disappear in the rubble of the world, leaving less trace of its presence than Greece or Rome, the Minoans or the Hittites.

In the following excerpts, President of the United States Harry S Truman announces the arrival of the Nuclear Age. Truman deemed his reasons sufficient for dropping the bombs on Hiroshima and Nagasaki, though the wisdom of his decision has often been questioned. He recognized, however, as did many of his contemporaries, that the atomic bomb had added a new dimension to the relations between men. Since August 6, 1945, Western civilization and the world have never for a moment been able to forget its presence.

Document 102

Statement by the President of the United States

August 6, 1945
The White House
Washington, D.C.

Sixteen hours ago an American airplane dropped one bomb on Hiroshima, an important Japanese Army base. That bomb had more power than 20,000 tons of T.N.T. It had more than two thousand times the blast power of the British "Grand Slam," which is the largest bomb ever yet used in the history of warfare.

The Japanese began the war from the air at Pearl Harbor. They have been repaid many fold. And the end is not yet. With this bomb we have now added a new revolutionary increase in destruction to supplement the growing power of our armed forces. In their present forms these bombs are now in production and even more powerful forms are in development.

It is an atomic bomb. It is a harnessing of the basic power of the universe. The force from which the sun draws its power has been loosed against those who brought war to the Far East.

Before 1939, it was the accepted belief of scientists that it was theoretically possible to release atomic energy. But no one knew any practical method of doing it. By 1940, however, we knew that the Germans were working feverishly to find a way to add atomic energy to the other engines of war with which they hoped to enslave the world. But they failed. We may be grateful to Providence that the Germans got the V-1's and the V-2's late and in limited quantities and even more grateful that they did not get the atomic bomb at all. . . .

We are now prepared to obliterate more rapidly and completely every productive enterprise the Japanese have above ground in any city. We shall destroy their docks, their factories, and their communications. Let there be no mistakes; we shall completely destroy Japan's power to make war.

It was to spare the Japanese people from utter destruction that the ultimatum of July 26 was issued at Potsdam. Their leaders promptly rejected that ultimatum. If they do not now accept our terms, they may expect a rain of ruin from the air, the like of which has never been seen on this earth. Behind this air attack will follow sea and land forces in such numbers and power as they have not yet seen and with the fighting skill of which they are already well aware. . . .

The fact that we can release atomic energy ushers in a new era in man's understanding of nature's forces. Atomic energy may in the future supplement the power that now comes from coal, oil, and falling water, but at present it cannot be produced on a basis to compete with them commercially. Before that comes, there must be a long period of intensive research.

It has never been the habit of the scientists of this country or the policy of this Government to withhold from the world scientific knowledge. Normally, therefore, everything about the work with atomic energy would be made public.

But under present circumstances it is not intended to divulge the technical processes of production or all the military applications, pending further examination of possible methods of protecting us and the rest of the world from the danger of sudden destruction.

I shall recommend that the Congress of the United States consider promptly the establishment of an appropriate commission to control the production and use of atomic power within the United States. I shall give further consideration and make further recommendations to the Congress as to how atomic power can become a powerful and forceful influence towards the maintenance of world peace.

The United Nations Charter, 1945

The United Nations officially came into existence on October 24, 1945, when twenty-nine victorious nations ratified the Charter drawn up four months before at San Francisco.

Its structure was similar to that of the defunct League of Nations, though its two chief bodies—the Security Council and the General Assembly—possessed somewhat greater powers. Hope in the United Nations, however, was less in its structure than in its widespread base of support. The League had been essentially a Western European institution, led by England and France. The United Nations drew its strength not only from Western Europe but from the United States and Russia and, to a lesser extent, from nations on every other continent. The United Nations thus came closer to being a global force, even if that force is frequently only moral. The United Nations has inherent weaknesses, some that were visible to its founders at San Francisco. But it was and remains the principal hope of the world for peace in the Nuclear Age.

The following document is the opening section of the United Nations Charter. It contains the preamble and the first chapter, which enumerates the noble purposes and principles of the organization. Though the United Nations has frequently faltered in the achievement of its high aims, it has already surpassed the League of Nations in longevity and continues to be a vibrant organism dedicated to the perpetuation and enrichment of life and civilization on earth.

Document 103

We the Peoples of the United Nations
Determined

to save succeeding generations from the scourge of war, which twice in our lifetime has brought untold sorrow to mankind, and

to reaffirm faith in fundamental human rights, in the dignity and worth of the human person, in the equal rights of men and women and of nations large and small, and

to establish conditions under which justice and respect for the obligations arising from treaties and other sources of international law can be maintained, and to promote social progress and better standards of life in larger freedom,

And for These Ends

to practice tolerance and live together in peace with one another as good neighbors, and

to unite our strength to maintain international peace and security, and

to ensure, by the acceptance of principles and the institution of methods, that armed force shall not be used, save in the common interest, and

to employ international machinery for the promotion of the economic and social advancement of all peoples,

Have Resolved to Combine Our Efforts
to Accomplish These Aims.

Accordingly, our respective Governments, through representatives assembled in the city of San Francisco, who have exhibited their full powers found to be in good and due form, have agreed to the present Charter of the United Nations and do hereby establish an international organization to be known as the United Nations.

Chapter I

PURPOSES AND PRINCIPLES

Article 1

The Purposes of the United Nations are:

1. To maintain international peace and security, and to that end: to take effective collective measures for the prevention and removal of threats to the peace, and for the suppression of acts of aggression or other breaches of the peace, and to bring about by peaceful means, and in conformity with the principles of justice and international law, adjustment or settlement of international disputes or situations which might lead to a breach of the peace;

2. To develop friendly relations among nations based on respect for the principle of equal rights and self-determination of peoples, and to take other appropriate measures to strengthen universal peace;

3. To achieve international cooperation in solving international problems of an economic, social, cultural, or humanitarian character, and in promoting and encouraging respect for human rights and for fundamental freedoms for all without distinction as to race, sex, language, or religion; and

4. To be a center for harmonizing the actions of nations in the attainment of these common ends.

Article 2

The Organization and its Members, in pursuit of the Purposes stated in Article 1, shall act in accordance with the following Principles.

1. The Organization is based on the principle of the sovereign equality of all its Members.

2. All Members, in order to ensure to all of them the rights and benefits resulting from membership, shall fulfil in good faith the obligations assumed by them in accordance with the present Charter.

3. All Members shall settle their international disputes by peaceful means in such a manner that international peace and security, and justice, are not endangered.

4. All Members shall refrain in their international relations from the threat or use of force against the territorial integrity or political independence of any state, or in any other manner inconsistent with the Purposes of the United Nations.

5. All Members shall give the United Nations every assistance in any action it takes in accordance with the present Charter, and shall refrain from giving assistance to any state against which the United Nations is taking preventive or enforcement action.

6. The Organization shall ensure that states which are not Members of the United Nations act in accordance with these Principles so far as may be necessary for the maintenance of international peace and security.

7. Nothing contained in the present Charter shall authorize the United Nations to intervene in matters which are essentially within the domestic jurisdiction of any state or shall require the Members to submit such matters to settlement under the present Charter; but this principle shall not prejudice the application of enforcement measures under Chapter VII.

Reading List

Reading List

This book has been made possible through the efforts of all those who have thought to preserve the important records of history. Many scholars have drawn on these efforts before. Among them, James H. Robinson, early in this century, reached back into time to collect and publish a wide selection of documents on Western civilization. The author gratefully acknowledges his debt to Robinson, just as Robinson acknowledged his dependence on those who recorded documents before him. The author is also grateful to the others whose work, if less extensive, contributed no less vitally to the balance and completeness of this book. The documents in this collection have been drawn from the following earlier works:

Chafee, Zecharia: *Documents on Fundamental Human Rights*, 3 vols., Harvard, Cambridge, 1951–2.

Columbia University Staff: *Introduction to Contemporary Civilization in the West*, 2 vols., Columbia University Press, New York, 1948.

Gantenbein, James W.: *Documentary Background of World War II, 1931–41*, Columbia University Press, New York, 1948.

Gilson, Etienne: *The Church Speaks to the Modern World*, Doubleday, New York, 1954.

Heffner, Richard D.: *A Documentary History of the United States*, New American Library, New York, 1952.

Langsam, Walter C.: *Historic Documents of World War II*, Van Nostrand, Princeton, 1958.

Lecuna, Vicente, and Bierck, Harold A., Jr.: *Selected Writings of Bolivar*, Bolivian Society of Venezuela, New York, 1951.

Mowat, Robert B.: *Select Treaties and Documents to Illustrate the Development of the Modern European States System, 1815–1916*, The Clarendon Press, Oxford, 1916.

Ogg, Frederick: *A Source Book of Medieval History*, American Book Company, New York, 1907.

Robinson, James H.: *Readings in European History, 2 vols.*, Ginn and Co., Boston, 1904–6.

Robinson, James H., and Beard, Charles A.: *Readings in Modern European History*, 2 vols., Ginn and Co., Boston, 1908–9.

Russell, Ruth B.: *A History of the United Nations Charter*, the Brookings Institution, Washington, 1958.

Scott, Jonathan, and Baltzly, Alexander: *Readings in European History since 1814*, Crofts, New York, 1930.

Snyder, Louis L.: *Documents of German History*, Rutgers, New Brunswick, 1958.

Stevenson, J.: *A New Eusebius*, Macmillan, New York, 1957.

* * *

The following works are recommended as useful supplementary reading to the information and interpretation offered in the commentaries. The list, not meant to be exhaustive, is based on the experience of the author and the recommendations of competent specialists in the various fields of Western history.

W. L. Langer's *An Encyclopedia of World History* (Houghton Mifflin, Boston, 1948) and *The Columbia Encyclopedia* (Columbia University Press, New York, 1963) are invaluable for providing basic information as well as a reliable check on dates and other facts. The Rand-McNally *Atlas of World History* often discloses graphically information that is difficult to obtain elsewhere.

General Works

BURNS, EDWARD MCNALL: *Western Civilizations: Their History and Their Culture*, New York, 1963.

CANTOR, NORMAN H.: *Medieval History*, New York, 1963.

COMMAGER, H. S., AND BRUUN, GEOFFREY: *Europe and America Since 1492*, Cambridge, 1954.

DURANT, WILL: *The Story of Civilization*, in nine volumes, New York, 1935 ff.

HAYES, CARLTON J. H., et al.: *History of Western Civilization*, New York, 1962.

KIRCHNER, WALTHER: *Western Civilization Since 1500*, New York, 1958.

MCNEILL, W. H.: *The Rise of the West*, New York, 1963.

PAINTER, SIDNEY: *A History of the Middle Ages*, New York, 1953.

PALMER, R. R., AND COLTON, JOEL: *A History of the Modern World*, New York, 1965.

STRAYER, JOSEPH R., AND MUNRO, DANA C.: *The Middle Ages*, New York, 1959.

Chapters I–III

ARTZ, F. B.: *The Mind of the Middle Ages*, New York, 1954.

BOAK, A. E. R.: *A History of Rome to 565 A. D.*, New York, 1929.

BOISSONNADE, PROSPER: *Life and Work in Medieval Europe*, New York, 1927.

CLOUGH, S. B., AND COLE, C. W.: *Economic History of Europe*, Boston, 1947.

COWELL, F. R.: *Cicero and the Roman Republic*, New York, 1948.

DAVIS, H. W. C.: *Medieval Europe*, London, 1948.

FLICK, A. C.: *The Decline of the Medieval Church*, 2 vols., New York, 1930.

HUIZINGA, J.: *The Waning of the Middle Ages*, New York, 1954.

LAMONTE, J. L.: *The World of the Middle Ages*, New York, 1949.

LATOURETTE, K. S.: *A History of Christianity*, New York, 1953.

LOT, FERDINAND: *The End of the Ancient World and the Beginnings of the Middle Ages*, New York, 1931.

MCILWAIN, C. H.: *The Growth of Political Thought in the West*, New York, 1932.

MOMMSEN, THEODOR: *The History of Rome*, Chicago, 1957.

MOSS, H. ST. L. B.: *The Birth of the Middle Ages, 395–814*, New York, 1935.

PAINTER, SIDNEY: *The Rise of Feudal Monarchies*, Ithaca, 1951.

PIRENNE, HENRI: *Economic and Social History of Medieval Europe*, New York, 1956.
PIRENNE, HENRI: *Medieval Cities*, Princeton, 1925.
RAND, E. K.: *Founders of the Middle Ages*, Cambridge, Mass., 1928.
ROSTOVTZEV, M. I.: *Social and Economic History of the Roman Empire*, New York, 1926.
TAWNEY, R. H.: *Religion and the Rise of Capitalism*, New York, 1947.
THOMPSON, J. W., AND JOHNSON, E. N.: *An Introduction to Medieval Europe*, New York, 1937.
TOUT, T. F.: *The Empire and the Papacy, 918–1273*, London, 1941
WADDELL, HELEN: *The Wandering Scholars*, London, 1927.

CHAPTERS IV–VII

ABBOTT, WILBUR: *The Expansion of Europe, 1415–1815*, New York, 1938.
ADAMS, G. B.: *Constitutional History of England*, New York, 1921.
BAINTON, R. H.: *The Age of the Reformation*, New York, 1957.
BECKER, C. L.: *The Heavenly City of the Eighteenth Century Philosophers*, New Haven, 1932.
BELOFF, MAX: *The Age of Absolutism*, New York, 1962.
BRUUN, GEOFFREY: *The Enlightened Despots*, New York, 1929.
CLARK, G. N.: *The Seventeenth Century*, New York, 1947.
ELTON, G. R.: *England Under the Tudors*, London, 1955.
HARING, C. H.: *The Spanish Empire in America*, New York, 1947.
HECKSCHER, E. F.: *Mercantilism*, 2 vols., New York, 1935.
KEIR, D. L.: *The Constitutional History of Modern Britain*, Princeton, 1960.
KIDD, B. J.: *The Counter-Reformation, 1550–1600*, New York, 1933.
LUCAS, HENRY S.: *The Renaissance and the Reformation*, New York, 1934.
MARTI, O. A.: *The Economic Causes of the Reformation in England*, New York, 1930.
MORISON, S. E.: *Admiral of the Ocean Sea: A Life of Christopher Columbus*, 2 vols., Boston, 1942.
OGG, F. A., AND SHARP, W. R.: *Economic Development of Modern Europe*, New York, 1929.
PACKARD, L. B.: *The Age of Louis XIV*, New York, 1929.
RANDALL, J. H., JR.: *The Making of the Modern Mind*, New York, 1926.
SABINE, G. H.: *A History of Political Theory*, New York, 1961.
SMITH, PRESERVED: *The Age of the Reformation*, New York, 1920.
WEDGWOOD, C. V.: *Richelieu and the French Monarchy*, New York, 1950.
WOLF, JOHN B.: *The Emergence of the Great Powers, 1685–1715*, New York, 1951.

CHAPTERS VIII–X

ASHTON, T. S.: *The Industrial Revolution, 1760–1830*, New York, 1948.
BRINTON, C. C.: *A Decade of Revolution, 1789–1799*, New York, 1934.
BRUUN, GEOFFREY: *Europe and the French Imperium*, New York, 1938.
FERRERO, GUGLIELMO: *The Reconstruction of Europe*, New York, 1941.

FISHER, H. A. L.: *Napoleon*, New York, 1913.
GERSHOY, LEO: *The French Revolution, 1789–1799*, New York, 1932.
GERSHOY, LEO: *The French Revolution and Napoleon*, New York, 1933.
GOTTSCHALK, L. R.: *The Era of the French Revolution, 1715–1815*, New York, 1929.
GRANT, A. J., AND TEMPERLEY, H.: *Europe: the Revolutionary and Napoleonic Eras*, New York, 1935.
MANTOUX, PAUL: *The Industrial Revolution in the Eighteenth Century*, New York, 1947.
MATHIEZ, ALBERT: *The French Revolution*, New York, 1928.
MUMFORD, LEWIS: *Technics and Civilization*, New York, 1934.
NEWMAN, P. C.: *The Development of Economic Thought*, New York, 1952.
SCHUMPETER, JOSEPH: *Capitalism, Socialism, and Democracy*, New York, 1942.

CHAPTERS XI–XIII

BEER, MAX: *History of British Socialism*, New York, 1942.
BROGAN, D. W.: *France Under the Republic*, New York, 1940.
CARROLL, E. M.: *Germany and the Great Powers, 1866–1914*, New York, 1938.
CARSTON, F. L.: *The Origins of Prussia*, London, 1954.
COLE, G. D. H., AND POSTGATE, R.: *The British Common People, 1746–1946*, New York, 1947.
DAWSON, W. H.: *Bismarck and State Socialism*, New York, 1891.
DAWSON, WILLIAM: *The German Empire, 1867–1914, and the Unity Movement*, 2 vols., London, 1919.
GRIFFITH, G. O.: *Mazzini, Prophet of Modern Europe*, New York, 1932.
HOVELL, M.: *The Chartist Movement*, New York, 1925.
LASKI, H. J.: *The Rise of Liberalism*, New York, 1936.
MCKAY, DONALD: *The National Workshops: A Study in the French Revolution of 1848*, Cambridge, Mass., 1933.
PIPKIN, C. W.: *The Idea of Social Justice*, New York, 1928.
THAYER, WILLIAM: *The Life and Times of Cavour*, Boston, 1914.
WOODWARD, ERNEST: *The Age of Reform, 1815–1870*, Oxford, 1938.

CHAPTERS XIV–XV

ALBERTINI, LUIGI: *Origins of the War of 1914*, New York, 1952.
ALPEROVITZ, GAR: *Atomic Diplomacy: Hiroshima* and *Potsdam*, New York, 1965.
ARON, RAYMOND: *The Century of Total War*, Boston, 1955.
BAKER, RAY STANNARD: *Woodrow Wilson and the World Settlement*, New York, 1922.
BIRDSALL, PAUL: *Versailles Twenty Years After*, New York, 1941.
BULLOCK, A. L. C.: *Hitler: A Study in Tyranny*, London, 1952.
CLARK, R. T.: *The Fall of the German Republic*, New York, 1935.
CURTISS, J. S.: *The Russian Revolutions of 1917*, Princeton, 1957.
DEAN, V. M.: *The United States and Russia*, New York, 1948.
DOLIVET, LOUIS, ED.: *The United Nations: A Handbook*, New York, 1946.
DRUCKER, P. F.: *The End of Economic Man*, New York, 1939.

FAY, S. B.: *The Origins of the World War*, 2 vols., New York, 1928.
FEIS, HERBERT: *The Road to Pearl Harbor*, Princeton, 1950.
HAINES, C. G., AND HOFFMAN, R. J. S.: *The Origins and Background of the Second World War*, New York, 1943.
HALPERIN, S. W.: *Germany Tried Democracy, 1918–1933*, New York, 1946.
LIDDELL HART, B. H.: *The Real War, 1914–1918*, Boston, 1930.
LIE, TRYGVE: *In the Cause of Peace: Seven Years with the United Nations*, New York, 1954.
LINK, A. S.: *Wilson: The Struggle for Neutrality*, Princeton, 1961.
MITCHELL, BROADUS: *Depression Decade: from New Era through New Deal, 1929 to 1941*, New York, 1947.
NICOLSON, HAROLD: *Peacemaking, 1919*, New York, 1946.
PARES, SIR BERNARD: *A History of Russia*, New York, 1953.
SCHMITT, B. E.: *The Coming of the War*, 2 vols., New York, 1930.
SHUB, DAVID: *Lenin*, New York, 1948.
TROTSKY, LEON: *The History of the Russian Revolution*, 3 vols., New York, 1932.
WILMOT, CHESTER: *The Struggle for Europe*, New York, 1952.
WOLFE, B. D.: *Three Who Made a Revolution*, New York, 1948.

Index